The Battlefield of
IMPERISHABLE MEMORY

The Battlefield of
IMPERISHABLE MEMORY
PASSCHENDAELE AND THE ANZAC LEGEND

Matthew Haultain-Gall

MONASH
UNIVERSITY
PUBLISHING

The Battlefield of Imperishable Memory: Passchendaele and the Anzac Legend
© Copyright 2021 Matthew Haultain-Gall
All rights reserved. Apart from any uses permitted by Australia's Copyright Act 1968, no part of this book may be reproduced by any process without prior written permission from the copyright owners. Inquiries should be directed to the publisher.

Monash University Publishing
Matheson Library Annexe
40 Exhibition Walk
Monash University
Clayton, Victoria 3800, Australia
publishing.monash.edu

Monash University Publishing brings to the world publications which advance the best traditions of humane and enlightened thought.

This book has been peer reviewed.

ISBN: 9781922464064 (paperback)

Design: Les Thomas

Typesetting: Jo Mullins

Cover image: Photograph of three unidentified soldiers looking at the corduroy track leading from Westhoek Ridge to Bellevarde Ridge. (Unknown Australian official photographer, 26 October 1917. Australian War Memorial, E01318.)

A catalogue record for this book is available from the National Library of Australia.

CONTENTS

List of Plates vi

About the Author viii

Acknowledgements ix

Foreword xiii

Prologue xvi

Introduction: A Salient Question 1

Chapter 1   Bean's Belgium 19

Chapter 2   Displaying the Ypres Salient 48

Chapter 3   Belgium Imagined 84

Chapter 4   Belgium Experienced 124

Chapter 5   Dead Trees and Withering Memories 157

Chapter 6   Lost in a Surfeit of Memory 198

Epilogue 243

Notes 249

Bibliography 285

Index 307

LIST OF PLATES

1 Supporting troops in the Ypres Sector, 1917.

2 Chateau Wood, 1917.

3 Official Australian photographs from third Ypres and images that draw inspiration from them.

4 Plan of the Australian War Museum, Melbourne, 1922.

5 Wallace Anderson and Louis McCubbin, *Nonne Boschen (Ypres)* 1922–23.

6 Frank Hurley, *The Morning of Passchendaele*, ca 1917.

7 *Australian Chivalry* frontispiece, 1933.

8 Septimus Power, *First Australian Division Artillery Going into the 3rd Battle of Ypres*, 1919.

9 Fred Leist, *Australian Infantry Attack in Polygon Wood*, 1919.

10 Paul Nash, *The Menin Road*, 1919.

11 Otto Dix, *Flandern*, 1934–36.

12 Will Longstaff, *Menin Gate at Midnight*, 1927.

13 Menin Gate Memorial, Ypres, 2017.

14 C.H. Percival's illustration for the poem 'Ypres', 1920.

15 Sketch of a proposed national Australian memorial for Broodseinde Ridge, 1919.

16 Sketch of a divisional memorial, 1919.

17 Survey of the mound at Polygon Wood, ca 1920.

18 J.C. Goodchild, *Divisional Monument, Polygon Wood*, 1920.

19 J.C. Goodchild, *Tynecot*, 1920.

List of Plates

20 Australian section, Memorial Museum Passchendaele 1917, 2015.

21 Australian section, Memorial Museum Passchendaele 1917, 2015.

22 'A Multicultural War' section, In Flanders Fields Museum, 2015.

23 Charles Web Gilbert's *Digger* at the In Flanders Fields Museum, 2015.

24 Stretcher bearers passing through Polygon Wood, 1917.

25 Polygon Wood, 2017.

26 *Planting the Australian Flag on Anzac Redoubt*, 1917.

27 Ypres: a multinational commemorative space.

ABOUT THE AUTHOR

Matthew Haultain-Gall is a scientific collaborator at the Université catholique de Louvain, Belgium. His research focuses on the cultural and social impacts of the First World War. In 2017 he completed a PhD at the University of New South Wales, Australia, in which he traced how Australians have remembered and commemorated the battle of Messines and the third battle of Ypres.

ACKNOWLEDGEMENTS

Beginning as a doctoral thesis, this book has taken the better part of a decade to research and write. Over that period of time, it has pulled more and more people – hopefully not unreluctantly – into its orbit. No one has influenced my work more than my former supervisors, Associate Professor Ruth Balint and Dr Peter Schrijvers. Their passion for history and dedication to their craft will always be a great source of inspiration. They did a fantastic job keeping me on track and their guidance at key moments throughout the PhD and beyond has been critical. The School of History, faculty support staff and especially the history postgraduate community at the University of New South Wales (Sydney) played an important role in fostering a welcoming environment which made the years when the bulk of the research was carried out considerably less arduous than they could have been. Special mentions go to Dr James Keating, Dr Liam Kane, Dr Jess Parr, Dr Isobelle Barrett Meyering and Dr Paul Irish who were all roped into proofreading proposals, abstracts, conference papers, articles and chapters at various times. I would also like to thank Dr Gen Dashwood and Dr Katherine Jacka for their enthusiasm in organising postgraduate workshops and writing retreats so the postgraduate community could regularly share ideas, research and writing. I am especially thankful that many of us have been able to keep in touch beyond our days at Kensington.

Outside of UNSW, I am deeply indebted to a number of people working within the academic community. Professor Joan Beaumont has been exceedingly generous, engaging with my work on several occasions and providing incisive feedback that has greatly strengthened the final product. He may not necessarily be aware of it, but Professor

Peter Stanley's interventions at key moments have helped my research reach a larger audience. In-depth conversations with Dr Bart Ziino and Associate Professor Martin Crotty on various aspects of the book proved highly enlightening and enjoyable to boot. I must thank Professor Laurence van Ypersele and Professor Mark Connelly for taking an interest in my project and providing me with opportunities to present my findings to Belgian and British audiences, with a Gateways to the First World War event held at the In Flanders Fields Museum being a particular highlight. The individualised nature of research can make the historian's job lonely at times and I am grateful to have had the opportunity to turn to some of the brightest early career researchers working in the field for support and guidance. Dr Alexia Moncrieff, Dr Romain Fathi and Dr Margaret Hutchison have all taken time out from their packed schedules to look over chapters and have also played key roles in organising some of the most thought-provoking conferences I have attended in recent years.

Of course, this book would not exist at all without the cultural institutions that care for the archives on which it is based. I have received invaluable assistance from the staffs of the Australian War Memorial, the National Archives of Australia, the National Library of Australia, the Belgian Embassy in Australia, the Department of Veterans' Affairs, the Commonwealth War Graves Commission, *les Archives du Ministère des Affaires étrangères de Belgique, Stadsarchief Ieper,* the In Flanders Fields Museum, the Memorial Museum Passchendaele 1917, Plugstreet 14-18 Experience interpretation centre, and the Australian Embassy in Belgium. In particular, I cannot thank the following individuals enough: Dr Dominiek Dendooven, Piet Chielens, Annick Vandenbilcke, Christophe de Nijs, Maria Choules, Andrew Fetherston, Freddy Declerck OAM, Peter Slosse, Steven Vandenbussche, Anny Beauprez, François Maekelberg

ACKNOWLEDGEMENTS

OAM, Jennifer Stephenson, Hilde Demoor and Jan Bartlett. They were incredibly patient in answering the numerous questions with which I bombarded them, often over a number of years.

It is important to acknowledge that this project would not have been possible without financial support provided primarily by the Australian government's Australian Postgraduate Awards scheme. In addition to this, I received support for research trips and conferences from UNSW's Faculty of Arts and Social Sciences and through the Australian Historical Association's Copyright Bursary scheme. These sources of funding ensured that I could focus my full attention on my research while completing the thesis. I would also like to thank the Australian War Memorial for allowing me to use the vivid photograph that features on this book's cover at a generously discounted rate; the webmasters of www.greatwar.be for allowing me to use a photograph from their site free of charge as well as the Société belge des Auteurs, compositeurs et éditeurs and bpk image agency for allowing me to reprint Otto Dix's evocative *Flandern* at a discounted rate.

That this book has seen the light of day is thanks to the team at Monash University Publishing, who took a chance on a title exploring the legacy of 1914–18 after the centenary and when (First World) War weariness had reportedly set in. I would like to acknowledge Joanne Mullins, in particular, who had the unenviable task of walking a green author based in Belgium through the publication process while locked down in Victoria. Special mention must also go to Penny Mansley, copyeditor extraordinaire, who went over the original manuscript with a fine-tooth comb and helped turn it into the cracking read it is now.

There is also a host of other 'unofficial agents' who have supported my work in one way or another that cannot go unmentioned. A big thanks to Claire Dujardin for her keen interest in my work and the wealth of information with which she has provided me; Johan Durnez OAM and Anny De Decker for their hospitality during one of my many visits to Belgium; Christophe Piron, for his photography skills; Sarah and Ray Boggiano for providing me with a roof to sleep under in the UK on two separate occasions; and Dr Delphine Lauwers for sharing her best seller with me. I must also thank members of the vibrant Dutch-speaking community in New South Wales: Dr Anne van Dongen, Dr Wim de Jonge and Amanda Thijsen, whose linguistic skills came in handy when decrypting certain sources.

Finally, eminent historian Jay Winter has often stressed the importance of family bonds in making and sustaining memory. With the addition of friends into the equation, the same can be said for books. My Australian and Belgian families and friends patiently put up with my incessant references to the First World War and gave me a reason to occasionally step away from the computer screen and get out into the real world. Marie-Jo et Pierrot Cordonnier, Marie Cordonnier et Christophe Piron, Mélanie Cordonnier et Thibaut Collard, *je vous remercie du fond du cœur pour votre soutien et votre patience.* To my parents, Meredith Haultain and Paul Gall, thank you for being such fantastic role models and supporting me from near and afar in whatever way you could. Nicola Haultain-Gall and Jennifer Mastrogiannidis, thank you for giving me plenty of suggestions of what to watch during my moments of down time. To Dr Aline Cordonnier, this would not have been possible without you. You inspired me, challenged me and supported me throughout. You are the real memory expert in our little family, and I am – and will always be – in awe of your resolve and intelligence. *Je ne saurais jamais te remercier assez.* Lastly, Félix, you were not around for most of it, but no one could make me smile like you on the long, trying days when it all seemed like a distant dream. To you and *maman*, I dedicate this book.

FOREWORD

For Australians, 1917 was clearly the worst year of the First World War. More than a third of the total deaths suffered in the war occurred in this terrible year. Most of them were on the Western Front, many in the Ypres salient. In November 1917, as the long battle of third Ypres finally ground to a halt, one clergyman at home wrote, 'This has been the blackest week in the whole hundred and seventy-three weeks of the war ... we seem to be up against a great black wall of darkness as high as the clouds and as deep as the bottomless pit'.[1]

Yet, in Australian popular memory and national commemoration, it is battles other than those fought in the Ypres salient that are commonly remembered: Pozières (1916), Villers-Bretonneux and Amiens (1918), and, of course, Gallipoli (1915), the inspiration of the foundational narrative of Anzac. To be sure, haunting visual images of the Ypres salient have come to represent all the horrors of the First World War: images of Australian soldiers marching past the ruins of the Ypres Cloth Hall; dead and wounded soldiers huddled in the railway cutting at Broodseinde; and five men in single file negotiating a duckboard track through the mud, water and gaunt, bare trees of the desolate Chateau Wood, near Menin Road. But the actual details of the associated battles of 1917 are less well known. Messines, Polygon Wood and particularly third Ypres are not familiar names to many Australians. The date of the first battle of Passchendaele, 12 October, is now remembered for the Bali bombing of 2002. Passchendaele has none of the popular resonance in Australia that it does in Britain, where for decades it has been a byword for Field Marshal Sir Douglas Haig's strategy of seemingly futile attrition.

The Battlefield of Imperishable Memory

In this important book Matthew Haultain-Gall explains the processes whereby 1917 suffered this puzzling eclipse in Australian collective memory. The relative neglect began with that most influential of memory makers, Charles Bean. *The Official History of Australia in the War of 1914–1918* included one (admittedly large) volume on 1917, but it was only one. Gallipoli and 1918 both merited two equally fat volumes. Bean, it seems, had simply seen too much killing on the Somme in 1916 to mourn again in 1917. Moreover, the Flanders campaign was problematic. It presented no scaling of cliffs, no climactic moment like the suicidal charge of the Light Horse at the Nek. Its outcomes were ambiguous. Its battles were largely 'bite and hold' operations, which gave centre stage not to courageous individuals, though there were plenty of these, but to artillery, poison gas, airpower and all the other lethal technology of mass industrial warfare.

This book shows that it was not only Bean who had trouble integrating the events of 1917 into the celebratory legend of Anzac. In the years after the First World War, returned servicemen, politicians and the Australian War Memorial all failed to accord the Ypres salient the prominence it deserved. Only one of the five memorials to Australian divisions hastily built in 1919 was positioned in this sector, at Polygon Wood. Although there were brief plans for a national memorial too at the site, it was Villers-Bretonneux that won out, in part because the dramatic recapture of that town in 1918 coincided with the semi-sacred Anzac Day. Of all the sites in the Ypres salient, only the Menin Gate, that massive monument to the missing, claimed a dominant place in Australian memory, thanks to the celebrated 1927 Will Longstaff painting *Menin Gate at Midnight*. However, the multinational character of that memorial inhibited its becoming a focal point for commemoration driven by national exceptionalism.

Foreword

Much has changed in the 'memory boom' of the last three decades, in which soldiers have come to be remembered as victims rather than heroic killers. From the 1990s on, the Australian government spent many millions on building new war memorials, installing interpretive plaques and, for the centenary of 1914–18, establishing the Australian Remembrance Trail along the former Western Front. Naturally, the battlefields of Belgium attracted some of this memory investment. New relationships with Belgian locals developed around practices of shared remembrance. But these activities were less grand and attracted less publicity than many others; and it was Villers-Bretonneux that was granted the starring role in centennial Western Front rituals, becoming the site of the $100 million Sir John Monash Centre.

Matthew Haultain-Gall has done us a great service in exploring this mystery of why Australians have failed to accord the Ypres salient a greater place in national memory over the past century. His meticulous, wide-ranging and insightful study confirms, compellingly, that the processes of collective-memory formation are always selective, serendipitous and – from the historian's perspective – unjust. Battles are remembered not for their strategic importance, their scale or even their casualties, but because, for a multitude of reasons, they attract the attention of agents of memory, ranging from individuals, filmmakers and community organisations to the media and governments. Memory, then, is not history – something that is worth remembering as Australia continues to accord the memory of war a dominant place in its national political culture.

Joan Beaumont

PROLOGUE

Driving back from a holiday in Brittany, my father-in-law stopped at Amiens so we could stretch our legs. As it is for so many Australians who grew up on a steady diet of Anzac proselytising in the 1990s, the name Amiens was immediately familiar to me. I felt compelled to let my partner's family know that it was on the outskirts of this city – Villers-Bretonneux, more precisely – that Australian soldiers broke the German offensive on the Western Front in 1918. They are French-speaking Belgians (Walloons), so this was news to them. In fact, they were surprised to learn that Australians had fought in Europe during the First World War. I was taken aback. I could forgive them for not knowing about the failed landing of 25 April 1915 on the distant shores of Gallipoli, but when the Australian Imperial Force got to Europe, it was fighting to liberate Belgian territory! Amiens was on their doorstep. And what about the Australians' enormous sacrifices at nearby Fromelles, during the bloodiest twenty-four hours in Australian military history? And Pozières, where poor British leadership left the soldiers of the AIF exposed to unrelenting artillery barrages? They had not heard of those either.

Then I played what I thought was my trump card. Surely they knew that the Australians had been at Ypres, that sliver of Belgian territory that had remained free from imperial Germany's yoke throughout the war? They hadn't, but they kindly showed some interest and asked what the Australians had done in Belgium. It was a good question. I didn't really know. It had been particularly muddy around Ypres, but then again, I vaguely remembered the Australian War Memorial diorama that most clearly depicted men struggling in the mud was of the Somme winter of 1916–17. The other engagements I could name all appeared to have some sort of clear narrative thread. Gallipoli stood for the death of innocence, a baptism of fire, the birth of a nation; Fromelles and Pozières were tragedies that further drove home the point that Australian troops had been used as cannon fodder by callous British generals; Villers-Bretonneux and Amiens symbolised the realisation of Australian martial potential. In my mind, the Australians' time at Ypres did not have any distinguishing features. Perhaps their involvement in the fighting in Belgium had not been as intense as that in France.

When I later delved into the history of the First World War, I was stunned to discover that the opposite was true. Had I missed something? Or were the AIF's battles in Belgium not as central to the Anzac narrative I had grown up with as those in France?

INTRODUCTION

A Salient Question

On 4 August 1914, imperial German troops marched into Belgium. The violation of the small kingdom's neutrality was the justification Great Britain sought to declare war on Germany. Bound to the mother country, the young Commonwealth of Australia had no legal right to remain neutral in the face of an imperial declaration of war. Not that Britain needed to dig into its constitutional arsenal to force the hand of Australian officials: the dominion enthusiastically committed itself to the empire's cause, immediately pledging 20,000 men to form an expeditionary force to be sent 'to any destination desired by the home [British] Government'.[1] On the home front, the plight of 'Brave' and then 'Poor Little' Belgium became a rallying point for public support for the war. In cities and country towns, community groups organised flag days and concerts to collect money for Belgian relief. Stories of German atrocities in the invaded regions were spread to bolster recruitment and mobilise hatred of the enemy.[2] However, it was not until nearly three years after Germany's invasion of Belgium that the men of the Australian Imperial Force finally found themselves fighting in a major engagement on Belgian soil.

The battle of Messines, which opened with a tremendous explosion of nineteen mines buried underneath German positions, was the AIF's first large-scale battle in Belgium. Before this, the AIF had seen action against the Ottoman Empire as part of the failed, but already legendary, Gallipoli campaign in 1915 and had fought several bloody battles against the Germans on the Western Front at Fromelles, Pozières and Bullecourt. Messines differed from the AIF's engagements in 1915 and 1916 in one significant way: it was a clear-cut victory. A similarly rosy appraisal did not apply to the Australians' involvement in the third battle of Ypres (now commonly known as Passchendaele), which began several weeks later.[3] During this campaign, all five of the AIF's infantry divisions were engaged in the same battle for the first time in the war. Fighting alongside other British units, the Australians initially met with some success, but their advance eventually ground to a halt as autumn rains drenched the devastated battlefield, turning it into an immense quagmire. By the time the AIF's main contribution to the third Ypres offensive petered out, the Australians had suffered over 38,000 casualties, including 10,000 dead, far outweighing Australian losses in any other campaign of the First World War.

After the war, the bodies that were recovered from the tortured Belgian earth were buried in British-administered cemeteries throughout the former salient. Among the numerous cemeteries in which Australians were interred in Belgium was Tyne Cot, the final resting place of more Commonwealth soldiers than any other Imperial War Graves Commission cemetery in the world. In addition to those who received proper burials, the names of more than 6000 Australians whose bodies were never identified or recovered were inscribed on the imposing memorial to the missing of the Ypres salient, the Menin Gate Memorial. Throughout the interwar period, the IWGC's cemeteries in the salient, and especially the Menin Gate, became key sites of pilgrimage for the bereaved from all corners of the British Empire.

The AIF's exploits in Belgian Flanders ought to be well known in Australia, the nation that most fervently commemorates its involvement in the First World War, given the extent of its losses in the salient.

Introduction

Certainly, a handful of official war photographs of the AIF taken during the Belgian battles are now among some of the most recognisable images of 1914–18 in circulation. They adorn the covers of numerous books, are printed alongside newspaper articles about the war and feature in First World War exhibitions (see plates 1 and 2). Frank Hurley's famous silhouette of 1st Australian Division support troops walking along a duckboard track even inspired the symbol of the Ngā Tapuwae New Zealand First World War Trails memorial project and featured on the poster for the Canadian war film *Passchendaele* (2008; see plate 3).[4] Yet, if these images now dominate the visual imagery of war on the Western Front, the actual campaign they represent and the nationality of the soldiers they depict are often obscured.

The proliferation of these photographs is a reflection of the now widely held view of war on the Western Front as a futile exercise that obliterated men and the terrain over which they fought, not of an increased interest in the specific events of 1917. On the contrary, Messines and third Ypres have received relatively little popular or even academic attention in Australia. Gallipoli and the Somme region of France remain the favoured destinations of Australian battlefield tourists, while the recent wave of memorial building on the Western Front has bypassed Belgium. In the words of Australian historian Joan Beaumont, 'The clashes on the Ypres salient … have a strangely ambiguous place in Australian national memory today'.[5]

The Battlefield of Imperishable Memory is the first study to seriously analyse how Australians have remembered and commemorated the AIF's involvement in the British campaigns fought in Belgium in 1917 over the last century. It is not a conventional military history of these battles, nor is it an appeal to remember the trials and triumphs of idealised Anzac soldiers, like so many other publications that invoke 'forgotten' battles. This is a cultural history that examines the evolution of war commemoration in Australia. Its main objective is to ascertain how these battles faded from Australian collective memory and why they have remained largely absent from the popular narrative of the war – the Anzac legend – despite a resurgence of interest in Australia's First World War exploits over the last few decades. Given that we have recently commemorated the centenaries of these engagements, this book also considers how Australians have cooperated with locals in Belgium in order to anchor these engagements more firmly in the popular narrative than has previously been the case.

Writing about Memory

Tracing the various ways in which Australians have engaged with, commemorated and overlooked the AIF's Belgian battles, *The Battlefield of Imperishable Memory* firmly positions itself within the burgeoning domain of memory studies. Academic interest in the study of memory is part of what is known as the 'memory boom', a term coined to describe Western countries' rediscovery of and confrontation with their past. It is as much the work of nations as it is of community groups, families and individuals. The boom began in the 1980s and has shown no signs of abating. Debates concerning remembrance and commemoration of the Holocaust, the nature of victimhood and the recognition of past traumas have contributed to the memory boom. So too have increased access to tertiary education and rising disposable incomes; the former has created a greater demand for cultural products, while the latter has ensured that individuals have the time and money to consume those products. Finally, a host of noteworthy anniversaries related to historically significant events have further amplified the memory boom.[6] In Australia, this can be seen in the interest aroused by the commemorative efforts put into events such as the bicentenary of white settlement, the centenary of federation and, of course, the 'Anzac Centenary'.

One of the most influential notions that has underpinned many historians' forays into the field of memory studies is that of collective memory. The term is usually defined along the lines of 'a group's representation of its past, both the past that is commonly shared and the past that is collectively commemorated, that enacts and gives substance to that group's identity, its present conditions and its vision of the future'.[7] There are two points worth highlighting here. First, collective memory includes representations of past events that are transmitted through everyday communication ('commonly shared') as well as more formalised representations ('collectively commemorated'). In the case of the latter, the war memorial is an example par excellence, but other formalised representations of the past can include rituals, museum exhibitions and books, to name just a few. Second, as long as they continue to evoke a shared and meaningful past, collective memories bind groups together even if the group members have never met each other. The best known of these 'imagined communities' is the nation.[8]

Agency is central to how historians approach the study of collective memory. They aim to identify those who seek to mobilise the past in the present, in which sociopolitical spaces these agents act and to what end. This concern with agency has seen a number of researchers focus on either bottom-up (psychological) or top-down (presentist) influences on collective memory. These divergent approaches inform one of the major questions in First World War historiography the world over: who is more influential in shaping war memory and commemoration? Arguing that the cultural impact of an event such as the First World War is 'virtually impossible for a government or ruling elite to engineer', scholars who adhere to the psychological approach downplay the political character of remembrance activities.⁹ Their studies thus focus on the memory work of 'small-scale' agents of remembrance, including families and returned veterans.¹⁰ For instance, when analysing war memorials in *Sites of Memory, Sites of Mourning*, historian Jay Winter argues that

> their ritual significance has been obscured by their political symbolism which, now that the moment of mourning has long passed, is all that we can see. At the time, communal commemorative art provided first and foremost a framework for and legitimation of individual and family grief.¹¹

In these studies, various acts of First World War commemoration were not the result of political intervention but 'expression[s] of mourning ... a human response to the death and suffering that war engenders on a vast scale'.¹²

Presentist studies of memory, on the other hand, emphasise the political character of commemoration. One of the best known examples of this approach is Eric Hobsbawm and Terence Ranger's *The Invention of Tradition*, which dissects how nations' elites mobilised history through 'invented traditions', defined as 'set[s] of practices ... of a ritual or symbolic nature', to legitimate action and cement group cohesion.¹³ In the Australian case, Anzac's dramatic revival has seen this question of political involvement in war commemoration take on a new immediacy for historians. Many have expressed concern that the state's extensive involvement in the promotion of a romanticised and sentimentalised Anzac narrative has 'effectively marginalised other formative experiences ... in the making of the nation'.¹⁴

Both approaches clearly have their weaknesses. Psychological studies that highlight the memory work of small-scale agents can downplay the role of the state in influencing and manipulating collective memory. As for the presentists, they 'can overplay the unity of social elites' as well as overlook the fact that in order to be accepted by the greater public, state-sponsored commemorative activities have to 'resonate with individual memories'.[15] This study aims to strike a balance between these two polarising approaches to the analysis of collective memory by applying the combined method suggested by Timothy Ashplant, Graham Dawson and Michael Roper. They cast the articulation of war memories as a struggle between 'different groups to give public articulation to … certain memories and the narratives within which they are structured', and they isolate several aspects of this struggle of articulation under the terms 'narratives', 'arenas' and 'agencies':

> Narratives of articulation refer to shared formulations within which social actors couch their memories … Arenas of articulation refer to those socio-political spaces within which social actors advance claims for the recognition of their specific war memories and … agencies of articulation refer to those institutions through which social actors seek to promote and secure recognition for their war memories.[16]

In other words, *The Battlefield of Imperishable Memory* examines the role and goals of multiple agents of memory, as well as the means deployed, intentionally or not, in representing and transmitting their visions of Messines and third Ypres. It does this through the examination of a wide range of mnemonic products and practices, including Charles Edwin Woodrow Bean's war correspondence and his *Australian Imperial Force in France in 1917* (the fourth volume of *The Official History of Australia in the War of 1914–1918*), which covers the AIF's 1917 campaigns; the Australian War Memorial's temporary exhibitions in Melbourne in 1922–25 and in Sydney in 1925–35; unit and family histories; articles published in the press and returned servicemen's journals; war novels and memoirs; the erection of memorials in Belgium; pilgrimages and battlefield tours; film and television productions; and the development of the Department of Veterans' Affairs' Australian Remembrance Trail on the Western Front. Each of these falls under the umbrella of what Jay Winter and Emmanuel Sivan have termed 'collective remembrance', defined as 'the act of gathering bits and pieces of the past, and joining them together in public', with the potential to influence the collective memory of the war.[17]

At the same time, it is important to keep in mind that not all agents or acts of collective remembrance are equally influential. For instance, as official war correspondent and official historian, Bean had the substantial backing of the state during and after the war, which allowed him to disseminate his interpretation of the war throughout the nation. With some exceptions, many unofficial agents working at the same time as Bean, including unit historians, soldier-authors and contributors to newspapers and returned services journals, would never have reached such a large audience. Rather, their accounts were shared within smaller groups, such as unit associations and returned services organisations. This is not to suggest, however, that these sources are not worth considering. As Alistair Thomson has argued, the dynamics within these smaller groups – or 'particular publics', as he calls them – are significant, as they can 'provide an important site for maintenance of alternative or oppositional meaning, a source of public strength for members to filter or even reject and contest more general meanings'.[18] Examining sources beyond those diffused to a mass audience thus allows for a more comprehensive understanding of how Australians have remembered and shared memories of the fighting in Flanders.

Since the late 1990s, there has been an explosion of studies analysing how Australians have remembered and commemorated various aspects of their participation in the First World War. There is also a rich body of literature concerning the origins and evolution of the Anzac legend in Australian society. Several of these mention official and unofficial commemorative initiatives related to the AIF's Belgian battles, such as the tour of Will Longstaff's famous painting *Menin Gate at Midnight* (1927; see plate 12), the memorials at Hill 60, in Zillebeke, and at Polygon Wood, and Australian pilgrimages to the former battlefields of the salient. However, they often fail to draw a distinct connection between these commemorative acts and the battles to which they are ostensibly linked. For example, in one particular article examining the significance to Australians of the Menin Gate Memorial and Longstaff's painting, there is not one reference to the battles of Messines or third Ypres, although most Australians whose names are engraved on the monument died in these campaigns.[19]

In addition to studies concerned with the general evolution of the Anzac legend and the commemorative practices it has engendered, there are also some histories that consider how specific campaigns have been remembered and commemorated. Unsurprisingly, historians have predominantly concentrated on Australian memory work surrounding the Gallipoli campaign, but there is also a trend for military histories of other battles to conclude with a discussion of the cultural legacies of the particular engagement or, at the very least, a brief description of how the battle is remembered today.[20] However, there is as yet no academic or popular history analysing Messines and third Ypres from a distinctly Australian standpoint. This gap in the literature is particularly marked when considering the bestselling work of journalist Peter FitzSimons, who has managed to avoid 1917 altogether in his rollicking accounts of other major AIF battles. Two minor exceptions to this state of affairs are historians Mark Connelly and Stefan Goebel's *Ypres* and Joan Beaumont's *Broken Nation*. The former covers representations of the campaigns fought around the Flemish town between 1914 and 1918 before tracing the evolution of mnemonic practices in the salient. Australian commemorative activity related to and in Belgium features in *Ypres*, but, in a publication that explores the transnational nature of remembrance in Belgian Flanders from British (imperial and commonwealth), French and German perspectives, the peculiarities of antipodean commemoration are quickly skimmed over. As for *Broken Nation*, of the hundreds of First World War books published in recent years, this study is the *only* one to consider in any detail the position of third Ypres in Australian memory. Yet, in a book that spans the entire war, Beaumont's analysis provides only a brief snapshot that does not consider the accumulation of acts that have led to the marginalisation of Messines and third Ypres in the popular imagination.[21] Drawing on Beaumont's astute analysis of the ambiguity of Belgium in Australian national memory, *The Battlefield of Imperishable Memory* extends her hypothesis in thinking about why this might be.

A Brief History of the Australians in the Ypres Salient

Before diving into our analysis of the 1917 Belgian campaigns in Australian memory, we must first consider what actually took place at the battles of Messines and third Ypres, as certain features of these engagements influenced the way they would be recalled and commemorated. When the AIF arrived in France in 1916, it was sent to a section of the line on the Franco-Belgian border known as the 'nursery', to be eased into combat on the Western Front. With the British preparing for a massive thrust further south, on the Somme, the Australians were only involved in raids, mainly in the vicinity of Armentières, in French Flanders. One raiding party did harass the Germans in front of Messines, but this could hardly qualify as a baptism of fire.[22] The AIF's first major engagements in France on the Western Front – a botched feint at Fromelles (5th Division) and brutal assaults on Pozières and Mouquet Farm (1st, 2nd and 4th Divisions) – occurred a few weeks later. By the time the Australians saw Belgian Flanders again, they had endured a bitterly cold Somme winter, had taken part in two wasteful assaults on Bullecourt and had suffered tens of thousands of casualties.

After a relatively quiet year by its already-infamous reputation, the Ypres salient became the centre of British attention in 1917. The British commander-in-chief, Field Marshal Sir Douglas Haig, launched a major offensive on the Belgian front for three main reasons: to hit the Germans in an area from which they would be reluctant to withdraw; to capture U-boat bases on the Belgian coast to reduce losses to British shipping; and to take the pressure off the French army, which had become increasingly demoralised after the failed Nivelle Offensive at the Chemin des Dames. Just how necessary and obtainable any of these aims were has been the subject of much debate among military historians, although it is clear that – as was often the case on the Western Front – the campaign's initial objectives were wildly optimistic.[23] The British forces eventually found themselves in a horrendous slogging match that ground to a halt in the shattered remnants of a Belgian village called Passchendaele. In British popular memory, Passchendaele – 'the very name with its suggestion of splashiness and of passion at once' – has become shorthand for the terror, stupidity and tragedy of the First World War.[24] However, the history of the third Ypres campaign is more nuanced, particularly when viewed from the Australian perspective.

The first major engagement the AIF fought in Belgium was the battle of Messines, in June 1917. Nominally a separate engagement, this battle, which aimed to straighten the British line to the south of the salient, was a necessary prelude to the third battle of Ypres, which was fought further to the north. The assault on Messines had been in the works for some time, and a number of mines had been laid under German positions in preparation for the attack. The explosion of these, two of which were detonated by the 1st Australian Tunnelling Company, obliterated the German garrison at the front and sent the survivors fleeing. The AIF's most recently formed division, the 3rd, was in the first wave of the British attack. Although its units had been hampered by intense gas shelling in the build-up, it advanced under the cover of a highly concentrated barrage and captured its objectives along with the rest of the British forces. Later, the 4th Division was also thrown into the fray, but the Germans had recovered from their initial shock by then, and as their resistance strengthened, the attackers' losses increased drastically. In total, the 3rd and 4th Divisions' casualties numbered some 6800.

With the British eventually achieving their main objectives, Messines was considered one of the Allies' more successful engagements of the war, but it is important to consider the context of this victory. The commander of the British Second Army, General Sir Herbert Plumer, who planned the Messines offensive, employed 'bite and hold', or 'step-by-step', tactics. These involved the attacking forces following an artillery bombardment known as a 'creeping barrage', 'which moved just ahead of [them] and so forced the front-line defenders to keep their heads down almost to the moment when they were about to be assaulted'.[25] Once the attackers had 'bitten' into the enemy line, they consolidated their position against counterattacks. If the barrage was heavy enough, these tactics were effective but also quite rigid, as they did not allow the infantry to exploit local successes. Moreover, each individual bite was rather shallow, making any breakthrough an unlikely proposition. Finally, the British success at Messines had been a long time in the making. There were no mines to blow away German resistance in the AIF's following engagements in Belgium.

With minor exceptions, the Australian infantry was not called on again until September 1917, when the 1st and 2nd Divisions were at the centre of the British forces for the battle of Menin Road. In between Messines and this engagement, the third battle of Ypres proper had not gone well for the Allies.[26] The British Fifth Army under General Sir Hubert Gough made little headway, as it became bogged down in a battlefield that was drenched in torrential rain for the better part of August. Frustrated by Gough's lack of progress, Haig looked to Plumer and his Second Army, which included the Australian divisions. Plumer was not only a more methodical planner than Gough; he was also luckier during his first major interventions in the campaign. The rain that had drowned Gough's ambitions of achieving a breakthrough stopped falling, and the battlefield began to dry out. When the Australians arrived at the front, the conditions were far more favourable to the attackers.

Having more or less abandoned the goal of reaching the Belgian coast before winter, the British set their sights on capturing the village of Passchendaele, the strategic value of which was questionable. Nevertheless, Haig insisted, and Plumer planned a series of bite and hold advances, the first of which was Menin Road, on 20 September. Preceded by an intense creeping barrage, the 1st and 2nd Australian Divisions captured their objectives with relative ease, especially when compared with previous engagements on the Western Front. German counterattacks over the following days nearly put paid to the British plans for a second push, but the 5th Australian Division managed to take back key positions in time. Although stretched to its limits, this division, along with the 4th, played a key role in the advance that captured

Polygon Wood, the local landscape feature after which this battle was eventually named. The following advance at Broodseinde Ridge, on 4 October, marked the Allies' third hard-fought victory in a row in the salient. This time, three AIF divisions – the 1st, 2nd and 3rd – were at the heart of the action. One of the outstanding features of this engagement was that the 1st and 2nd Divisions encountered German troops massing in No Man's Land for an attack that was due to take place at the same time and engaged them in fierce hand-to-hand combat. More generally, German command had decided to pack its front with troops to counter Plumer's bite and hold attacks. This was a woeful decision, as these men were exposed to the heavy Allied barrages accompanying the infantry's advance. According to the German official history, the battle of Broodseinde was 'the black day of October 4'.[27] And yet, for all their successes, the Australian divisions involved suffered upwards of 17,000 casualties during these battles alone.

Unfortunately for the AIF, the rain that had begun to fall during Broodseinde became stronger over the following days. The victory of 4 October reinforced Haig and Plumer's belief that the Germans were reaching their breaking point, and they did not wish to halt their offensive lest it give their enemy time to recover. It was a poor decision. The rain saturated a battlefield whose intricate drainage system had been decimated by artillery bombardments, making it nearly impassable for the infantry, let alone the artillerymen and their horses, who had to drag guns and ammunition through thick mud. Stripped of effective artillery support and with a shorter build-up time than the previous attacks, the Allies had little chance of success. The battle of Poelcappelle (also spelled Poelcapelle), on 9 October, which involved the 2nd Australian Division, was a particularly fruitless affair with no notable gains. For his part, Plumer appears to have been unaware of this failure, and, believing his forces were on the cusp of capturing the ruins of Passchendaele, he ordered a follow-up attack to take place on 12 October. The 3rd Australian Division was tasked with the dubious honour of capturing Passchendaele. Unsurprisingly, the first battle of Passchendaele ended as an unmitigated disaster. The losses endured during this battle, Poelcappelle and Broodseinde, along with 'wastage' each unit sustained while in the salient, ensured that October 1917 was the deadliest month of the war for the Australians. So ended the AIF's major role in the third Ypres campaign, an offensive which had promised so much in its early stages but ended up profoundly shaking Australian morale and costing the force over 38,000 dead, wounded and captured soldiers.

A Century of Remembering Messines and Third Ypres

The memory of the 1917 campaigns fought in the infamous Ypres salient lies at the heart of this book. The most logical place to start our examination of how Australians have collectively remembered these battles is with the work of official correspondent and historian Charles Bean. Bean was a central agent in the creation and propagation of the Anzac legend, and he was in Belgium in 1917 reporting on the AIF's experiences in the salient. This book's first chapter analyses Bean's various writings on the latter half of 1917 in order to discover how he viewed the fighting personally and how he communicated what he witnessed to his compatriots during and after the war. The following chapter examines another key agent – and a brainchild of Bean – responsible for disseminating an official narrative of the war to the Australian public: the Australian War Memorial. The focus here is on the representation of Belgian battlefields in the temporary exhibitions held by the AWM in Melbourne (1922–25) and Sydney (1925–35), as well as the tour administered by the AWM of Will Longstaff's painting *Menin Gate at Midnight*.

Chapters 3 and 4 primarily explore the memory work of unofficial agents. The first of these looks at how Messines and third Ypres were portrayed in a variety of media, including unit histories, popular war books and returned servicemen's publications. It finds that neither battle was a popular topic of discussion when compared to other engagements. The terrible conditions faced in the salient were difficult for many returned men to look back on with any sense of nostalgia. The second takes us overseas, to consider both official and unofficial Australian acts of remembrance in Belgium throughout the interwar period. During that time, Australia established a permanent – if rather shallow – 'memory footprint' in the salient, but this ultimately mattered little to many contemporary Australians.[28] Those who could afford to travel to the salient were often drawn there for intensely personal reasons, not by some abstract national narrative of Anzac glory.

Chapter 5 covers a rather turbulent period for First World War commemoration in Australia, spanning from the beginning of the Second World War to the end of the 1980s. During this time the Anzac legend was initially reinvigorated, but the experiences of the Second World War quickly overshadowed the memory of 1914–1918. Messines and third Ypres all but disappeared from popular memory during these decades. However, there was one key development further afield. In 1967, arrangements made between the Australian embassy in Brussels and the town of Ypres saw the establishment of a small annual Anzac Day service in the Belgian town, marking the beginning of a sustained relationship between the Flemish locals and Australia.

The final chapter follows developments in Australia and Belgium from the Australian bicentenary, in 1988, to the centenary of the First

World War. Although the war moved out of living memory with the passing of the last Anzacs during this period, following generations of Australians became increasingly proactive in its commemoration. The intersection between family and national history was an important factor, as was the increasing interest shown by officials in promoting the Anzac legend. Amid all the feverish remembrance activity of these years, Messines and third Ypres were not overlooked; however, they continued to receive comparatively less attention than other Western Front engagements.

Gallipoli, Fromelles, Villers-Bretonneux and Pozières: these battles resonate with meaning for many Australians. Not so Messines or third Ypres. Largely overlooked by both the public and historians, these costly engagements, fought in the AIF's worst year of the war, have long remained on the periphery of Australian memory. And yet their position there can tell us much about how the Anzac legend has evolved over the last century, as well as how Australians define themselves in the world. Tracing how Australians have portrayed and commemorated the 1917 campaigns in Belgium, *The Battlefield of Imperishable Memory* brings a fresh perspective to the memory work of familiar agents such as Bean while shedding light on the contributions of lesser known actors in shaping the Anzac legend. In looking beyond the Anzacs' campaigns in Turkey and France, this study furthers our understanding of how legends simplify and silence certain histories in order to survive.

Chapter 1

BEAN'S BELGIUM[1]

> As we drove to Bailleul between those flattened fields
> it seemed a part of the senseless fatuity of the world that
> a great nation's good cause can be ruined and a just war lost
> in spite of the devotion of millions of lives by some blind trick
> of the weather. Of course the only thing is to allow
> for the weather in your plans and assume that it may
> be the worst.
>
> *Charles Bean, 2 August 1917*
> *Diary, AWM: AWM38, 3DRL 606/84/1*

By the end of the First World War, Australia was a divided nation. The apparent unity of the early war years papered over divisions within pre-war Australian society, but war-weariness, industrial strikes and two bitterly contested conscription referendums shattered this illusion. Industrial unrest and a sluggish economy racked the country as it welcomed home 270,000 Anzacs bearing the physical and mental scars of four long years of conflict. Politically, the landscape at both federal and state levels was overwhelmingly conservative. Prime Minister William 'Billy' Hughes, having defected from the Australian Labor Party over conscription in 1916, ruled the Commonwealth with the Nationalists, who had managed to associate themselves with loyalty to the Australian (and British) cause during the war. By 1919, the Nationalists had further advanced their loyalist credentials by aligning themselves with the

Returned Sailors' and Soldiers' Imperial League of Australia, Australia's largest returned servicemen's organisation.[2] The Labor Party, on the other hand, had not only opposed conscription, but certain elements within the party had also sought a negotiated peace at all costs instead of pushing for outright victory over the Central Powers. This allowed conservatives to brand the party as disloyal, a slur that saw it banished to 'the political wilderness federally for many years'.[3] It was in this overly conservative political climate that the official narrative of the war took shape.

Historians concerned with the impact of the war in Europe have noted that the societies of the Old World found themselves in a state of 'cultural flux', unsure of how to imagine or remember the war.[4] Highlighting the concerted modernist turn in 'high' cultural productions, Samuel Hynes, Paul Fussell and Modris Eksteins argue that the industrial-scale carnage of the First World War led to, in Hynes' words, 'a sense of radical discontinuity of present from past'. For these scholars, the experiences of 1914–18 undermined traditional values steeped in classicism, romanticism and religion and reversed the idea that human history was inexorably progressing towards perfection thanks to scientific advancements.[5] Others, such as Jay Winter, George Mosse and Stefan Goebel, reject these arguments, demonstrating that many turned to the traditional forms of expression they knew so well for solace.[6] Such a debate is strikingly absent in Australian historiography. Indeed, 'Australia shared some of these [European] cultural dilemmas, but from the very first, public opinion was shaped by a less ambiguous embrace of the classical and nationalist traditions' – traditions which were rooted in notions of Edwardian militarism and social Darwinism.[7] Seen through these notions, the Gallipoli landing, and the war in general, provided Australians with a coming-of-age moment that proved the young commonwealth worthy of a place among the established nations of the world.⁸ As historian Stephen Garton argues, 'This emphasis on the nobility of war and the glory of Anzac achievement is not surprising; especially given the nationalist longings of many Australians'.⁹ Moreover, the irony and despair proffered by modernists provided scant consolation to those who had suffered loss. The high diction, romantic imagery and triumphalism that had become so jaded for some still appealed to and comforted the vast majority of Australians. Consequently, it is of little surprise to find that the official narrative – the Anzac legend – disseminated by a conservative state that believed in the righteousness of the conflict, drew heavily on these traditional themes.

In the immediate aftermath of the First World War, the Australian state's plans to foster the memory of the conflict were in their infancy. In fact, the Australian National Memorial in Villers-Bretonneux was only unveiled in 1938, the Australian War Memorial opened its doors in 1941, and the final volume of Charles Bean's *Official History of Australia in the War of 1914–1918* was published in 1942. Thus, it was not until the second global conflict in a generation that the official narrative of the first was finally enshrined in ink and stone. The Australian public, however, did not have to wait for the completion of memorials or the *Official History* to be exposed to the predominant narrative of the First World War. From the moment the Australian Imperial Force faced its first major test of the war, the landing at Anzac Cove, the legend began to take shape, and Charles Bean – Australia's official war correspondent and, eventually, official historian – was one of the principal agents behind the creation and elaboration of this narrative.¹⁰ In addition to the steady stream of reports he sent from the front, Bean had a hand in numerous official projects publicising the AIF's achievements throughout the war. He edited the extraordinarily popular *Anzac Book*, a collection of writings and illustrations 'by the men of Anzac', along with two more Anzac annuals: *Letters from France*, in 1916, and *From the Australian Front*, in 1917.[11] He was also instrumental in the establishment of the Australian War Records Section – a unit tasked with collecting war records – the creation of which 'marked the beginnings of the Australian War Memorial'.[12] Bean's work with the section also saw him closely involved in Australia's official photography and war art schemes.[13] Nor did his efforts to commemorate the Anzacs slacken with the end of hostilities. Although the *Official History* took up the lion's share of his time, this did not prevent him from becoming a key figure in the foundation of the Australian War Memorial, the monument and institution that gave the Anzac legend a physical form.[14] Given his integral role in nurturing the legend, no study of Australian First World War memory can afford to overlook him.

When the bulk of the AIF transferred to Europe, Bean found the conditions of trench warfare throughout 1916 and 1917 challenged several romantic, bush-tinged ideals upon which his conception of Australian manhood was largely based. In particular, the crushing artillery bombardments at Pozières in 1916 left a deep impression on the journalist, and this engagement became his benchmark for Anzac endeavour in Europe.[15] Gallipoli could be interpreted as a glorious baptism of fire, but Pozières was an 'uglier', more testing ordeal, and Bean was awestruck by the heroism, humour and mateship the Australian infantry displayed there. Moreover, the sacrifice of so many Australians at Pozières set Bean on a course that saw him establish the Australian War Memorial. From the 'gigantic ash heap' of a ruined French village arose one of the young commonwealth's most symbolic monuments.[16] Just under a year later, Bean observed the Australians' major engagements in Belgium:

the limited victory at Messines in June 1917 followed by the third battle of Ypres proper. It was a longer, bloodier affair than Pozières, involving all five AIF divisions, and the losses suffered during this campaign contributed to another recruitment crisis for the Australian military and helped trigger a second conscription referendum. Yet, despite the campaign's particular significance for Australians, Bean's published and unpublished accounts suggest that, for the most part, what he witnessed in Belgium moved him less than that at other battlefronts, especially Pozières.

In the introduction to the fourth volume of the University of Queensland's edition of the *Official History*, Bill Gammage claims Bean found 1917 difficult to write about, as events of that year 'contributed relatively little to his essential purpose, to show how Australian citizens passed the test of war and founded a national tradition'.[17] While this is a useful starting point, the argument is rather narrow. The reasons Gammage cites – the death of several of Bean's 'heroes' and the soldiers' vulnerability to artillery – were not confined to 1917. In order to comprehend Bean's interpretation of the Flanders campaign, it is necessary to look more critically at his correspondence and diaries as well as the finished product of the *Official History*. Bean's private writings during the campaign reveal he was suffering under an increasingly heavy workload. This meant he was not as focused on or as emotionally invested in either Messines or third Ypres as he had been during previous engagements. More importantly, as Bean's writings show, the AIF's experience of the offensives was not confined to the soldiers' passivity in the face of enemy bombardments, as Gammage claims.[18] Instead, the Allied artillery's effectiveness, as opposed to the Australian infantry's much-vaunted audacity, was often the decisive element in deciding a battle's outcome. Moreover, many Anzacs displayed a disquieting brutality towards surrendering Germans in Belgium. These features combined to further undermine key elements of Bean's romantic vision of Australian military manhood.

Bean's Public and Private War

Before radio and television, the newly literate populations of the developed world relied on print media for the latest news. In Australia, the major dailies 'were the sole ciphers of overseas news to the public'.[19] The German invasion of Belgium and the subsequent British declaration of war meant that Australian newspapers and press associations were hungrier for overseas news than ever before. Utterly reliant on the various media outlets in the early days of August 1914, Australians gathered in front of newspaper offices awaiting the most up-to-date reports from Europe. Over the next four years, news outlets maintained this interest in the war by providing daily, instead of intermittent, reports from the various fronts. Yet, as the war became an increasingly rich source of news, press censorship narrowed the scope of what could be reported. Australians were doubly affected by this state of affairs: news reports published in the dominion were subject to the critical eye of British censors before undergoing a second treatment at the hands of locals.[20] Moreover, censorship had a general levelling effect on the media. According to historian John Williams, 'The mainstream press … constituted a homogenous mass of apparently like-minded newspapers, which had become, to all intents, semi-official propaganda organs espousing the national cause'.[21] In other words, Australians were hardly spoiled for choice when it came to keeping abreast of events in the Middle East and Europe.

It was within this restrictive environment that Bean's dispatches reached the Australian public. Other war correspondents' reports were regularly published in Australia during the war too, but Bean was unique. The British government allowed the dominion governments to appoint a single war correspondent each. Employed by the Commonwealth, Bean's brief was to

> satisfy the poignant anxiety of Australians for news of their own men – their daily life, their behaviour in action, their peculiar Australian interests ... and who was also specially charged with the writing after the war of an account of the Australian part in it for a permanent record for Australian libraries, schools and the Australian people generally.[22]

Censorship still applied, but in order to attain his objectives, Bean (as well as the other dominion correspondents) had the freedom to roam unhindered by General Headquarters' chaperones. Consequently, he saw much more fighting than the typical war correspondent. Nor was Bean beholden to any one media outlet, as his articles were available for publication in any newspaper.[23] This ensured that an officially mediated narrative of the war was available to the widest audience possible.

Yet Bean's influence on public opinion cannot be taken for granted. Bean himself admitted that the public gradually became 'accustomed to over- or under-emphasis in the press'.[24] While the earliest reports of the Australians at Gallipoli incited men to enlist like never before, come 1917, war-weariness had set in. Casualty lists were still mounting, and a tightly contested conscription referendum had divided the population. Nevertheless, the re-election of Prime Minister Billy Hughes and the landslide victory of his 'Win the War' party in May 1917 showed that an overwhelming majority of Australians had not lost the will to fight either. Journalists' reports from the front may no longer have been effective at encouraging men to enlist, but ongoing reports of the heroic deeds of AIF soldiers, who were not just compatriots, but sons, brothers and relatives of many Australians, surely played a role in maintaining popular support for the war. These reports did not say anything drastically new, but they did give Australians further proof of their soldiers' courage.

At the other end of the spectrum, Bean's diaries were unavailable to the public until well after the war. When writing as a correspondent, Bean respected censorship restrictions and refrained from questioning military authorities. His diary entries, on the other hand, offer more candid qualifications of the war, thereby revealing biases omitted from newspaper articles or tucked away in one of the *Official History*'s copious footnotes. Bean planned for the diaries to serve as a blueprint for the *Official History*.[25] Consequently, his entries differed greatly from those of a soldier living through the First World War. Paid to observe, Bean had to 'detach himself from his surroundings and analyse his emotions in a manner rarely available to the soldier under fire', while thinking of the grander narrative behind each individual event.[26] This also meant that, unlike most journal-keeping soldiers, he edited passages retrospectively. In certain instances, then, a diary entry was not the spontaneous work of an eyewitness but a 'carefully constructed narrative written after the event'.[27] Familiarity with these relatively private writings allows for a deeper analysis of Bean's work carried out under the gaze of the public eye during and after the war. In this sense, the diaries draw back a curtain on the Anzac myth-making process that marginalised the AIF's experiences in Belgium.

Bean in Belgium

At 3:10am on 7 June 1917, the detonation of nineteen mines on the southern flank of the Ypres salient heralded the beginning of the battle of Messines and, more generally, Field Marshal Sir Douglas Haig's great Flanders campaign. The explosion created by the mines was recorded as the largest ever made by man. The encounter also saw the introduction to the battlefield of the 3rd Australian Division – 'the baby of the AIF, untried so far as major operations went' – commanded by Major-General John Monash, fighting alongside New Zealand and British troops.[28] They achieved all of their objectives, and Messines is still considered one of the more successful engagements of the war. However, it is interesting to note that Bean's correspondence and diary entries dealing with this battle were fairly prosaic. Monash himself was particularly unimpressed, noting that Bean's coverage of Messines was 'the apotheosis of banality'.[29]

As many scholars familiar with Bean's work have noted, the language he used to describe the action at the front was never as jingoistic as that of other correspondents.[30] Nonetheless, even by Bean's usual standards, his initial reports of Messines were overly restrained. For example, when writing about the Australians at Fromelles and Pozières, he had declared that they were 'worthy of all the traditions of Anzac'.[31] At Messines, however, it is surprising to see that the reunion of the Australians with their Anzac kin, the New Zealanders, did not culminate in a similar attempt to wax lyrical about the past glories of the Gallipoli campaign. At least one correspondent was awake to the symbolic importance of the event, claiming that, although thousands of the Australians and New Zealanders involved had not fought at Gallipoli, they were 'of the Anzac breed' and that Messines was 'the proof of it'.[32] Bean, on the other hand, does not seem to have been as moved, merely stating that it was the 'first great common battle' in which men of the two dominions had fought together since Gallipoli.[33] This was the first of several instances in which Bean's description of the fighting in Belgium was rather uninspired.

Even Bean's handling of the detonation of the mines in the opening phase of the battle was rather fleeting, especially given the 1st Australian Tunnelling Company's role in protecting the Hill 60, in Zillebeke, and Caterpillar mines laid underneath the German lines. Other British war correspondents drew considerable attention to the 'man-made earthquake' that 'broke out in a vast roar, like a cliff falling down a precipice, as Hill 60 opened and let forth a great eruption of flaming clods', leaving the defending Germans in the area shaking 'with the terror of the explosion'.[34] Bean, on the other hand, was content with a single, banal line noting 'the explosion … of seven great mines'. Well after the battle, two longer, more graphic accounts of Bean's covering the fighting at Messines did appear in the papers, but they added little to what had already been reported by other correspondents.[35]

Bean's diary entries concerning Messines were a reflection of his official correspondence. Bean recorded the details of the fighting for the *Official History* in his usual blow-by-blow fashion but wrote very little of his own appreciation of the battle. That Bean was so sparing in his evaluation of Australian achievements at Messines largely boiled down to two factors. First, he was hardly enamoured with two generals involved in the battle: Monash and Lieutenant-General Sir Alexander Godley, commander of II ANZAC Corps. Bean's well-documented disdain for Monash was far more palpable during other episodes of the war – notably his attempt to block the general's appointment to the command of the Australian Corps in 1918 – than at Messines.[36] Nevertheless, the correspondent did note that certain 3rd Australian Division commanding officers were 'a bit shy of fire' and that Monash was 'not the man to keep them up to it'. As for Godley, Bean did not find him particularly 'sincere' and wrote that the general's indecision at

Messines left his divisions 'longing to get back' to Lieutenant-General Sir William Birdwood's I ANZAC Corps. Second, when he recorded comments made by members of the 48th Battalion that the fighting had been 'nothing like so trying as Pozières', Bean probably summed up his own position on the matter as well. This was the first of several occasions on which Bean referenced Pozières (or noted others' comments about it) over the course of the 1917 Belgian campaigns. Messines, on the other hand, was just a prelude to something grander, 'an attack made to get out of the way a big obstacle before the real offensive was made in Flanders'. Reassured that this larger offensive following Messines would be 'quite a separate move', Bean decided to 'hurry across to England and get a real holiday in order to store up nerve and freshness for the strain which ought to come later on'.[37]

Unfortunately for Bean, the four weeks in England did not give him enough time to lessen his workload. Instead, the timing of the campaign in Flanders clashed with his efforts to have the Australian War Records Section's collecting duties extended from unit war diaries to also include objects for 'future Australian museums'.[38] By the beginning of September he was finding it difficult to perform his main tasks to the best of his ability:

> It is obvious that the record work makes it impossible to do the correspondent work properly, and they both suffer. There are battalions I have not visited since Bullecourt and Messines and I have only written a couple of articles in the last month.

Despite these concerns, Bean did not relinquish the record work. Instead, in an effort to make up for lost time, he headed off to Pozières 'to get what relics' he could find there.[39]

At least in the months preceding September, the AIF's role in the third Ypres campaign was minimal. For most of July and August,

Bean had little to report apart from inspections of various units by King George V or Birdwood.[40] Nonetheless, he addressed two subjects worth highlighting. First, Bean's writing during the initial stages of the campaign drew liberally on the symbolism of the salient, which – although the war was far from over – had all but attained the status of a sacred site, thanks to the press coverage of the first and second battles of Ypres.[41] It was the determined last stand of the British regular army in November 1914, in particular, that appealed to Bean. Tapping in to this recent history, he reported that the current battle was taking place on 'ground of imperishable memory … ground sacred to the memory of that little British regular army which made its last and greatest sacrifice'. Such writing added colour to the current battle and helped set the scene for the eventual involvement of the Australians, who were yet to play a leading role in the fighting around the salient. Of course, the Anzacs had already proved Australia worthy of her place among the great nations at Gallipoli and during the battle of the Somme, but soon they would be proving themselves on a battlefield that had attained particular significance to the British Empire, fighting over 'historic soil' hallowed by the blood of the best soldiers the empire had to offer.[42]

The second intriguing aspect of Bean's correspondence during this period, and eventually throughout the entire Flanders campaign, was his treatment of the Australian artillery. Never before had the British amassed so much artillery for any operation on the Western Front, and the Australian gunners were in the thick of the action from the beginning.[43] The infantry and light horsemen may have forged the Anzac legend on the shores of Gallipoli, but now the artillerymen were demonstrating to Bean that they too belonged to this famous tradition. Those natural soldierly qualities that the frontline Anzac possessed in abundance were on display in Australian batteries. The gunners proved to be just as unflappable under shellfire and strafing as their mates in the trenches. In one episode, the men did not weather heavy counter-barrages; they thrived under them:

> The Australian batteries carried out every order which reached them through the long day, exactly as if on the practice ground. 'I liked those first six hours,' said one gunner to me, 'more than any other day in my life'.[44]

This report set the tone of Bean's later articles concerning the artillery. In his summary of the campaign months later, he wrote, 'The Australian infantry has long since made its quality known. In this battle the Australian artillery has laid down a glorious and wonderful tradition'.[45] The correspondent's focus had always been on the fighting combatant, which usually meant the infantry.[46] Now, for the first time in the war, Bean carved a niche for the gunners and drivers into his vision of the Anzac soldier. They were to be considered Anzacs by simple association no longer, but rather by proud contribution.

The shift to an emphasis on the artillery was problematic, as the highest romantic ideals of the superior Australian soldier came to be represented by those operating anonymous killing machines. John Williams suggests that switching attention away from the infantry to other arms of the AIF, such as the artillery, was simply a technique to broaden a correspondent's scope. Yet, Bean's interest in the artillery at Ypres went beyond the occasional reference.[47] Neither the engineers nor the pioneers received nearly as much attention. The focus on the Australian artillery was a tacit admission of the realities of modern industrial warfare, weakening elements of the Anzac legend that emphasised the fighting ability of Australian citizen soldiers. Whether readers in Australia picked up on these conflicting ideas is impossible to say. But the fact that Bean highlighted the work of the artillery signalled a slight shift in his correspondence. Warfare on the Western Front had never been conducive to demonstrating the Australian infantryman's supposed fighting superiority, and the tactics employed during the third Ypres campaign left even less room than previous engagements for romantic representations of infantry action. For a correspondent dedicated to the 'truth', regular glorifying references to the artillery were perhaps sometimes the only consolation available.[48]

Crucially, the achievements and suffering of those who best exemplified the Anzac legend – the men in the trenches – remained Bean's measure for judging a battle throughout the war and beyond. In a postwar summary of 'great battles', he again identified Pozières as the 'hardest fight' because of 'the strain it placed on the endurance of the troops'. Other battlefields, like Bullecourt and Lone Pine, also stood out thanks to the intensity of the hand-to-hand fighting there. Bean did briefly note that Ypres was the 'heaviest experience of the latter part of the war, *but* the chief weight of that experience fell upon the artillery'.[49] His use of 'but' implied the battle was less significant, as the infantry did not endure the worst of the campaign.

After weeks of fighting in the salient, the Australian infantry finally made its appearance in 'one of the world's mightiest battles' on 20 September, at the battle of Menin Road.[50] Like so many offensives before it, the third Ypres campaign had not lived up to the expectations of the British High Command. General Hubert Gough's Fifth Army had failed to attain its objectives, so Haig turned to General Sir Herbert Plumer's Second Army, which contained all five Australian infantry divisions. As it was only the first of Plumer's 'steps', or 'bite and hold' attacks, at Ypres, the Australians' success at Menin Road was favourably reported by Bean without eliciting too much excitement.[51]

The battle was unique in that it was the first time two Australian divisions (the 1st and 2nd) had attacked side by side. However, censorship prevented Bean from naming the units involved, and his readers in Australia remained unaware of this historic first. Bean was able to report that Australians were at last advancing over the 'ground of imperishable memory':

> Three years ago this ridge was clothed by the great trees of Polygon Wood around the Zonnebeke racecourse where the first small British army was made for ever glorious, and where the Canadians and British held on fighting inch by inch after the Germans had broached their first vile gas cylinders.

With the battle of Menin Road, the Australians had taken their first stride towards writing themselves into the history of the region. Nonetheless, Bean did not hesitate to remind his readers where the AIF had already made its name, adding, 'One can only say that they went into this great test beside British troops, the same grand wholehearted Australian boys who took Pozières and who stormed Gallipoli'.[52] The Anzacs would have to achieve something very special in the salient if Bean was to consider Ypres as important as those two legendary battlefields.

Bean's diary entries contained few differences from his official correspondence concerning the assault along the Menin Road, as had been the case with his records of Messines. They did, however, reveal that Bean was barely distracted from his war records work and his attempts to sacralise all that the Anzacs had touched. It may have been a 'remarkably excellent bit of work' by the 1st and 2nd Australian Divisions, yet the following day Bean was not solely focused on writing reports of the action. He also wired Australia with the suggestion that the government should purchase the Pozières battleground.[53] Making such a proposal at this point in time was another indication that Bean had already drawn his conclusions about which of the AIF's battles on the Western Front was most worthy of commemoration.

On the eve of Plumer's second step, Bean's diary entries painted the picture of a man who had spread himself too thinly. On this occasion it was not only the quest for relics that impinged on his valuable time, but also his work on the souvenir AIF Christmas book *From the Australian Front*, which led him to confide in his diary:

> I have so much to do in the way of administration – arranging for records and photos and the Christmas Book and other things, that I have scarcely any time to get the history of this battle [Menin Road]. Add to it that my car is laid up and that another has not come – I am at my wits['] end how to cope with this work.[54]

Evidently, Bean was becoming increasingly overwhelmed by his numerous responsibilities, which left him precious little time to focus on the present situation. His diary entries compound this impression: the description of third Ypres is no more than a pale imitation of those concerning earlier battles, notably Pozières.[55] Bean's response to an invitation to lecture on the 'fighting in Flanders' after the war further demonstrated that he had been more alert to events at Pozières than to those at Ypres, as he claimed, 'I find Pozières a good deal easier to speak of than Flanders, since I know so much more about it'.[56] Third Ypres was the largest campaign in which Australians were involved that year, and yet Bean did not give it his full attention.

Bean did manage to send off several articles outlining the battle of Polygon Wood. The second successful advance in a row, achieved under more trying conditions than those at Menin Road, gave Bean the chance to highlight the work of the infantry while once again referring to the AIF's past exploits. The Victorians on the right flank, in particular, came in for special praise, as they had been subjected to the hardest fighting the Australians had faced so far at Ypres, where 'the heaviness and the constancy of the barrage brought it more into comparison with Pozières than perhaps any other fight Australians were ever in'. Bean even went so far as to claim that 'the fight of the Victorians in Polygon Wood will be one of the most famous of many terrible struggles which history will associate with that name'.[57] Having reinforced their successes at Menin Road, the Australian soldiers, like the British and Canadians before them, could now lay claim to their place in the history of the famous Ypres salient. This may seem like simple exaggeration on the part of the war correspondent, but after the war, the 5th Australian Division, which had not endured the Pozières bombardments, erected its divisional memorial on top of the Polygon Wood butte.

The optimistic tone of Bean's correspondence continued with the British triumph at Broodseinde Ridge on 4 October. It was the third successful push in a row, and the Australians had played a leading role in the attack. While still unable to give the names of the units involved, Bean was at least able to report that

> the centre in today's great thrust is made up by a solid phalanx of Australian troops ... Never before were troops so content to enter battle beside one another as this great line of Australians who were just loosed upon the Germans.

Pushing the Germans off a crest, which once again teemed with 'undying associations', the Australians 'swept over almost the exact position ... where General French's line before Ypres originally ran in the earliest days of the war'.[58] At that moment, the Australians were not only reliving history by equalling the achievements of armies past; they were making it.

Whether Bean himself was wholly convinced by this victory is unclear, as he neglected to record any observations in his diary.[59] According to his correspondence, however, the Broodseinde triumph seemed so complete that he could see an end to the conflict. Eager to share it with his fellow Australians, he wrote:

> Many of us today feel an optimism we have not before felt, realising that means at last have been worked out for delivering upon the German, whenever desired, smashing blows which he cannot avoid nor parry ... Personally one feels that for the first time a weapon has been worked out which opens the prospect of real success leading to finality.[60]

That the Australians proved to be the effective cutting edge of this new weapon was even better:

> It should be a matter of tremendous pride to Australians to realise that in the battles of Messines and Ypres the solid striking force of their troops helped in an outstanding way to deal the blows by which this weapon has been proved.

Back in Australia, the major dailies published these passages under titles such as 'Haig's Success' and 'Hapless Plight of the Enemy'.[61] It is hard to know how much enthusiasm this stoked in a public that had seen its fair share of grand titles and predictions over the years. Nevertheless, proclaiming a possible end to the war, these dispatches were among the most upbeat of Bean's reports from the front in 1917.

Even as these bold forecasts went to print, Bean's following cable put a dampener on them. Autumn had descended 'too late to do any harm' during the most recent Australian push, but the weather had now turned. The battles of Poelcappelle and Passchendaele, launched on 9 and 12 October respectively, were fought in highly unfavourable conditions, and their outcomes were far from inspiring, although Bean avoided such an admission. Instead, when referring to Poelcappelle, he wrote, 'The results of this fight are less complete than the three previous ones'. Moreover, without such positive results to draw upon, he found little else to highlight in this battle. Sure enough, the men had shown 'extreme endurance', but Bean also noted that he had not 'seen any depression or any exhaustion similar to which showed in the faces of the men who came out of the Pozières battle'.[62] Thus, another engagement failed to measure up to Bean's yardstick for Australian achievement and suffering on the Western Front.

After the failure of Poelcappelle, the first battle of Passchendaele only served to prolong Australian misery in the salient. It was yet another bitter pill for the AIF and Bean to swallow after similarly trying experiences at Fromelles, Pozières and Bullecourt. Once again, Bean's correspondence did not state this in so many words, but the tone and scope of his articles had changed significantly since the optimism of Broodseinde. There were no more all-conquering advances, and Bean had to content his audience with anecdotes relating to minor actions. Furthermore, it was clear that at Passchendaele the Australians were fighting against not just the Germans but the rain-drenched terrain as well – so much so that Bean felt it necessary to state that 'the weather – and the weather alone' was the reason for the poor outcome.[63] It was a sorry end to Australian involvement in the campaign.[64] For all the correspondence doublespeak available to him, Bean was unable to disguise the fact that the AIF's big push had ended with a whimper, when he had promised a bang.

Omitted from his correspondence, Bean's personal frustration with the assaults on Passchendaele Ridge was palpable in his diary entries. In particular, he was highly critical of the Second Army command and Field Marshal Haig. As Bean saw it, the accumulation of obstacles facing the attackers was too great. A combination of poor weather, more distant objectives than before, a thinner barrage and only one day's artillery preparation – most of which went unmentioned in his newspaper correspondence – meant that each push had a low chance of success. German morale had been believed to be near breaking point after the events at Broodseinde, but in the follow-up assaults 'the object was so badly carried out' that the Allies 'won not an inch of ground'. As a result, German morale rose while that of the Allies was eroded. Bean asked himself, 'What excuse is the very best strategic or psychological object in the world if the plan you pursue does not and cannot get it?'[65]

The inability of certain British commanders to fully comprehend the reality of the situation was, unfortunately, nothing new in the AIF's overall experience of the war. Bean had already seen his fair share of bungling, and for him, General Hubert Gough's incompetence at Bullecourt was the absolute nadir.[66] General Herbert Plumer's earlier operations in the salient had at least made some headway, and he had seemed to be aided by somewhat capable men. After speaking to Major-General Sir Charles Harington, Plumer's second-in-command, about the failure of the recent attacks, Bean admitted that, despite being unimpressed with his reasoning, at least Harington appeared to have

> room for a finer brain and character than he showed on the surface … [as] he was clearly not one of those society cavalry generals … He has the face, the lines, the slight raggedness of moustache, and other unconventionalities, of the scholar.[67]

In short, he was close to the antithesis of the much-maligned Gough, whose 'Lancer background' and preference for dash rather than solid staff work had cost many Australian lives.[68] Poelcappelle and Passchendaele were abysmal, but for Bean a disaster of colossal proportions would be needed to replace Bullecourt as the worst Australian experience under British leadership. There seemed to be some method in the madness of third Ypres.

Bean's private and public writings after the campaign emphasised that Haig's Flanders offensive was neither a debacle of the proportions of Bullecourt nor the summit of Australian heroism and endurance. Recording a meeting with two old hands from the 5th Battalion in November, Bean noted that they had described the fighting in the Ypres salient as 'hot'. However, when he pressed them on this point, enquiring, '"Was it as stiff as Pozières?" They shook their heads at once and said decisively "No, not by a long chalk. Oh that was a bloody muddle. This time the staff work was good"'.[69] The articles Bean sent to Australia during the northern winter took up this theme. Despite the Flanders campaign being by far the bloodiest of the AIF's engagements, Bean concluded, 'to the Australian infantry there has been an immense difference between the Ypres battle and the nightmare of Pozieres'.[70] Of course, this conclusion depended on how Bean qualified 'nightmare'. The bombardment at Pozières may have been more severe in intensity, but the average casualty rate per division was roughly the same in both battles. Moreover, with all AIF divisions engaged at Ypres, there were approximately 15,000 more casualties and 2000 more deaths overall.[71] Unable to state this in so many words, Bean fell back once again on his Pozières trope. This served to minimise the consequences of the Belgian campaign while further elevating the mythic proportions of that first major engagement on the Somme.

In view of its meagre results, it was difficult for Bean to summarise the third Ypres campaign in a positive manner. Due to their relative success, the actions at Polygon Wood and Broodseinde were the subjects of much post-campaign correspondence. Broodseinde, in particular, turned out to be all the more astonishing, as Bean revealed that the Australians had met the Germans in No Man's Land and simply rolled over them 'as a wheel crushes the stones of the road'. However, for all the promise of that battle, its potential went unfulfilled. When turning to Poelcappelle and first Passchendaele, Bean could only describe these ineffectual advances as 'incompletely successful'.[72] The reality was more sombre; the only notable 'success' of these two poorly conceived operations was to further weaken a battle-weary AIF that was struggling to replace its losses.[73]

It was not until several weeks later, however, that the full consequences of the failed campaign became apparent. A heavy defeat for the Italians at Caporetto and the collapse of the Russian army as a result of the October Revolution 'completely changed the complexion of the war'.[74] In response to these events and the losses in Belgium, Australians were again asked to vote for conscription, and they rejected it once more. Not long before, the British had been 'breaking down the German resistance by a series of great and crushing blows [and] the end never seemed more certain'. Now, Bean reported, 'it would be idle to pretend' that the AIF's prospects were 'bright'.[75] In the end, the third battle of Ypres had failed to live up to Bean's optimism and had left the AIF in a precarious position. It was neither a grand victory nor a total defeat, but a steady wearing down of the AIF, which fell short when it hinted at offering more.

Official History

Compared to Bean's regular correspondence and edited publications produced during the war, the *Official History* is often considered to have had less direct influence on the broader memory of the conflict. This is not to suggest that it had no influence. Speakers read passages from the

Official History on special occasions, particularly Anzac Day, and excerpts were included in school readers.[76] Nevertheless, it was published too long after the conflict to have any grand impact on the public's understanding of the war, which had already been shaped by exposure to numerous representations of the Anzacs between 1914 and 1918 and, after the war, by publications in circulation several years before the bulk of the *Official History* was completed, such as Monash's *Australian Victories in France in 1918*, various unit histories and descriptive newspaper reports. Appearing so soon after the conflict, it was these unofficial texts that helped cement the memory of the Anzacs' achievements firmly in the mind of the Australian public in the interwar years.

Nevertheless, the *Official History* has had a remarkable impact on how Australian *historians* have written about the war. In fact, Bean's monument to the men of the First AIF has dominated popular and academic studies of Australian military history. His central question was 'How did the Australian people – and the Australian character … come through the universally recognized test of this, their first great war?'[77] This meant that questions of higher command, overall strategy, training and logistics were under-analysed. As the *Official History*, with its focus on the frontline soldier, has become the staple source in consequent studies, many have drawn on the 'tradition of "democratic military history"' that it established.[78]

The *Official History*'s soldier-centred focus is not its only idiosyncrasy. The narrative of the conflict itself is also incredibly imbalanced. Bean devoted two full volumes to the Gallipoli campaign, which only lasted eight months. When it came to recounting the Australian engagements on the Western Front between 1916 and 1918, he wrote just four volumes, two of which are dedicated to the final year of the war. Yet, the AIF spent more time in the front line during 1917 than in any other year of the war. As Gammage has noted, 'None of the twelve volumes of the *Official Histories* treat so much so briefly'. The accounts of Messines and third Ypres are particularly short. Admittedly, Messines was not one of the AIF's largest or longest battles, but the *Official History* covers it in fewer than 100 pages. And at 265 pages, the description of the third Ypres campaign is barely longer than that of the smaller Bullecourt battles, which take up 245 pages, and it is dwarfed by Bean's epic portrayal of Pozières, which is over 400 pages long. While it cannot be said that Bean's narrative glosses over the Flanders engagements, by allocating them so little space he minimised their place within the official narrative. As with the tendency to focus on the infantry's experience, this relative neglect of the AIF's Belgian battles has continued in subsequent studies.[79]

Bean's brevity on the subject aside, his description of the Flanders campaign is also far from awe inspiring. The accounts of Messines and third Ypres reaffirm much of what was evident in his correspondence and diary entries. There are, however, key differences. The salient is no longer a place of 'imperishable memory' linked to the British Expeditionary Force's exploits in the opening years of the war. Bean only made one mention of the Anzacs 'looking out upon a landscape … hidden from British infantry since May 1915'.[80] The symbolism of the salient is therefore altered, for the AIF has left its own impression in the region. Still, the particularities of fighting in the salient and the final outcome of Haig's Flanders offensive mean that this impression is not wholly positive. Unhindered by the censorship regulations of wartime, in the *Official History* Bean acknowledged the more contentious aspects of Messines and certainly third Ypres. Consequently, readers are left with a darker, more brutal impression of the Australian presence in the Ypres salient. The baptism of fire at Gallipoli in 1915, the first great trial of Pozières in 1916 and the march to victory in 1918 all have a place in the Anzac tradition. On the other hand, 1917 is 'the year in between',[81] a year when the battles at Bullecourt plumbed the depths of inept British command and the Flanders campaign posed new challenges that did not always conform to Bean's Anzac model.

The first of these challenges relates to the increasingly dominant role artillery played on the battlefield. Bean's war correspondence had acknowledged the artillery's prominent role in the salient; in the *Official History* he admitted that artillery was more important than it had ever been before – so much so that the indomitable Australian infantryman is displaced as the protagonist in the successes of September. According to Bean, at Menin Road:

> the advancing barrage won the ground; the infantry merely occupied it, pouncing on any points at which resistance survived. Whereas the artillery was generally spoken of as supporting the infantry, in this battle the infantry were little more than a necessary adjunct to the artillery's effort.

In an official history that 'usually makes much of the travails of the infantry', this passage is particularly telling. Bean did not entirely forgo praising the man in the front line, proclaiming that 'infantry such as the Australian gave the artillery the best prospect of success'.[82] Yet, this was hardly glorious work for an infantry force that had proved itself so capable in previous engagements. The admission that the Australian troops played a secondary role in the successful undertaking of attacks at Ypres runs counter to the historian's original thesis.

Even when the narrative does focus on the infantry, Bean had to address a second challenging aspect of warfare particular to the salient: the presence of German pillboxes. These concrete shelters provided better protection than traditional dugouts for defenders in the waterlogged terrain of Flanders. Often able to withstand heavy bombardments, they posed a significant threat to attacking troops. Bean's correspondence during the war had mentioned their presence, but he had been restrained in reporting the struggles that took place around them. Free of his obligations as official correspondent, in the *Official History* Bean the historian did not shirk from the reality, stating:

> The tension accompanying the struggles around these blockhouses – the murderous fire from a sheltered position, followed by the sudden giving-in of the surrounded garrison – caused this year's fighting in Flanders to be marked by a ferocity that renders the reading of any true narrative peculiarly unpleasant. Where such tension exists in battle, the rules of 'civilised' war are powerless.[83]

Bean's forewarning of unpleasantness is accurate. Descriptions of engagements around blockhouses do not make for easy reading, and anecdotes of Australians killing surrendering garrisons stack up over the course of the narrative, some described in vivid detail, while others are simply hinted at. The most confronting of these tells of a Victorian who, in retribution for the death of a fellow Australian, goes to bayonet a surrendering German. Upon realising that his bayonet is not attached to his rifle, the soldier proceeds to fix it and then stab the defenceless man, in spite of the victim's pleas for mercy. Ignoring the cruel composure the Australian exhibited in preparing his weapon, Bean justified this incident as inevitable in the heat of battle. He thereby exonerated the soldier of his actions while placing the blame squarely at the feet of 'those who make wars'.[84] Had this been but one extraordinary incident, it is unlikely the actions of a single individual would be worth defending, but it was not the case. This passage suggests a certain callousness on the part of Australian soldiers that had rarely been acknowledged before. Throughout the *Official History*, Bean presented the Anzacs as natural soldiers and highlighted their efficacy at killing, but his image of the chivalrous Anzac, cultivated in previous volumes, is weakened in his description of third Ypres.[85]

The domination of artillery during the assaults and the brutal confrontations around pillboxes would not seem so important had the Australians' actions led to a breakthrough. Instead, the 'complete success' at Broodseinde is the closest they get to such an achievement. Bean claimed that by that battle's end there was

> the unmistakable feeling, not to be experienced again by the A.I.F. until the 8th of August, 1918, that the British leaders now had the game in hand and, if conditions remained favourable, might in a few more moves secure a victory which would have its influence on the issue of the war.

That the weather held was an important prerequisite, and it was a message Bean reiterated in his conclusion, noting that 'the success of those strokes could be made a certainty, provided good weather continued. Granted this condition, there was little doubt that the commanders could at last powerfully affect, if not decide, the issue of the war'.[86] Unfortunately, as Bean had witnessed firsthand, the weather did not hold. Thus, Broodseinde is not only the AIF's crowning achievement in the salient but a sign of the disappointment to come.

Bean noted how the British command had been lulled into making rash choices against better judgement when describing the battles of Poelcappelle and Passchendaele.[87] The decision to carry on with the campaign 'contain[ed] the seeds of a classical tragedy'. Stripped of much of their artillery support and struggling through the quagmire of No Man's Land, the Australians suffer for limited gains. Bean could find no redeeming features in either of these engagements, writing that 'so closely had the events of October 9th been repeated that those who took part, reading an account of the last fight [12 October], might easily believe that their own action was being described'. As for the results, 'much of the effect of the antecedent successes was thus thrown away on October 9th and 12th'. All the headway made in the salient then comes to nothing, and the Australian casualty figures of 38,093 officers and men give 'rise to much anxiety' about the future of the AIF's five divisions.[88] It is an undignified end to the campaign, with the Australian troops once again suffering for British hubris.

In his summary of 1917, Bean concluded that, for the Anzacs, 'the Third Battle of Ypres was in the main a successful offensive, at one stage brilliantly so'. Losses had been heavy but apparently lower than those suffered per division at Pozières. Moreover, Bean reaffirmed that, 'with the exception of parts of the 2nd and 3rd Divisions ... the infantry never came out of action in the condition in which it had issued from Pozières and Flers' (the Somme winter campaign). Despite these conclusions, Bean conceded that the losses 'furnished an acute problem for the AIF'.[89] He had always cast 1916 as the AIF's most difficult year, yet in his conclusion to the *Official History*'s third, 1916 volume, he wrote, 'They [the Australians] slowly emerged, recovering in numbers, health, and spirit, their area one of the best furnished, and their corps recognised as among the finest fighting machines at the disposal of the British command'.[90] By the end of the fourth, 1917 volume, no such recovery was in sight for those who had survived the Belgian front. Instead, with the failure of the second conscription referendum, it was likely that the AIF had passed 'its zenith of achievement' and would 'face the fighting of 1918 in weaker numbers and with overstrained and inelastic material'.[91] The tragedy of third Ypres was complete, and, according to the *Official History*, it had driven the AIF closer to the brink of destruction than any previous campaign.

***

The AIF's 1917 battles in Flanders were difficult for Bean to cover as Australian war correspondent and official historian. The campaign's timing clashed with his many side projects. Forced to juggle his journalism and other responsibilities, Bean was less invested in the offensive than he had been during previous engagements. Yet, in the long run, it was the particularities of the fighting at Ypres that had the greatest impact on his representations of the battles. Despite the relatively positive beginning, once the offensive foundered in the mud, there was little to extol about it. The *Official History* confirmed the AIF's Belgian battles' peripheral position within the Anzac legend. The elements that made the engagements in the latter half of 1917 unique – the dominance of the artillery, the pillbox fighting, the sense that victory was near before hopes stuck fast in the quagmire of the salient – did not fit easily into Bean's narrative of the war. Brutal, bloody and devoid of grand, awe-inspiring moments, Ypres provided Bean with little that he could use to advance his romantic characterisation of Australian military manhood.

Chapter 2

DISPLAYING THE YPRES SALIENT[1]

> Although war itself is beastly, there are things about war that are far above the things of the beast. There are imperishable and lovely things; there are the associations so sacred they are almost divine.
>
> *Article on the opening of the Australian War Museum in Sydney,* Sydney Morning Herald, *3 April 1925*

If Charles Bean's *Official History of Australia in the War of 1914–1918* was the major literary interpretation of the Anzac legend, then the Australian War Memorial was, and still is, its physical incarnation. Responsible for its conception and remaining heavily involved throughout the AWM's development was the ubiquitous Charles Bean. Inspired by Canadian efforts to organise record-collecting schemes independent of the British, Bean helped establish the Australian War Records Section in 1917. Initially, the section was tasked with gathering official documentation related to the Australian Imperial Force – notably, unit war diaries – but the remit quickly expanded to include object collection as well as managing war art and photography schemes. Although officials first viewed the section's activities as providing the foundations for a national *museum*, Bean had long envisaged a grander commemorative monument and, with government backing, got his way. By the time the AWM had finally settled into its prime location, facing Parliament House at the base of Mount Ainslie, Canberra, in 1941, it was a unique institution: 'a museum, a repository of records, and a shrine ... alone among Great War memorials anywhere in the world in combining these purposes'.[2]

The AWM may have lacked a permanent location before the 1940s, but it was not invisible during the interwar years. On the contrary, its staff engaged in a variety of activities publicising its work, propagating its narrative of the war and raising funds. These activities included organising battle lectures; selling souvenirs, photographs and books; and working on joint ventures with the Returned Sailors' and Soldiers' Imperial League of Australia. The most important of these interwar initiatives were two major temporary exhibitions of the AWM's collections and the tour of Will Longstaff's painting *Menin Gate at Midnight* (1927; see plate 12). The temporary exhibitions were the brainchildren of Bean, who felt that they would

> give all Australia an opportunity of seeing these fine collections and would keep alive Australian interest in the AIF at a time when it [was] very desirable that this should be done. It would awaken the enthusiasm of Australians in this memorial of their countrymen who fought and fell during the war.[3]

In the end, only Melbourne (1922–25) and Sydney (1925–35) hosted major exhibitions showcasing the AWM's collections, but these still managed to attract close to 3 million visitors.[4] Far smaller in scope, *Menin Gate at Midnight*'s tour saw the painting pass through all the capital cities as well as a number of regional centres, regularly drawing audiences of thousands.

Examining the interwar exhibitions in Melbourne and Sydney and *Menin Gate at Midnight*'s tour, this chapter analyses how the objects, dioramas, photographs and paintings related to the Australian Imperial

Force's Belgian battles fitted into the AWM's portrayal of the war. With their focus on supposedly unique Australian fighting qualities and the AIF's grand achievements – the 'imperishable and lovely things' – the exhibitions' narrative structure served to downplay the magnitude of the losses as well as the terrible conditions endured in Belgium. As a consequence, despite being reasonably well represented in the collection, neither Messines nor third Ypres was held up in the exhibitions as an exceptional example of the AIF's most trying ordeals, and certainly neither was counted among its most triumphant achievements. Once again, they sat somewhere in between. Even the tour organised by the AWM of *Menin Gate at Midnight* – a painting depicting Ypres' most iconic war memorial – did not do all that much to shed further light on these battles. Instead, they remained overshadowed by a promotional campaign emphasising the commemoration of all Australian dead and not just those lost to the salient.

The Australian War Memorial Museum and Memory

The presentist nature of museums has long been a given. While these institutions purportedly display the 'past', such representations also reveal much about their present milieu. In this way, the museum is 'a receptacle and a reflection of a group of people at a present point in time … that [aims to] project itself in the past'.[5] This act of projection is not a passive undertaking. As scholars of nationalism, such as Benedict Anderson, have pointed out, the establishment of museums serves a legitimising purpose.[6] This legitimisation is achieved by 'showing how smoothly the processes of the past led to the present day, suppressing dislocation, fragmentation and false starts, and reinforcing local value systems'.[7] Nevertheless, it is important to note that museums may not only be memory agents aiming to produce for visitors 'a new and different set of memories as the basis for a collective identity'; they can also be contested 'arenas of articulation' that provide spaces for a plurality of viewpoints.[8]

This understanding of museums as contested arenas is useful when considering the current Australian War Memorial's exhibitions, which are now somewhat open to input from unofficial stakeholders.[9] The interwar AWM, however, was firmly under the custodianship of Charles Bean and John Treloar. A former head of the Australian War Records Section, Treloar was the AWM's director from 1920 until his death, in 1952. Supporting them was a conservative board of management made up of ex-AIF officers, politicians and other 'men of prominence' who shared similar interpretations of Australia's First World War experience.[10] Thanks to Bean's standing in official circles and the federal government's patronage of the project, which was eventually guaranteed in the *Australian War Memorial Act 1925*, the AWM was able to remain sheltered from most outside influences. As long as financial constraints were respected, the official historian and the AWM's director were more or less free to pursue their vision for the institution. This ensured that the AWM's narrative of the war in its temporary exhibitions 'convey[ed] a coherent vision of Australian character and achievement'.[11]

As did Bean's *Official History*, the AWM recounted the events of the First World War through the pre-modern ideals upon which the Anzac legend was founded. In Melbourne and Sydney, the values of a martial Anzac tradition were displayed in forums that downplayed the harsher realities of industrial warfare. According to Craig Melrose, the principal narrative framing these values was the arrangement of the collection in a manner that 'was strongly reminiscent of saga and epic'. This narrative divided the war into three parts: test, which covered the Dardanelles campaign; ordeal, which focused on the AIF's engagements on the

Western Front in 1916 and early 1917; and triumph, which focused principally on 1918.[12] Within this epic framework, the AIF's first major engagement in Belgium, at Messines, was the turning point between ordeal and triumph. Yet, this initial shift in the narrative could only be temporary, as the AIF finished third Ypres mired in the morass of the salient, in October 1917. Thus, the principal battles in Belgium sat awkwardly between the ordeal and triumph stages and provided no superlative examples of either.

The Hunt for Relics

The positioning of the AIF's Belgian actions in the grey area between ordeal and triumph began with one of the cornerstones of the AWM's collection: the objects. Bean and Treloar believed that objects souvenired from ravaged battlefields – 'relics', as Bean termed them[13] – provided physical proof of Australian endeavours, and these were eventually exhibited 'in such a way as to create an imaginative link between the war and the visitor' as well as to present a coherent, romanticised and ultimately triumphalist account of the war.[14] That the AWM's exhibitions would have a strong triumphalist bias had already been largely determined by the belated implementation of official collection policies during the war. It was not until September 1917 that the Australian War Records Section was charged with collecting objects, and its attempts to inculcate an AIF-wide culture of collecting were only in their infancy while third Ypres raged. The first section order encouraging units to look out for souvenirs defined relics as 'all articles of interest found on the battlefield or, in certain cases, used by units on memorable occasions. Relics of our own, and Allies' forces, are as interesting to posterity as those of the enemy'.[15] A later order clarified this vague statement by providing a list detailing 'articles of interest', which included enemy weapons, uniforms, equipment, tools, transport signs and German paper money.[16] However, issued long after third Ypres, this order had no impact on the collecting practices of Australians in the salient. Moreover, the section found that many units lacked 'enthusiasm for the work' during the early stages of the scheme, and it strived to generate interest in relic collection through a variety of strategies. It regularly issued circulars and held lectures on the importance of collecting for Australia. Officers of the section also stoked inter-unit rivalry while reminding soldiers that by collecting relics they were 'ensuring their future public recognition … [and] paying a tribute to their fallen comrades'.[17] According to the figures, these approaches had quite an impact. From September 1917 to April 1918, only 1157 relics had been collected. Over the course of the following year, the AIF amassed some 24,000 more.[18]

Other battles that had taken place before September 1917 also lacked significant representation in the Australian War Records Section's collections, but Bean and the section worked hard to rectify this situation. During and after the war, several journeys were arranged to the AIF's previous battlefields, including the Somme and Messines, in order to make up for lost time.[19] For example, Bean spent three weeks in the Dardanelles as part of the Australian Historical Mission to Gallipoli, painstakingly putting together the pieces of the campaign as well as actively searching for relics.[20] In the meantime, the section engaged the assistance of the Australian Graves Detachment, which was working around Villers-Bretonneux, to further augment its collection of relics from the Somme region.[21] Yet, the Belgian battlefields, with the exception of Messines, were ignored in this postwar scramble for relics. Perhaps this was because those heading collection efforts felt that the Australians, having received orders 'to souvenir' during the third Ypres campaign, had already scoured the fields of Flanders. However, the difference between the numbers of relics collected before and after April 1918 suggests the Australians were hardly thorough collectors during September and October 1917.

The disparity between the collection figures is also indicative of how the Australian War Records Section obtained its relics. The section had only a handful of officers it could rely on, so the bulk of collecting fell to the soldiers themselves. This approach, while working within constraints imposed by the nature of the conflict, had its weaknesses. If a soldier could not reach an area, he could not be expected to souvenir anything from it. This issue is most evident when considering the returns from the AIF's various engagements at Ypres. The battles of Menin Road, Polygon Wood and Broodseinde all saw reasonable advances, and various objects in the section's collections represent each battle. The battles of Poelcappelle and Passchendaele, on the other hand, ended without any noteworthy gains, and the Australians participating in them did not manage to souvenir any objects from those failed advances.[22] Apart from references in certain exhibition labels, neither Poelcappelle nor Passchendaele was represented in the AWM's collection. They were thus subsumed into the broader Anzac saga, which resulted in the narrative somewhat obfuscating the less-than-glorious end to the Australians' participation in the 1917 Flanders campaign as well as sidestepping the tragic interpretation of the campaign that marked Bean's correspondence and *Official History*.

Treloar's decision to arrange the displays at the Melbourne and Sydney exhibitions in a chronological order also ensured that pride of place was given to the AIF's opening and closing campaigns. Of the seven 'courts', or sections, devoted to specific phases of the war in Melbourne, only two were reserved for the bloodier, middle years of the conflict. This approach left little room for clarity, with the battles of Fromelles,

Pozières, Bullecourt and Messines lumped together in one court and the third battle of Ypres and the winter of 1917–18 in another.[23] Even the *Nonne Boschen* (Nun's Wood) diorama, which depicted an assault on a pillbox, was hidden from direct view within the main body of the exhibition if visitors followed the proposed circulation route (see plate 4).[24] The Sydney exhibits were only marginally more clear, with relics from 1916 separated from those related to the fighting in 1917. However, the 1916 and 1917 display cases were included in the same court, as if to suggest there was little difference between them, whereas the 1918 cases – representing seven months of fighting – occupied three and two courts in Melbourne and Sydney respectively.[25] These arrangements leaned heavily on the triumph stage of the AWM's narrative, to the detriment of the battles that took place in 1916 and 1917.

Judging from the section titles and descriptions in the AWM's guidebook and from press reports on the exhibitions, artefacts from Gallipoli and several French battlefields were far more worthy of attention than those from Belgium. Signifying the Anzac legend's 'Immortal Beginning' at Gallipoli, objects such as 'the actual boats used in The Landing' were presented as among the most 'sacred' and 'precious war relics' on display.[26] In its portrayal of the Australians on the Western Front, the guidebook asserted that 'Relics of Terrible Bombardments' were emblematic of the ordeal battles. This included the remains of the famous Pozières windmill, which 'was the most heavily bombarded point in what proved to be one of the most devastated areas along the front', along with

> fragments shovelled at random from the site of the village of Pozières, showing the condition to which the whole area was reduced, literally a desert of hummocks and hollows … [In addition, a] portion of the railway line taken from near Pozières Copse [bore] evidence of the fury of the same bombardment.

The symbolism of this rubble was not lost on journalists, who were drawn to this 'sample of Pozieres after the Australians had done with it'; one opined that it was 'merely a couple of shovelsful of broken debris'.[27] Concerning the 1918 courts, the guidebook was dominated by descriptions of objects stripped from defeated foes during key moments, such as the 'Defence of Amiens & Hazebrouck: Where the Tide Turned' and 'Germany's Day of Doom' or when the AIF went 'Smashing Through' the Hindenburg Line. Neither the guidebooks nor the journalists reviewing the AWM's exhibitions identified such a series of defining relics among those representing the AIF's Belgian battles.

The Salient in Three Dimensions

Given the relatively banal nature of relics from Belgium and their unfavourable position within the overall display, all that remained to give visitors a lasting impression of the AIF's presence in Belgium were the models (dioramas and a contour map), photographs and paintings depicting Flanders. With no two models or paintings quite alike, these elements of the AWM's collection highlighted unique aspects of fighting in the salient. Bean conceptualised the dioramas, in particular, as art that would do more than just provide 'a sort of three-dimension map of the place … to explain it to your brain'; they would also evoke the 'utter fatigue, or the danger, the feverish unreality which comes over everyday landscapes during battle times'.[28] The dioramas aimed to draw the spectator into the experience of the AIF, and Bean considered them essential, second only to the war diaries in importance within the AWM's collections.[29]

As one 'of the more important Australian Battle Fields', there was no doubt that Flanders would be represented in the modelling scheme.[30] The AIF engagements in Belgium were initially allocated two inset picture models (a series of smaller dioramas), with one series depicting Messines and the other Broodseinde; one picture plan model (large diorama), depicting fighting in Nonne Bosschen during the battle of Menin Road (20 September 1917); and one plan model (raised contour map) of the Flanders battlefield. A similar number of models were to be dedicated to each of the battlefields on which the AIF had fought in 1915, 1916 and 1918.[31] However, this was altered once it became obvious that the scheme was advancing more slowly than originally projected and was seen as posing an unnecessary financial burden on the AWM. The future of the program was assured largely thanks to Bean's lobbying, but its scope was significantly narrowed.[32] Plans for the Broodseinde inset picture models series were jettisoned, leaving two large models – the *Nonne Boschen* diorama and the plan model of the region – as well as the smaller Messines series to represent the fighting in Flanders. Several years later, Bean did float the idea of a second large diorama depicting the battle of Messines. However, this was rejected, because Treloar was 'unable … to think of any special feature which will enable the modellers when treating this subject to strike a distinctive note'.[33] Of the Flanders dioramas that survived the cutbacks, *Nonne Boschen* was completed first, but all were finished before the AWM moved to Sydney.[34]

The *Nonne Boschen* diorama was the most specific of the Flanders models, representing an assault on a pillbox in waterlogged terrain (see plate 5). The accompanying exhibition label detailed the background to the scene, highlighting the invaluable contribution of the British artillery, the battlefield's wet nature, which was unsuitable for deep entrenchments, and the presence of the Germans' 'small concrete forts' spread throughout the area. Although the original label was already relatively detailed, an updated version, edited by Bean, appeared in

1932 and included additional information emphasising the formidable obstacle these pillboxes presented. Sheltered in these structures, which were able to 'withstand direct hits from anything less than an 8-inch [200-millimetre] shell', the Germans were protected from barrages, and some of the forts were 'loop-holed' to allow enemy machine gunners to remain inside while firing on advancing troops.[35] These were particularly difficult to capture, and, unsurprisingly, the pillbox confronting the Australian attackers in the diorama was designed with this feature. The edited caption read,

> The bombers (on the left) and rifle-bombers (right), having advanced by short rushes ... to within range of the 'pill-box' and having knocked out a German machine-gun, have subjected the 'pill-box' to an intense fire, the bombers hand-throwing Mills grenades and the rifle-bombers firing similar grenades from rifles ... In the meantime part of the platoon have crept up until they are within charging distance, and wait for the platoon commander's orders. At last he decides the enemy's resistance has been sufficiently beaten down and orders the charge. A German, caught sheltering near a minenwerfer [short-range German mortar] in the open, is surrendering.[36]

It is worth noting that although the AWM did not shy away from relating Australian fighting prowess in killing the enemy, the *Nonne Boschen* label did not explicitly describe the events that occurred following this scene. Perhaps this was considered self-explanatory, but its vagueness about the outcome of the Australians' charge (originally called a 'determined onslaught' in the Melbourne caption) also avoided any reference to the ruthlessness displayed by some Australians when wresting control of the concrete pillboxes from the Germans.[37]

Why Bean selected this particular episode in place of other engagements in Flanders is unclear. The Menin Road battle was not the most impressive of the AIF's victories during the third Ypres campaign. Moreover, the diorama somewhat misrepresented this particular engagement. While the Australians who advanced in the Nonne Bosschen sector did so over sodden ground, Menin Road and the following battle of Polygon Wood were actually fought in reasonably dry conditions. Although some rain did fall during the evening prior to the attack on 20 September, it did not turn the battlefield into anything like the quagmire the Australians encountered the following month.[38] Nevertheless, if the terrain encountered at Nonne Bosschen was not necessarily typical for the specific Menin Road engagement, the diorama was consistent with many of the AWM's photographs and paintings on display, which also gave the impression that the AIF had fought the entire third Ypres campaign in the mud.

The diorama also portrayed several familiar tropes of the Anzac tradition. As Anne-Marie Condé has argued, each diorama was most likely made as a homily illustrating certain fighting qualities of the AIF, and several elements of *Nonne Boschen* supported this.[39] For example, the timing of the depiction, showing the advanced stage of an assault on a pillbox, conveniently bypassed the role of the British artillery at Ypres. This allowed the diorama to focus on the Australians' skill and initiative. Although Bean wrote in the *Official History* that the artillery took the ground while the infantry simply occupied it at Menin Road, the stances of the figures suggested that the men in this scene were far from passive.[40] The model thus reinforced the overall image of the Anzacs in the AWM exhibitions, where traditional, warrior-like attributes won out over industrialised warfare. At the same time, the diorama's themes fitted neatly into the AWM's narrative framework. Placed after the *Gueudecourt* (*Somme Winter 1916–17*) and *Bullecourt* models, which portrayed Australians bravely enduring, as opposed to dominating, trying conditions on the Western Front, *Nonne Boschen* handed some initiative back to the Anzacs. However, when compared to the subsequent 1918 dioramas, *Dernancourt* and *Mont St Quentin*, which respectively depicted the crucial, steadfast defence of a French village and an audacious, glorious advance, it appeared rather limited in nature: a local success rather than a resounding triumph, a metaphor for third Ypres' position in the AWM's interwar narrative.

A Flanders plan model and a series of small inset picture models depicting Messines also touched on the AIF's presence in Belgium, but their objectives were more didactic than those of *Nonne Boschen*. The Flanders plan model was a simple raised map. Notably, its accompanying label included the only reference to the casualty figures for both Messines (8999) and third Ypres (38,000) to appear in the AWM. It also briefly hinted at the terrible conditions facing the Australians, particularly in the latter stages of third Ypres:

> The fine weather which permitted the rapid progress of August and September broke early in October. The ground became a veritable quagmire in which even the tanks became bogged, and strewn with corpses and damaged material of all descriptions.[41]

Of all the third Ypres exhibits' labels, this brief reference was one of the most unambiguous when acknowledging the terrible conditions of that battle. The most striking aspect of this particular passage is not its admission that Australians fought over a battlefield littered with the cadavers of their mates, but the fact it was linked to a banal raised map which did not depict any of the aforementioned devastation. Marrying such a short, blunt description with the plan model's neutral subject matter ensured the horrors of third Ypres appeared abstract and distant, in stark contrast to the immediate and overwhelming visual proof of the Australians' glorious achievements portrayed in the relics and picture models.

As for the smaller models portraying the Messines battlefield, they were part of a series that focused on 'typical places and scenes' as opposed to specific engagements.[42] As a consequence, they did not depict any aspects of fighting along the ridge or even the explosion of the nineteen great mines. Instead, this particular series concentrated on the process involved in evacuating the wounded. Messines was chosen as the starting point for this scene simply because it happened to be the best example Treloar had of medical evacuation on the Western Front. Since the AWM's director was just as concerned as Bean with the realism of the models, he contacted Colonel Graham Butler, author of the *Official History of the Australian Army Medical Services*, in order to get his opinion on the most efficient chains of evacuation. While having a limited knowledge of that particular battle, Butler suggested Messines to Treloar because the evacuation system was 'extremely good and well organised'. Yet, had another battle presented itself with similar credentials and with more 'intimate associations for the Australians', there is little doubt that Treloar would have selected it instead.[43] Whatever made Messines distinctive was consciously ignored so that it could stand for a 'typical' war scene.

The Salient in Two Dimensions

Adorning the walls of the Melbourne and Sydney Exhibition Buildings were the fruits of the official war photography and war art schemes. Heavily involved in the development of these, Bean demanded that official photographers and painters capture 'the plain, simple truth' of the war in their work. Although Bean's understanding of what constituted the 'truth' occasionally led to disagreements with the men working in these schemes – most famously with the photographer Frank Hurley over his use of composite pictures – the end products functioned in much the same way as the battlefield relics and dioramas: they highlighted the values of the Anzac tradition while downplaying the more unsavoury elements of modern warfare.[44] The Australian war art scheme favoured traditional forms of realism and visual accuracy, ensuring that any dabbling in modernism, which Bean classified as 'freak art', was avoided.[45] The official Australian photographers, Hurley and Hubert Wilkins, also shared with Bean a rather traditional understanding of modern war and a deep admiration for the Australian soldiers. Hurley and Bean may not have seen eye-to-eye on the issue of how best to capture the Australian experience of the war. Nevertheless, the photographer 'was still conditioned by prewar images of beauty, cohesion, and harmony' and strove to depict 'the fighting ability and spirit of the Australian soldiers he encountered, representing them not as individuals, but as a collective force whose energies were directed towards good'.[46] As for Wilkins, his photographs may have 'rarely matched Hurley for artistry', but they still had a 'timeless humanity' to them.[47]

The majority of the photographs depicting the Western Front in the exhibitions were arranged in chronological order, mirroring the overarching narrative that applied to the relics and dioramas. The photographs of 1916 – including images entitled *The Scene of a Gallant Failure*, *To Fallen Comrades*, *Somme Mud* and *Flers – Of Evil Memory* – predominantly accentuated the AIF's ordeals, while those depicting 1918 focused on martial triumphs, showing the Australians in action, as well as captured trenches, prisoners of war and dead enemies.

The themes covered in the 1917 photographs occupied the middle ground between these two opposing poles of the AWM's narrative. There was only a small selection of photographs from Messines, and those depicted the elaborate planning that went into the battle, Anzac chivalry towards the defeated enemy, and wounded – but relaxed

– Australian soldiers. Third Ypres, on the other hand, was particularly well represented, with forty-two photographs displayed in Melbourne and forty-eight in Sydney. Although Hurley and Wilkins had begun their work early enough to experience the drier conditions in the salient before the October rain set in, many of the photographs depicted the battlefield as a 'sea of fathomless mud' that the Anzacs had to slog their way through. As with the *Nonne Boschen* diorama, these images reinforced the notion that the entire campaign had been fought in a morass. Nonetheless, with the exception of Hurley's photograph of a regimental aid post, they captured the terrible conditions facing the Australians in Flanders without presenting too bleak a picture of the campaign. Hurley himself had actually used the aid post photograph as the bottom half of the composite, *The Morning of Passchendaele*, to which he added a dramatic sunburst, hinting at the divinity of the Australian sacrifice and the redemption of the squalor in which the wounded Anzacs lay (see plate 6). That the AWM did not include this more uplifting version was probably due to Bean's stance on composites. Instead, the caption accompanying the aid post image attempted to draw the viewers' attention away from the prostrate men to how captured pillboxes 'made admirable shelters for the wounded'.

The photographs from third Ypres also included several pictures of captured German positions and soldiers as well as Hurley's evocative composite *A Hop-Over*, which showed two lines of Anzacs leaping out of their trenches to engage the enemy. Given Bean's quest to show Australians the plain truth of the war, it is not clear how *A Hop-Over* came to be included in the exhibition. The Australian literary scholar Robert Dixon has suggested the AWM 'may have used the image because Hurley's own publicity made it so famous that it was difficult to ignore in a series of exhibitions that were meant ... to feed public enthusiasm and raise funds for the Museum project'.[48] Whatever the reason for its inclusion, this photograph, along with those portraying the fruits of Australian martial achievement, at least casts the Anzacs' struggles in the salient in a somewhat positive light. This was in stark contrast to those taken in 1916, which, with the exception of an image of the ruined concrete covering of a captured strong point titled *'Gibraltar'*, presented next to no evidence of Australian victory.

Although there were more photographs on display related to third Ypres than to any other engagement, a significant percentage of these did not actually focus on what made the campaign unique. Rather, they aimed to provide visitors with an appreciation of 'typical places and scenes' Australians encountered throughout the war, functioning much like the medical evacuation models nominally set at Messines. In fact, there was a similar series of photographs showing the various stages of medical care in the salient, including German prisoners carrying Australian wounded, a regimental aid post, an advanced dressing station and a field operating theatre. There were also several representative scenes of the Australians' daily lives, such as the popular *Telling the Latest*, which captured a group of men listening attentively to one of their mates back from leave. The guidebook described this as 'a typical scene, for billet life with the Australian was as cheerful as his fighting was terribly earnest'. Finally, a number of the photographs portrayed, or were at least linked to, the travails of the Australian artillery. While this reflected the artillery's drawn-out participation in the 1917 campaign, no other section in the exhibitions gave anywhere near a proportionate amount of space on the gunners, or on other 'typical' themes, for that matter.[49]

It was not until mid-1917 that Australia's official war art scheme was well established. Before then, only the illustrator and cartoonist Will

Dyson had been working as an official artist on the Western Front. He had been in Europe since late 1916 but missed the battle of Messines, as he was in London between May and July 1917. Consequently, there was no official artist on the front to witness the engagement, and it was not until 1921 that the AWM commissioned the artist Charles Wheeler to paint a scene of the battle.

There was no such shortage of artists in Belgium several months later. By September 1917, Dyson was back at the front, along with two more artists, Fred Leist and Septimus Power. These three produced the majority of the official paintings and sketches portraying the Australians' experiences in the Ypres salient, and several of their works from the battlefield were displayed in Melbourne and Sydney.[50]

There does not appear to have been a definitive list of paintings included in the interwar exhibitions, but a number of works were mentioned in the guidebooks and press. It is also useful to consider the images that featured in a folio of Australian war art, *Australian Chivalry*, published by the AWM in 1933, as a distillation of the pictorial narrative displayed among the relics and models. Treloar edited this folio in order to counter 'the debased point of view commonly adopted in war books', such as Erich Maria Remarque's *All Quiet on the Western Front* (1929), which described the war in disillusioned and tragic terms. Showcasing the Australian war art scheme's traditional realism and stridently anti-modernist approach to the depiction of war, the folio harked back to an epoch when 'knights in glistening mail on richly caparisoned steeds' rode off 'in search of honourable adventure'. The Anzacs, it claimed, were the contemporary incarnations of these 'paladins', embodying their 'high sense of honour, disdain of danger and death, love of adventure, compassion for the weak and oppressed, self-sacrifice and altruism'.[51] The frontispiece of the folio's slip case even depicted an Australian soldier standing with a knight from the Middle Ages (see plate 7).

Of the paintings portraying the fighting in the Ypres salient, several of Leist's and Power's works must have stood out for Treloar, as he had pictures of both artists printed in *Australian Chivalry* and numerous guidebook editions of the Melbourne and Sydney exhibitions. Two of Power's paintings, *First Australian Division Artillery Going into the 3rd Battle of Ypres* (1919; see plate 8) and *Bringing up the Guns* (1921), were published in *Australian Chivalry*, and a third, *Bringing Up the Ammunition, Flanders, Autumn 1917* (1920), in the Melbourne guidebook.[52] Leist's *The Cloth Hall, Ypres* (1917) was printed in the folio, and his *Australian Infantry Attack in Polygon Wood* (1919; see plate 9) was so evocative that it featured in both publications.[53] *Australian Infantry Attack* was the only one of these five paintings to portray the Anzac infantry in action at third Ypres. Charles Wheeler's painting *The Battle of Messines* (1923), was also included in *Australian Chivalry*, probably in order to ensure that the folio featured images from all the AIF's major engagements, but it went unmentioned in the guidebooks.[54]

Given the involvement of all five Australian infantry divisions at third Ypres, the imbalance between representations of the infantry and artillery highlighted in *Australian Chivalry* and the AWM guidebooks may seem surprising, but it reflected a similar, if somewhat less marked, trend discernible in the photographs on display at the exhibitions. With the infantry well represented in depictions of other battles in *Australian Chivalry* and through the objects and models of the exhibitions, the Power paintings filled a gap in the AWM's exhibits: the role of Australian artillerymen in Belgium. On this modern battlefield, it was the weight and efficacy, or lack thereof, of the British guns that made, or broke, the 1917 offensives, and the Australian gunners paid dearly for being more heavily engaged in this campaign than in any preceding offensive on the Western Front.[55] This fact was highlighted by the guidebook:

> In the battles in Flanders in the autumn of 1917 the Australian artillery was subjected to its most searching test, the constant fighting in the waterlogged fields imposing the greatest hardships upon men and animals. These are vividly suggested in the pictures and sketches by Septimus Power hung in this court.

Yet, for all the vivid suggestion of Power's work, representations of the gunners' trials in carrying out their duties and being subjected to counter-barrages were virtually non-existent. In two of the paintings, the guns and ammunition were barely included in the frame, and in *First Australian Division Artillery Going into the 3rd Battle of Ypres*, the charging arrival of a gun team overshadowed the one artillery piece in action. Power ignored the relationship between the men and the technology of war – a trope that was very much present in several well-known modernist works, such as those of official British and Canadian war artist Percy Wyndham Lewis – and focused on the traditional imagery of man and horse united instead.[56]

A gifted painter of animals in particular, Power often 'used horses to portray the energy, tension and sheer hard going of war', whereas the men were often only included as subsidiary figures.[57] His Ypres paintings dovetailed neatly with the knightly ideals espoused in *Australian Chivalry*. The union between man and beast in overcoming the trials of the war was the central element in these pictures, and in none of the reprinted works was there any hint of a wounded – let alone a dying or dead – horse, although the Allied mounts suffered terribly. This is hardly surprising given that Bean and Treloar 'overlaid Australia's war paintings with a memorialising purpose'.[58] Power's paintings, like all those commissioned for the AWM, aimed to inspire and comfort visitors with their depictions of antipodean gallantry, not to disturb them with images of the horrors Australian soldiers – and their animals – endured in a modern war.

Of Leist's paintings, *The Cloth Hall, Ypres* – depicting arguably the most famous ruins on the Western Front – was standard fare within any Allied war art collection. Images of northern European cities and villages in ruins had long served to highlight the 'frightfulness' and brutality of the enemy and his kultur in Allied propaganda.[59] The inclusion of *Cloth Hall* in *Australian Chivalry* (and most likely in the exhibitions) served to highlight the altruism of the AIF who fought to defend it and other landmarks from wanton German destruction. It was not unique in the folio – Power's painting of the battered Albert cathedral with its Madonna hanging precariously from the main tower was also included in *Australian Chivalry* – nor was it specifically Australian in character, as the figures moving around the ruins were of an unidentifiable nationality. It said more about German barbarity and the Allies' selflessness than about the actual presence of the AIF in the salient.

The apotheosis of such altruism was reached in Leist's second painting, *Australian Infantry Attack in Polygon Wood*. At first glance, this painting resembles the *Nonne Boschen* diorama, and the similarities between the two must have appeared so striking to Treloar that he mistakenly entitled it *Attacking a Pillbox in Nonne Bosschen* in *Australian Chivalry*. It actually portrays a scene from the battle of Polygon Wood (26 September 1917) that took place several days later, and there are also key differences in content: a distinct lack of mud pervades Leist's battlefield, and the skill involved in conquering the blockhouses is not the central element. Rather, it is the valiant sacrifice of Lieutenant J.E. Turnour of the 59th Battalion that dominates the scene.[60] As with Power's paintings, Leist's portrayal of Turnour laying down his life so that his men might capture the deadly pillboxes underlined the traditional values of the Anzacs. According to one review of the Melbourne exhibition, the scene 'was a typical instance of bravery and sacrifice'.[61] That the painting was based on a specific event and its central figure was clearly identified in the description was significant insofar as it served to further strengthen the symbolism of the AWM's more generic works.

The most striking element of Power's and Leist's paintings is the lack of space they dedicated to the Ypres battlefield itself. For artists who were less concerned with traditional forms of realism, the singular landscape of the salient in 1917 was a source of terrifying inspiration. It is hardly surprising then that a number of the war's most confronting and memorable paintings were set in Flanders, such as Paul Nash's modernist *The Menin Road* (1919; see plate 10) and Otto Dix's apocalyptic allegory *Flandern* (1934–36; see plate 11). Despite their differing styles, the historical contexts in which they were produced and their political undertones, the battlefield in these paintings is omnipresent and oppressive, threatening to swallow whole the human figures depicted in the lunar wastelands.[62] Such iconography is absent in the AWM's artworks, as Australian protagonists impose themselves on the landscape, not the other way around. For example, mud slows Power's horses but does not stop them, while in Leist's *Australian Infantry Attack* the little refuse of war there is poses no direct obstacle to Turnour's men as they dash over the trenches to seize the pillbox. In the AWM's narrative, the Ypres landscape did not dominate the Australians but was dominated by them.

The AIF's battles in Belgium were not the only engagements official war artists treated in this manner. A perusal of *Australian Chivalry* or the initial list of paintings planned for the Australian war art collection reveals that, while it was important to include each major AIF action in the collection, the principal subjects were the Australians themselves, not the terrains over which they fought. A little more mud could be seen in certain works depicting Flanders in 1917, but ultimately there was little to differentiate these paintings from portrayals of fighting elsewhere on the Western Front. The emphasis of the art scheme on capturing the Australian experience of 1914–18 in a traditional manner that privileged visual accuracy over aesthetics effectively shackled the official artistic response to the conflict. As the historian Margaret Hutchison has argued, 'The consolation and inspiration which Bean and Treloar hoped visitors would discover in the AWM's [art] collections was found not in canvases which strove to capture "accuracy" ... but in evocative images such as Will Longstaff's *Menin Gate at Midnight*', to which we will now turn.[63]

Menin Gate at Midnight

In addition to the Melbourne and Sydney exhibitions, the AWM was involved in many side projects that further promoted the Australian role in the First World War. One such project, organised with considerable success, was the national tour in 1928–29 of Will Longstaff's painting *Menin Gate at Midnight* or, as it was popularly known at the time, *The Ghosts of Menin Gate* (1927; see plate 12). The painting's broad symbolism and spiritualist sentiments resonated deeply with the interwar population. Exhibited in each state capital as well as larger towns, it attracted thousands of viewers. The central object of Longstaff's work was the Imperial War Graves Commission's monument to the missing of the Ypres salient, the Menin Gate Memorial (see plate 13). Designed by Sir Reginald Blomfield, the imposing archway was unveiled in the rebuilt town of Ypres before thousands of British pilgrims in 1927, and the ceremony received extensive coverage in major Australian newspapers. Carved on panels throughout the memorial are the names of more than

54,000 British soldiers, including close to 6200 Australians, who died in the salient and have no known graves.

While Ypres was never central to the Australian experience of the war, it had captured the British public's imagination early on and remained dominant in imperial memory well after the final shots had been fired. Therefore, there was little doubt that a memorial to the empire would be raised in the Belgian town. The form it would take, on the other hand, was less certain. In early 1919, IWGC chairperson Winston Churchill suggested the devastated town be left in its current state, 'a beautiful monument' to the empire's dead, because 'a more sacred place for the British race [did] not exist in the world'.[64] This proposal did not sit well with locals who returned to Ypres intent on rebuilding their homes. Fortunately for the Belgians, Churchill's plan was eventually rejected on practical grounds. This did not dampen British enthusiasm for some sort of monument in the town, and, after negotiations with the Belgian government and recommendations from Blomfield, the Menin Gate – a gap in the town's ramparts – was selected as the most appropriate site for a memorial. Initially conceived as a monument to the military exploits of the British armies in the salient, it was eventually combined with the Imperial War Graves Commission's project to commemorate the empire's missing in Belgium.[65] Like their counterparts in the other British dominions, Australian officials were not initially interested in the IWGC's plans, believing that the inscription of names on nearby cemetery walls would be sufficient to commemorate the missing.[66] The IWGC eventually convinced them to agree to the proposal, but the Australians nearly pulled out when Stanley Bruce's government decided that the national memorial at Villers-Bretonneux would include the names of Australia's Western Front missing. Bruce wrote to the commission's director Fabian Ware, '[We] consider essential that names of all Australian missing both in France and Belgium should be recorded there'. Ware responded quickly, noting that work had already begun and the IWGC would be 'seriously embarrassed' should the Australians withdraw. He also claimed, without any evidence, that the move would leave the Belgians 'undoubtedly disappointed if these [names] transferred to monument in France'.[67] These arguments evidently convinced the Australians, and the names of the Commonwealth's missing in the salient were inscribed on the arch. Fortunately for the Australian government, the popular reaction to the memorial and Longstaff's painting vindicated the decision to bend to the commission's will.

The Menin Gate Memorial's unveiling, in 1927, was a profound moment for many Britons. Thousands travelled across the English Channel to Ypres, and the ceremony was broadcast on BBC Radio. In Australia, neither distance nor the absence of a notable, official antipodean presence tempered media interest in the occasion, and the unveiling received substantial coverage across the nation. Headlines such as 'Britain's Dead Honoured' and 'A Symbol of British Courage' highlighted the imperial nature of the memorial. This was further reinforced by King Albert of Belgium's powerful declaration:

> If bloodshed in a noble cause sanctifies the ground where it was spilt, no ground in the world is more sacred than that of the Ypres salient. For 50 months Ypres was the threshold of the British Empire, and its name will stand for ever as a symbol of British courage and endurance. Ypres was for the British Empire what Verdun was for France.[68]

Yet, to Australians, the Menin Gate was more than a symbol of imperial commemoration and British glory. It also stood as a 'surrogate tomb' for relatives and friends of the missing, providing a solid reference point in the face of oblivion.[69] Herbert Plumer's famous declaration, 'He is not missing; he is here', at the unveiling was a personal message to all who recognised a name inscribed on the arch. Beyond comforting the bereaved, the memorial was also a reminder of the Australians' own martial efforts in Belgium framed within a broader, imperial context. *The Western Mail* captured this sentiment better than most:

> Naturally we are apt to pay chief attention to the actions in which our troops engaged and sometimes our perspectives need adjusting. There was much more than rhetoric in the words of King Albert … Ypres was the threshold of the Empire, not only of Britain. The men who held Ypres held it for Australia as well as England. The Menin Gate memorial is one through which Australia's remembrance passes as well as Britain's for she recalls her own 6,200 unfound dead.[70]

In Australia, then, the Menin Gate Memorial was indelibly linked with the empire, the AIF missing and the Ypres salient. Longstaff's painting of the same memorial had broader meanings still for the Australian public.

Menin Gate at Midnight came into the Australian War Memorial's possession thanks to the generosity of Lord Woolavington (formerly Sir James Buchanan) who donated it to the Commonwealth in 1928. It had been well received in Britain, and Woolavington purchased it for 2000 guineas, a record for an Australian artist's work at the time. The painting was then displayed in London, Manchester and Glasgow and even lent to King George V so he might view it in private at Buckingham Palace, before it was shipped to Australia.[71] There does not seem to have been a particular reason as to why Lord Woolavington decided that Australia should have the painting, especially considering the imperial nature of the Menin Gate Memorial. As John Williams has pointed out,

> The spirits of the dead soldiers that rise up wearing their British helmets are the spirits of *British* soldiers; *Menin Gate at Midnight*

is an imperial painting, therefore acquiring national meaning only through the context of the place in which it is displayed.[72]

Perhaps the fact that Longstaff had been a war artist for the Australian War Records Section during the war had swayed Woolavington's decision, but this went unmentioned in official correspondence. All he wrote when making his offer was that he 'would be proud to present it to the gallant Australians who served in the Great War'. This general statement was often repeated in articles explaining how the AWM acquired the painting.[73] Significantly, no explicit link was drawn between the donation and the Australian achievements at Ypres or the terrible losses they endured there. Whatever the reason for Woolavington's offer, Prime Minister Bruce formally accepted the gift on behalf of the Commonwealth.[74] Longstaff also offered 400 large, signed copies, desiring 'that these should be sold for the benefit of some fund connected with the AIF at ten guineas each'. These reproductions were subsequently given to the Returned Sailors' and Soldiers' Imperial League of Australia, which earmarked the eventual funds raised by their sale for the relief of distress among ex-soldiers.

The next step was to consider how the painting would be displayed. Canberra was still too far removed from the average Australian, so it was decided that 'it be exhibited in all the State Capitals before going to the Federal Capital'. Such a tour would reach the widest audience possible and was viewed as 'an opportunity for selling the [RSSILA] reproductions and so raising an important sum'. In order to arrange this, responsibility for the painting and its tour was passed on to the AWM. Always alert to ways of propagating the AIF's memory, Treloar also saw a potential fundraising opportunity, through admission charges and the sale of reproductions. The latter would be smaller, unsigned copies that would be more affordable than the larger versions in the RSSILA's possession. Nevertheless, Treloar was keen to avoid competing with the RSSILA and approached them about managing the sale of Longstaff's signed copies, to which they agreed.[75]

The painting's broad appeal lay in its successful harnessing of emotionally laden symbolism. Longstaff, who had attended the Menin Gate unveiling ceremony, claimed to have been inspired by visions of steel-helmeted spirits after a midnight stroll along the Menin Road; his painting captured this moment. Upon his return to London he set to work. The result, which became his chef-d'oeuvre, depicted the Menin Gate arch overlooking fields ripe for harvest, in which an ethereal host had risen, marching through blooming poppies and into the night. It was a highly spiritualist work, and although Longstaff professed not to be a spiritualist himself, his phantom army had considerable appeal in the aftermath of the war. Spiritualism had already been somewhat in vogue before 1914, but the mass death precipitated by the conflict ensured that an 'interest in the paranormal and the after-life naturally deepened' and remained popular well after 1918.[76] *Menin Gate at Midnight* was not the only painting to draw on this subject matter – Longstaff himself painted several similar works after *Menin Gate*, which 'gradually became little more than a formula' – but it was one of his most evocative. Moreover, the spiritualist element was but one facet of the painting, which used several other 'well-known motifs to trigger emotion', such as blood-red poppies and reference to the 'harvest of men'. According to Anne Gray, this potent mix of symbols allowed the painting to mean 'many things to many people'.[77] It was this versatility on which the AWM capitalised to market the painting's tour.

On the whole, *Menin Gate at Midnight*'s voyage throughout Australia was a great success, drawing large crowds and generating a considerable amount of publicity. Undoubtedly, the painting held a particular attraction for those who recognised names carved on the memorial. Recording the reaction to the painting, Bean wrote in a press release for the exhibition,

> Some of the crowd are affected by the site of this beautiful memorial as they would be by visiting the grave of a friend ... Some visitors clearly find it difficult to tear themselves away from what seems a link with precious memories.[78]

Even judging by the lowest estimates, at least 100,000 people saw the painting during the countrywide circuit. It is therefore unlikely that each visitor had a close, personal connection to the physical memorial in Belgium.[79] Ken Inglis has suggested that the impressive public response was due to the fact that the Menin Gate 'had a wider significance, commemorating as it did casualties of the only battle region, the Ypres salient, in which men of all sixty Australian battalions had been engaged'.[80] However, neither the general media coverage nor the AWM's publicity campaign and its scheme to sell reproductions highlighted this Australian connection to the Ypres salient. In fact, the strong Australian connection to Belgium and the Menin Gate was considerably underplayed in both articles and sales pitches, while the allegorical significance of the painting was accentuated. This focus served to move the public response to the painting 'beyond the commemoration of Australia's wartime achievements and closer to a pilgrimage of the bereaved'.[81]

The emphasis on spiritualism and remembrance during the tour, as opposed to the AIF's achievements in Belgium, was evident from *Menin Gate at Midnight*'s first appearance in Australia, at the Public Library, Museum and Art Gallery of Western Australia. The AWM had minimal input regarding the organisation of the painting's display at this stage, so the publicity campaign surrounding this exhibition was less pronounced than it became later on. Nevertheless, Western

Australian newspapers enthusiastically covered the arrival of Longstaff's work. Regular articles reminded readers that time to see the 'famous picture' was slipping away, and one paper printed a large colour copy for those unable to view the painting in person.[82] In all this coverage, there was a conspicuous absence of context. The reason for the erection of the Menin Gate Memorial was barely mentioned, if mentioned at all, and there was no explicit reference to the Australians' sacrifices in Flanders. On the other hand, the painting's spiritualist overtones and its wider meaning were stressed. For example, an article in *The West Australian* noted,

> The mysticism of the picture is its great quality ... [it] is a vision conceived under the stress of reflection upon the war's toll of humankind ... The memorial is only a part of the picture's motive, which is the whole scene of shadowy hosts rising from the field of battle.[83]

Evidently, Longstaff's subject was already being interpreted not only as representing the memorial to those lost in Flanders but also as a reflection on loss during the war in general. This was further highlighted in an editorial summarising the exhibition's success towards the end of the painting's time in Perth:

> The interest shown in Captain Will Longstaff's picture, 'The Ghosts of Menin Gate,' which has been on exhibition at the Perth Art Gallery during the past month, is nothing short of extraordinary ... But it may safely be concluded that this interest was not generally speaking, an art interest, but one almost wholly due to the subject of the painting – the war and its dead – a topic which strikes memory chords in the hearts of almost all today.[84]

The ghosts rising before the archway need not have fallen in Belgium; they symbolised all Australian dead, no matter where they lay.

After Perth, the AWM took a more active role in explaining the Menin Gate Memorial to the Australian public. This included the publication of a booklet – sold at the exhibitions and offered with reproductions – and the organisation of elaborate unveiling ceremonies, during which dignitaries spoke of the monument's history. The most substantial information regarding the AIF's actions in Belgium was provided in the booklet, which presented a brief overview of Ypres' importance to the British throughout the war before quickly moving on to the battles in which the five Australian infantry divisions had participated in 1917.[85] These were hardly detailed descriptions, simply naming the major assaults and referring to the deteriorating conditions that defeated the final pushes on Passchendaele. Yet, for those who read the booklet, it did clarify the Australian connection to the Menin Gate in a way that was largely ignored by the press. The unveiling ceremonies were another opportunity to draw attention to the strong link between Australia's war experience and the memorial. Three of the events were overseen by General John Monash, and they attracted considerable interest from newspapers, for which the AWM was only too happy to provide press releases, while several were broadcast on the radio. Monash was particularly direct in hailing the work of the AIF, but the speeches recorded in newspapers drew heavily on the *British* past at Ypres, appealing to the image of an unvanquished imperial army.[86] As a result, the rhetoric surrounding Longstaff's painting ended up primarily highlighting the British Expeditionary Force's achievements, to the detriment of the AIF's experiences. The governor of New South Wales called Ypres a 'new Thermopylae' where the 'little army' of Sir John French – the original commander of the British Expeditionary Force in 1914 – 'first stemmed the torrent of invasion'. Meanwhile, Queensland's governor highlighted the combined effort of 'troops from all parts of the Empire'. The overall trend of this reporting was to ignore the failed 1917 offensive in favour of praising grim British stoicism in the face of German onslaughts in 1914 and 1915.[87] In any case, once the unveiling ceremonies had taken place, the media turned their attention back to the mystic properties of Longstaff's painting, and the battles, whether they involved Australian or British troops, were seldom mentioned again.

The arrangements for *Menin Gate at Midnight*'s display during the tour also emphasised its broader significance. The AWM's other paintings were exhibited in the museum-like setting of the Sydney Exhibition Building, but *Menin Gate*'s presentation demanded solemn reverence. A journalist who saw the painting at a private viewing in Adelaide described its position for the *Advertiser*:

> The picture is surrounded by a beautiful frame of imitation gold and black, and is fixed in centre of dark brown drapines ... There are khaki-colored cloth panels, and on the top panel are placed representations of golden wreaths with ribbons of a light purple shade hanging from them. The effect is arresting.[88]

To further enhance this impression, the painting was also 'lit by electric light' and 'accompanied by a gramophone record of Schubert's *Unfinished Symphony*'. These details evidently had the desired effect, as visitors treated the painting with a veneration bordering on the religious, with men removing their hats in the picture's presence.[89] In a detailed report on the exhibition, another journalist distilled the sober atmosphere that reigned:

> Twenty feet [six metres] away was the street with its crowd hurrying on its noisy business. But here was an attitude of worship, or at least the silence of worship, for the few who spoke at all did so in subdued tones, almost ... in a whisper.

While the writer did not see the painting as 'superlative', he felt that

> the key note of the whole situation was certainly set by the allegorical meaning of the picture. Life, death, the indestructibility of spirit, these themes usually capture interest: But they have not always moved to reverence, and to the artist therefore must be attributed the sincerity and capacity which alone can inspire.[90]

Several days following the publication of this piece, Arthur Bazley, Bean's assistant during and after the war, wrote to Treloar to inform him of this 'excellent article on the exhibition'. Yet, there was no allusion to Ypres in this article. The Menin Gate's physical location was of limited importance to those organising the painting's tour. What really mattered was *Menin Gate at Midnight*'s ability to draw the largest audience possible, thereby helping the AWM to 'keep alive and evergreen the memory of the AIF'.[91]

A second, unique exhibition in Sydney did give viewers a chance to see *Menin Gate at Midnight* set in a context highlighting the AIF's presence in Belgium. Arranged in order to make up for relatively low turnout during the work's first visit to Sydney, this exhibition did not focus solely on remembrance but included representations of Australia's wartime achievements in Ypres. For the event, Treloar commandeered Power's *First Australian Division Artillery Going into the 3rd Battle of Ypres* and Leist's *Australian Infantry Attack in Polygon Wood*, as well as other works that gave 'dramatic and sympathetic impressions of actual fighting conditions [in Flanders]'. However, the proposed press campaign to support the exhibition, for which Bean was to provide 'descriptions of the battles on the 20th and 26th September and 4th October, 1917, with special reference to New South Wales units', did not eventuate.[92] Furthermore, Sydneysiders were the only Australians to see the display in its altered form. This new-look exhibition was simply a novel approach to attract the largest audience possible for a painting that had already been displayed in the city several months prior. When *Menin Gate at Midnight* moved on to large regional towns, the display reverted to its standardised reverential format, and the contextualising narrative of Australians in the Ypres salient was cast aside.[93]

Not even the sales campaign surrounding the reproductions of Longstaff's work emphasised the connection between the Menin Gate Memorial and the AIF's battles in Flanders. Despite Bean's initial misgivings, Treloar engaged the services of a third party, United Distributors Ltd, to undertake the sale and distribution of the reproductions. In keeping with AWM policy, only ex-servicemen were employed to sell, frame and distribute the copies.[94] As door-to-door salesmen they roamed the country, spreading the word about Will Longstaff's 'beautiful picture which has a very deep significance for *all* Australians'. That the painting had such a broad appeal was a key point in their pitches. Many sales scripts contained the line 'Capt. Longstaff might well have named his inspired work as Kipling named one of his finest poems, *Lest We Forget*. WE MUST NOT FORGET'. This was a call to remembrance not of specific wartime events but simply of the essence of Australian 'self-sacrifice, selflessness and devotion to duty' on all fronts. Unsurprisingly, references to Australians in Ypres were all but non-existent. In some interview scripts even the number of Australian names on the Menin Gate was only included in brackets, suggesting that this information was not relevant enough to make it into the full text.[95] Selling the history of Australia's role in the salient was not deemed a profitable exercise.

* * *

Throughout the interwar years, the Australian War Memorial – under the direction of Treloar and with close support from the indefatigable

Bean – was a key agency behind the propagation of the Anzac legend. Although the institution did not move into its permanent home in Canberra until 1941, millions of Australians flocked to see its temporary exhibitions of the 'sacred things' their fellow Australians had brought home from distant battlefields. Between 1922 and 1935, the major Melbourne and Sydney exhibitions attracted large crowds which viewed objects and read captions that portrayed the Australian experience of the war in traditional, romantic terms, with a particular emphasis on martial triumph and sacrifice. In these settings, which largely omitted the more confronting elements of industrialised warfare, the battles the AIF fought in the second half of 1917 came across as tough and, in the case of third Ypres, muddy engagements in which the Australians had achieved some notable successes. However, when compared to other campaigns in the AWMs' exhibitions, they clearly did not rank among the Australians' most testing or glorious battles.

The tour of *Menin Gate at Midnight* was an opportunity for the AWM to highlight the AIF's struggles in Belgium. Yet, in spite of more than 6000 names of missing Australians being chiselled into the stone panels of the Menin Gate Memorial, this connection between Longstaff's painting and the Flanders campaigns was not as concrete as one might assume. The Menin Gate itself was not a specifically Australian memorial but an imperial one, and this was reflected in the language used to describe both the monument and the painting at respective unveiling ceremonies. In any case, the commemoration of Australian or imperial military accomplishment in Belgium was of decidedly secondary importance to the AWM's plans for exhibiting the painting. The picture's overly broad symbolism and Lord Woolavington's vague reasoning for offering it to the Commonwealth meant that it had taken on a grander significance by the time it reached Australian shores: commemorating the loss of Australians wherever they fell. The AWM fostered this wider interpretation through reverence-inducing display techniques as well as in publicity and sales campaigns. It was, after all, in the best interests of Treloar to ensure that *Menin Gate at Midnight* appealed to as many Australians as possible, in order to keep the memory of the AIF alive while raising a considerable amount of money for the institution as well. As a consequence, the painting was more or less severed from the specific Belgian landscape that it represented, and the AIF's experiences at Ypres were once again folded into a grander, overarching narrative, not of triumph this time, but of loss.

Chapter 3

BELGIUM IMAGINED

Passchendaele is a distressing pen picture. It cannot be otherwise.

'Non-Com', West Australian,
18 September 1928

Charles Bean and the Australian War Memorial may have been the two most influential agents shaping the memory of the First World War in interwar Australia, but their narratives were not the only ones Australians recounted and shared during the interwar years. Everyone who lived through the war had their own experiences on which to draw. As is clear from the erection of thousands of war memorials, as well as the organisation of and participation in Anzac Day ceremonies, many Australians also chose to engage in 'collective remembrance'.[1] These often-unofficial agents of memory – including returned soldiers and bereaved family members – did not take part in such commemorative acts with the aim of shoring up abstract notions of the nation; they did so in order to fulfil their own commemorative needs. Alongside federal initiatives, their acts of commemoration served to keep the First World War alive in the memory of the population. Their acts also simplified the memory of the war, elevating what was considered worthy of recollection while simultaneously minimising the rest.

With the exception of the explicit links between Anzac Day and the Gallipoli landing and, to a lesser extent, Villers-Bretonneux, an overwhelming majority of these manifestations of remembrance did not focus on specific battles – and certainly not on Messines or third Ypres. This meant that the only time Australians might routinely hear the names of places where Australians fought was on 25 April, and this was dependent on different speakers. The names intoned were not set in stone, and the fighting at the Dardanelles remained central to the rhetoric of the day. Still, at least other Australian engagements were mentioned on Anzac Day; they were all but absent on most local memorials, which concentrated on naming the dead and those who served.

There were other avenues for individuals and groups to partake in acts of collective remembrance that shed light on the Australian Imperial Force's many First World War engagements, including Messines and third Ypres. This chapter examines how Australians portrayed the 1917 Belgian campaigns in regimental histories, returned services' journals, popular memoirs and novels. These texts show that contemporaries had not forgotten the Flanders battlefields, but their accounts of the Belgian campaigns did not always fit the framework of the dominant Anzac legend. As Iwona Irwin-Zarecka has argued, 'Collective remembering has to be out in the open ... there is a need for records, markers, stones, reminders, the full information base of remembrance'.[2] The 'information base of remembrance' of Messines and third Ypres was fragile and disparate when compared to that of the Gallipoli narrative. As the war faded from living memory, brief, often-critical accounts in dry unit histories, Returned Sailors' and Soldiers' Imperial League of Australia magazines, memoirs and novels were unlikely to sustain Belgium's place in the national memory – and as it turned out, they did not.

Reviewing the War

In the months following the signing of the armistice, the press, far from losing interest in the past four years of conflict, printed frequent if ultimately shallow accounts of the war. While the battles of Messines and third Ypres were big enough to merit several sentences, if not a paragraph or two, in many synopses, it was clear that journalists did not consider the Australian Imperial Force's engagements in Belgium to be as significant as other battles on the Western Front, especially those of 1918. Descriptions of Messines often centred on the work of the tunnellers, as opposed to the efforts of the much larger infantry contingent involved. Accounts of third Ypres condensed its individual phases into one or two battles, and the dreadful weather conditions experienced during the battles of Poelcappelle and Passchendaele came to represent the whole campaign: 'Our men had to overcome not only the Germans, but that fifth element – neither earth, air, fire, nor water – [but] the mud of Flanders'.[3] The articles had much in common with, though considerably less nuance than, the later-published official narratives of Bean and the Australian War Memorial. At best, journalists cast 1917 as a year in between the first trials on the Western Front and the triumph of 1918 or, at worst, a year that 'exhausted and dispirited' the British armies.[4]

For Australians who wished to learn more about the Australian Imperial Force's battles shortly after the war, there were three histories available: Frederic Cutlack's *The Australians* (1918), John Monash's *The Australian Victories in France in 1918* (1918) and Staniforth Smith's *Australian Campaigns in the Great War* (1919). In keeping with the triumphant mood permeating newspaper articles of the period, *The Australians* and *The Australian Victories* concentrated exclusively on the war's final year. There were practical as well as ideological reasons for this. In Cutlack's case, he based his work on expanded notes and dispatches written after his appointment as assistant official war correspondent in 1918. Monash, having commanded the 4th Australian Infantry Brigade at Gallipoli and the 3rd Australian Division on the Western Front, had a considerably longer history with the AIF, but 1918 was the year in which he became commander of the Australian Corps. According to both authors, the emphasis on 1918 was logical, as it was the first year in which the Australian divisions had been 'brought together under a single leadership'. For Cutlack and Monash, this position did not downplay the Australians' achievements before that year, which were 'all epics themselves'.[5] But the banding together of the five Australian divisions in Europe was a moment when the AIF became a truly *national* force, which further accentuated the fighting prowess demonstrated from 1915 to 1917. Monash's and Cutlack's works implored Australians to remember 1918 as a year of 'brilliant successes ... which far overshadowed those of any earlier period of the war'.[6] From this triumphalist perspective, there was little point in looking further back.

Smith's *Australian Campaigns* was the only book-length history that specifically addressed the AIF's battles in Belgium. However, as Smith stressed, his work was 'in no sense an official history', and he did not attempt 'to describe the strategy and tactics of the Great War'. Drawing on divisional staff diaries, *Australian Campaigns* lacked detailed description of the AIF's engagements and resembled something akin to the regimental histories that were beginning to appear, albeit with a much broader scope. In describing Messines, Smith spent as much time hailing the Irish contribution to the battle as that of the Australians. His portrayal of third Ypres did go into more detail concerning Australian 'spirit and ardour' in the 'sea of mud' that was the salient, and he pointed to the Anzacs' key roles in the three 'sledge-hammer blows' struck against 'the most vital defensive positions of the Germans' at Menin Road, Polygon Wood and Broodseinde. Yet, his greatest praise was reserved for soldiers of other countries:

> The magnificent stamina, heroism and dogged determination of the British and French troops during that terrible period form one of the brightest pages in the glorious annals of these two great nations, equalling in lustre the most heroic actions in the campaigns of Marlborough and Wellington in the earlier battles of Flanders, but the casualties were enormous.

Smith usually differentiated between British and Australian successes, so such praise did not implicitly include the Australians, although the AIF was at the heart of the most successful British advances and had also suffered enormous casualties in the salient. This decision to portray the 1917 battles in Flanders as a 'bright page' in the long and established histories of Britain and France, while overlooking their place in Australia's much shorter history, is therefore rather surprising.[7]

Reading on, it becomes apparent that Smith's omission of any grand rhetoric about the AIF and its role in third Ypres was deliberate. The overly positive focus on the British and French at third Ypres can be explained by the manner in which the narrative of *Australian Campaigns* – like that of Monash's and Cutlack's books – implicitly broke the AIF's war experience into two distinct periods: before and after the formation of the Australian Corps. Smith argued that, as the Australian divisions had generally fought in different sectors of the front before 1918, 'it was … not possible to know what the Australian infantry, fighting as one body, was capable of achieving. Right up to the last great campaign this nullified to some extent the national pride in achievements'.[8] This was a somewhat disingenuous claim, as all the Australian divisions had fought at third Ypres, a detail Smith failed to mention when describing the battle. Smith's suggestion that the Australian divisions had not reached the zenith of their martial proficiency before 1918 because they had not fought 'as one body' also glossed over the realities of fighting on the Western Front in that last year of the war. Nonetheless, this argument evidently held great weight with ex-AIF members such as Smith and Monash, who stoked the myth.[9] Messines and third Ypres, which sat on the wrong side of this crucial juncture in the AIF's history, were undoubtedly significant in terms of men involved and casualties, but they were not symbolic of national unity.

For the Glory of the Unit and the Fallen

While newspapers and publishers were releasing broad accounts of AIF exploits, another type of war-related chronicle began to appear: the unit history. In the long term, these publications had little influence on the wider memory of the war. Most print runs did not exceed 1000 copies, and no unit histories were reprinted during the interwar period. Nevertheless, surveying their content is useful, because they show how returned men who wished to commemorate their units' achievements during the war framed their experiences within the Anzac legend, reflecting and reinforcing this predominant narrative. The most common type of publication in the genre was the infantry battalion history. This is unsurprising, given that the infantry was the largest branch within the AIF and the battalion itself was seen as 'a self-contained community'.[10] By the beginning of the Second World War, nearly forty per cent of the AIF's sixty infantry battalions had published a history, with two more appearing shortly after hostilities had broken out in Europe again. Some specialist units also produced their own histories, but these were less numerous. Out of the larger formations, only the 5th Division saw fit to publish an account of its involvement in the war. These works provided some of the most detailed accounts of fighting in Belgium available during the interwar period.

Returned servicemen, often ex-officers, were responsible for producing the bulk of the unit histories published at the time. These passionate men were keen to promote their units' exploits to ensure that they would not be forgotten. Since a unit's reputation was based on its work at the front, authors structured their chronicles around the engagements in which their formation had fought. Consequently, many histories passed over Messines, as only two out of the five Australian divisions played a part in the battle. As every division had fought at third Ypres, it was one of the few battles covered in all unit histories concerned with Australian formations in Europe.

Given their relatively narrow scope, the publications proffered specific – sometimes even intimate – accounts of the war to ex-members and relatives of deceased members. Composed by men who had a firm conviction that the war had been a positive, nation-affirming experience for Australia, the histories also largely toed the official line. In fact, the overwhelming majority of unit histories received official aid and were therefore subject to government oversight. Bean and Department of Defence officials were eager to see units publish histories, and they actively encouraged potential authors. The Unit History Scheme, launched in 1919, adopted the following objectives:

> firstly, to provide a thoroughly accurate narrative for the benefit of those who belonged to the units; secondly, to keep alive its traditions; and thirdly, to enable the relatives of those Australians who died to have some knowledge of the fights, journeys, and other incidents in which their son, brother, or husband took part.[11]

As part of the scheme, units that wished to publish a history were eligible for an advance from the Anzac Book Trust Fund. The small lump sum was not meant to completely pay all publication costs but covered those incurred contacting ex-members and the next of kin of deceased members as well as other preliminary expenses.[12]

The support from the trust fund came with conditions. Unit historians had to submit manuscripts to the scheme's literary officer, Charles Barrett, or to Charles Bean or his assistant Arthur Bazley. This condition allowed Barrett, Bean or Bazley to cast an editorial eye over the work of these enthusiastic amateur historians before permitting publication. The stipulation was mutually beneficial: while the scheme's administrators could monitor authors' claims and guarantee that the histories did not challenge the official narrative of the war, many of the unit historians appreciated the critical evaluation of their writing and placed considerable faith in the official editors, yielding to their suggestions on many occasions.[13] An exchange of letters between Bean and Newton Wanliss, author of the 14th Battalion history, neatly captures the balance of power between unit historians and the official editors. Wanliss was an atypical unit historian, as he had not served but was the father of a 14th Battalion officer killed at Polygon Wood. He wrote to preserve not only the memory of the battalion but also that of his son – a passionate undertaking into which he threw himself completely for close to a decade. Nevertheless, when Bean wrote to Wanliss regarding several points of contention in his Bullecourt chapter, including exaggerated criticism of British tanks, the 62nd Division (2nd West Riding) and the AIF leadership, the unit historian acquiesced to Bean's demands, despite remaining convinced of his initial position, replying:

> I realise that you were on the spot and saw the battle whilst my information was secondhand. I shall accordingly modify my account of the battle. In reference to the tanks perhaps justice has not been done to them by our people. They were (like the infantry) set an

impossible task but some of them certainly failed. There should have been 120 instead of 12 of them. In my opinion Bullecourt was a classic example of incompetence in leadership.[14]

Of the published unit histories, only a minority – those written within months of the war's end – avoided this editing process and the benefits of the Unit History Scheme's support.

For all Bean's vigilance, official oversight was hardly required. Several authors admitted they had drawn liberally on Bean's *Official History of Australia in the War of 1914–1918* and Monash's *Australian Victories in France in 1918*.[15] In any case, interwar unit histories proved to be considerably more selective and less contentious than Bean's own publications, as amateur historians focused on the positives. These authors saw ex-members as the principal beneficiaries of their books and wanted them to take pride in their achievements. According to the compilers of the 2nd Battalion's history, their objective was

> to place on permanent record the individual and collective exploits of the Second, to preserve the link that [bound] all its members in a common Diggerhood, and hand down to posterity a record of the battalion's achievements in one of the greatest wars of history.[16]

Less common were references to families and friends of deceased unit members, but occasionally regimental historians addressed them too. The author of the 22nd Battalion's history noted that his work was 'for relatives in particular', and in order to satisfy their interest there was 'no striving after literary effect, but, instead a detailed attention to dates and names of places' so they could 'identify more easily the period' that interested them.[17] Just as Bean conceived his *Official History* as a monument to the men of the AIF, unit history authors envisaged their works as memorials to their regiments' accomplishments and comrades left behind.

Unit historians had little trouble fitting Messines, when it was discussed, and third Ypres into their narratives. Most infantry battalion histories omitted the artillery's predominant role in the salient. Some paid lip service to the artillery, which they noted as having paved the way for the victories at Menin Road, Polygon Wood and Broodseinde, but they were primarily concerned with the successes of the frontline soldier, the iconic Anzac. As the author of the 3rd Pioneer Battalion's history noted, 'What the gunners suffered in those bad days was only equalled by the perils and discomforts of the infantry'.[18] Apart from rare allusions, ruthless clashes near German pillboxes went unmentioned, so the image of Australian chivalry remained uncontested. The recurring themes in interwar histories concerning the Flanders engagements were the trying conditions, particularly at third Ypres, and a sense the British had lost several opportunities to break through the German lines. By engaging with these topics and failing to acknowledge the campaign's broader strategic aims, certain histories flirted with a sense of futility. Several writers even expressed bitterness at the campaign's outcomes. These negative elements, however, were nearly always redeemed by exhortations of Australian bravery and deprecating remarks about 'English generalship and staff methods'.[19] Framing the Belgian battles in this manner was evidently acceptable, as no unit historian's account of the Ypres campaign caused any noticeable indignation. Such portrayals did not prompt much interest either, with review articles rarely referring to histories' descriptions of the Flanders fighting as key moments in the text.

Little more than a sidenote in the postwar press, Messines did not elicit much excitement from most unit historians either. The one unit that was regularly hailed for its work at Hill 60, at Zillebeke, the 1st Australian Tunnelling Company, did not publish a history. Still, the

Australians had contributed more than a single company of tunnellers to the engagement; it was the 3rd Division's baptism of fire, and the veteran 4th Australian Division also participated in the attack. Two battalion historians did note, in off-the-cuff remarks, that their formations' experiences south of the salient were particularly testing.[20] The overall impression of the Messines battle, though, was one of stringently limited and limiting objectives in which the British failed to press the advantage sufficiently for the 'temperamentally aggressive' Anzacs. The 14th Battalion historian Wanliss was outspoken in his summary of the engagement:

> There was a feeling among all ranks that a great opportunity – such as had never before presented itself to the AIF in France – was being lost. A great victory had been gained: there was indisputable ocular evidence both of the enemy's heavy losses and demoralisation and all were eager to push forward and exploit the victory. They were, much to their disappointment, held back ... The great tactical victory yielded only local results and little strategical use was made of it by the General Headquarters staff.[21]

Messines was thus a stunted victory in which the Australians had indeed triumphed; but it was also cast as an opportunity that had gone begging.[22] The 3rd Pioneer Battalion's historian distilled an appreciation of the attack better than most: 'Messines was not the greatest battle of the war. There were many others greater and more lasting in their gains', but it did give many a sense of 'satisfaction in smashing back the Hun with sheer might of arms'.[23]

Third Ypres presented the Australians with another opportunity to 'smash back the Hun', and it was certainly a 'greater' engagement in every sense: greater in scale and hardship, and greater in disappointment when it petered out in the mud. Most descriptions of the first steps – Menin Road, Polygon Wood and Broodseinde – were positive, given the Anzacs' successes, although several unit historians lamented the fact that opportunities to push on had been lost. Summarising the 7th Battalion's experience at Broodseinde, Arthur Dean and Eric Gutteridge claimed that the rigid set piece battles of the campaign 'galled' them:

> Having reached our objective we were bound to stay there, and not able to exploit our attack as we should have liked, and as we did in the closing battles of the war. In each of these operations we simply followed our barrage and cleaned up as we moved forward.[24]

Such claims ignored the fact that going beyond the set limits for each push meant quitting artillery support, which would have drastically decreased the infantry's chances of further success. They also served to highlight the Australians' offensive spirit while bringing into question British leadership, both common tropes of the Anzac legend.

Third Ypres was more than a tale of lost opportunities, though. Focusing on the terrible conditions allowed unit historians to accentuate Australian courage. Some historians have strongly criticised the emphasis on the mud of Passchendaele in popular memory. Brian Bond bemoans the fact that 'no one wants to be told … of the dry and dusty spell during the Passchendaele campaign'.[25] His critique is reserved for the works of modernist authors and artists, which have been influential in shaping present-day understandings of the First World War. Yet, Australian regimental historians did not tell their readers about that dry and dusty spell at Passchendaele either. Only *two* histories mention dust in the salient, and one of those references is highly ironic, with the author of the 5th Pioneer Battalion history finding a sign that read 'Don't raise dust' particularly 'sardonic' given 'the whole country round about was a festering mass of mud and slush'.[26]

While the dry conditions went unmentioned, unit historians provided their readers with an abundance of descriptive language to depict the abysmal state of the battlefield when the weather broke in October. They employed the terms 'morass', 'quagmire' and 'sea of mud', among others, suggesting the campaign at Ypres was an interminable struggle against the elements.[27] In some instances, narratives gave way to harrowing depictions of futility. Frank Green, the 40th Battalion historian, described one such pathetic episode: that of a wounded German trying to follow two Australians back to Allied lines during first Passchendaele.

> As they [the Australians] were unable to take him they tried to induce him to go back, but he was badly wounded, and only seemed to realise that it was a stretcher, and a stretcher – German or otherwise – meant help. He tried to follow them on his hands and knees. His progress became slower and slower till he stopped, and his head sank forward and buried in the sea of mud.[28]

Horrendous as it is, the Australians in this anecdote did not die, and no unit historian dared describe a similar situation with the roles reversed. Moreover, the confronting nature of Green's passage was an exception. Overwhelmingly, the evocation of torrid conditions served to eulogise formations' achievements and aggrandise Australian bravery. In this way, the 2nd Battalion's compilers could claim that, despite the unit's losses, Passchendaele added 'another brilliant chapter to the history of the Second … and out of this inferno it emerged richer in tradition'.[29] This approach reassured traditional-minded ex-servicemen as well as family members and friends of those who had died in action.

For all the traditions upheld in Flanders, very few unit historians indicated that the battle had surpassed other engagements in exertion or sacrifice. Rather, it was the first battles on the Western Front in 1916 that held a special place in the memory of many regiments. The chroniclers of 1st, 2nd, 4th and 5th Australian Division units often couched these engagements in reverential terms. 'Oh Pozières, resting place of heroes!' exclaimed the author of the 24th Battalion history,[30] while the 1st Battalion's historians declared:

> The mind of every Australian is stirred to proud and sombre memories by the name Pozières. Few who took part in the Great War can hear without some sort of emotion the mention of the insignificant but now famous mud village of Picardy.

Such high diction was generally absent in the 1st Battalion's history when it came to third Ypres. Broodseinde, the most successful battle of the campaign, came across as another costly action carried out at the behest of the 'heads', who no doubt 'had weighty strategical reasons to advance'.[31] The majority of authors writing about 3rd Division units, for which Messines and third Ypres were their first major engagements, even used moderate language to describe the battles. Perhaps this was because the authors of these histories were keenly aware of their regiments' inexperience, compared to that of other formations. They had not participated at Fromelles or Pozières, so they did not – as older units did of the 1916 battles – claim the Flanders offensive as anything like a defining moment in their First World War experience.

Concluding one of the more outspoken unit histories, the author of the 37th Battalion's chronicle noted that 'the bitterness and tragedy of such places as Passchendaele have been softened. The horrors are forgotten, or at any rate dimly remembered, and the war's humorous incidents live on'.[32] He was right. The Anzacs' larrikin spirit and bravery – captured in numerous anecdotes circulating during and after the war – remain among the defining characteristics of Australia's First World War citizen soldiers. Despite providing some of the most detailed descriptions of the battles available at the time, the unit histories did not challenge the official narrative, with its focus on Gallipoli, Pozières and the victories of 1918. They reaffirmed it.

The Returned Remember

Magazines and newspapers that regularly printed articles recounting the experiences of Australian soldiers had far wider audiences than unit histories. Returned services organisations, the largest and most influential of which was the Returned Sailors' and Soldiers' Imperial League of Australia, were responsible for producing many of these publications. State, territory and local RSSILA branches produced monthly magazines, including *Reveille* (New South Wales), *The Queensland Digger*, *The Listening Post* (Western Australia) and *The Duckboard* (Melbourne, Victoria). While these were published under different editors and focused on issues in the RSSILA branch's home state, territory or city, the wider content of the magazines was fairly similar across the board. This included an abundant supply of nostalgic anecdotes, articles on battlefield pilgrimages, book reviews and excerpts of longer soldier tales, including extracts from novels and histories. Available to a wider public were *Smith's Weekly* newspaper and the revamped trench magazine *Aussie*. Both were 'popular and populist' productions – *Aussie* less than *Smith's Weekly* on both counts – that courted, but were not exclusively aimed at, a returned soldier readership.[33] These newspapers and returned services publications were central to the maintenance of the stereotypical 'digger' image.[34] They also helped keep Messines and third Ypres in the margins of the Anzac narrative throughout the interwar years.

Given their pro-Anzac roots, RSSILA magazines, *Smith's Weekly* and early issues of *Aussie* staunchly promoted any narrative that asserted the Australian soldier's unique character and fighting qualities. RSSILA journals heralded the efforts of Bean and the Australian War Memorial in spreading the Anzac gospel. These same journals enthusiastically promoted unit histories and praised those motivated enough to produce them while expressing dismay that more had not been published. Occasionally, contributions to RSSILA publications mildly contested the dominant interwar narrative. When former war prime minister Billy Hughes wrote an article for *Reveille* claiming that the attack spearheaded by the Australians on 8 August 1918 had 'brought the war to an end' two years early, an ex-serviceman chided Hughes for adopting 'an American attitude' by unnecessarily boasting about Australian success. However, the writer did not make such a critique to downplay the AIF's role in ultimate victory; he simply suggested that the focus on 1918 was wrong and argued that it was the men who had fought at Bullecourt and Messines 'who won the war'.[35] Debates such as these certainly did not bring Australian fighting prowess into question.

When Australians were criticised, publications closely linked with returned servicemen leaped to their defence. An example of this can be found in the response to certain books published in the late 1920s. Initially, journals like *Reveille* and *The Duckboard* reviewed some of the earliest disillusionment novels, such as Erich Maria Remarque's *All Quiet on the Western Front* (1929), rather favourably. They lauded Remarque's depiction of 'what the war meant in the *German* lines' for its 'plain speaking indictments against war'.[36] Yet, as the number of anti-war novels swelled, the journals' response hardened. The tipping point for *Reveille* came when English poet Robert Graves charged an Australian with killing German prisoners at Morlancourt in *Goodbye to All That* (1929). From then on, according to the historian Humphrey McQueen, '*Reveille*'s reviews and comments either attacked the war novels as unbalanced and degenerate, or defended war as a necessary, inevitable and ennobling experience'.[37] Around the same time, the author of *War Is War* – A.M. Burrage, a returned English soldier writing under the pseudonym of Ex-Private X – incensed *Smith's Weekly* with the suggestion that the Australians' reputation as brave fighters was an exaggeration. He even had the temerity to claim that, due to the prominence of 'black sheep' in the AIF's ranks, he was 'sorry' that the Australians had been on the British side.[38] In response, the newspaper commissioned a series of bombastic articles based on interviews with AIF hero John Monash. Over the following weeks, the series refuted 'slanderous attacks', suggested that those of the disillusioned clique should have been 'strangled at birth' and reaffirmed the glory and romanticism of Australia's participation in the war.[39] The magazines did not brook criticism of the AIF soldier, and their laudatory content was even less critical of the Australian war experience than was that of the official narratives.

As we have seen, Bean's *Official History* and the unit histories offered rounded, chronological accounts of the war interspersed with colourful anecdotes. The ephemeral periodicals, on the other hand, despite an uncritical embrace of the Anzac legend, were not concerned with providing anything like a complete narrative of the war. In their pages, AIF battles were little more than a backdrop for 'digger yarns'. Yarns were an important medium for projecting and reinforcing the Anzacs' self-image, both between themselves and with the world at large. They drew on pre-federation concepts of Australian national identity – the bush and pioneer legends – whose attributes had become associated with Anzac exploits on and off the battlefield.[40] A yarn's strength relied not on where or when the events recounted took place but on the Australian qualities emphasised. For example, *Smith's Weekly* included a yarn about a Major Taylor, 'one of the best', who 'disobeyed his own order' by giving his dressing to a 'wounded cobber', only to be subsequently wounded himself.⁴¹ The fact that this event took place during Broodseinde was of little significance. What mattered was the illustration of the Anzac spirit embodied in the officer's selflessness. Belgium was a regular setting for digger yarns, but these did not suggest anything notable about fighting in the salient.

Returned services publications, which had more war-oriented content than *Smith's Weekly* and the postwar *Aussie*, did not print solely digger yarns to fill their pages. They made efforts to remind members of glorious actions in which Australians had participated, and therefore, important events and dates did matter to a certain extent. *The Duckboard* was one of the more conscientious RSSILA publications in this respect, printing 'war diaries' recording all the AIF's major engagements between 1914 and 1918 during the month corresponding with the date of each particular issue. These were included 'not to keep the war alive, but "lest we forget"'.⁴² Still, these were not complete articles, just lists, and they rarely included more information than a date and a title for numerous events. They extolled readers to remember dates without explaining why the dates were worth remembering.

Other publications were less consistent in reminding readers of key moments in the war. In 1929, *The Queensland Digger* printed an article listing all 'important battles' in response to questions that were 'constantly being asked in relation to the doings of the AIF'. However, only the 1918 battles were the subjects of a longer, descriptive passage at the end of the article.⁴³ This triumphalist attitude was even clearer in *Reveille*. In July or August each year (*Reveille* was published at the end of the month), special August 1918 issues went to press, with editorials and articles relating specifically to battles that took place in that historic month.⁴⁴ April was the only other month in which these types of periodicals paid close attention to the events of corresponding months during the war. Gallipoli and the 1918 victories dominated analyses of the AIF's battles in the RSSILA's interwar journals.

Messines and third Ypres were seldom recalled in detail in the returned services publications and, falling outside April and August as they did, certainly not on their respective anniversaries. Messines, in particular, was as overlooked as it was in the unit histories. The battle was rarely the subject of specific articles, although it did feature in *Reveille*'s abridged version of Bean's *Official History*, biographies of AIF 'celebrities' and extracts of George Mitchell's memoirs, which were published in 1937. More often than not, however, Messines was simply cited as one of many 'memorable names' that attested to the AIF's success as a fighting force, without any further explanation to back up the claim.[45] It was just not a battle that inspired much interest. Third Ypres, although evoked more often, was evidently a challenging action to recall. The infrequent articles describing third Ypres rarely referred to the AIF's successes at Menin Road, Polygon Wood and Broodseinde in glowing terms. Occasional criticism of British leadership during the campaign was also rather subtle when compared to the accusations of incompetence levelled at generals in relation to Fromelles and Bullecourt. Articles about third Ypres once again tended to focus on the deplorable conditions in the salient, portraying the campaign in uncompromisingly miserable terms. This is unsurprising, given that most articles and short stories about the battle were written from individual viewpoints that failed to acknowledge the broader strategic reasons for and consequences of the campaign's various phases. As Brian Bond highlights in his critique of British modernist literature, an ignorance of greater military strategy served to render 'the whole war effort meaningless'.[46] But, in journals that constantly reminded readers of the glories of Gallipoli and the 1918 victories, there was no danger of the war appearing 'meaningless'. In the few articles concerning third Ypres, however, the campaign was depicted as little more than a gruelling, bloody experience that achieved no meaningful results apart from the killing and maiming of mates en masse. Only the evocations of Australian bravery, sacrifice and humour ensured the battle did not come across as entirely futile, but, even then, it remained little more than an 'ugly memory': too horrific in its nature and too inconclusive in its results to arouse anything like nostalgic relish.[47]

Articles by Frank Green, Jas Pollard and a returned soldier writing under the pseudonym Emma Gee were among the most detailed accounts of fighting in Belgium to appear in RSSILA magazines. Green, formerly of the 40th Battalion, had already written a damning account of third Ypres in his unit's history and, in a rare piece printed on third Ypres' anniversary, once again he did not mince his words. He noted the Anzacs honoured many dates 'according to the memories they bring', such as 8 August 1918, when they had the 'German army on the run'. October and its connection to third Ypres, however, belonged to a separate 'hell of memory'. The victory at Broodseinde, much feted by Bean, was 'a grim fight' in Green's view, but at least the Anzacs had demonstrated discipline and courage throughout, exemplified by Sergeant Lewis McGee, who won the Victoria Cross for his gallantry that day. There was nothing redeeming about the following push towards Passchendaele, which died, like McGee, on 12 October on the Broodseinde Ridge. Green detailed the severe hardship the troops endured as well as their appalling casualties in a battle during which 'even the enemy seemed sick of the slaughter'. Worse still was his implication that the attempt to wrest Passchendaele from the Germans was pointless:

> The attack on October 12 was a severe defeat. Why it was undertaken when doomed to failure under the conditions *has never been explained*. It failed on account of the wet weather and consequent

mud, which made it impossible to get artillery forward ... We had to advance 2,000 yards [1800 metres] to reach Passchendaele, and though after our attempt attacks were made by the Canadians, the town was not captured until November 6 after six weeks of constant fighting.[48]

Green's sidelining of greater strategy, his reluctance to explicitly question British command and his rejection of traditional terms such as 'sacrifice' and 'fallen' departed from the dominant Anzac narrative. The article's abrupt conclusion, which focused on the 40th Battalion's harrowing casualty figures, further reinforced the break from this narrative. There was, however, another important element to Green's account: numerous examples of Australians sticking out the engagement and then leaving their trenches the following day to bring in the wounded. There is something grimly heroic in these details that prevents the episode slipping into utter futility. Still, these thin silver linings did not reverse Green's representation of third Ypres as a thoroughly wretched experience for the Australians.

Both Emma Gee and Jas Pollard produced more literary portrayals, which enhanced the nightmarish aspects of the Flanders campaign. Published under the title 'Fragmentary Memories', Gee's serialised memoirs offered detailed and disturbing images with flourishes of irony common to European war writing. Gee's first night at Ypres was spent in a 'lunatic asylum', and his experiences in Belgium only became more grotesque. Heading out to the line, he heard the rumour that the main artery to the front, the infamous Menin Road, was supported by bodies, which gave it a 'springiness', to prevent one from sinking too far into the mud: an ominous sign of things to come. Having sought shelter in a pillbox during the fighting at Polygon Wood, Gee leaned back on a 'shelf' to rest, only to find that he had put his hands 'into the face of a semi-decomposed man'. This led him to choose the floor as a more suitable resting place, until he was startled by 'an uncanny gurgle as my weight forced the gases from another corpse'. In spite of these experiences, Gee managed to veer away from absolute disillusion. The memoirs were buoyed by touches of sardonic humour and even a reference to the romance of bygone wars, encapsulated by the imagery of a gun team galloping through Ypres – a description that recalls Septimus Power's *First Australian Division Artillery Going into the 3rd Battle of Ypres* (1919; see plate 8). Such references often concluded Gee's contributions, allowing the narrative to end on a somewhat brighter note.[49] Nevertheless, the portrayal of third Ypres in 'Fragmentary Memories' remained deeply disconcerting.

Jas Pollard's contributions to *The Listening Post* comprised four loosely linked vignettes. Although not quite as horrific as Gee's depiction of third Ypres, they were consistently more pessimistic. Throughout, Pollard touched on attributes that typified the Australian serviceman: initiative in tight spots, strong sense of mateship and cool character. When the narrative was focused on these attributes, which were embodied in battle-hardened protagonist Johnnie, the conditions in Belgium featured little. Yet, when the narrative turned away from Johnnie's casual bravery and towards notions of futility, the salient battlefield was thrust to the forefront of the action. The most emphatic example of this came in the ominously titled finale, 'Annihilation's Waste'. The first half of the story follows the nonchalant advance of Australians under a creeping barrage. Once the objective is captured and no German retaliation is forthcoming, Johnnie is ordered to deliver a message to headquarters. During his return, he takes in his surroundings, where

> he found his glance straying often over the stagnant fields ... seeing again something of the tragedies and comedies of the day – and

of the ways and weeks before ... A terrible brooding field of death spread away before him, strangely, horribly fascinating.

This passage and the following description described a war as close to futile as did any contribution to an RSSILA publication, counterbalanced only by the survival of Johnnie, who wonders, 'What shall the harvest be?' Perhaps a future harvest, reaped from these 'men from everywhere, drawn together at the end of things' and 'sown over this field of stagnation', would herald a new world. But Pollard did not provide readers with the answer. Instead, his conclusion was as sombre as ever, with Johnnie spotting

> a long line of diminutive figures stretched away into the distance. This was a Labour battalion, part of a Legion, cleaning up, salvaging, burying the dead, miles behind the advance. And once more there was a question to which he could get no answer, though it reiterated over and over again through his mind ...

'Will they ever catch up?'[50]

This was a thoroughly depressing end to the series. Although the Anzacs' reputation remained unblemished, the general destruction and death that third Ypres engendered had no comforting justification. In Pollard's writing, the campaign encapsulated the worst of a terrible war.

Aussie and *Smith's Weekly* also addressed third Ypres aside from digger yarns at various moments, although such occasions were even scarcer than those in RSSILA magazines. After all, these publications' content did not solely cater for returned men, and consequently, they did not revisit specific episodes of the war often or in detail. Within two years of the war's end, *Aussie* did publish a poem entitled 'Ypres' by Sydney George. Framed by drawings by C.H. Percival of dead men lying in a ruined city and a pockmarked landscape (see plate 14), the verse mirrored themes embraced in RSSILA journals: terrible conditions and ugly memories. The poem follows the thoughts of a returned soldier as he watches men 'shift beneath the lights' of a park. He cannot shake the image of holding 'those shadows on his rifle-sights'. During his reverie, 'mundane reason intervenes', and he realises there is nothing in the figures 'to affright'. Nonetheless, his dark reminiscences come rushing back:

> I have no lust to-night to maim and kill
> But reason shudders when the memory wakes:
> Lord God! I see that writhing German still ...
> I wonder if his mother's heart still aches.

Apart from George's dark portrayal of the psychological challenges ex-soldiers faced upon their return to civilian life, his decision to locate these confronting recollections in Belgium is significant. It is hard to imagine contributors to *Aussie* or *Smith's Weekly* expressing similar sentiments regarding Germans killed in the purposeful and decisive attacks of 1918. The inconclusive 1917 campaign on the 'Belgian flats', however, was far more easily associated with 'waste' and provided an appropriate setting for such a nightmarish scene.[51]

Smith's Weekly concentrated on contemporary issues facing returned soldiers and rarely concerned itself with their literary flourishes, unless these were short enough for its digger yarn section, 'The Unofficial History of the AIF'. As mentioned above, the exception to this was the periodical's response to the 'damnable lies' it found in the anti-war novels of 'catchpenny scribblers'.[52] In addition to the articles by John Monash, the paper commissioned Brigadier-General H.G. Bennett to write a series of short vignettes capturing the Anzac spirit. Entitled 'Great Deeds of the AIF', they were

> dedicated to the children of the Diggers though, they have a tremendous appeal to the adult. They are tales of individual heroism,

> giving names, dates and places ... They are written in the memory of those who fell, bravely, and in evergreen praise of those AIF heroes who live.[53]

Appearing in no apparent order, the episodes on which Bennett chose to concentrate principally covered fighting on the Western Front; descriptions of Broodseinde and Menin Road featured in his sixth and thirteenth articles respectively. Given the young target audience and the glorifying objectives, Bennett's writing recalled the *Boy's Own* language of brash regimental histories and typical contributions to RSSILA magazines. As a result, the articles concerning third Ypres were quite different in tone and content from texts like those of George and Pollard; Bennett's articles trivialised or ignored the memories that haunted these men. In his account of Broodseinde, Bennett addressed the difficulties of fighting in a European winter, but this was not used to paint an ominous picture of the dreaded salient in wet conditions. The description served to highlight the Australians' fighting prowess. Bennett also completely avoided any discussion of the draining and ultimately abortive attempts to capture Passchendaele by falsely claiming that the Broodseinde Ridge was the Australians' last objective of the campaign.[54] His account of Menin Road was little different. Although he acknowledged the artillery's vital role, he concluded that 'the Australians confirmed the previous good reputation they had earned, and from this date were considered at least equal to any troops who took part in the Great War'.[55] Depicted in this light, third Ypres was just another glorious chapter in the AIF's history. Yet, Bennett's positive portrayals of this campaign were also anomalies in publications that catered to Anzac nostalgia.

Elegies of 'Mud, Blood and Darkness'

In the late 1920s and early 1930s, the boom in war books that swept through many formerly belligerent countries reached Australia.[56] During this period, several international and national war memoirs and novels became bestsellers in the Commonwealth, while dozens of returned Anzacs were caught up in the trend with less success. Unlike some of the better known European writers, most Australian authors did not portray the war as a brutal, bloody, emasculating experience. Rather, they cast the conflict as an ennobling, thrilling event. These antipodean authors did acknowledge the conflict's industrial nature, with its mass death and maiming. At the same time, they sought to redeem the experience by affirming that the conflict had made them better men for having served, as well as by confirming the status of their young nation on a global stage. In the words of Clare Rhoden, they found 'purpose in futility'.[57] Whether they flirted with irony or told tales of swashbuckling adventures, few Australian books that achieved critical acclaim or reached wide audiences mentioned the Belgian battles. When they did, their depictions often mirrored or even surpassed RSSILA magazine articles for horror and hopelessness.

Australian soldier-writers' ability to salvage purpose from the wreckage of 1914–18 was important to the interwar population. Conservative-minded Australians reacted vehemently to books deemed anti-war, particularly those questioning the Anzacs' honour. Imported modern war novels sold well in Australia, but home-grown literature was held to a different standard. Despite critical acclaim, the two Australian works recognised as being closest in style to modernist books, Leonard Mann's *Flesh in Armour* (1932) and Jack McKinney's *Crucible* (1935), were commercial failures, and neither was reprinted before the Second World War. In Mann's case, despite his winning the Australian Literary

Society's Gold Medal and receiving support from successful writers, Angus & Robertson, the leading publisher of Australian war books, rejected him twice, claiming his 'book could not be put into everyone's hands'. Subsequently, the author was forced to self-publish.[58] Although rather tame by European standards, Mann's and McKinney's novels, which had distinctly unheroic protagonists, evidently did not appeal to a broad Australian audience.

Conversely, novels and memoirs featuring protagonists that embodied Anzac stereotypes found publishers and a large audience more easily. Angus & Robertson's Gallant Legion series provides the best cross-section of Australian war literature. Comprising twelve books, the series included memoirs written by men and one woman who had seen action in different theatres of the war, as well as Monash's *Australian Victories in France in 1918*. Marketed as the opposite of ironic European First World War depictions, the works in the series purportedly revealed 'the courage and resource, the endurance and grim humour, the comradeship and gaiety, the vision and self-sacrifice of those who answered their country's call'.[59] Striking a balance between traditional, romantic themes and irony, these were decidedly 'middlebrow' works.[60] They were not as excessively boastful about Australian achievements as one might expect, but they reflected and reaffirmed the dominant narrative, positing that 'war had measured the worth of Australian manhood and found it more than satisfactory'. It was this type of book that publishers worked hard to 'put into everyone's hands', and many sold well.[61]

In these novels and memoirs, the Western Front was the scene of most of the action. However, detailed descriptions of the AIF's involvement at Messines or Ypres were rare. As fate would have it, while every Australian division on the Western Front fought at Ypres, many war book authors had found themselves out of the line for various reasons during that battle. This meant that memoirists, not having been present at the engagement themselves, could only allude to the battle. Even authors of fictional accounts often only focused on events of which they had 'intimate knowledge'.[62] This situation compared unfavourably with accounts of the AIF's 1918 battles, although Pozières and Fromelles also figured in a surprising number of interwar memoirs and novels. Pozières regularly featured in the best publicised or bestselling works of the period, while Fromelles – a battle in which only one of the five AIF divisions was engaged – appeared nearly as often as the 1917 Belgian battles. The position of Messines and third Ypres in Australian war literature mirrored that in RSSILA magazines.

References to the Flanders campaigns in war books also reflected returned soldiers' journals in overall content. In the case of Messines, excerpts recounting this battle from George Mitchell's memoir *Backs to the Wall* (1937) had already featured in *Reveille* and *The Queensland Digger*. Mitchell was clearly a favourite of RSSILA magazine editors, who published several of his articles throughout the interwar period. His bombastic tone interspersed with moments of pathos suited the audience of these publications and was firmly middlebrow. Mitchell's discussion of Messines constituted one of the most complete portrayals of the battle in a popular Australian war book. Early in his account he confessed to having a foreboding premonition that the 'power or fate that guards some so carefully' had deserted him at Messines. Although his presentiment turned out to be incorrect, his experience of the battle was trying. His narrative included graphic imagery, such as 'carefully stacked piles' of Germans, 'black faced from the manner of their deaths, swollen and already putrefying', and a tortured description of his 'skipper' bleeding out. At one moment, the industrial nature of the carnage led Mitchell's mind to 'wander back in dream paths through the ages' to reflect on 'heroic times' when English muskets or crossbows dominated warfare. Yet, such moments hardly led Mitchell to any ironic conclusions. Despite the horrors he witnessed there, Mitchell summarised Messines as 'child's play [compared] to any other battle we had ever encountered'. Although the difficulties faced at Messines were personally significant, Mitchell's downplaying of them suggested it was less worthy of remembrance than other battles. Certainly, his gallant descriptions of Australians stemming the German offensive and then smashing 'the unbreakable [Hindenburg] line' later in the memoir overshadowed the Belgian engagement.[63]

Recounting the experience of third Ypres proved even more difficult for Australian memoirists and novelists. Harold Williams and Edgar Rule salvaged something positive from the Flanders campaign with descriptions limited solely to the fighting at Polygon Wood, but their memoirs are exceptions. Notably, neither writer witnessed firsthand the events he described. Williams, author of *The Gallant Company* (1933) and *Comrades of the Great Adventure* (1935), was not in the salient during the fighting and instead had survivors 'regale' him with 'a stirring tale of battle' when he returned to his unit.[64] Rule was at Ypres during the battle of Polygon Wood but did not take part in the engagement. Still, in a memoir entitled *Jacka's Mob* (1933) – so called because the author was in the same unit as Albert Jacka VC – Rule could not let glowing reports of his hero's bravery go unmentioned. Consequently, he bent the rules of the memoir genre in order to recount Jacka's achievements. The outcome of his initiative in attack and then his steadfast resolve in holding off enemy counterattacks ensured that Polygon Wood 'was the most successful achievement of the unit up to this time', exceeding 'previous efforts [which], in spite of many brave achievements, had usually been barren in their results'. Admittedly, the engagement was not an entirely happy one, and Rule juxtaposed Jacka's triumphs with the death of Harold Wanliss, who, 'in the loftiness of his vision, the splendor of his ideals, and the nobility of his actions', was equalled by few. According to Rule, Wanliss' death 'was a loss for the whole of the force and for the nation'. Nevertheless, in focusing principally on Jacka's heroism, *Jacka's Mob* provided readers with a relatively optimistic account of third Ypres. Rule missed the rest of the campaign when he left for England to train reinforcements.[65] One might wonder, then, how he would have portrayed the Australians' wholly unsuccessful actions of two weeks later.

Most Australian interwar literature portrayed third Ypres in substantially darker terms. Even in books that made only passing remarks about the campaign, the Flemish city was a byword for appalling conditions, death and pointlessness. Although Mitchell had not fought in third Ypres, he noted in *Backs to the Wall*,

> The blood-bath of Passchendaele had drained our battalion … The whole British army had been shaken to its foundations by the blind fury and futility of the third Ypres offensive. The year 1917 had been one of disaster for our arms in all save the Messines attack.[66]

Obviously, highlighting the dire situation in which the Australians and British found themselves at the end of 1917 made the following successes in 1918 all the more dramatic in Mitchell's narrative. It also reinforced the notion that third Ypres was the last, and possibly the most, futile battle of the war, and Mitchell was not the only Australian writer to make this claim. Another, more subtle reference to the engagement can be found in McKinney's *Crucible*. While the novel's protagonist, John Fairbairn, did not participate in third Ypres, McKinney painted a bleak picture of the engagement in a digger yarn recounted between 'old hands'. In the scene, each character spun a yarn that covered a wide range of AIF experiences and stereotypes. These included the larrikin officer, who found himself in a Victorian unit having fled Queensland after various misdemeanours, and the 'bushwacker' who embarked with the Light Horse without enlisting and became a major. Then came the padre's tale, which he began by asking whether his audience 'remember[ed] the mud around Ypres'. Of course, the listeners did. The humorous story that followed involved the padre coming across an Australian 'buried to the neck in mud' but failing to realise that the man's pants slipped off while he was being extricated from the mire. Only when the pair went in search of coffee was the naked condition of the padre's charge remarked upon: 'The padre in charge of the Wild Man from Borneo!' The padre's audience could not believe they had never heard this amusing tale and wondered why the 'Wild Man from Borneo didn't spread the story'. This forced the preacher to admit that the 'Wild Man' did not make it back to his battalion, as he had been injured internally when he was dragged from the mud and had died soon afterwards. The padre had not intended to mention this detail: 'the story was going to be amusing'. At that point, the mood turned sombre, and the passage ended with the yarn spinners drinking to those who had been 'marked off strength' – that is, killed.[67] In choosing to situate the anecdote that curtailed the group's general bonhomie at Ypres, McKinney reinforced the loathsome reputation the salient had garnered throughout the interwar period.

The interwar books dealing with third Ypres in more detail – Leonard Mann's *Flesh in Armour*, Joseph Maxwell's *Hell's Bells and Mademoiselles* (1932), Mary Tilton's *The Grey Battalion* (1933) and Thomas Prince's lesser known *Purple Patches* (1935)– were more confronting in nature. These writers had fought or, in the case of Tilton, who was a nursing sister, had been just behind the lines at Ypres throughout the campaign, and they avoided grandiose claims of triumph linked to Menin Road, Polygon Wood and Broodseinde. Their descriptions of the salient's horrors were not used to extol Australian bravery and sacrifice. Instead, their grotesque depictions of death and destruction portrayed the very worst of the First World War. They included subjects that were often avoided in official and glorifying narratives, such as direct and unsettling depictions of dead and seriously wounded Australians. These were best captured in Prince's *Purple Patches*:

> Men sprawled in twisted attitudes over the ground with torn limbs and blackened faces. One moved feebly the reddened stump of an arm blown off above the elbow, from which blood gushed in copious jets. Another lay on his back, a ball of white foam streaked with red covering his face. The horrid whistlings of his breath broke flecks from the mass. A third twitched with his mouth in a pool of muddy water, which his expiring gasps blew out in black frothy bubbles. Yet another thrashed the mire with awful gurgles, hands pressed to where his entrails had been. Bodies, some without heads and some without limbs, with clothing ripped from flesh, lay without movement.[68]

This depiction, and others like it in Maxwell's and Mann's writings, was a long way removed from the nationalistic propaganda often associated with Australian war literature. While Prince, Mann and Maxwell did switch between moments of realistic aestheticism to panegyrising the qualities of Australian soldiers, the Ypres battlefront remained impervious to eulogistic moments in their works.

These accounts pointed to the engagement's psychological consequences, which pushed many to their breaking points. Significantly, as trying as the fighting was on other fronts, it is in Belgium that the psychological vulnerability of key figures in Maxwell's, Tilton's and Mann's books is most evident. In *Hell's Bells and Mademoiselles*, the moment that threatens to unhinge one of the memoir's most heroic characters, a typically larger than life (and possibly fictional) Anzac by the name of Shamos Doherty, is only fleeting.[69] Up to this point, Doherty has stoically endured his baptism of fire at Gallipoli and the hell of Pozières. Maxwell recounts how, at Ypres, his mate's courageous facade momentarily cracks:

> Doherty's face was pale and drawn. The old humorous twinkle had vanished from his eyes. The pallid glow from another German flare awakened a sparkle near his eye. He stifled a choking sob. Here was Stewart dead in the bottom of the trench – a man who had shared with us so much terror and so many pleasant hours out of the line. Doherty noticed my glance. He hated to be thought emotional.[70]

Doherty, being the true warrior that he is, recovers quickly enough. However, this moment, followed by a passage that is distressingly comparable to the tale of the mortally wounded German pathetically seeking aid in Frank Green's 40th Battalion history, arguably signals the lowest point of Maxwell's memoir. War's horror is evident throughout Maxwell's book, yet only third Ypres draws such a raw emotional response from this irrepressible Anzac stereotype.

Mary Tilton, in *The Grey Battalion*, and Mann's fictional Frank Jeffreys, in *Flesh in Armour*, suffer far more complete breakdowns. Tilton's experiences at the No. 3 Australian Casualty Clearing Station, among others, in Belgium most likely contributed to her return home in early 1918. In *The Grey Battalion* she recalls being shunted between overflowing casualty clearance stations and a field hospital as well as being subjected to artillery and aerial bombardment. The strain of the conditions begins to tell, and soon after the beginning of the third Ypres offensive fifteen English girls come down 'shell-shocked', but the Australian women remain strong 'to give their best for the men who [are] dying so bravely'. However, as the campaign drags on, Tilton's tone shifts. She still hails the courage of the wounded in her care, but the unceasing 'butchery' appals her: 'to watch them die in such numbers [is] ghastly'. The tipping point comes in mid-October when Tilton reads the name of her fiancé 'under the big, black heading, "Killed"' on the most recent casualty list and feels 'an overpowering sense of desolation' sweep through her. The following week, a friend's death compounds her grief. Shortly afterwards, Tilton's unit leaves the salient. She notes, however, 'No matter where I go or what I do, the best part of me will always remain in this Passchendaele area where lie many of the friends I loved best'. She is given time to recover in the south of France, but within a few weeks of her return she is suffering from 'terrific headaches', and boils break out on her arms and wrists. She blames poor food, but it is difficult to imagine that the physical and personal strains of her experiences in Belgium have not taken their toll. With her health failing, she is transferred back to Australia, where she arrives 'tired and weary', her mind full of the 'losses, the beastliness, the destruction, the waste, the agonies and endurance' of war.[71]

While Tilton survived her ordeals, third Ypres fatally breaks the spirit of *Flesh in Armour*'s Frank Jeffreys. In an incident mirroring Mann's own experience in Belgium, a shell buries Jeffreys alive, with devastating personal consequences. A loner who lacks the fighting spirit of those around him, Jeffreys is hardly a model Anzac, and his mental fragility means that his eventual death, at the end of the book, comes as no surprise. Nevertheless, Mann's portrayal of the hapless corporal at third Ypres, before his burial in the mud, does not suggest that Jeffreys is completely broken as a soldier. It is once the fighting at Ypres reaches its climax, with the Australians' unsuccessful assault on Passchendaele Ridge, that Jeffreys' nerves are shattered irreparably. The traumatic incident occurs in the midst of a passage that draws unnervingly on many of the unsavoury and futile elements used to describe third Ypres in non-fiction works: the mud, the pillboxes, the killing of men in the act of surrendering and the sense that 'the bloody fools' in charge had lost an opportunity to press the advantage at Broodseinde. The shock of being buried alive in the thick Flanders mud does not affect Jeffreys immediately, but once his unit repels a counterattack, he finally breaks down. His unit's withdrawal the following day forces him to cross a 'dark, glutinous sea' fearful that 'when he fell down into the thick stinking ooze … he would fall one time or another into one of the black, putrid pools where the water was deep enough to drown a man'. Increasingly panic stricken, Jeffreys soon becomes separated from his unit and possessed with the terror of a man who,

> lost in the bush, and seeing still the eternal sameness of the green trees, but, in particular, one oddity distorted to a shape like one he had seen before, believes that he has at last completed the dreadful circle. Never so dreadful a circle as this. Never was such a ghastly, dark desolation ever imagined.

Jeffreys eventually finds his way out of a morass, but he suffers one final torment when he strays too close to an artillery battery. The guns suddenly fire, sending the wretched man running and screaming. From this point on, Jeffreys' fear is ever present, compromising his ability to be a comrade in the line – a serious failing for an Anzac. Even the respite offered by a 'Blighty wound' (a wound that required treatment in England) and, upon his return, the sentiment of being imbued with the spirit and morale of the newly formed Australian Corps, is only temporary. While his suicide, at the end of the book, is attributed to a number of factors, there is no doubt the horrific experience in 'the darker country' of Flanders sowed the seeds of his demise.[72]

Postwar Polemics

If Australian soldier-writers had difficulty finding a purpose in their struggles against the Germans and the Flemish mud more than a decade after the campaign, so too did their former leaders. Memoirs and biographies of key political and military figures gave readers perspectives on the war beyond the trenches. Among the best publicised of these in Australia were Billy Hughes' *The Splendid Adventure* (1929), Frederic Cutlack's compilation *War Letters of General Monash* (1934), and *War Memoirs of David Lloyd George* (1933–36). Each contained damning accounts of third Ypres. All three writers, but especially Lloyd George, were more vociferous than the Australian soldiers who publicly recounted their experiences at Ypres in asserting that the offensive had been a tragic, avoidable waste. They also largely omitted the positive references to Anzac heroism and humour that redeemed or softened the most graphic accounts of fighting in Belgium given in the unit histories, RSSILA magazines and war books. Their scathing portrayal of British military leadership was certainly compatible with the Anzacs' disdain for brass hats. However, their denigration of High Command was such that third Ypres came across as completely futile; this further isolated the campaign from the triumphant Anzac legend of the interwar years.

Published as a book and serialised in the Hobart *Mercury* and Adelaide *Advertiser* in 1929, Hughes' *Splendid Adventure* provided Australians with one of the earliest and frankest denunciations of third Ypres by a public figure. It was not solely a memoir but a 'review of Empire relations within and without the Commonwealth' in which Hughes passed judgement on the British civil and military leaders' handling of the war and its aftermath, particularly in relation to the dominions. The former prime minister spent few words on the war's various battles, but he did briefly consider two campaigns in his analysis: Gallipoli and Passchendaele. He did not treat the former uncritically, suggesting that failures in British decision-making processes contributed to the 'glorious tragedy' of the Dardanelles campaign. Nevertheless, his language was measured and stopped well short of any suggestion that Gallipoli had been a futile adventure: 'on a fair review of the facts, as far as they are known, there was reasonable probability that it would have succeeded if it had been pushed home at the right time and in the right way'. Such nuance was lacking in his summation of third Ypres, which he contemptuously branded as 'the most useless, bloody and deplorable battle of the whole war, which swept away the flower of the British Army, left the troops utterly worn out, their *moral* [sic] seriously impaired, and won nothing'. His justifications for discussing the two engagements were essentially the same: unimaginative British leadership and inflexibility between military and civil circles had led to failure. But the difference between them could not have been greater. Although not entirely beyond criticism, that immortal first engagement at Gallipoli was 'glorious', while third Ypres was painfully 'long, desperate and bloody'.[73]

The *War Memoirs of David Lloyd George* offered Australian readers an even more sustained and scornful critique of Douglas Haig's Flanders offensive. Published in six volumes over four years, the memoirs were hugely successful, largely thanks to their polemic nature. The fourth volume, which dealt with the 1917 'campaign of the mud', was not only the most controversial but the most popular.[74] Lloyd George condemned Haig's planning and execution of third Ypres. In '110 blood-curdling pages' he reduced it to a desperate struggle in which 'artillery became bogged, tanks stuck in the mire, unwounded men drowned by the hundreds and wounded men by the thousands sank into the filth … It was a tragedy of heroic endurance enacted in mud'. Moreover, it was a tragedy that achieved nothing, apart from being 'one of the greatest disasters of the War'.[75] Historians have highlighted the bias and questionable accuracy of the memoirs' claims concerning the 'Passchendaele fiasco'.[76] Yet, most articles in the press parroted Lloyd George's words with little or no analysis. The lack of a visible public response, not only in the papers but also in RSSILA magazines, is telling. Lloyd George's claim that third Ypres had been 'senseless' was not met with opposition in Australia, because many accepted this conclusion.[77]

Cutlack's *War Letters of General Monash*, excerpts of which also appeared in several newspapers, revealed that Monash was just as disparaging of British command at third Ypres as Hughes and Lloyd George. As the general wrote the letters to his wife and daughter in 1917, his depiction of the battle was not as acerbic or as retrospectively damning as those of the former prime ministers. While his early letters cast the campaign's initial stages in a positive light, his final appraisal was highly critical and added further weight to the argument that the offensive had been an exercise in futility. The Australians' successes impressed him, particularly at Broodseinde, where his 3rd Division was 'brilliantly victorious in [the] "greatest battle of the war"'. But following the failed assault on Passchendaele, this optimism gave way to full-blown pessimism. In a letter dated 15 October 1917, the general noted that 'the operations of 12 October [were] deeply disappointing', but he restrained himself from judging the British leadership too severely:

> It is bad to cultivate the habit of criticism of higher authority and, therefore, I do so now with some hesitation, but chiefly to enable you to get a correct picture of what the situation was …
>
> I am inclined to believe that the plan was fully justified and would have succeeded in normal weather conditions.

He went on to outline the various difficulties confronting his division in a relatively balanced manner. Yet, just three days later, his faith in High Command had plainly deteriorated:

> Our men are being put into the hottest fighting and are being sacrificed in hair-brained ventures, like Bullecourt and Passchendaele, and there is no one in the War Cabinet to lift a voice in protest … So Australian interests are suffering badly, and Australia is not getting anything like the recognition it deserves.[78]

Australia's most famous soldier had branded the campaign as pointless, and newspapers serialising the letters jumped on the 'hair-brained' comment to grab readers' attention.[79] As with Lloyd George's memoirs, however, there was no strong refutation of the claims in Monash's letters. The accounts of Hughes, Lloyd George and Monash stripped away any notions of triumph related to third Ypres, leaving behind a narrative of unnecessary and tragic waste.

* * *

A concentrated analysis of written sources focusing on the Australian battles in Belgium risks suggesting that Messines and third Ypres occupied a central place in collective memory throughout the interwar years. We need to put these writings about Messines and third Ypres into perspective. In newspapers and RSSILA magazines of the period, Gallipoli and the events of 1918 dominated accounts of the war, while Pozières and Fromelles also received a fair share of attention. These more numerous accounts drowned out descriptions of the AIF in Belgium. The handful of books and articles that did deal with Messines and third Ypres never put forward a case to suggest those engagements were worth remembering and commemorating ahead of other battles. For the writers of the earliest unofficial accounts of the AIF's performance in the war, the Belgian engagements were on the wrong side of that historic moment when the Australian divisions were brought together to form the Australian Corps. In the regimental histories, a unit's involvement in the Flanders campaigns was just another honour to add to a long list of impressive achievements. But at least these were relatively positive ways of framing Messines and especially third Ypres. For the majority of returned men writing about their experiences in RSSILA journals or in longer memoirs and novels, there was little to extol in the fighting in Flanders. In *Hell's Bells and Mademoiselles*, one of Maxwell's chapters addressing these months is entitled 'An Elegy of Mud, Blood and Darkness'.[80] The description captures the spirit of much of the interwar writing concerning third Ypres, which often posited it as a low – if not the lowest – point of the war. This was reinforced by the publications of key wartime figures. Messines may not have been all that memorable, due to its limited scope and outcomes, but third Ypres was a bitter memory and one that did little to advance the young, triumphalist Anzac legend.

Chapter 4

BELGIUM EXPERIENCED

Can this be the old Salient?

'Five-One', West Australian,
23 October 1928

Barely mentioned in the various forms of writing on Australia's war experience, the former battlefields of Belgian Flanders were regular features in the travel itineraries of the small proportion of Australians who visited the Western Front throughout the interwar period. This chapter explores why the region's popularity as a significant destination for those on a battlefield pilgrimage or tour did little to ensure the Australian Imperial Force's trials at Messines and third Ypres became fixed in Australian war memory. As we shall see, there were several reasons for this. In particular, the burial of the Commonwealth's dead and erection of memorials to the missing were carried out within a broader imperial project managed by the Imperial War Graves Commission, which strived for a message of equality of sacrifice throughout the empire. For all overseas battlefields, Australia shared its commemorative space with other countries, and this was particularly pronounced in Belgium. While visitors to Anzac Cove and the Somme region could find cemeteries in which the vast majority of burials were Australian, the quarter of a million British buried and commemorated on memorials to the missing around Ypres easily dwarfed the approximately

12,000 AIF dead lying in the salient region. Australians did manage to establish a shallow memory footprint with a division and unit memorial at Polygon Wood and Hill 60, in Zillebeke, respectively. Nevertheless, the Australian government's failure to erect a memorial of national importance in Belgium to match the national memorial at Villers-Bretonneux, in France, hampered any chance that the AIF's battles in Belgium might be recalled beyond living memory. Finally, although there were official and unofficial trips to Flanders in the first half of the 20th century, these were sporadic and followed much the same patterns as tours to other sites on the Western Front. In Belgium, as on other former battlefields, bereaved relatives sought out the graves of their loved ones, curious travellers visited famous locations, politicians inspected the state of cemeteries, and returned men searched in vain for old haunts in a fast-changing landscape. Individual rather than collective memory was central to these interwar pilgrimages.

Australia and the Postwar Belgian Landscape

At the war's end, close to 60,000 Australian soldiers had died on active service, but British policy did not allow for the repatriation of their bodies. Instead, they were interred close to where they fell. The recovery and burial of the dead were carried out under the auspices of the Imperial War Graves Commission, which retained responsibility for the remains of empire soldiers long after the belligerents had cast aside their weapons. By the time the commission had finished its work, hundreds of cemeteries had been built throughout in Belgium and northern France. They were based on a common design, built from similar materials and filled with uniform headstones, a Cross of Sacrifice – 'a tall finely proportioned stone cross, with a symbolic sword of bronze attached to its face' – and, in all but the smallest cemeteries, a Stone of

Remembrance – a stone altar on which was carved 'Their name liveth for evermore'.[1] This equality of treatment extended, as best it could, to the missing. Although the IWGC rejected out of hand Prime Minister Billy Hughes' suggestion that Australians whose bodies had not been found or identified might have their own headstones and plots of land, it did erect memorials at important sites naming the missing men.[2] The Menin Gate Memorial, commemorating close to 55,000 British missing of the Ypres salient – including over 6000 Australians – was among the most famous of these. The imperial scope of the IWGC's projects ensured that Australia's dead on the Western Front and elsewhere were, in theory, treated no differently from those of other countries within the British Empire.[3] In an area like the former Ypres salient, however, where Australian graves were a minority in many cemeteries and the names of the AIF's missing were vastly outnumbered on the Menin Gate, Australian sacrifice was subsumed within a landscape of generalised British sacrifice. The 'immortal salient of Ypres' was a site of British or imperial memory first, an Australian site second.[4]

Australian officials did not leave the commemoration of the AIF's engagements and its war dead in Belgium – and northern France – entirely up to the IWGC. In 1919, Hughes suggested that each infantry division that had served on the Western Front have a memorial raised at a site in either France or Belgium. These were to be erected where the divisions 'had performed some outstanding feats of arms'. The prime minister also proposed that another 'memorial for the whole of the AIF', which quickly became cast as a 'national memorial', be erected in France. The divisional memorials, paid for by the government, were to take 'the form of a plain obelisk in stone' and were very different from those erected by local communities throughout Australia.[5] As Ken Inglis states, these memorials were 'the 1914–1918 equivalent of regimental memorials raised on sites of earlier wars'. Eventually erected in locations that dominated the landscape around them, they were dedicated to the men 'who *fought* in France and Belgium'.⁶ They were not conceived as sites of mourning; rather, they celebrated the battle prowess of a specific division and the heroism of its men. The proposed national memorial was to be of a similar nature, and Villers-Bretonneux was selected as the most appropriate site, because, as *The Sydney Morning Herald* informed its readers, it was where 'the Australian Divisions stamped their influence upon the war … in the hours of highest critical importance to the Allies'.⁷

On the whole, the AIF commanders agreed with Hughes' proposals and earmarked five sites for the divisional memorials.⁸ Only one of these – the 5th Division's monument at Polygon Wood – was located in Belgian territory. The same commanders also (rather accurately) predicted that 'the next generation will have forgotten the separate divisions and think only of Australia'; they were therefore of the opinion that 'a single memorial for the whole of the AIF … is not adequate'. Instead, they suggested 'an Australian memorial, similar to that proposed for Villers-Bretonneux, should also be erected in the Ypres area'.⁹ When this proposal was presented to the Australian Battle Memorials and Soldiers' Graves Committee, its members agreed, and the 'Broodseinde Cross Roads' was selected as the most appropriate location.¹⁰ At the meetings during which the motions for a second national memorial were passed, the only voice missing was that of the prime minister. Having reached a provisional agreement, the Australians then had to seek permission from the British to erect the memorials. The British Battle Exploit Memorials Committee, 'formed in order to consider claims made by [imperial] units to erect permanent memorials of their exploits on the battlefields', approved all the sites, with the exception of one divisional memorial, and informed the Australians the IWGC would approach Belgian and French officials so that they might make the locations available.[11] The lone site whose fate hung in the balance was Polygon Wood, as apparently another unit had also claimed the location. Eventually, permission was given for this monument too, but the decision turned out to be fatal to the plans for an Australian national memorial in Belgium.

By the time the Australian memorials committee met again, the British had confirmed that the 5th Division's claim to Polygon Wood would be upheld. During the meeting, committee chairperson Major-General Sir Joseph Talbot Hobbs informed the members that he had approached Billy Hughes about the proposed second AIF memorial, at Ypres, and had received a negative response: 'Mr Hughes did not think the monument at Broodseinde Ridge was necessary as the monument at Polygon Butte would be less than a mile [1.6 kilometres] away'. It is unlikely the proximity of the 5th Division's memorial was the sole element to sway Hughes' decision on this matter. The fact that the preliminary design of the Broodseinde memorial was based on the divisional memorial obelisks – albeit of considerably greater dimensions – probably did little to convince him of the project's importance (see plates 15 and 16).[12] Another element worth considering is that perhaps Hughes having already formed an overly negative view of the third Ypres campaign, as suggested in *The Splendid Adventure*, was keen to give it as little attention as possible. The national monument in the salient had no grand design, was facing competition from a near-identical memorial within two kilometres of its proposed location and would refer to 'the most useless, bloody and deplorable battle', as opposed to a meaningful victory like Villers-Bretonneux; Hughes' objection to it is hardly surprising.[13] This position denied Australia a stronger memorial presence in the region, especially when compared to the concentration of structures built in the vicinity of Péronne, in the Somme region of France, which included not only the national memorial at Villers-Bretonneux, but four out of the five divisional memorials *and* a section of Australia's 'most sacred acre', around the Pozières windmill site, purchased by the government in 1932 and upon which a commemorative tablet and fence were erected in the following years.[14]

Hughes' rejection of a national memorial at Broodseinde meant there were only two Australia-specific monuments in Belgium: the 5th Division's memorial at Polygon Wood and the smaller obelisk erected by the 1st Australian Tunnelling Company at Hill 60. Perhaps aware that the shelving of the national memorial left Australians with a fairly minimal memorial presence at Ypres, officials working at Australia House in London requested the IWGC change the layout of the Buttes New British Cemetery, in which the 5th Division memorial had been erected. While the monument itself, located on top of the Polygon Wood Butte, was visible from a good distance and dominated the surrounding area, the Australians wished to extend the cemetery and lay out the grave plots in a manner that evoked the rising sun of the AIF, all at the expense of the IWGC (see plate 17).[15] This idea was less impressive than a national memorial and also a little perplexing, given that fewer than half of the identified graves in the cemetery actually belonged to men who had fought in the AIF. Nevertheless, the plan to stamp the symbol of the Australian forces into Belgian soil was an oblique way of commemorating all five AIF infantry divisions' involvement in fighting around the region.

The IWGC's director of works was far from enamoured, and he raised his concerns with the commission's land and legal adviser, pointing out 'there would be very serious objections to graves being set out in a formal garden design … It appears to me a very incongruous suggestion'.[16] In the end the idea was dispensed with when an officer from the Australian Graves Services reported that it was 'not practicable, for the ground in question is an absolute swamp'.[17] Withdrawing the plan avoided potential conflict with the IWGC, but the Australian Graves Services officer's evaluation of the terrain was undoubtedly short-sighted; not only did the wood eventually grow back, covering the swamp, but New Zealand erected one of its seven monuments to the missing on the Western Front in approximately the same position as the Australians' proposed rising sun layout. Several years later some gum trees were planted in the cemetery, giving it 'the fragrance of the bush', but Australia had passed up another opportunity to stake a stronger and more visible claim on the Belgian landscape.[18]

The 1st Tunnelling Company's memorial at Hill 60 was even narrower in scope than the 5th Division memorial. The tunnellers originally erected it in honour of comrades killed in the lead-up to the battle of Messines between 1916 and 1917, but its location also clearly referred to the company's exploits in exploding the Hill 60 mine. That such a monument to a relatively small unit remained in place throughout the interwar years was somewhat fortuitous. The 1st Tunnelling Company was not the only AIF unit to raise a memorial to its dead; several battalions and specialist companies also erected memorial crosses in Europe. These were made from wood and were unable to withstand long-term exposure to the elements; the IWGC viewed them as 'temporary' monuments. To avoid further decay in the open fields or destruction by the commission, Australian authorities requested they be sent to the Australian War Memorial.[19] The 1st Tunnelling Company memorial, on the other hand, was made of stone, and although it had fallen 'into a state of bad repair' in the early 1920s, Australian officials erected a new monument at the site. The memorial's survival may also have been due to the 'historic character' of its location and the fact that the tunnelling company, which had never been an Australian Corps unit, 'was not represented by any other Australian memorial'.[20] Whatever the reason for the government's decision to restore the monument, by the beginning of the 1930s, it was the sole remaining memorial on the Western Front raised by an Australian unit smaller than a division – a symbol of Australian valour in Belgium, but hardly a clear-cut site of national significance.

In spite of their relatively parochial nature, the monuments at Polygon Wood and Hill 60 did provide travellers to the Ypres salient with uniquely Australian sites of memory to seek out during the interwar years. The Hill 60 memorial often attracted comments on the work of the tunnellers before Messines, ensuring the memory of their efforts did not fade into oblivion.[21] Nevertheless, these sites did not receive anywhere near the amount of public attention given to Villers-Bretonneux. The latter remained in the spotlight thanks to the national scope of the memorial project, its drawn-out design and construction processes and the links forged between the local French community and the citizens of Melbourne, who helped fund the village's reconstruction.[22] The divisions' and tunnellers' memorials had been designed behind closed doors and did not have any grand unveiling ceremonies to herald their completion. Moreover, their simplistic designs were hardly awe inspiring. Their austere nature incensed at least one Australian visiting the Western Front, who claimed:

> Three of the memorials are 'completed,' and are a jest and a jeer against us by visitors of other nationalities. The design is mean and conventional, being, in fact, nothing but a built up angular obelisk, such as is sometimes used for traffic refuges in large cities; the material is bad, and the workmanship slip-shod …

> The obelisk at Polygon Wood is built on a mound ... used by the Germans for dug-outs, and also pounded by our big guns for a considerable period. The result is that the weight of the obelisk, some 300 tons, has smashed down the ground ... I am no engineer, but the glaring ineptitude of putting a monument of 300 tons on a foundation like a rabbit warren would be apparent to a school girl.[23]

Still, such objections were rare. Instead, it was the beauty of the cemetery and the 'most imposing' position of the memorial overlooking it that most impressed Australian travellers to Polygon Wood, not the structure's 'plain' design.[24]

Even if the 5th Division's memorial had been given a more striking design, there was no guarantee Australians would have visited it. A monument that was only divisional in scope was of less interest than a national one, and this had lasting consequences. As Joan Beaumont's work on Australian First World War commemoration demonstrates, Australians have long neglected most divisional memorials on the Western Front. Conversely, it is worth considering what might have been the outcome had Hughes agreed to erect a *national* memorial in Belgium. Historians Linda Wade's and Romain Fathi's studies of Villers-Bretonneux have shown that, despite fading into obscurity after the Second World War, the Australian National Memorial in France was rediscovered in the 1990s, becoming a focal point for Australians who wished to look beyond Gallipoli on Anzac Day.[25] Its national dimension helped channel this renewed interest. Across the Franco-Belgian border, the 5th Division's Polygon Wood monument has never achieved the same broad appeal.

Bereaved Pilgrims and Solemn Sightseers

In *The Ship of Remembrance* (1926), a book about a British interwar pilgrimage to Gallipoli, Ian Hay suggested that most ex-servicemen did not qualify for the sacred status of pilgrim; only 'relatives with a grave or graves to visit' could truly be considered 'pilgrims proper'.[26] This view would not have been shared by many returning to the battlefields on which they served. Even travellers with less concrete connections to such sites would not have considered themselves tourists, with all the pejorative baggage the term entails. Nowadays, much of the secondary literature about postwar journeys to battlefields avoids this strict pilgrim–tourist binary, demonstrating that acts of pilgrimage and tourism were not (and still are not) mutually exclusive. Bereaved 'pilgrims' often engaged in touristic activities while travelling, and 'tourists' approached war cemeteries and memorials with a solemn reverence.[27] Regardless of whether battlefield wanderers were 'pilgrims proper' or tourists, they had the potential to influence collective memory if their journeys received public attention.

Of particular relevance is the intersection between travellers' individual experiences and the public acts of commemoration they undertook when visiting battlefields and cemeteries. For historians concerned with the influence of nationalism, pilgrimage to First World War cemeteries and memorials has a distinct element of 'nation worship' to it. However, in a reflection of the larger debates surrounding the field of memory studies, others have sought to counter such nation-centred narratives, which are seen as overstating the role of official agency. Instead, they analyse pilgrimage from below, focusing on the personal elements of these voyages to distant battlefields set against a backdrop of wider national commemoration.[28] In the case of Australian interwar pilgrimages to Belgium, it is impossible to ignore either the individual or the national implications of such trips. However, there were very few cases of overt nation worship: Australian pilgrims and tourists occasionally expressed pride in their compatriots' sacrifices in the name of Australia and the British Empire, but they were much more concerned with ensuring Australians were well cared for in imperial cemeteries, visiting the gravesides of loved ones and seeing the former battlefields.

The interplay between the individual and public aspects of interwar pilgrimage is most easily traced in the publicity generated by large-scale pilgrimages. Yet, despite public agitation at regular intervals, a lack of official support and the inability of potential organisers to agree on crucial issues – including who would be invited to participate – meant only two major ventures launched from Australia ever reached the Western Front before war tore Europe apart again.[29] These were the independently organised United Services Association Tour, in 1929 – dubbed by the press as the 'Australian War Graves Pilgrimage' – and the official Coronation Contingent tour, in 1937, which comprised a group of servicemen who visited continental Europe after representing Australia at the coronation of King George VI. A third substantial pilgrimage involving a large number of Australians was arranged for the unveiling of the national memorial at Villers-Bretonneux in 1938; however, due to the financial constraints of the post-Depression years, the federal government only paid for one returned serviceman to travel from Australia to participate in the ceremony. The other participants included politicians who were already in Europe for a trade conference, and a number of ex-AIF servicemen who had taken up residence in Britain.[30] Moreover, in a sign of this pilgrimage's ultimately limited significance for many Australians, no concessions were made for the party to embark afterwards on a more extensive tour of the Western Front beyond Villers-Bretonneux.

Many Australians would surely have visited the sites linked to the Australian experience of the war if they could have done so. However, trips to the former battlefields were prohibitively expensive and well beyond the financial means of the vast majority, and undertaking the journey was no simple matter, due to the time involved in travelling over the great distances separating Australia from the Middle East and Europe. Those able to overcome these barriers – small numbers of bereaved relatives, ex-servicemen and women, state and federal politicians, and others with weaker personal connections to the First World War – had varying relationships with the locations they sought. The bereaved travelled to see the grave or name of a loved on carved into a memorial to come to terms with their grief, while those who had served returned to 'the battlefields in search of their past'.[31] Many politicians, on the other hand, had no explicit connection to the battlefields, but they often wandered through cemeteries searching for familiar names and partook in ceremonies on behalf of their constituents. Curiosity drew other travellers: after four years of conflict, particular sites had become 'places of historic interest' whose names 'resonated with meaning'.[32]

Not only dotted with thousands of AIF graves but also boasting the famous martyred city of Ypres, Belgian Flanders was certainly a place of 'historic interest' and a key destination on many Australians' itineraries. Moreover, the region was relatively easy to reach when compared to the hallowed, but largely inaccessible and inhospitable, cliffs of Gallipoli. In the two decades separating the end of the First World War from the beginning of the Second, both of the major pilgrimages from Australia passed through Ypres, in addition to a small number of independent travellers and groups.[33] Australian graves, the imposing Menin Gate

Memorial – at which there was a nightly Last Post ceremony[34] – and, to a lesser extent, the 5th Division and tunnellers' monuments acted as focal points in Belgium, but individual rather than collective memory remained central to most interwar pilgrimages.

Unsurprisingly, the larger pilgrimages and voyages of elected officials attracted a considerable amount of publicity, but dozens of other travellers also wrote about their experiences, their reports appearing in various press outlets. The articles of pilgrims and tourists could be interpreted as a simple continuation of the popular travel writing that had cropped up regularly in Australian newspapers for years. Yet, there was an added emotional impetus for all those who had travelled to the battlefields to act as 'adoptive kin' and share their experiences with the broader public.[35] The accounts became one of the main ways in which Australians who could not make the trip learned about the state of the previously war-torn landscapes and gained reassurances that their loved ones were well cared for in foreign fields; indeed, these were regular – if not predominant – themes in many reports. Analysing the rhetoric employed at Anzac Day ceremonies in Brisbane before 1939, Martin Crotty and Craig Melrose have argued that commemoration in Australia was not exclusively characterised by notions of 'sacrifice and bereavement' but that the language of 'triumphalism was the dominant force in the interwar years'.[36] The language surrounding the pilgrimages and even the politicians' tours of the former battlefields is another matter. Belgium, as well as the other battlefields, was frequently described as a place where one could find thousands of 'scrupulously tended' Australian graves 'as evidence of the tremendous sacrifices made', while the actual battles – victories and defeats – in which so many men died were rarely, if ever, recalled.[37]

It was highly uncommon for bereaved travellers who engaged in collective remembrance to discuss the battles of 1917 when recounting their overseas experiences. According to the historian Bart Ziino, pilgrims were 'intimately attuned to the anxieties and desires' of mourners back home, who did not need platitudes from an abstract Anzac legend but concrete information about the state of graves or memorials to the missing.[38] A pilgrim whose interviews with the press exemplified how the bereaved with the means to travel communicated their experiences to those in Australia was Barbara Jeffries. Jeffries' son, Captain Clarence Jeffries, was no average soldier but one of the elite sixty-four Australians awarded the Victoria Cross during the war 'for most conspicuous bravery' demonstrated during the first battle of Passchendaele.[39] He was killed in the same battle and was eventually buried in the largest of the IWGC's cemeteries, Tyne Cot. In her interview with *The West Australian*, Barbara Jeffries recounted her impressions of the IWGC's cemeteries and the Menin Gate Memorial 'for the benefit of those mothers whose sons are buried in Flanders' and 'mothers of sons who have no graves'.[40] While she praised the IWGC's work of burying the dead and maintaining their graves, her comments spoke to the very heart of the impotency many felt:

> Although for years I have wished to bring back my son's body for burial here, when I saw the war graves and the love and care with which they were tended, I could not want him to be elsewhere than with his comrades in arms.[41]

She told the mothers of the missing that the Last Post ceremony performed by buglers at the Menin Gate Memorial every evening ensured that 'although these boys have no graves, they are really remembered almost more than those who have'.[42] While not all pilgrims were afforded as much space in the press to describe their own impressions, their chief emphasis was, understandably, on the IWGC's sacred labour.[43]

Thanks to the IWGC's work of bringing order to the chaos of former battlefields, the industry of 'hardy Flemish peasants' and the natural rejuvenation of the ravaged landscapes, it was difficult for travellers with no firsthand knowledge of the battlefields to imagine what the AIF had experienced, and their reports tended to concentrate on the 'beautifully kept' silent cities rather than refer to the fighting that had occurred.[44] Many noted that some evidence of devastation remained, but this was usually contained at specific sites, such as the Ypres Cloth Hall, which did not give visitors a deeper appreciation of the trials their compatriots had been through.[45] Only the few Australians who arrived within a year or two of the armistice witnessed the tension between the shattered Flemish countryside and the serene burial grounds under construction. For W. Crowle, who sought out his brother's grave accompanied by his wife, the beauty of his sibling's resting spot did not hide the nature of the war:

> I have seen enough on this trip to convince me of what our soldiers went through to stem the tide of the mighty force which faced them. No history books will ever be able to convey 10 per cent of what is visible here.[46]

As the uniform cemeteries and monuments were completed, effacing or at least sanitising the vestiges of devastation on the former Western Front, such reflections became a rarity.

There were occasional instances when writers without direct war experience did overtly link the Australian graves in Belgium with the AIF's battles in the Ypres salient. The most noteworthy example of this stemmed from the Australian War Graves Pilgrimage, in 1929. Other studies have dissected the specifics of this unofficial pilgrimage, highlighting its rather successful binding together, in a 'community of grief', those who stayed at home and the pilgrims. This was achieved by engaging general public interest through the 'wattle tribute', an initiative that encouraged mourners to purchase artificial wattle sprigs to send with the pilgrims, who would subsequently place the 'fluffy yellow balls' on specific graves and memorials to the missing. It was a uniquely Australian public gesture of remembrance that permitted the bereaved who could not make the long trip to participate vicariously. The tribute added to the pilgrimage's public standing so that it came to 'represent the grief of a nation'.[47] This was adoptive kinship on a much broader scale than anything that could be offered by individual travellers or small groups. Moreover, the pilgrimage's public dimension ensured sustained press coverage, with many newspapers tracking with great interest the peregrinations of the long-distance voyagers.

Melbourne's *Herald* was particularly keen to obtain detailed reports on the pilgrimage and assigned one of its journalists, John Waters, to accompany the group. The correspondent did not have any personal connection to the war himself, but he had a journalist's flair for weaving together past and present tableaus for the Australian public. In his longer articles, Waters described important sites in Belgium in terms of their poignancy for mourners and touched on their significance within the wider narrative of the war. He noted that the enormous Tyne Cot Cemetery, at Zonnebeke, would 'for ever … remain close to Australia', and not just because it was 'another beautiful cemetery' that had more Anzacs buried in it than any other. The site was also significant because it 'immortalised the famous battles of Passchendaele Ridge' and even contained physical evidence of Australian valour in those engagements: the central blockhouse was marked with a plaque stating that the Australians had captured the position. The journalist also hailed the empire's 'splendidly conceived memorial' to the missing of the salient, the Menin Gate. Yet, unlike many battlefield visitors, he did not forgo briefly grappling with the torturous conditions in Belgian Flanders, pointing out that the memorial marked the exit from the city to 'gouged and shattered' battlefields, a gateway through which 'went the Diggers to Passchendaele'.[48]

Waters later expanded on his articles for *The Herald* in a book about his experience on the pilgrimage. Entitled *Crosses of Sacrifice* and written in the language of high diction, it had a 'special appeal' for Australians with 'fathers or sons, husbands or brothers still "over there"', although the frightful scale of losses on the Western Front, and particularly those in Belgian Flanders, were not always easily cast in a comforting light.[49] In a passage that reflected many interwar descriptions' focus on the terribly muddy conditions the AIF encountered in October 1917, Waters declared,

> Menin Road, Zonnebeke, Hell Fire Corner, Glencorse Wood, Broodseinde, Messines, Passchendaele! To our troops who took part in the desperate fighting along this world-renowned salient … these names will call up pictures of utter ruin and devastation, morasses of mud, holding a dreadful death for men who fell wounded there, a pock-marked countryside oozing water and slime … Probably no part of the front holds for them such ugly memories.

The author did not go into any great detail concerning the engagements, nor did he question the broader strategic aims of the battles, which allowed him to stop well short of probing notions of futility. Instead, Waters' work served to confirm Australian bravery and sacrifice as well as reassure the bereaved that this sacrifice had been sufficiently commemorated. Places like 'the field of death' surrounding Tyne Cot Cemetery were now covered by 'peaceful' cemeteries of 'beauty and nobility', which stood as testaments to 'the valour of all who were Britons'. In locating his pilgrimage experience within a broader narrative of the war, Waters created in *Crosses of Sacrifice* a unique publication. Unlike the one-off, ephemeral accounts in the press of bereaved relatives, inquisitive travellers and politicians, it attempted to clearly posit a connection between the contemporary state of the battlefields and the 'historical facts' of the AIF's participation in the First World War. *Crosses of Sacrifice* received a number of positive reviews, but a second edition was never printed, suggesting that interest in such a book was limited.[50]

Official Representatives of the Bereaved

Politicians and government officials played an important role in communicating information about the IWGC's work in Belgium to Australian mourners unable to travel to the final resting places of loved ones. One of the earliest official attempts to reduce the distance between the bereaved and the dead overseas was the publication *Where the Australians Rest* by Lieutenant Alfred Hampson. Distributed to the kin of dead and missing Australians in 1920, the booklet was 'designed to bring comfort to relatives and friends of fallen soldiers' by responding to their need for 'a sense of place' when imagining faraway marked or unmarked graves.[51] It did this by providing readers with brief descriptions of IWGC cemeteries and their surroundings, accompanied by illustrations from 'each district' (see plates 18 and 19). There were also brief references to AIF engagements that had taken place in each location, but this information was of secondary importance. The depictions of most engagements, including Messines and third Ypres, were patchy at best. Hampson did include some basic information about the battles – for example, 'the names of Hill 60, Wytschaete and Messines are all closely associated with the terrific fighting in which the Australians were engaged' – and he named the various divisions involved – 'in this area [the Ypres salient] the 1st, 2nd, 3rd, 4th and 5th Divisions were heavily engaged' – but there was little else distinctive about the descriptions.[52] Charles Bean, who reviewed the original manuscript, was not impressed with its quality or accuracy and initially suggested it be 'completely re-written'. He softened his stance a month later, noting that despite its 'very meagre' content, it would be 'a real comfort' to the bereaved, and that was, after all, the main goal of the publication.[53]

A small number of public officials also took advantage of overseas voyages to keep their compatriots informed of developments concerning AIF graves.[54] The Ypres salient regularly featured on the itineraries of these trips, and, with the exception of Hughes, every Australian interwar prime minister – Stanley Bruce, James Scullin and Joseph Lyons – visited the Belgian battlefields. With Australian mourners relying 'on their nation's leaders for a vicarious experience of [the] graves', the visits were a form of adoptive kinship, in which officials became representatives of the absent bereaved.[55] Press reports describing the tours revealed that Australian prime ministers and other officials were at pains to stress how well the IWGC's work was progressing. At the beginning of 1924, Bruce reported that

> he could confirm all they [Australians] had heard of the loving care with which the graves of the soldiers were tended by the Imperial War Graves Commission … The simple dignity of the cemeteries and the note of equality and sacrifice in design was most impressive.[56]

In case this reassurance was not sufficient, Bruce also requested the Commonwealth's substitute delegate to the League of Nations Stella Allan visit the battlefields so 'she might be able to inform Australian mothers and widows of the work of the War Graves Commission'.[57]

Plate 1. Frank Hurley's photograph of 1st Australian Division supporting troops walking on a duckboard track near Hooge, in the Ypres Sector, 5 October 1917.
Australian War Memorial, E00833.

Plate 2. Members of a field artillery brigade passing through Chateau Wood in the Ypres Sector, photographed by Frank Hurley on 29 October 1917.
Australian War Memorial, E01220.

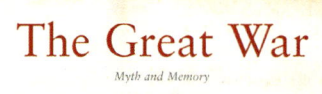

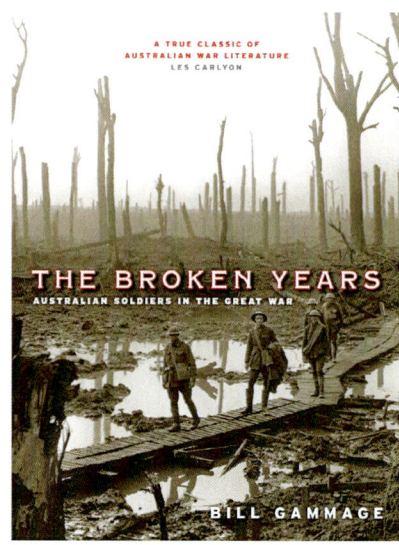
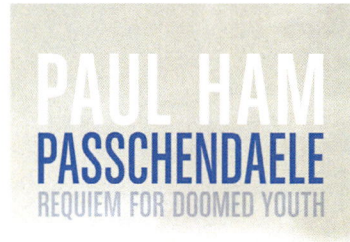

Official Australian photographs from third Ypres and images that draw inspiration from them appear in a variety of contexts that do not refer explicitly to the Passchendaele campaign or the Australians' role in it.
Top left: cover of Dan Todman's *The Great War* (London: Hambledon and London, 2005), analysing British First World War myths.
Top right: cover of Bill Gammage's *The Broken Years* (Carlton, Vic: Melbourne University Publishing, 2010), which traces the experiences of Australian soldiers throughout the entire war.
Bottom left: cover of Paul Ham's *Passchendaele* (North Sydney, NSW, Penguin Random House Australia), which is a general history of third Ypres.
Bottom right: symbol of New Zealand's Ngā Tapuwae (the footsteps) memorial trail project.
Images reproduced with permission of Bloomsbury Publishing Plc, Melbourne University Publishing, Penguin Random House Australia, and the New Zealand Ministry for Culture and Heritage.

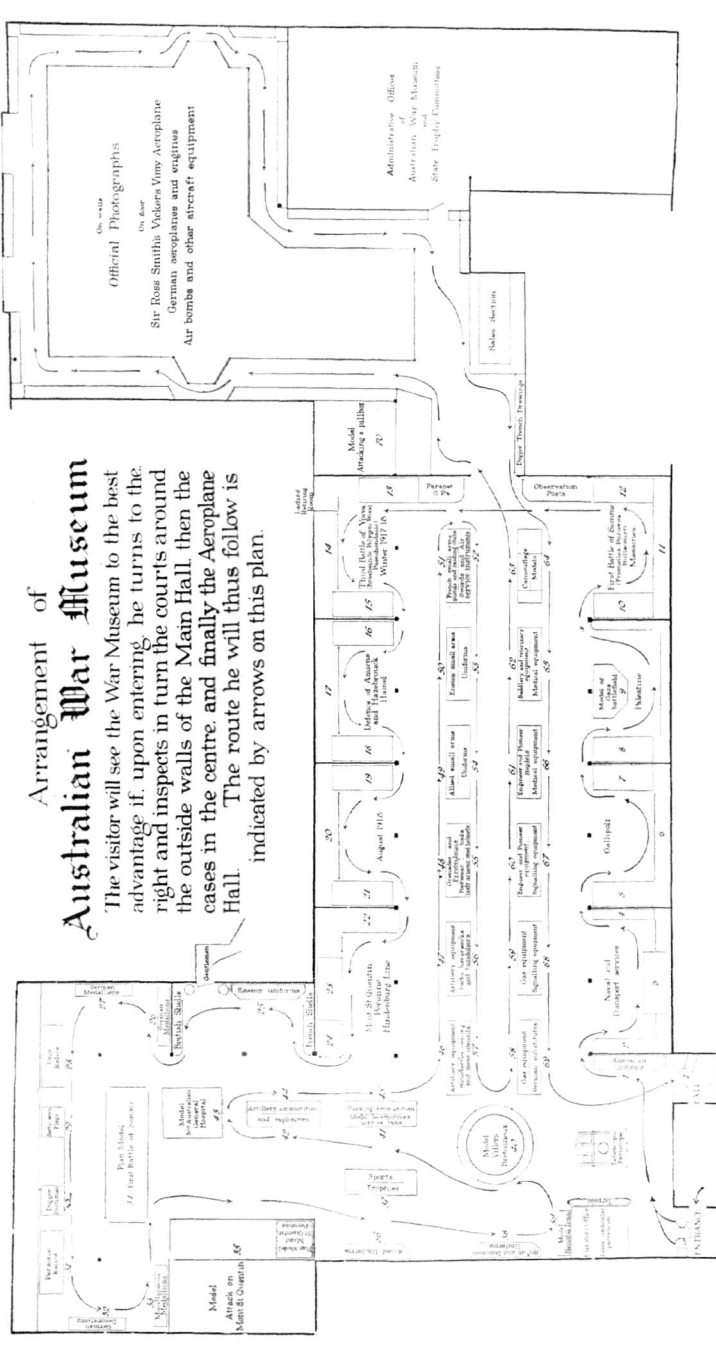

Plate 4. Plan showing the layout of the Melbourne exhibition and a suggested circulation route around the Australian War Museum, 1922. Note the *Nonne Boschen* diorama (no. 70) is clearly separated from the third Ypres section (nos 13, 14 and 15) when following the suggested route. Australian War Memorial, J00292.

Plate 5. Wallace Anderson and Louis McCubbin, *Nonne Boschen* (*Ypres*), diorama, 400 × 730 × 215 cm, 1922–23.
Photograph by the author; Australian War Memorial, ART41023.

Plate 6. Frank Hurley, *The Morning of Passchendaele*, ca 1917.
Australian War Memorial, P04060.005.

Plate 7. Frontispiece of *Australian Chivalry*, edited by John Treloar (Canberra: Australian War Memorial, 1933).
Photograph by the author; Australian War Memorial, EF 704.94994 A938.

Plate 8. Septimus Power, *First Australian Division Artillery Going into the 3rd Battle of Ypres*, oil on canvas, 121.7 × 245.0 cm, 1919.
Australian War Memorial, ART03330.

Plate 9. Fred Leist, *Australian Infantry Attack in Polygon Wood*, oil on canvas, 122.5 × 245.0 cm, 1919.
Australian War Memorial, ART02927.

Plate 10. Paul Nash, *The Menin Road*, oil on canvas, 182.8 × 317.5 cm, 1919.
Imperial War Museum, Art. IWM ART 2242 © IWM.

Plate 11. Otto Dix, *Flandern*, oil and tempera on canvas, 200 × 250 cm, 1934–36.
Staatliche Museen zu Berlin – Preussischer Kulturbesitz, Nationalgalerie, B 658.
© SABAM Belgium 2020 and bpk image agency.

Plate 12. Will Longstaff, *Menin Gate at Midnight*, oil on canvas, 137 × 270 cm, 1927.
Australian War Memorial, ART09807.

Plate 13. Menin Gate Memorial, Ypres, 2017.
Courtesy of Christophe Piron.

Plate 14. Illustration by C.H. Percival that accompanied Sydney George's poem 'Ypres' in the October 1920 edition of *Aussie*.
National Library of Australia, nla.cat-vn879709.

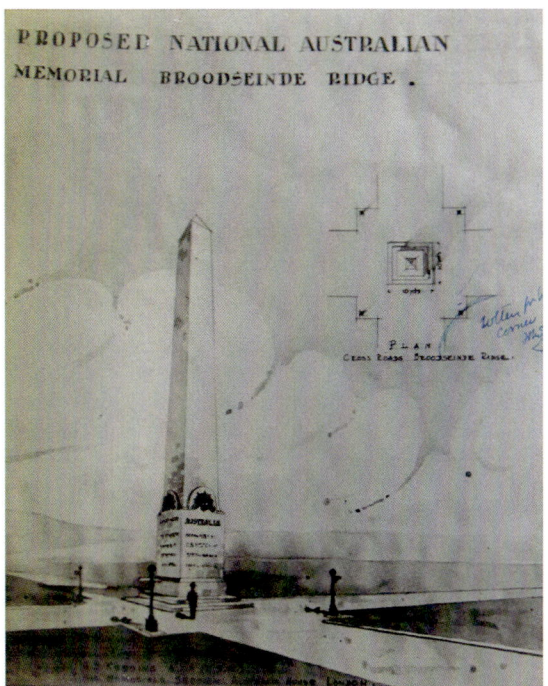

Plate 15. G.S. Keesing's sketch of a proposed national Australian memorial for Broodseinde Ridge, 1919.
Photograph by the author; Commonwealth War Graves Commission, WG 857/3 pt. 1, box 1124.

Plate 16. G.S. Keesing's sketch of a divisional memorial, 1919.
Photograph by the author; Commonwealth War Graves Commission, WG 857/3 pt. 1, box 1124.

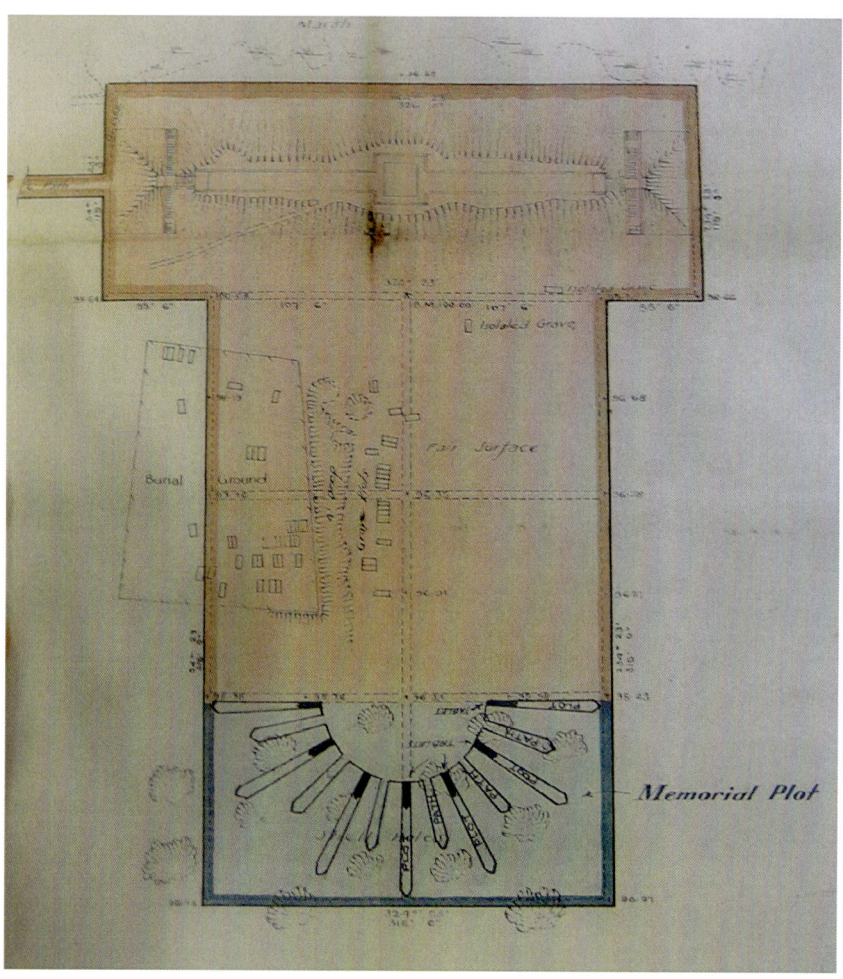

Plate 17. Survey of the mound at Polygon Wood, ca 1920.
Photograph by the author; Commonwealth War Graves Commission, WG 857/3/1, box 1060.

Plates 18 and 19. J.C. Goodchild, *Divisional Monument, Polygon Wood, Broodseinde* and *Tynecot* [sic] *British Cemetery, Broodseinde*, in *Where the Australians Rest* (Melbourne: Government Printer, 1920), 19, 21.
National Archives of Australia, MP367/1, 446/10/3447.

Plate 20. Australian section, Memorial Museum Passchendaele 1917, 29 September 2015.
Photograph by the author.

Plate 21. Australian section, Memorial Museum Passchendaele 1917, 29 September 2015. Note the Seabrook brothers' death plaques just above the 'Roll of Honor'.
Photograph by the author.

Plate 22. 'A Multicultural War' section, In Flanders Fields Museum, 30 October 2015. An II ANZAC Brodie helmet can be seen on the right, next to the New Zealand 'lemon squeezer' hat.
Photograph by the author.

Plate 23. Charles Web Gilbert's *Digger* at the In Flanders Fields Museum, 30 October 2015.
Photograph by the author; In Flanders Fields Museum.

Plate 24. Stretcher bearers passing through Polygon Wood two days after the eponymous battle, 28 September 1917.
Australian War Memorial, E01912.

Plate 25. Polygon Wood photographed by Ilse de Groot on the morning of the Australian centenary commemorative offensive, 26 September 2017. 'Centenary of the Battle of Polygon Wood: Reflective Program – Zonnebeke'.
® WO1.be – GreatWar.be (www.greatwar.be), 26 September 2017,
www.wo1.be/en/youwerethere/11649/centenary-of-the-battle-of-polygon-wood-reflective-program.

Plate 26. *Planting the Australian Flag on Anzac Redoubt*, by an unknown artist, 1917. *Sydney Mail*, 3 October 1917.

Plate 27. Ypres: a multinational commemorative space. Top: British, French, European Union, Canadian, American, Belgian and English flags adorning the Boerenhol cafe; the Australian flag is notably absent. Middle left: The painting depicts soldiers of different backgrounds, including an Australian (to the left). Bottom right: The shop window has numerous British curios, and an Australian postcard under another depicting a maple leaf. Shops and bars in Ypres have names that clearly draw on the British link to the city, including 'The Old Bill Pub' (bottom left), 'Old Tom', 'The Times' and 'The British Grenadier Bookshop'.
Courtesy of Christophe Piron.

Unsurprisingly, her message – printed under the title 'The War Cemeteries: A Labour of Love' – supported Bruce's claims and unequivocally hailed the IWGC, whose 'gardens of the dead' made 'fitting homes for the bodies of brave men'.[58] While Scullin's rapid battlefield tour several years later was set against the backdrop of the Great Depression and barely made the news,[59] Lyons' 1935 trip attracted substantial public attention. At Tyne Cot Cemetery, Lyons and his wife, Enid, were 'overcome with emotion by the scene and all it conveyed'.[60] Upon their return, Enid Lyons gave a 'vivid lecture', describing the cemeteries as one would a garden, 'with the scent of clove pinks and roses in the air, the buzzing of bees and the song of birds'.[61] The sentiments expressed regarding these trips were of a personal nature, addressed to the bereaved who would never make the long journey to Europe and for whom the resting place of the fallen could only be imagined.[62]

The focus on comforting Australians by keeping them informed of the state of war graves and memorials to the missing dominated reports of officials' tours, while references to the fighting were kept to a minimum. Politicians made no overt statements about the AIF's experience on the Western Front – or such statements went unreported if they did – and the media seemed content to follow the legislators' lead. For example, articles on Bruce's and Lyons' tours of Ypres noted that they visited Tyne Cot Cemetery yet failed to highlight why this imposing graveyard was significant to Australians. The reports did not address the extraordinarily high number of Australian burials there, among which were two Victoria Cross winners, nor did they point out that it was the AIF that had captured the four German pillboxes on top of which the cemetery had been built.[63] Even outside the emotionally charged grounds of Tyne Cot, officials appear to have avoided overly militarist or triumphalist comments about the AIF's exploits in

Belgium. This is best exemplified by Lyons' reported response to the burgomaster of Ypres who, having 'fought in the ranks side by side' with the Australians, claimed they were 'daredevils'. This was surely an opportunity for the prime minister to join his host in extolling the virtues of Australian military prowess, but, if Lyons did so, the press did not report it. Instead, Lyons said that 'he had been impressed by the peace, beauty and orderliness of the "silent cities" he had just visited'.[64] References to the AIF's trials and triumphs were standard fare in many representations of the war in Australia at the time, including Bean's *Official History of Australia in the War of 1914–1918*, the Australian War Memorial's exhibitions and popular literature. However, they were evidently not suitable when the nation's leaders toured a region that contained one of the IWGC's most daunting cemeteries and well over 10,000 Australian war dead.

The discourse surrounding tours of cemeteries and memorial sites in France followed a similar pattern to that in Belgium, but with two chief exceptions: Villers-Bretonneux and Amiens. This is somewhat unsurprising, given the sites' intimate association with the AIF's victories in France in 1918. The unveilings of a memorial tablet at Amiens Cathedral in 1920 and the Australian National Memorial at 'Villers Bret' eighteen years later were particularly significant moments when speakers and journalists deployed triumphalist rhetoric.[65] Similar remarks were also publicised during the European trips of Hughes and Bruce. Hughes' comments were particularly bombastic: he declared his countrymen were 'foremost among the braves' and 'of heroic breed … [who] fought to the end and fell gloriously', claims that were echoed by locals in no fewer than '*eleven* speeches, all emphasising that the Australians saved Amiens'.[66] Several years later, at Amiens, Bruce was so impressed with the warm greeting he received from the bishop, who referred to the

Australians as the 'Saviours of Amiens', that he wrote to the prefect of the Somme to show his appreciation in language that evoked the grand Anzac narrative. In the letter, an excerpt of which was published in a number of major dailies, Bruce declared there were

> strong bonds between the people of Amiens and Australia, and recalled the most critical hours in March, 1918, when French and Australian troops, side by side four miles [6.5 kilometres] from Amiens, countered the Germans' final desperate attempts [to capture the city]. 'This ... changed the fortunes of the conflict, and assured the eventual triumph of the Allied cause.'[67]

On the whole, when visiting the battlefields, Australian officials employed rhetoric that reflected the success of the IWGC's memorial project. The commission had designed its monuments and cemeteries as poignant sites of memory that captured 'the emotion of the Empire after its most terrible ordeal'; the idyllic English garden landscaping of the cemeteries, in particular, served to displace memory from modern battle to the sacrifice of those whose names would 'liveth forever more'.[68] It would have been out of place to herald martial achievements while standing before the tens of thousands of names inscribed on the Menin Gate Memorial or the endless rows of headstones in IWGC cemeteries. Documents relating to Bruce's tour of the Western Front and Gallipoli reveal his reluctance to broach the national war narrative alongside the topic of war graves. Following his return to Australia, his staff prepared two statements to be released to the press for Anzac Day 1924, explaining the reason for this in an attached note:

> The statement, re Soldiers' Graves, has been written as a separate message since it is *hardly appropriate* to the special Anzac Day message. However, it, or something on the same lines, could be issued additional to the Anzac Day message.[69]

Bruce's Anzac Day messages were kept apart because one asserted the 'glorious history of the Australian Imperial Force' and its role in making 'Australia a nation', while the other fulfilled a 'solemn duty to convey to relatives of Australia's soldier dead a record of his [Bruce's] recent observations in France and Gallipoli'.[70] Australian officials following in Bruce's footsteps maintained the distinction between these two themes, steering clear of triumphalist declarations and focusing on their role as adoptive kin instead.

Returning to the Battlefields

Ex-servicemen's return journeys to the battlefields were quite different from the visits made by curious travellers, politicians and the bereaved. Many former soldiers expressed a longing to pay respects at the gravesides of 'old mates', but the predominant motive appears to have been a nostalgic longing to recapture a sense of their war experience.[71] One ex-soldier best summed up this sentiment in a letter to the editor of Brisbane's *Telegraph* criticising the lack of financial support, official or otherwise, for a pilgrimage of former servicemen:

> I have lost a lot of interest in life and pre-war ambitions but I have a great desire (which I may describe as my one and only ambition) to revisit the battlefields of France and Anzac, to see the places I once described as hell, the places where some of the truest and best Australians gave their lives in a cause they believed just.[72]

This desire to retrace their steps across the former battlefields was reflected in the accounts of those who recorded their experiences of return. This is not to suggest that returned men were so focused on their own personal journeys that their reports did not engage with the needs of mourners. Indeed, many wrote messages 'to those fathers and mothers whose sons remained there [overseas] that nothing could be better than the way the cemeteries were being looked after'.[73] Nevertheless, the most consistent theme in former soldiers' accounts of their voyages was their impressions of old haunts.

Returned soldiers writing about trips through Belgian Flanders focused primarily on the difficulties they had reconciling the rejuvenated landscape of the present with the 'shell-swept quagmire' of their memories. This was a common enough subject throughout accounts of pilgrimages all along the Western Front. However, the salient's evolution from morass to 'green fields' interspersed with 'new red brick villages' happened more quickly and was more complete than changes to other significant locations, including Pozières and Villers-Bretonneux.[74] In early 1922, Clarence Seccombe, a former officer attached to Australia House, reported that the Belgians were 'working extremely hard' and 'were very systematic in clearing up the old battlefields', whereas at Villers-Bretonneux rebuilding continued 'but not so fast', and Pozières was still 'very little altered from what it was in war-time'.[75] Just over a year later, another returned man, Loftus Hills, noted that it was becoming difficult to recognise the Somme he had known, but at certain places, including Pozières, traces of war were still visible. The changes at Ypres, on the other hand, were 'the most impressive … there were not the slightest signs of a war having been fought'.[76] Even as late as 1938, Geoff Stillman, a pilgrim present at the unveiling ceremony of the national memorial at Villers-Bretonneux found that although 'few conspicuous signs' remained of the war in the Somme region, 'a close examination by anyone who was there on active service [would] reveal many signs of interest'. In Belgium, he found that conditions were different and that 'it was impossible to recognize any particular point'. Even the 'better-known places' had to be 'designated by notice boards'.[77] The particularly rapid transformation of the salient denied all but the earliest soldier pilgrims the chance of encountering a familiar landscape.

Some changes were seen as reassuring – notably, those brought about through the work of the IWGC. Henry Slater, a member of the Returned Sailors' and Soldiers' Imperial League of Australia's Killara sub-branch, was especially impressed with the Buttes New British Cemetery, at Polygon Wood, whose design provided 'a wonderful atmosphere of calm dignity about the locality which makes it impossible to connect it with the place we knew in 1917'.[78] Other transformations, however, were disorienting: 'places once so well known, and never to be forgotten were impossible to find', reported a disheartened John Massey after visiting Belgium.[79] Dramatic changes were even distressing to some returning servicemen who went on to write highly critical accounts of Belgian civilians' attempts to begin their postwar lives by building over, for example, 'the most sacred battleground in British history'.[80] Clarence Seccombe complained that the 'new town' that had sprung up at Ypres was 'a collection of hideous square houses of red brick, with red high-gabled, tiled roofs'. Indeed, the 'glaring redness' was 'unrelieved', and he found the town 'extraordinary in its ugliness'.[81] Nor was it solely the locals' efforts to physically transform the devastated region into a place fit for farming and habitation that rankled. According to reports in newspapers and RSSILA magazines, former servicemen also 'deplored the manner in which the Belgians were commercialising the dead' and the former battlegrounds by charging visitors fees to see memorials and selling souvenirs at key sites, such as Hill 60, all of which was seen as trivialising the sacrifice of the dead.[82]

In certain cases, some were so disillusioned by their return that they regretted having made the journey at all. This was best expressed by Frederic Cutlack, author of *The Australians* (see chapter 3), who lamented that 'the anticipated pleasure of renewing acquaintances with old scenes was working out all wrong ... The diggers had gone, and with them had departed the life of these places as we had known it'.[83] Such accounts were nostalgic lamentations for experiences that were receding into the past.

As soldier pilgrims were seeking to recapture something of their war experience in Belgium, their accounts were mostly short on historical details but more intimate than many articles in RSSILA magazines or the longer personal narratives that served to reinforce elements of the Anzac tradition. Writing about his experience touring the 'famous spots' at Ypres, Henry Slater noted that 'the old familiar names arouse many recollections in my mind'.[84] In another account, a returned man's wife revealed the emotional toll these journeys could take:

> He took me to Passchendaele, where, after pointing out several places, he turned sharply to me and said, 'You go away. You do not belong here. This is mine.'
>
> Naturally, I was astonished and was about to remonstrate, but the soft, pitious holy light in his eyes showed me that he was right; that his heart was full, and I silently left him to commune with his dead comrades.[85]

Others were more explicit in addressing what the Australians had endured in the salient. Predictably, the terrible weather conditions experienced during third Ypres were a consistent theme, although few travellers went into much detail about 'those terrible muddy days of October 1917'.[86] On the rare occasions soldiers did more than simply name specific locations and battles, it was the physical reminders of the AIF's presence in Belgium – the monuments at Polygon Wood and Hill 60, as well as the plaque on the central blockhouse in Tyne Cot Cemetery – that triggered brief descriptions. For example, *The Listening Post* published an account by 'Jockand' of the 'tunnelling epic' at Hill 60 after he had visited Belgium. Although the author was 'not sure what the Tunnellers ha[d] done' to merit a monument before his trip overseas, most of the article went on to describe the 'Herculean effort' of his countrymen in the build-up to Messines.[87] On the other hand, with no monuments to trigger fading memories, the victories at Menin Road and Broodseinde were overlooked in ex-soldiers' accounts.

Also influencing returned servicemen's expeditions to and their impressions of the Ypres salient was the Menin Gate Memorial. Its location within Ypres itself, as opposed to being in an isolated field in the countryside, ensured pilgrims travelling through the town could not miss it. The local community's spontaneous establishment of a regular Last Post ceremony under the archway had also added an element of solemn pageantry to the already-imposing monument.[88] The publicity generated by the grandiose unveiling ceremony and the tour of Will Longstaff's *Menin Gate at Midnight* meant that many soldier pilgrims took their audience's knowledge of the memorial for granted. Consequently, they did not elaborate on its importance for the British Empire or Australia beyond occasionally citing the number of names engraved on its panels.[89] One pilgrim clearly acknowledged this when he noted that it was a 'very fine memorial to those whose graves are unknown ... but this has been so often described that Tasmanian readers will already know about it'.[90]

The same writer proceeded to describe another striking monument in the salient: Canada's memorial to those 'who fell in the first gas attack at St. Julien'. This was not a unique reference to the fellow dominion's monument in soldier pilgrims' accounts; others also expressed their admiration for the *Brooding Soldier* memorial.[91] That returned Australian servicemen drew attention to this memorial is somewhat unexpected, given it did not have any tangible association with their war experience.

In fact, the battle it commemorated occurred just as the Australians were about to land at Gallipoli. Still, thanks to a combination of its unique, moving form – that of a soldier, head bowed, emerging out of a eleven-metre-tall block of granite – and its location in a 'delightful park of distinctive Canadian shrubs and trees', the monument had a striking presence in the salient region, and it left a strong impression on those who saw it. The site was interpreted as unequivocally Canadian, exposing the shortcomings of Australia's memorials in the Ypres salient, with their 'plain', 'unobtrusive' monuments and comparative lack of antipodean flora causing them to become subsumed within a broader landscape of imperial memory. 'The maple leaf is still known in Flanders', declared Leonard Robb, president of the RSSILA's New South Wales branch, when reporting on his tour of the battlefields.[92] No similar claim about the gum leaf was forthcoming in Robb's or any other returned man's account of pilgrimage in Belgium.

In addition to a shortage of truly moving Australian-centred sites in Belgium, many battlefield tours lacked any grand sense of ceremony that might have captured the public's imagination in an enduring way. At least the press was able to highlight the atmosphere of 'pathos' accentuated by the wattle tribute during the Australian War Graves Pilgrimage.[93] It did fall short of providing awe-inspiring scenes like those of the British Legion pilgrimage in 1928, which was led by the Prince of Wales and included over 11,000 participants (without counting day-trippers at various locations). But the intimate, well-publicised actions of the bereaved on the Australian pilgrimage were far more engaging than the rare ceremonial events involving returned men throughout the interwar years.[94] A prime example of this was RSSILA federal president Gilbert Dyett's involvement in an IWGC ceremony organised for the unveiling of the Cross of Sacrifice at Tyne Cot Cemetery during a tour of Flanders. Although the event attracted considerable local attention, it received very little exposure in Australia: the press did not even address Australia's close connection with the burial ground or the pillbox on which the cross was located.⁹⁵ Ceremonies like this were just too small, irregular and lacking a distinctive Australian slant to warrant much attention from the general public.

The official pilgrimage of the Coronation Contingent, in 1937, could have been the exception to this state of affairs. However, the pilgrimage was too exclusionary and came about as the result of incidental factors rather than being a painstakingly planned venture. RSSILA branches and former soldiers had envisaged a contingent of up to 5000 ex-servicemen heading overseas to participate in the coronation ceremony and then tour the war graves of Europe. Once it became evident that federal assistance would be needed and government officials took over the pilgrimage's organisation, the scale and objectives were pared back, and only 150 *serving* men and 7 nurses were chosen from the army, navy, air force and militia, barely half of whom were former AIF members.⁹⁶ Furthermore, those selected were chosen for their physical appearance, to maintain the 'illusion of a nation of natural warriors who were tall and strong'. These changes meant the pilgrimage came close 'to the heart of the Australian memory of war because it emphasised the achievements of Australian servicemen and the Anzac tradition'.⁹⁷ They also ensured that those who did not fit the Anzac mould – the wounded, unfit, frail and elderly – were excluded. Official pragmatism and pride in the Anzac legend won out over a deep-seated desire of many returned men to revisit the Western Front.

The pilgrimage's capacity to resonate with the broader public was also hampered because the tour of the battlefields themselves was more of an afterthought than a carefully orchestrated commemorative exercise.

The government's initial plans did not actually involve a voyage to the European continent at all. Indeed, officials do not seem to have given much thought to the idea until contingent members agitated for a tour while in London. Early correspondence suggested only returned soldiers would be permitted to visit the battlefields before all members finally received permission to participate, although the official arrangements were not completed until only four days before the Australians left England for Belgium and France.[98] The last-minute nature of the trip gave all involved little time to prepare. The Belgians were certainly caught off-guard; one local Ypres newspaper reported the town had barely been given any warning of the contingent's arrival.[99] From the Australian perspective, the tardiness of the decision-making process ensured that no touching, uniquely Australian gestures that might appeal to a national audience – like the wattle tribute – were organised. The result was a rushed tour of the Belgian and French battlefields that missed the kinds of impressive ceremonies that had accompanied grand tours organised by other countries, such as the United States, Britain and Canada.[100]

The disparity between the press reports of the contingent's time in Britain and those of the European leg of the voyage drove home the relatively mundane nature of the latter. Comprehensive accounts from London confirmed the martial image of the contingent, and the strapping Australians were found to be the equals of renowned English units and outshone dominion counterparts.[101] Many articles also recalled, in general terms, Anzac feats of arms accomplished with the support of other empire troops.[102] When the contingent arrived on the continent, the focus shifted from narratives lauding imperial solidarity and the Anzacs' place among the elite of the empire to unimpressive summaries of commemorative activities. Perhaps this was, in part, because no newspaper had arranged for a special correspondent to accompany the contingent to provide gripping accounts of its progress. It was also significant that, once in continental Europe, the pilgrims did little beyond partake, like many Australians before them, in the standard rites of commemoration: they inspected war graves, laid wreaths and, at Ypres, attended the Last Post ceremony at the Menin Gate Memorial. The Belgians did welcome them with a bit more fanfare than they did most other Australian visitors, but this tour ultimately lacked the grandeur and coverage of other ventures, such as the aforementioned British Legion pilgrimage and the Canadians' Vimy Ridge pilgrimage of 1936, which had 6000 participants.[103] The resulting accounts of the cemetery tours and ceremonial events were incredibly light on detail. If press coverage reflected and reinforced public interest surrounding the tour, it was evidently the pomp and ceremony of the coronation that stood out for many, not the subsequent pilgrimage to the Western Front.

Specific elements of the pilgrimage received more attention once the contingent returned to Australia, with some members sharing their experiences with various newspapers and RSSILA magazines. The ex-AIF men, like others who had returned to the battlefields, were stunned by the disappearance of any visible evidence of the war's ravages – 'no longer was it [the salient] the Valley of Desolation' – and found it 'consoling' to see the graves of old mates well cared for.[104] Despite being 'received with generous compliments in Ypres', the travellers found that Villers-Bretonneux made the deepest impression on them. The close links Australians had fostered with French locals captivated the commander of the contingent, Colonel Edmund Lind:

> The town of Villers-Bretonneux was like an oasis in a desert of indifference. The school children were fully aware of the sacrifices made by the Australian troops in the defence of the town, and the

community, generally, regarded Australia as a place to be looked up to.[105]

Ypres, on the other hand, lacked this distinctly Australian feel. In any case, whether a handful of ex-AIF men spoke about locations in Belgium or France in reverent terms or not, their accounts could hardly be expected to make up for the lost opportunity to organise a more widely accessible endeavour commemorating the AIF's actions on the Western Front. A year later, Villers-Bretonneux had another chance to bask in the limelight, when King George VI unveiled the Australian National Memorial there in the presence of Australian and French officials and a ragtag group of former Australian servicemen who had travelled there not from Australia but from their homes in Britain. A visit to Belgium afterwards was not on the cards, and so slipped by the final opportunity to make a large-scale pilgrimage to the salient in memory of Australian achievements and sacrifices before war again engulfed Europe.

* * *

Australian commemorations in Belgium throughout the interwar years did little to reinforce the memory of the AIF's struggles around Ypres. The Flemish town was a common destination for the few Australians with the means to travel to Europe, but this did not reflect its position within the Anzac legend. The bereaved travelled there to see where their loved ones lay and to share their experiences with other grieving Australians who could not make the long journey; politicians also acted as adoptive kin, inspecting the gravesites of countrymen in order to reassure constituents in mourning; returned men visited to rediscover the sites that had so marked them in 1917; and tourists were drawn to the town because of its infamous reputation. Once in Belgium, pilgrims and travellers were confronted with a landscape dominated by numerous IWGC cemeteries and the Menin Gate Memorial, which conspicuously linked the former salient with the sacrifices made by men of all countries in the British Empire. The presence of the 5th Division's obelisk at Polygon Wood and the 1st Tunnelling Company's Hill 60 memorial ensured there were two uniquely Australian memorials in the region, but these were too narrow in focus, too isolated and too plain to become national sites of memory. The eruption of a second worldwide conflict heralded the end of Australian commemorative activities on the Western Front for several decades, and over half a century went by before significant numbers of Australians walked the Belgian battlefields again. By then, the passing of those who had experienced the war firsthand, cheaper international travel and a proactive local population had radically changed the nature of memorial initiatives in Belgium.

Chapter 5

DEAD TREES AND WITHERING MEMORIES

Inspecting recently liberated areas of Belgium in 1944, the Imperial War Graves Commission's deputy director of works, Major Andrew Macfarlane, wrote a short report on the state of the 5th Australian Division's obelisk at Polygon Wood. On the whole there was little to be concerned about, especially considering the state of other memorials, such as the 2nd Australian Division's monument at Mont St Quentin, whose bellicose stance had evidently offended German sensibilities: it had been removed by the Germans during their occupation of France. More banal in design, the 5th Australian Division's monument had only suffered minor wear and tear from exposure, not wilful vandalism. It was 'in an excellent state of repair'. The same could not be said for the horticultural manifestations of Australian remembrance in the memorial's proximity – the gum trees that had been planted in the wood during the interwar years. Unable to survive without external care and intervention in a climate that did not favour them, they had withered and died. As the deputy director reported bluntly, 'The eucalyptus trees are dead'.[1]

There is a poignant symbolism in the death of those Australian trees in Belgium. Likening memories to plants, Marc Augé has argued that they need tending if they are to burgeon; those deprived of care will fade into oblivion.[2] Although the Australian Imperial Force's Belgian battles could make for an uneasy fit within the dominant Anzac legend, certain agents did at least tend to their memories during the interwar years, keeping them alive. With fewer individuals fostering their remembrance after the Second World War, however, Messines and third Ypres withered in collective memory. Even when a resurgent popular interest in Anzac led to a rediscovery of the Western Front in the 1990s, the 1917 battles were once again left largely on the periphery of the nation's evolving First World War narrative.

Charting the trajectory of Messines and third Ypres in Australian memory from the outbreak of the Second World War to the end of the 1980s, this chapter covers a particularly turbulent period for Anzac commemoration. These were fallow years for First World War remembrance in Australia, when not only the Belgian battlefields but the entire Western Front essentially disappeared from the Anzac narrative. In part, this was due to the memory of the Second World War displacing that of the First. Yet, there was another, fundamental shift taking place. The numbers of men and women who had experienced the conflict firsthand were dwindling, and the influence they once had over the Anzac legend was shifting inexorably to those who had not lived through 1914–18: the war was moving from living memory to 'cultural memory' with increasing speed.[3] At the same time, contemporary issues cast Anzac in an unappealing light. The disintegration of Britain's empire and the abolition of the White Australia policy saw the rise of a 'new nationalism', which sought to distance Australians from their British past. The nation's involvement in the Vietnam War also complicated war commemoration. As a result of these developments, many observers felt the Anzac legend occupied an increasingly tenuous position within Australian historical consciousness, and there were predictions that it would be forgotten altogether. But these bleak forecasts turned out to be premature. Thanks to the publication of several powerful social histories, renewed political attention and the subsequent reimagining of the Anzacs in film and on television, Australians rediscovered an interest in the First World War. The successful reframing of the Anzacs' experience at Gallipoli for a contemporary audience was central to this resurgent wave of First World War commemoration, but certain Western Front engagements eventually benefited from Australians' growing fascination with 1914–18. Messines and third Ypres were not among them.

Anzac and Another World War

Official commemoration of the Australian Imperial Force's actions on the Western Front belatedly reached its apogee with the unveiling of the Australian National Memorial at Villers-Bretonneux, in July 1938. That no effort was made to arrange a pilgrimage to Belgian Flanders or to Fromelles, in French Flanders, after the unveiling spoke volumes about the marginalisation of those sites in official war memory. However, Villers-Bretonneux did not maintain its prominent position in the Anzac legend for very long. Just over a year later, the Second World War began. This new war did not initially eclipse the memory of 1914–18; it had Australians casting their minds back to the previous conflict, and although it was not mobilised to the same extent as that of Gallipoli, the memory of 1918 provided commentators with optimistic talking points. Brisbane's *Courier-Mail* ran an article reminding readers of 'What the First AIF Did' between 1914 and 1918. In particular, the paper's special correspondent highlighted the Australians' 'big captures' during 1918, their efforts in liberating 116 towns and villages 'from enemy hands' and the Australian Imperial Force's role in the famous Allied advance on 8 August, 'which Ludendorff afterward described as "the black day for the German Army"'.[4] Another journalist declared that Australia's decision to send 20,000 men to Europe as the *Second Australian Imperial Force* would 'certainly not be reassuring to the Germans', as the Australians had already 'met and defeated the soldiers of Germany in some of the fiercest and bloodiest battles ever fought in Europe'. Citing an unnamed British historian, the journalist also claimed that the AIF's 'onslaught at Villers-Bretonneux … saved Amiens and Hazebrouck' and that this was the turning point of the war. The article then ended on a grimly resolute note: Germany had 'good reasons to remember the Australians – and she [would] have added reason for doing so' before the end of the new war.[5] The rhetoric of triumph fostered throughout the interwar period was alive, and its contemporary message was clear: as the First AIF had prevailed in 1918, so too would its second incarnation. After all, the Second AIF was following in the footsteps of 'the old AIF, an army of citizen soldiers who made history and gave Australia an enduring glory'.[6]

While recalling the events of 1918 aimed to reassure readers, some commentators also expressed an underlying fear that previous lessons might not have been learned. In particular, Passchendaele, became a shorthand term for 'a lack of intelligence' that was said to have plagued British military strategy in the First World War. The simplified reference lacked the nuance of Charles Bean's appraisal in the *Official History of Australia in the War of 1914–1918* and the semi-triumphant gloss that Australian War Memorial exhibitors and many battalion historians had applied to the campaign. Third Ypres had become 'the greatest tragedy in military history', and the memory of its long casualty lists still 'haunted' men. A widely reported cable from British authorities even stressed that the Allies did not 'intend to repeat the losses suffered at Passchendaele'. Thus, the overwhelmingly negative view of third Ypres suggested in Australian soldier literature and made explicit in the fulminations of Billy Hughes and David Lloyd George – as carnage involving little more than the 'throwing [of] wave after wave of men at an enemy position of rocklike impregnability' – was now a terrifying yardstick against which to measure the current global conflict.[7] Once the Second AIF had faced combat, commentators availed themselves of this yardstick to highlight the Australians' successes, such as the comparatively bloodless victory at Bardia, in Libya, in 1941, and to take the sting out of their defeats. Referring to the British defeat in Greece, Charles Bean – who was still working on the official history of the First World War – pointed out that although losses were 'great in comparison with those suffered' in Libya, they were 'not heavy in proportion to those incurred by the AIF in 1914–18 … In the whole First Battle of the Somme the AIF lost in 7 weeks 28,000 men, and in the Third Battle of Ypres it lost 38,000'.[8]

As the conflict wore on, it was cast in terms of 1914–18 less frequently, and Australians began to hear of 'new and imperishable battle honours' that reinvigorated the Anzac tradition, such as Bardia, Tobruk and Kokoda.[9] These battles were far more relevant to contemporary Australians in relation to time and experience, and in the case of those engagements fought in the Pacific theatre, they were much closer to home as well.

This general shift of Anzac rhetoric to the events of 1939–45 did not fundamentally change the characterisation of the Australian warrior. Certain elements, however, did not fit easily into the original legend – namely, the enforcement of conscription, which signalled the end of the First AIF's proud volunteer tradition; and several noteworthy defeats, which led to a large number of Australians being taken prisoner. The latter issue was particularly disturbing, as the prisoners' emaciated bodies and experiences of captivity were initially difficult to reconcile with the martial warrior image cultivated in the First World War. Authorities were so concerned about this that they banned the public from the wharves when the worst affected former prisoners of war reached Australia.[10] Even after they had been nursed back to health, it took several decades for the stories of former prisoners 'to be more fully integrated into the rituals of national commemoration and remembrance'.[11] Despite these challenges to the legend, most popular representations throughout the war and beyond explicitly linked the new generation of Australian citizen soldiers with their First World War forebears. As Graham Seal has argued,

> There was no need to invent a new group persona for the Australian foot soldier at the front – it was ready and waiting, already full-blown, polished and resplendent with over two decades of sacred polish applied around the land each Anzac Day.

Upon their return, many veterans joined the ranks of the Returned Sailor's, Soldier's and Airmen's Imperial League of Australia (later known as the Returned and Services League, or RSL), which had done much to foster the interwar 'digger tradition'.[12]

While the Second World War initially did little to alter the popular image of the Australian citizen soldier, the articulation of the Anzac legend itself softened. Acknowledging the sacrifice of the dead remained imperative, but displays of triumphalism were toned down. Some thirty years earlier, communities had fought over German trophies captured by the AIF to crown local war memorials so they might bask in the glow of the Anzacs' martial achievements. Very few did so after 1945. Nor were there any sustained official attempts to erect memorials at every overseas site where the Second AIF's divisions had performed with distinction.[13] The rhetoric of commemoration reflected this change. The 1914–18 generation had drawn succour from high diction that expressed pride in martial triumph and sacrifice. As one commentator declared on Anzac Day in 1922, 'On the morning of April 25, 1915, in the fire of Gallipoli, a piece of steel was forged. On the morning of April 25, 1918, at Villers Bretonneux [sic], it was thrust into the heart of the Hun'.[14] The generation of 1939–45, on the other hand, was markedly more subdued. For instance, Prime Minister Ben Chifley's 1947 Anzac Day address could hardly have been termed triumphant or celebratory:

> Twice in our time the flower of our manhood suffered the scourge of war, and so many of our homes have been darkened by sorrow. In the name of those whose memory we now recall, let us bend our efforts to ensure that it shall never happen again.[15]

This shift was due to the Second World War being, on the whole, a more chastening experience for Australians. Throughout the interwar period, the most vocal propagators of the Anzac legend had found comfort in the belief that the Commonwealth's citizen soldiers had been instrumental in helping the Allies achieve a lasting victory, thanks to their role in apparently decisive engagements, such as Villers-Bretonneux, Amiens and Mont St Quentin. By 1945, such claims appeared 'pathetically innocent'.[16]

A consequence of this was the increasing marginalisation of the First World War in collective memory. Events in 1914–18 had already cast doubt on 'the might of the British Empire and the superiority of all things British'. The experiences of 1939–45 further eroded such beliefs.[17] The failure of the British to protect their outposts in South-East Asia forced Australians to realise just how vulnerable they were, and the threat of Japanese invasion drove them to seek aid and protection from the United States. The Second World War also inflicted thousands of losses for the second time in under thirty years and saw white Australia under direct attack for the first time in its short history. Gallipoli, enshrined in a national holiday and buoyed by three decades' worth of rhetoric that declared it the birth of the nation, remained central to the popular war narrative. The rest of the Anzac epic – the ordeals of 1916 and 1917 and the Australian victories of 1918 – did not fit easily into a broader imagining of the more 'problematic, and in some sense anti-climactic, nature of Australia's involvement' in the Second World War.[18] Humbling defeats in Greece, Crete and Singapore made it difficult to cast 1939–45 in a triumphalist manner, and even if one ignored these disasters, no engagement in which the Australians were involved was recognised as having a substantial bearing on the war's outcome. As a writer in *Reveille* framed it,

> In 1918, we were part of the world shaking happenings. We had five divisions in France – and what divisions! The Australian Corps had been the rock on which the great German offensive of April 1918 had smashed itself to a standstill. And it had been the spearhead of our counter-offensive of August 8, 'the black day' on which Ludendorff's bleak military mind finally accepted the premise of defeat. To-day, there is not a slouch hat in France.[19]

In the same vein, an *Argus* journalist jealously noted that Australia's fellow dominion Canada was 'luckier', as its soldiers had had the opportunity to 'blaze their way from Caen to Rouen, and from Ypres to Amsterdam. The Maple Leaf was as familiar as the Union Jack in Brussels and Paris'.[20] Conversely, the Southern Cross was missing in action.

There was also a generational shift under way, as the numbers of those who had fought in the First World War gradually shrank, although this was not so marked immediately after 1945. Prior to 1939, veterans of 1914–18 had been a dominant force moulding Australia's war memory. The Returned Sailors' and Soldiers' Imperial League of Australia played a central role in shaping Anzac Day pageantry; Bean, admittedly never a combatant, was an eyewitness and a dedicated propagator of Anzac lore; and Treloar and other important figures managing the Australian War Memorial were ex-servicemen, as were the authors of the most popular literary accounts of the war.[21] In post-1945 Australia, however, the memory work of those who were left failed to inspire broad public interest. Younger generations with no living memory of the war had to pick up the torch if the Anzac tradition were to survive. Initially, they dallied, and it seemed that public enthusiasm for Anzac was in terminal decline. By the end of the 1970s, however, contemporary interpretations gradually began to appear, reinvigorating the ageing legend and giving it new meaning for those who had no firsthand experience of the conflict.

Aleida Assmann's notions of social, cultural and political memory are useful for interrogating shifts in the Australian memory of the First World War at this time and over the following decades. For Assmann, social memory refers to the exchange of lived memories through oral communication.[22] Political memory and cultural memory, on the other hand, are types of 'long-term collective memory' that are distinguished from living memory by generational distance and from cold, hard, 'objective' history by their emotional appeal to contemporaries.[23] They are 'founded on more durable carriers of external symbols and material representations' than social memory, such as 'affectively charged and mobilising narratives', 'sites and monuments', 'visual and verbal signs' and 'rites of commemoration'.[24] The distinction between political and cultural memory will be discussed in chapter 6, but what is particularly important to note here is that the transition from short-term social memory to these longer term memory forms is often viewed as a fundamentally reductive process.[25] As the historian Dan Todman has argued in his study of British First World War memory, from the 1970s onwards,

> a combination of rapidly declining numbers of veterans ... and the loss of active participation by veterans in public discussion, all exercised a reductive effect on what was remembered ... The complex emotions that those involved had felt at the time could not be brought back.[26]

Similar circumstances, in conjunction with Australia's experience of the Second World War and then the Vietnam War, led to a simplified understanding of the 1914–18 conflict that saw the First AIF's engagements on the Western Front marginalised for many years. However, the veterans' weakening grip on the various manifestations of the nation's war memory permitted younger generations to find *new* meaning in Anzac, without which it may have completely passed into oblivion.[27]

Fading Fast

Given that after the Second World War Australians stopped widely commemorating their most impressive feats in the First, it is unsurprising that during the same period they all but ignored or forgot the earlier conflict's engagements with more questionable outcomes, like Messines and third Ypres. There were minor exceptions throughout the late 1940s and 1950s, but they were usually part of broader commemorative projects and hardly unique to the Belgian battlefields. More importantly, they were limited in nature and generated little publicity. Emblematic of this was the fleeting concern shown for the First AIF's overseas memorials. With the liberation of Belgium and France, reports on damage to various sites filtered through to Australians. There was little to say about the sites in the Ypres salient; the region had been relatively untouched by the fighting, and in most cases, the Germans had not gone out of their way to vandalise Imperial War Graves Commission cemeteries and memorials during their occupation of the low country.[28] Cabinet approved funding for minor repairs to the divisional monuments, as some had become 'eyesores' due to lack of maintenance, but there was no public pressure to do more. The miserly figure of £150 was set aside to restore the 5th Division's memorial, at Polygon Wood; it did not cover the replacement of the dead eucalypts. No longer would pilgrims smell 'the fragrance of the bush' in Belgian Flanders.[29] More significant still was the fact that the completion of the memorial's restoration heralded a decades-long suspension of official interest in the region as an Australian site of memory.

How far Belgium, and the Western Front in general, had slipped in the official Australian commemorative agenda soon after the Second World War is apparent from the Anzac contingent's trip to Great Britain for the coronation of Queen Elizabeth II, in 1953. The 1937 Coronation Contingent's pilgrimage to the battlefields had been a slapdash affair, but the idea of an official pilgrimage had at the time aroused considerable enthusiasm. There was no such interest in public or official circles the next time around. The Returned and Services League involved itself in the planning of the contingent's tour once again, demanding that at least half the group be made up of veterans, but, as Prime Minister Robert Menzies remarked in a memo to his Defence minister, it was, 'of course, referring to ex-servicemen of the 1939–45 war'.[30] The government accommodated the league, but its decision to send a 'purely service contingent' of 250 currently serving men and women meant that most First World War veterans were ineligible for the voyage.[31] As Defence officials noted, elderly ex-servicemen were unable 'to reach the desirable standard of medical fitness for the Contingent'.[32] The contingent's leader, Sir Edmund Herring, was the exception, but he had fought with the British Expeditionary Force, not the First AIF.[33] Unsurprisingly, neither Herring nor his charges lobbied the government to arrange a trip to the former Western Front.

The final itinerary reflected more recent preoccupations in the nation's war memory. Provisions were made for a stopover in Tobruk, where the contingent held a memorial service commemorating the Australians' brave defence of the town in 1941, and for a return via North America. The extended detour for the return leg of the trip was considered particularly important, because it would be used as an opportunity to 'show the Australian flag in American waters' and 'repay the visit made to Australia by a Canadian cruiser some time ago'. Moreover, the Defence department hoped it 'would have some value from the standpoint of the ANZUS Pact'.[34] In terms of war commemoration, Australian attention had turned away from Western Europe.

This was further illustrated by the unofficial laying of two plaques in St George's Memorial Church, Ypres, in the same year as Queen Elizabeth's coronation. The church had been built by private British subscriptions during the interwar years, and members of its board had approached the Australian government in the late 1920s hoping to raise funds for 'a window in memory of the Australians who fell in the Ypres salient'. Concerned that the church was denominational and that a substantial contribution had already been made towards the Menin Gate Memorial, government officials decided that 'the proposal ... should not be supported by public funds'. The request was passed on to the Returned Sailors' and Soldiers' Imperial League of Australia and the Anglican archbishops of Melbourne and Sydney, to see if they wished to canvass their supporters for private subscriptions. The RSSILA was 'much impressed with the proposal', as were the clergymen, but neither took any concrete action, and the idea was forgotten.[35]

A quarter of a century later, the federal executive of the Returned and Services League and the unit association of the 4th Machine Gun Battalion had plaques prepared for St George's. By then, the church was no longer recognised exclusively as a monument to the British Empire's dead of the Ypres salient, or even as being related distinctly to the First World War, but as a memorial raised 'to those of the British and Commonwealth Forces who [also] fell in the 1939–45 War'.[36] Thus, the decision of the two organisations to lay plaques should not be read as an action made in order to remember the fighting at Ypres in particular. The machine gunners acted because they felt 'their numbers were fast diminishing' and they wanted 'to establish some form of permanent memorial to their fallen comrades' before they had all passed away. Their offering was specific to their unit, not a particular battle: a commemorative gesture that had no wider significance for those unrelated to the battalion. The league's plaque was considerably broader in scope, but once again, as it was placed 'in memory of the Australian Forces who fell in two World Wars', it was clearly not only referring to the dead of the First AIF in Belgium.[37]

The exact reasons why the unit association and the league decided to lay plaques at St George's, rather than in other locations, are not entirely clear. In the case of the machine gunners, it is probable that selecting a location in Australia would have been difficult, as it was made up of members from all over the country. The church's appeal may have also resided in the fact that it was a rare place at which smaller units could make unique offerings to their dead and it was located in a region where 'many of their comrades lay'.[38] The inspiration underpinning the league's approach seems to have been more cynical; the idea was first floated when the federal executive learned that 'the New Zealand delegation to the 12th British Empire Service League Conference intended unveiling a plaque at Ypres'. Not wishing to be outdone by their antipodean cousins, the federal executive carried a motion for the creation of a similar plaque and organised a ceremony for the unveiling to take place after the empire league's conference in June 1953. The leader of that year's Australian Coronation Contingent, Herring, was still in Europe at the time and unveiled both plaques.[39] However, as the 250 members of Herring's party had long since left Europe by then, the event was all but completely ignored back home.

The general apathy towards the Western Front was also clear from waning enthusiasm for journeys to the former First World War battlefields. As we have seen, during the interwar period, reports from those foreign fields had regularly featured in newspapers and returned servicemen's publications as they responded to a public yearning to know that the dead were being cared for appropriately. After 1945, accounts of First World War cemeteries and battle sites in the press were rare. This was partially due to the fact that, without financial support, such a long voyage was still unaffordable for most Australians. Added to the imposing physical distance was the irreversible passage of time, which was reducing the First World War's relevance for contemporary Australians. A new generation of mourners wished to visit the sites of those who had died between 1939 and 1945 – most of whom were buried in the Pacific and the Middle East – while a significant number of potential pilgrims from the interwar period had become too old and frail to undertake the long journey to Europe. With politicians and the younger generation failing to show much interest, the 1914–18 battlefields held little appeal for anyone but the ageing cohort of First World War veterans, and most of those who made the trip were more interested in paying respects to old mates than in making grand commemorative gestures.[40]

Bean's account of a battlefield tour that he made in the early 1950s best exemplifies the interests of men returning to the former battlegrounds in that period. While not a veteran himself, Bean was driven by the same impulse to revisit the sites he had known so well:

> For years I have wondered whether one could find one's way about them [the old battlefields]. I had heard from others that the ground was unrecognisable. I can only say that, in this respect, for me it was as though I had left it yesterday ...
>
> Roadways, then only recognisable where traces of a straight bank or ditch led across some shell-flayed area, are again green flowering lanes; but there they are exactly where one expected to find them.

Pozières still held a magnetic attraction for Bean, and he devoted most of his initial report to describing the battlefield and reminiscing about the scenes he had witnessed in 1916. Three-quarters of the way through the report, he admitted he was indulging his own specific interests – 'I have only mentioned the landmarks at Pozières' – but by then, he had only left enough space to half-heartedly name several other sites he visited.[41] His account was published in a major paper, but unlike much of his earlier work, it was an overwhelmingly sentimental piece that did not attempt to place his wanderings within the broader narrative of the First World War. Written in such a way, Bean's and other veterans' accounts resonated little with the growing number of Australians to whom names like Pozières and Mouquet Farm were completely foreign.

On the Verge of Oblivion

By the end of the 1950s, it was not just the memory of the Western Front that was at risk of being consigned to the annals of cold, distant history, but the Anzac tradition itself. Attendance numbers at Anzac Day services were reportedly falling, and a host of commentators were forecasting Anzac's demise. One of the main reasons behind this perceived fall was the inability of the tradition's guardians, the aggressively conservative Returned and Services League, to adapt commemoration to the public at large and effectively communicate to the younger generation wider meanings behind the tradition.[42] Interrogating the gap between myth and reality, two plays written and performed around this time – *For Valour* (1958) and *The One Day of the Year* (1960) – best captured the frustration many felt towards Anzac. *For Valour* was written by Ric Throssell, son of the renowned Western Australian soldier Hugo Throssell VC, and was based on his father's struggles to run a farm in interwar Australia and subsequent suicide.[43] Alan Seymour's *One Day of the Year* approached the legend from a different angle, critiquing the boozy antics of returned men on 25 April through an exploration of the relationship between Second World War veteran Alf Cook and his son, Hughie.[44] Seymour's play, in particular, struck a chord; several productions were arranged in the early 1960s, with one company performing it in ninety-five towns throughout New South Wales and Queensland, thanks to funding from the Arts Council of New South Wales. It was also adapted for television and named best television drama in 1962.[45] Three years later, Geoffrey Serle observed, 'The natural tendency of many of the younger generation is to regard a military legend as sorry stuff on which to build a tradition'.[46] With the ex-servicemen who fought in the First World War gradually passing away and the traditional Anzac rhetoric and ritual holding no appeal for the younger generation, the legend's future was in question.

Australia's prolonged involvement in the Vietnam War between the mid-1960s and the early 1970s added to growing disillusionment with the perceived militarism of war commemoration and tarnished the romantic image of the Anzac soldier. Initially, a majority of Australians had backed the government's decision to commit troops, including conscripts, to the conflict in support of the United States.[47] However, as the war dragged on, it became an increasingly divisive issue. The 1968 Tet Offensive shook the public's faith in the United States' capacity to eventually triumph, while reports of Australian soldiers torturing a young Vietnamese woman and the infamous My Lai massacre involving American soldiers further damaged popular support for the war.[48] By 1969, public opinion was turning against the war, and in the 1970s, there were several high-profile moratorium marches held throughout Australia.[49] Growing anti-war sentiment helped to undermine the traditional ideals of aggressive masculinity and martial proficiency that had been the key tenets of the Anzac legend since the Gallipoli landing.[50]

Anzac's association with the British Empire also harmed its standing in the eyes of contemporary Australians. Before the 1960s, conceptualisations of Australian nationalism had never really questioned the Australia's place within the empire. The 'I' in AIF stood for Imperial, after all, and even though popular iterations of the Anzac legend could be highly critical of the British officer class, they 'did not challenge the hegemonic discourse about loyalty to Britain'.[51] Certain events during the Second World War may have strained relations between dominion and mother country – particularly the fall of Singapore to the Japanese in 1942, which saw 15,000 Australians taken prisoner – but Australians remained proud of their British heritage and the empire in the aftermath of the conflict.[52] However, two major developments in the postwar period gradually led to a decline in the importance of Britishness to Australian conceptions of nationalism. First, according to the historians James Curran and Stuart Ward, global decolonisation challenged 'the moral and racial assumptions of European imperialism', which helped 'accelerate the liquidation of Britain's empire', undermined the White Australia policy and forced Australian policymakers towards closer strategic association with the United States.[53] The second key development was Britain's economic turn towards Europe, which eventually brought an end to the privileges of the imperial trade preference system, threatening Australia's economic future. In attempting (and eventually succeeding) to join the European Economic Community, the mother country effectively turned its back on Australia.[54] The sense of Britishness that had long underpinned Australian nationalism now rang hollow, and efforts were made to forge a new nationalism freed from its imperial origins. In the 1960s and 1970s, the shift further dampened the appeal of Anzac, 'steeped as it was in the ritual and imagery of the "old" imperial patriotism'.[55]

Increasing disdain for Anzac was not just a popular phenomenon. With the exception of contributors to the world wars' official histories, no historians paid much attention to the experience of Australians at war. Liberal historians found the topic unpleasant, while those influenced by Marxism largely ignored 1914–18, because it was 'a war between nations … not a class war'.[56] Viewed as a conservative narrative, the Anzac legend also had an uncomfortable relationship with the leftist tradition. The Anzacs barely featured in Russel Ward's *Australian Legend* (1958) – a radical social history that proposed a vision of Australian national identity based on the egalitarian bushman – and this was in spite of nearly half a century's worth of rhetoric linking the formidable performance of Australia's citizen soldiers to their (supposed) bush origins.[57] When Ken Inglis drew attention to this lacuna in his seminal 1965 article, 'The Anzac Tradition', other historians began to follow suit, and the First World War and its legacy became viable subjects for academic interrogation.[58] Still, the impact of this new scholarly attention was not felt beyond the academy for over a decade.

In 1965, the Australian government and the Returned and Services League spent thousands of pounds partially subsidising the first major veteran pilgrimage to the Dardanelles, for the fiftieth anniversary of the Gallipoli landing. Despite the apparently wavering appeal of Anzac, *The Canberra Times* and the Australian Associated Press clearly felt the event was worthy of close media coverage and had two journalists, Ken Inglis and Norman Macswan, accompany the pilgrims. While there may have been shortcomings in the organisation, the event did not pass by unnoticed.[59] Conversely, when two reasonably large veterans groups organised pilgrimages to the former European battlefields in 1968 and 1971, they received no direct support from the Returned and Services League and little media coverage, and they failed to elicit much excitement among contemporaries. The first trip commemorated the fiftieth anniversary of the victorious 1918 Somme battles, and the second corresponded with the unveiling of a new sculpture for the 2nd Division memorial at Mont St Quentin. Had these pilgrimages been organised during the interwar years, there is every chance they would have captured the public's imagination. One of the key reasons for their failure to do so was that they were ostensibly limited to former members of specific divisions.[60] The 9th Brigade (3rd Australian Division) AIF Veterans' Association, which organised the 1968 pilgrimage, must have been aware that confining participation to its former brigade members alone would be too restrictive, but it only allowed other 3rd Division units, as well as wives and widows related to the division, to join the trip.[61] The 2nd Division veterans who arranged the 1971 voyage were a little more flexible, noting in an early circular to potential travellers:

> The pilgrimage is primarily for 2nd division veterans, wives however will be welcome. Furthermore, widows and next of kin of deceased veterans are eligible to join and will be included in the official receptions, which will be held in London, Paris, Amiens, Peronne and Ypres. Diggers who served in France or Belgium in

1916–18 are invited to join the tour and enjoy all the privileges except the official 2nd division receptions.[62]

It is unclear if any veterans from outside the 2nd Division took up the offer. In aiming their pitches to members of specific divisions, the organisers of the two trips limited prospective participants and diminished their pilgrimages' wider relevance. The 1968 voyage was, 'essentially, a service reunion', and there is little to indicate the 1971 venture was any different.[63]

The organisers of both pilgrimages applied for government support, on the basis that their charges should be viewed as representatives of the entire nation. Thanks to political connections, the 1968 pilgrimage's coordinators, Fred Cahill and Les Irwin, obtained the patronage of the Australian minister for External Affairs Paul Hasluck and the promise of support from Australian embassies. There were limits, however, to how many of their demands the government would entertain. Even with Hasluck's backing, Cahill and Irwin failed to convince the treasury to offer concessions to participants 'who could not meet their expenses', as it had done for the Gallipoli pilgrimage in 1965. The treasury's decision to reject the funding was indicative of how far the Somme had been pushed to the margins of contemporary Anzac remembrance. Not only did the 1968 trip attract a considerably smaller number of participants than the 1965 voyage – '314 members formed the Gallipoli pilgrimage. It is expected that between 30 and 40 members will join the Somme pilgrimage' – but, crucially, the government felt the event did 'not rank as highly as the Gallipoli Pilgrimage in national significance'.[64] The 1971 pilgrimage organisers did not even broach the issue of funding, probably because they had extensively lobbied the government for a new $23,000 statue at Mont St Quentin.[65] Nonetheless, they believed they were entitled to 'the accolade of officialdom', because the pilgrimage's grand objective was 'to cement the bonds uniting Anglo-Australian, Franco-Australian and Belgique-Australian relations and make these bonds imperishable'. Foreign affairs staff were less sanguine in their views of what the venture could actually achieve, but they ensured the pilgrims had embassy support for key ceremonies, giving them official lustre.[66]

The 1968 and 1971 pilgrims saw themselves as engaging not only in commemorative and nostalgic journeys but also in what has been termed 'memorial' or 'commemorative diplomacy' – that is, 'a dimension of diplomatic practice that seeks to materialise and mobilise a shared sense of the past at the intersection of collective memory and transnational history'.[67] They cast themselves as makeshift ambassadors charged with reaffirming links with various localities, particularly Amiens, Villers-Bretonneux and Mont St Quentin, in France. They also visited Belgium, but the brief forays across the border were not given any particular prominence in the respective itineraries. Informing the burgomaster of Ypres of the impending visit, Cahill noted that his group's timetable would not permit them to stay 'very long'. Not even a full day was set aside for the Belgian leg of that voyage, during which the party was scheduled to attend ceremonies at Ypres and Messines, as well as squeeze in visits to other local sites of interest. The second group of pilgrims at least spent a night at Ypres, to catch the Last Post ceremony at the Menin Gate Memorial. Judging from the two pilgrimages' programs and the absence of references to official Belgian ceremonies in the post-pilgrimage reports, the travellers' interest in Belgium focused on 'nostalgic' tours of 'villages with names well known to the Diggers', as opposed to formal observances that might have strengthened a Belgian-Australian bond.[68]

In France, the veterans retraced their footsteps over familiar battlefields and rest areas, but as the Somme had always been the main destination for both groups, considerable effort went into arranging official events of genuine import as well. While the ceremonies around Ypres made limited demands of locals, the veterans expected the participation of local mayors, *anciens combattants* and leading citizens in France.[69] Adding to the significance of these occasions was the inclusion of gestures such as a medal presentation ceremony in 1971 and the naming of streets after Australia, in Amiens in 1968 and in Mont St Quentin in 1971. For the 1968 pilgrimage, Australian prime minister John Gorton even provided an address to be read out at Villers-Bretonneux, in which he paid tribute to the French villagers who had 'so faithfully remembered the glory and the sacrifice' of the AIF in the town fifty years earlier.[70] Organisers and embassy officials considered these events as playing a substantial role in the success of both pilgrimages. According to their reports, the 1968 journey 'publicised Australia very favourably, arousing great interest everywhere' while 'reaffirming warmly the links forged in the First World War between Australia and France'.[71] Officials commenting on the 1971 pilgrimage were more circumspect, perhaps because the affair 'occupied the Embassy [in Paris] heavily for a period of some weeks'. They did note that, thanks to the cooperation of French authorities, the events were successful and the embassy was able to make 'a wide range of contacts in the Péronne and Amiens areas'.[72] However, the ventures had no apparent long-term effect on Australian commemoration in Europe. They did not reawaken any desire for pilgrimage to the French battlefields, and the sole attempt to establish an enduring official, albeit local, link with the Somme region – a proposal from the mayor of Newcastle to twin his city with Amiens – was unsuccessful.[73]

Origins of a Belgian Anzac Tradition

Paradoxically, while a growing number of Australians no longer found succour in the Anzac legend in the 1960s and 1970s, steps were being taken to establish an annual Anzac Day ceremony at Ypres, and the first one was held on 25 April 1967. The advent of this tradition predated the pilgrimages in 1968 and 1971, but those major veterans' voyages were the last of their kind. The commemoration of Anzac Day at Ypres, on the other hand, heralded the beginning of a long-term commemorative relationship between Australia and the Belgian town. In terms of participation and ritual, this event paled in comparison to the more elaborate ceremonies and festivities linked with 25 April in Australia. A combined party of eight from the Australian and New Zealand embassies participated, along with the burgomaster of Ypres and a handful of local officials, including the town's tourism officer. With the exception two other invitees – the military commander of the province and a Reverend Powell from Ghent, whom the Australian embassy suggested be invited to read prayers in English – the event was very much a local affair, with no state or provincial civil servants or ministers invited to attend.[74] The restrained nature of the day was reflected in its short program, which began at 10am and ended with a civic reception at 11:30am. In between, there was just enough time for a ceremony at the Menin Gate Memorial, the laying of a wreath at the Ypres War Victims Monument and a visit to St George's Memorial Church. Significantly, no arrangements were made to see the memorials at Polygon Wood or Hill 60, both of which lay outside of the Ypres council area. Despite the day's fairly limited scope, Australian and New Zealand officials were evidently pleased with how it proceeded, and they contacted the burgomaster of Ypres the following year indicating that they wished to make it 'an annual event'.⁷⁵ Ypres officials were happy to oblige, and so an Anzac Day tradition in the salient was born.

The commemoration of Australian dead in Europe was not a novel phenomenon when the tradition was finally introduced to Ypres in 1967. Throughout the interwar period, French villagers had tended Australian graves and laid wreaths at sites like the 2nd Division memorial and Villers-Bretonneux.⁷⁶ Not all such gestures were uniquely local undertakings. In Mont St Quentin, a year after Charles Web Gilbert's memorial for the 2nd Division had been unveiled with considerable fanfare in the presence of former Allied general Ferdinand Foch, the Australian prime minister's department provided funds for the town council to place a wreath at the monument on the anniversary of the battle, on 31 August 1926. The Australians intended to make this an annual event, and the mayor of Mont St Quentin agreed, although he proposed a slight date change. The parish's patronal fete fell on the first Sunday in September, and on the following Monday, a mass was held for parishioners who had died. In light of this, the mayor suggested that on the Monday 'a little ceremony could take place – quite simple and without speeches'. The Australians accepted this compromise and set up an account to finance the ceremony's continuation, but the locals also included the memorial in other unfunded events, such as 11 November commemorations and the unveiling of the town's own war memorial, in 1927.⁷⁷ The outbreak of the Second World War initially curtailed commemorative activity related to the First AIF's exploits in France. However, thanks to the personal enterprise of Keith Officer, the Australian ambassador to France, small Anzac Day ceremonies were held at Mont St Quentin, Corbie, Péronne, Sailly-le-Sec, Pozières and Villers-Bretonneux in the early 1950s. While Anzac Day did not become an annual event at most of these locations, motivated locals at Villers-Bretonneux soon took steps to officially recognise the continuing Australian interest in their town by forming a welcoming committee in order to properly receive antipodean guests and facilitate the ritualisation of the day.[78]

That Ypres was comparatively slow in establishing an Anzac Day tradition was due to two major factors. We have already noted how Australians put less effort into commemorating Anzac achievements in the salient than they did in the Somme region. It is just as important to note that Ypres – unlike Villers-Bretonneux, Pozières and others – was a key site of memory for the entire British Empire by the end of the war. Between 1914 and 1918, the salient had come to epitomise the Allied, and particularly the British, determination to defend the world against the Central Powers' aggression, while the gradual destruction of the region's majestic medieval architecture under artillery bombardment served to highlight the perceived barbarity of the enemy's kultur. By the end of 1918, the British Expeditionary Force had lost up to a quarter of a million men in the infamous salient, leaving many corners of Belgian Flanders, in the words of Rupert Brooke, 'for ever England'.[79] Consequently, British interest in the town did not subside with the signing of the armistice, in 1918.

As discussed in chapter 2, the erection of the Menin Gate Memorial and its grand unveiling, in 1927, reinforced Ypres' significance to Britons, attracting thousands of pilgrims from across the English Channel.[80] But the strong imperial connection to Ypres did not revolve around the Menin Gate alone. Years before Blomfield's memorial was completed, the British had already awarded the town the Military Cross in the presence of King Albert of Belgium.[81] Other reminders of the city's significance to the empire were manifest in numerous battle monuments and Imperial War Graves Commission cemeteries scattered throughout the region. Many unofficial organisations and individuals also contributed to Britain's deep memory footprint at Ypres during the interwar years. They included large numbers of independent travellers who journeyed to the city, drawn not only by its 'iconic, spiritual importance', but also because 'it was logistically easier to visit than the Somme'. Moreover, the township contained a large community of British expatriates, many of whom worked for the IWGC and, having married local women, had settled down in the region. Their numbers were so substantial that they even established a school to ensure their offspring could receive a British education.[82] Through both pilgrims and permanent residents, the British maintained a living as well as monumental presence at Ypres after 1918.

Arguably the most important unofficial agency working to keep the British memory of the salient 'green' at the time was the aptly named Ypres League. Founded in 1921, long before the IWGC had been able to fulfil its sacred mission of commemorating every empire soldier killed in Belgium, the Ypres League's main object was 'to perpetuate the memory of all that Ypres means to us by keeping alive the spirit of comradeship, and by commemorating the 200,000 dead now lying out in the Salient'.[83] It had powerful backing, counting Field Marshal Sir John French, first Earl of Ypres, the former commander of the British Expeditionary Force, and the author Arthur Conan Doyle among its members, as well as being patronised by King George V and Edward, Prince of Wales (later Edward VIII). It undertook commemorative initiatives, such as publishing a regular newsletter, *The Ypres Times*, played a leading role in the construction of St George's Memorial Church and supported British pilgrims (ex-servicemen and bereaved relatives, not 'tourists') travelling to the town.[84]

There was little in the Ypres League's activities to excite much attention in Australia. Its assistance to pilgrims did not extend to travellers from the Commonwealth, and the St George's Memorial Church proposal was of little interest to those unlikely to ever see it – hence a tepid Australian response to funding requests in the late 1920s. The league's imperial focus can be seen in its selection of 31 October as the most appropriate date on which to commemorate Ypres Day. Marking the anniversary of the 'crisis' of the first battle of Ypres, in 1914, the date may have been an 'ever memorable' moment in the history of the British Expeditionary Force, but it meant little to the dominions, because none of their forces played a part in the engagement. Only a handful of Australians became league members, and through lack of interest, its branches in Melbourne and Sydney closed shortly after they were founded.[85] The league's activities served to weave the British Empire tightly into the fabric of Ypres' commemorative landscape, but its message failed to resonate with those living far from the empire's epicentre.

Belgian locals were keenly aware of their town's significance to the British. Many enterprising individuals began catering for their wants and needs in various ways. Some Flemings ran commercial activities, such as temporary bars and war souvenir shops, which were a source of tension between locals and British visitors. Other Ypres residents, particularly council officials, were more attuned to British sentiments; they worked to ensure a civil and military presence at various imperial ceremonies and organised receptions for large groups of visitors.[86] These gestures were appreciated and set a precedent for future interactions between town authorities and pilgrims.

The establishment of the daily Last Post ceremony at the Menin Gate Memorial, a regular Belgian tribute to the British dead of the salient, also added significantly to the town's appeal for pilgrims and tourists. The driving force behind the ceremony was local chief of police Pierre Vandenbraambussche. The Last Post ceremony performed at the unveiling of the monument had so impressed the commandant that he formed a Last Post Committee of equally enthusiastic residents whose aim was to make the ceremony a daily event. On 2 July 1928, the committee's buglers sounded the first of these daily performances at the Menin Gate.[87] It quickly became one of the best known and most enduring commemorative acts of the interwar years. Occasionally, there were controversies surrounding the ritual that echoed the criticism of 'vulgar' tourist traps and betrayed many a British pilgrim's implicit distrust of the Belgians. These centred on rumours suggesting the ceremonies were funded by British ex-servicemen and the Belgians were abusing the arrangement by failing to provide a sufficient number of appropriately attired buglers. Such claims missed the point that the nightly ritual was a *locally* inspired tribute that survived thanks to subscriptions and did not necessarily adhere to British standards concerning dress because the musicians were 'Belgian peasants [dressed] in their working clothes', not professional soldiers. Still, many pilgrims reported favourably on the solemnity of the 'wonderful' and 'inspiring' ceremony, and some veterans groups showed their gratitude by offering silver bugles and financial support to the Last Post Committee.[88]

The German occupation of Ypres during the Second World War did not bring a definitive end to the locals' relationship with the empire; it was merely a period of enforced hiatus. On the very day the Germans left the town, the Last Post ceremony, which had been put on hold throughout the occupation, was resumed. Despite this, British interest in Ypres dwindled after the Second World War.[89] Into this void stepped the local community, which began to play a larger role in the organisation of activities associated with British commemoration than it had before 1939. The 1960s, with a host of important anniversaries – the 10,000th sounding of the Last Post (1960), the 50th anniversaries of the beginning of the First World War (1964) and the third battle of Ypres (1967), and the 40th anniversary of the Menin Gate Memorial's unveiling – provided motivated locals with several high-profile occasions to reaffirm the town's links to Britain. The 50th anniversaries, in particular, were seen as big drawcards, and the town's tourism department took a proactive stance in distributing advertising material to the countries of the British Commonwealth, while the burgomaster announced through the press that all veterans who had fought in the salient should return 'to pray for the dead and strengthen peace'.[90]

This publicity piqued the interest of at least a few Australians. Several veterans were so moved after seeing the burgomaster's invitation that they wrote to him, in some cases just to share their experiences – for example, one wrote that he had always remembered the fighting at Ypres and that, although he was unable to go back, he would be thinking of those who had passed, 'praying for them and peace'. Others made practical enquiries, about the timing of events and possible concessions.[91] These commemorative plans inspired the Australian ambassador to Belgium Ralph Harry to float the idea of an official Anzac Day ceremony at Ypres. On receiving the 'official program of events for 1967', the embassy wrote to Ypres' burgomaster Albert Dehem,

> The Ambassador ... is at present considering some suitable way in which we might most fittingly, on April 25 next year, observe Anzac Day – the Australian and New Zealand national day of remembrance of those who died in war. Obviously the most suitable place for a ceremony would be in the former battlegrounds of West Flanders.

Several months later, Harry confirmed the New Zealanders' interest, and the town council commenced planning an event 'worthy' of Australia and New Zealand.[92] Town officials and representatives of Belgian veterans associations were invited to the ceremony, and the public was informed through a short newspaper article that provided readers with a summary of the day's program as well as outlining the significance of the day to Australians and New Zealanders and describing the Anzacs' involvement in the battles of 1917.[93] Satisfied with the results of this inaugural event, the Australian and New Zealand ambassadors arranged to take turns organising more or less identical annual tributes in concert with the Ypres town authorities.[94] It had taken fifty years, but belated interest shared by local and Australian officials finally ensured the regular commemoration of Anzac in Belgium. Nevertheless, even with the extension in 1981 of the day's official program to include visits to Polygon Wood and Tyne Cot Cemetery, it remained a minor event in the Anzac calendar for many years.[95] The founding of an Anzac tradition in Belgian Flanders did little to increase the public profile of Messines or third Ypres back in Australia. It did, however, provide a platform from which to launch more elaborate commemorative initiatives as the First World War centenary approached.

Reinventing a Tradition

In *The Invention of Tradition*, Eric Hobsbawm argues that factors such as the 'rapid transformation of society' and the inflexibility or disappearance of 'institutional carriers and promulgators' of 'old' traditions pave the way for the invention of new ones.[96] These factors were clearly evident in 1960s–70s Australia, at least as far as Anzac was concerned. The waning influence of ageing and conservative Returned and Services League members, youthful disinterest, the Vietnam debacle and a belief that the British had abandoned Australia in its economic rapprochement towards Europe had all eroded the appeal of the traditional legend. Yet, from the mid-1970s onwards, there were signs Anzac was beginning to undergo a revival, thanks to subtle but significant shifts in the legend's emphasis. These changes did not come about as a result of political investment in Australia's First World War memory; they came from below. Bill Gammage's scholarly *The Broken Years* and Patsy Adam-Smith's bestseller *The Anzacs* were at the forefront of this revival, inspiring a raft of 1980s films and television series that reinvigorated the legend for a generation that had never experienced war firsthand.[97] The new representations reaffirmed the claim that Australia's involvement in the First World War had defined the nation and retained the prominence of the much-vaunted qualities of sacrifice, mateship, classlessness and larrikinism – universal qualities that apply just as easily to civilians as to soldiers – while toning down the martial and imperialist elements, key themes in the earliest portrayals of the legend. The Anzacs were still antipodean heroes, but they were no longer Charles Bean's aggressive, all-conquering warriors, 'always keen for the experience of plunging a bayonet into the enemy'.[98] Instead, they largely became young victims of war, sacrificed on the altar of British incompetence. The Gallipoli campaign provided the necessary threads – heroism, victimhood, imperial betrayal – for a new generation to patch up the old, fraying interwar narrative. Accounts of fighting on the Western Front further illustrated these themes but were far from central to the reinvigorated legend. In particular, Messines and third Ypres had little to add to narratives that cast every battle as a bittersweet victory at best and an utter tragedy at worst.

Gammage's *Broken Years* was published in 1974 and drew heavily on the diaries, letters and memoirs of soldiers in the Australian War Memorial's collections. It focused unabashedly on the experiences and sentiments of individual soldiers, and this emphasis fitted neatly into the 'new' social history of the 1960s and 1970s. It was also similar to Bean's own approach in the *Official History*. Other similarities included *The Broken Years*' affirmation of 'key themes of the *Official History*, in particular, Bean's assertion that the characteristics of the Australian soldier were derived from the bushman's code of behaviour'. However, Bean 'mainly told what soldiers *did*, rather than what they *felt*'; Gammage was concerned with the inverse.[99] While Bean argued that Australian nationhood had been confirmed through 'the test of a great war', Gammage's outlook was more tragic.[100] By relying on personal accounts as opposed to operations files, Gammage's analysis 'lack[ed] tactical and strategic explanations of events ... This lack of overarching view makes war seem pointless'.[101] The result was a narrative that tempered the aggressive masculinity and martial nationalism of the early Anzac legend, instead proffering a lament for the loss of the social paradise Australia could have become, had it not been for the 1914–18 conflict.

Four years after *The Broken Years* appeared, Patsy Adam-Smith's popular history of Australians in the First World War, *The Anzacs*, was published. While Gammage's book met with modest commercial success, Adam-Smith's work – a joint winner of *The Age* Book of the Year Award – appealed to a far greater number of Australians, going through numerous reprints and editions after its release. Recounting the war through diaries, letters and memoirs of individual participants, as well as through interviews with ageing veterans, *The Anzacs* was not all that dissimilar to *The Broken Years* and was just as candid in its focus on the horrors of war. 'War *is* hell', Adam-Smith declared on the opening page, but her vision of 1914–18 and its consequences for the young Australian nation was not quite as tragic as Gammage's, and her account took pride in Australian achievements and sacrifices:

> You [the veterans to whom she dedicated the book] had the greatest number of casualties per men on the field of all the Allied armies;

> you travelled furthest, were away the longest. You were the only volunteers. You came from a newer land, were a younger race than any who entered that awful arena. When time has removed this age to a distance, our descendants will speak of you as we now speak of the three hundred at Thermopylae.

Moreover, while Adam-Smith did address unpalatable aspects of the Australians' involvement in the war, her approach was less critical than Gammage's. She allowed the sources to speak for themselves – a method that has been imitated in many personal First World War narratives published by the descendants of Australian ex-servicemen – the result of which was a text largely made up of quotations taken verbatim from various sources with very little analysis.[102]

The appeal of both *The Broken Years* and *The Anzacs* for a contemporary audience lay in their capacity to condemn the First World War, lionise the fighting man and show empathy for the hardships he endured. This approach had much in common with the modern futility narratives that many Australians had found odious during the interwar years. In a post-Vietnam era in which symbols of militarism had lost much of their gloss, it was possible to portray the First World War as largely pointless without rousing widespread opposition. The depiction of the Anzacs as brave but vulnerable individuals who bore the brunt of seemingly meaningless, industrialised warfare, as opposed to bellicose warriors seeking to kill the enemy, also tapped into a growing 'interest in the "traumatic" impact of war'. With particular reference to the 1980s, Christina Twomey has argued that

> the concept of trauma has … allowed Australians access to the 'reality' of past wars: emotion can be a substitute for experience. The older language of manhood, glory and heroism did not allow for the same degree of identification; trauma, through the very breadth of its definition, is something anyone can experience.[103]

Gammage's and Adam-Smith's works were in the vanguard of this traumatic turn. They may have included numerous sources that referenced Australian martial prowess, but the overall tone of their works was one that highlighted the suffering and trauma of the Anzacs. Nowhere was this clearer than in Adam-Smith's preface: 'we must remember not to castigate the victims of war – and *every* man who fights is a victim' (italics added). This conception of the fighting man as victim proved to be a potent factor in Anzac's revival.

As early as the interwar years, the fighting in Belgium in 1917 had lent itself to exceptionally tragic portrayals in popular accounts and academic histories. It had also spawned one of the most enduring (and probably false) tales of the war – the Kiggell anecdote – which recounted the story of Douglas Haig's chief of staff Lieutenant-General Sir Launcelot Kiggell breaking down when he arrived close to the front lines at Passchendaele. 'Good God, did we really send men to fight in this?' he apparently exclaimed; the reply he received was that it was far worse further ahead.[104] It is hardly surprising then that, unlike Bean, neither Gammage nor Adam-Smith had much trouble integrating the AIF's Belgian battles into their narrative. For example, even though Gammage claimed that Messines was 'the swiftest and greatest British victory' up to that point in the war, his view of the battle was utterly pessimistic, as he went on to point out that 'victory could not avert tragedy; 6,800 Australians were killed or wounded during the battle'. His appraisal of third Ypres was equally negative. General Herbert Plumer's step-by-step method, which more enthusiastic writers ever since have hailed as grinding down the Germans, became 'a tactic of caution and despair' in *The Broken Years*, while Adam-Smith's account suggested there were no real tactics or strategy at all: 'Neither side knew exactly what it was fighting for ... They just ranged backwards and forwards over the churned-up sickened soil'. Before 1939, most Australian accounts had been able to salvage something positive from Messines and Ypres; no such redemption was forthcoming in *The Broken Years* or *The Anzacs*.

Gammage's and Adam-Smith's descriptions of Messines and third Ypres were brief. Gammage spent fewer than ten pages on them, in a chapter entitled 'Fighting in *France*' (italics added). Adam-Smith was equally sparing in her account; indeed, barely half of her 'Wipers' (an anglicisation of the word 'Ypres') chapter, addressing third Ypres, was given to the campaign, and she made no explicit mention of Messines at any point in her book. Messines and third Ypres were not the only campaigns the authors glossed over. As their aim was to explore the unique experience of Australian soldiers, rather than analysing the battles in which they fought, *The Broken Years* and *The Anzacs* tackled *all* of the AIF's Western Front engagements with considerable brevity. This is clear from the structures of the books. One-third of Gammage's work dealt with the Australians' time in 'France', yet only one chapter out of three provided readers with descriptions of the 1916–18 battles, while the other two identified and examined the particularities of the Anzac character throughout the same period. Adam-Smith's discussion of the various engagements was just as narrow but spread out over a handful of chapters in which she addressed a multitude of other topics, ranging from venereal disease to the Royal Australian Navy. In this context, the specifics of Messines, third Ypres and the other Western Front battles were largely ignored or lost in the detail, with the exception of their respective casualty figures, which Gammage and Adam-Smith included, to highlight the extent of Australian suffering and sacrifice. Analysing the state of Australian military historiography, Joan Beaumont and Vijaya Joshi have argued that for many, 'the battles fought have become secondary to the legacy left by the soldiers who fought them'.[105] Nowhere is this more evident than in *The Broken Years* and *The Anzacs*, which were the pioneers of the trend.

Gammage's and Adam-Smith's treatments of Gallipoli, the campaign that gave 'an almost epic-less land' a founding narrative, was more developed than those of the Western Front. Each author devoted comparatively more space to the Dardanelles campaign than to any other of the war. In the chapters discussing this theatre of the war, the salient arguments concerning the horror of war, the courage and suffering of the troops and the questionable British leadership were all present. Gammage even called his second chapter dealing with the Australians at the Dardanelles 'Nationhood, Brotherhood and Sacrifice', and Adam-Smith divided her narrative into two parts, 'The Beginning' and 'After Gallipoli', suggesting that an anno Domini had been reached in the history of the young Australian nation. After recounting the events at Gallipoli, that pivotal campaign in Australian history, all that followed in *The Broken Years* and *The Anzacs* was used to confirm what had been learned about the Anzacs during their eight months on the peninsula.

Anzacs on Screen

Gammage's and Adam-Smith's books rekindled enthusiasm for the First World War, but it was the following cinematic and televisual representations of Anzac that thrust the war back into popular memory. Over a dozen Australian-produced war films had been released between 1915 and 1940, but then interest in the First World War subsided, and it was not until the 1980s that popular accounts of the Anzac experience of 1914–18 returned to Australian screens. The appeal of these works lay in their capacity to reinforce the link between the Anzac and Australian nationalism, which had been weakened in previous decades, not least due to the legend's outdated warlike and imperialist implications. In the 1960s and 1970s, Australian governments and other proponents of new nationalism turned their backs on Anzac with its tangled connections to the British Empire when seeking symbols to unite an imagined national community within post-imperial Australia. However, their ventures largely 'failed to provide any cohesive means of invoking the much vaunted "spirit of the people"'. Britain's decline had left a 'conceptual void' at the heart of Australian nationalism.[106] A reinterpreted Anzac legend popularised in cinema and television filled this void. Combining the anti-militarist message of Gammage and Adam-Smith with largely negative – if not downright hostile – portrayals of the British, the films and television series of the 1980s severed the popular narrative of the First World War from its imperial roots. Unflattering descriptions of the British had never been alien to Anzac rhetoric, with many Australians drawing unfavourable comparisons between themselves and the 'curiously bovine' Tommies, as well as criticising British leadership during and after the war.[107] Still, these criticisms did not ultimately undermine notions of British race patriotism. With the collapse of Britishness as one of the central pillars propping up Australian nationalism, the context had shifted, and the British became antagonists who had 'duped' Australians into fighting imperial wars and sacrificed them in poorly planned and unnecessary battles.[108]

Released in 1981, Peter Weir's film *Gallipoli* ushered in a wave of Australian films and television series dealing with the First World War. Culminating in the dramatic death of one of the main characters during the infamous diversionary assault on the Nek, on 7 August 1915, this tale of youthful sacrifice clearly struck a chord with Australian audiences; *Gallipoli* dominated box office takings and the Australian

Film Industry awards that year.[109] A key reason for *Gallipoli*'s popularity lay in Weir's successful blending of the old elements of the Anzac narrative with the new, which reflected the work of the film's historical consultant, Bill Gammage, and its source material: *The Broken Years* and Bean's *Official History*.[110] Linking the well-worn themes of mateship, egalitarianism and sacrifice with contemporary notions of Anzac victimhood and British callousness, the film reinforced the Dardanelles campaign's position at the heart of the Anzac legend. Crucially for the evolution of the First World War narrative in Australia in subsequent years, the Western Front did not feature at all.

Several other productions broaching the Anzacs' experience of 1914–18 were released over the following decade, including the three mini-series *1915* (1982), *Anzacs* (1985) and *A Fortunate Life* (1986), and the film *The Lighthorsemen* (1987). With the exception of *Anzacs*, none covered the campaigns on the Western Front. This meant the 1985 mini-series was the only production to give the Belgian battles any screen time during the Anzac renaissance. Broadcast on Channel Nine and produced by Geoff Burrowes, the five-episode, eight-hour epic shared several elements with *Gallipoli*, employing the services of a contemporary knowledgeable about Anzac exploits, Patsy Adam-Smith, and drawing liberally on her work and Bean's *Official History* for inspiration.[111] Although its main characters were inventions of the scriptwriters, the series grounded its drama in the history of the war, with each episode structured around key battles in which the non-fictional 8th Battalion was involved between 1915 and 1918. *Anzacs* reaffirmed the major elements of the modern legend: British commanders were depicted as upper-class gentlemen who were uncaring or incompetent, or both, whereas the bulk of the Australian characters came from the bush and embodied noble traits such as 'initiative, courage, mateship and humour'.[112]

Only the first episode dealt with the Dardanelles campaign, leaving the following four to explore the Australians' experience on the Western Front, with the events of the final year being the main subject of episodes 4 and 5. In taking viewers beyond the shores of Gallipoli, *Anzacs* undercut the centrality of 1915 to the legend. The series also explicitly displaced the notion that the Australians lost their 'innocence' on Turkish beaches. In an echo of Bean, one of the characters declares the beginning of the battle of Pozières as the 'last day of our [the Australians'] innocence'.[113] Moreover, by positing the 'death of innocence' as having occurred in only the second episode, the series questioned this trope's 'traditional importance' in the Anzac narrative.[114] The real climax is reached in the fifth episode, when the AIF's five divisions are united into a single army corps under the command of the Australian general John Monash. Liberated from the constraints of British leadership, the Anzacs achieve their greatest victories. The mini-series thereby presented an updated interpretation of the triumphalist interwar epic without the imperialist connotations and with a somewhat toned-down emphasis on martial prowess.

With the exception of an oblique reference to the detonation of the mines on 7 June 1917, the battle of Messines went unmentioned in *Anzacs* as the 8th Battalion was not involved in the engagement. The battalion did fight at third Ypres, and the depiction of this campaign took up a significant portion of episode 3's runtime and a few minutes at the beginning of episode 4. However, unlike many interwar representations, which focused on the action at the front, *Anzacs* spent more time cutting between locations behind the lines in the build-up to the battle – David Lloyd George's office, various military headquarters, an estaminet, a field hospital – than portraying the fighting. The focus on scenes that revealed a sceptical British prime minister, a bloody-minded

Douglas Haig and fatalistic British troops was in keeping with the series' depiction of the Anzacs as victims of their own achievements, continually driven to slaughter by perfidious British generals.

Anzacs cast the Australians' victory at Menin Road as a harbinger of doom, setting the scene for a grand, inevitable tragedy. As one character declared, 'Some thought the end was in sight. [But] as we found out later, it would have been better if we had failed'. In the very next scene, Lloyd George laments that the Australians' victory means he cannot order a halt to Haig's offensive, with the consequence that 'the wealth and youth of Britain' will continue to be 'bled out for a few bleak acres of Belgium'.[115] These ominous predictions never fully materialise onscreen, as *Anzacs* – perhaps constrained by or sufficiently deferential to historical accuracy – depicts the 8th Battalion's action at Broodseinde as a success, which it indeed was, when considering the objectives captured on 4 October 1917. Admittedly, one of the main characters is severely wounded and another is blinded, which cuts short premature celebrations, as does the rain that has begun to pour down on the Australians as they dig in. Nonetheless, this conclusion is at odds with the grim premonitions made throughout. It certainly pales in comparison to the harrowing depiction of the artillery barrages at Pozières and the haggard state in which the survivors return from the front in the preceding episode. The imprint of Bean's *Official History* on the series' narrative arc is particularly evident here. *Anzacs* addresses many aspects that made third Ypres unique, including the hazardous and bloody struggles over German pillboxes, and airs the predictable recriminations against British command, with comments such as 'brains in their arses' and a scene giving form to the well-worn Kiggell anecdote.[116] Still, the mini-series does not highlight the extent of the Australian losses in Belgium. Although characters refer to third Ypres as a tragedy, it is clearly not as tragic as other engagements, nor is it as successful as what follows once the AIF's divisions are united. Once again, third Ypres was neither nadir nor zenith, but somewhere in between.

* * *

The period between the Second World War and the 1980s was critical in the evolution of the Australian memory of the First World War. As age gradually wore down 1914–18 veterans and younger generations of Australians became increasingly uncomfortable with the militarist and imperialist elements of the Anzac legend, the public's appetite for commemorating the First World War entered a decline. During these years, the First AIF's battles in Belgium, and the Western Front in general, largely faded from collective memory. Some ex-servicemen did engage in acts of remembrance related to Messines and third Ypres, but these were often too personal in nature and too poorly publicised to interest anyone outside the returned services community. Similarly, the introduction of an Anzac Day ceremony in Belgium may have laid the foundations for future collaboration between Australian officials and Ypres locals, but it went unnoticed at the time. Weakening the original Anzac legend's British origins, toning down its martial triumphalism and accentuating the tragedy of war, the influential works of Bill Gammage, Patsy Adam-Smith, Peter Weir and Geoff Burrowes revitalised the outdated narrative for younger Australians. While some of these contemporary interpretations included portrayals of fighting in Europe, they reasserted, with few exceptions, the Dardanelles campaign's place at the heart of Australia's 1914–18 experience. At the dawning of a new Anzac era, Gallipoli completely overshadowed the Western Front in Australian memory.

Chapter 6

LOST IN A SURFEIT OF MEMORY

In 1991, the Australian War Memorial finally placed two of its most physically impressive relics related to the Australian Imperial Force's battles in Belgium – the Menin Gate lions – on permanent display. The stone beasts originally flanked the Menin Road entrance to Ypres, that ill-reputed thoroughfare that thousands of Allied troops had trod on their way to the front.[1] The AWM obtained the sculptures in 1936, thanks to the efforts of an Australian officer with the Imperial War Graves Commission and the Australian high commissioner in London Stanley Bruce, who had convinced Ypres' burgomaster to offer the statues as gifts to Australia. AWM director John Treloar felt the acquisition was a 'great scoop' because of the lions' 'historical value'.[2] When they arrived, however, it was apparent the damage they had sustained during the war meant they would need to be restored before going on display. Little progress was made before the outbreak of the Second World War. They languished in storage and, like the battles they signified, were largely forgotten over the following fifty years. Their sudden appearance in prominent positions just inside the AWM's entrance in the early 1990s, therefore, was surprising. Despite their installation's coinciding with a wave of official commemorative activity, it did not generate any discernible fanfare and certainly did not herald the beginning of a newfound interest in Messines or third Ypres.

The initial motivation to put the lions on permanent display came from influences outside the AWM. During a trip to Europe in 1985, Australia's federal minister for Veterans' Affairs had found himself on the receiving end of 'pointed questions' posed by Ypres' burgomaster concerning the wellbeing of his city's former guardians.[3] This was not the first time the Belgians had enquired after the lions, but previous queries had failed to galvanise AWM officials into action.[4] On this occasion, the burgomaster cannily took advantage of the minister's presence in Belgium to put him on the spot. As there was 'a possibility of the Minister being embarrassed by the situation', the Department of Veterans' Affairs was keen to resolve the issue and pressured the AWM to find out what had happened to the lions. An investigation revealed the lesser damaged lion was located in an alcove off the Gallipoli gallery, while the second was in storage, having never been displayed.[5] This was hardly in keeping with Bruce's promise that the statues would 'be given a place of honour' among the AWM's collections.[6] In order to make up for the years of neglect, AWM director Jim Flemming instructed that urgent repairs be undertaken to bring the lions up to 'exhibition standard' so they might be put on display together.[7]

The AWM's decision to restore the lions in a manner that ensured the original stone was distinguishable from the reconstructed elements meant that the work took several years to complete. In 1991, the statues were finally ready to go on permanent display, but they did not find themselves in the AWM's First World War galleries. Instead, in a decision mirroring Treloar's belief that they should not be 'treated as relics and placed in a gallery', they were installed at the entrance to the AWM, among the site's most sacred features.[8] Having occupied this position for three decades, they are among the first statues visitors see when entering the AWM, and yet their public display has done little to anchor the Australian Imperial Force's Belgian campaigns in Australian memory. While a plaque located near to each lion informs visitors of their significance, only the most inquisitive pays them any heed. Subsumed within the AWM's monumental structure, the Menin Gate lions are there for all to see, but they inspire few to look more closely.

This chapter, which covers the late 1980s to the early years of the First World War centenary commemorations, makes apparent significant parallels between the case of the Menin Gate lions and broader trends in Australian efforts to commemorate Messines and third Ypres. In the 1980s, popular reinterpretations of Anzac propelled the legend into the public consciousness. From that point, there was increasing interest in many sites of Australian exploits in 1914–18. Gallipoli remained the epicentre of the contemporary Anzac narrative, but Australians 'rediscovered' several former battlefields in France. Villers-Bretonneux and Fromelles were standout examples, but both Bullecourt and Le Hamel were also sites of persistent efforts to commemorate Australian achievements on the Western Front. It is clear that neither officials nor the public entirely overlooked Messines and third Ypres during the period, but their interest in these battles was not sustained in any substantial, lasting manner. Just as the Menin Gate lions became part of the scenery at the AWM, Messines and third Ypres remained in the background of the modern Anzac legend, overshadowed by more fervently commemorated battles.

A Past Australians Could Live With

During the 1980s, the memory work of individual unofficial agents was largely responsible for reshaping and rekindling interest in the legend, but Anzac had not by that point 'assumed a central place in the construction of national [Australian] identity'.[9] This began to change from the end of the decade, when politicians and official agencies themselves – particularly the Department of Veterans' Affairs, which was responsible for the federal government's commemorative initiatives – took a more proactive approach towards commemorating Australia's military heritage.[10] Mark McKenna has argued that a key reason for this increased political interest in promoting Anzac as a defining national narrative was the failure of the 1988 bicentenary project to define a positive, coherent image of Australian identity that resonated with the public.[11] Marking the anniversary of the arrival of the British First Fleet at Port Jackson (Sydney) on 26 January 1788, Australia Day was largely devoid of elaborate ritual and had long occupied an ambivalent position for many in the calendar. The bicentenary festivities did little to change this. The attention devoted to the occasion further undermined its legitimacy in several ways. In spite of overtures from Bob Hawke's government, Indigenous Australians saw little to celebrate in an event marking 200 years of British colonisation and engaged in 'a year-long program of non-participation and protest' that sought to remind the population that 'white Australia had a black history'. Conservatives, on the other hand, were hardly enamoured with a perceived focus on multiculturalism and criticised the Australian Bicentennial Authority for 'subverting the core values of traditional Australia and presenting Australia as a land of incoherent diversity without unifying traditions and values'. Walking a tightrope between these criticisms, the bicentennial was heavy on spectacle, light on substance. As Peter Cochrane and David Goodman have noted, although 'the Bicentenary began in parliament with a bipartisan affirmation that there was a united Australian community', it ended as 'a postmodern affirmation of diversity'.[12] The bicentenary's shortcomings confirmed the unsuitability of 26 January as the date to celebrate the nation. Australia Day was simply not made of the stuff that tightly bound the imagined national community together.

The world wars and their impact on Australia were not overlooked during the bicentenary, but the Anzacs jostled for position with many other exemplars of the national character. Outside Australia, though, it was possible for countries to acknowledge and celebrate their relationship with Australia on more narrow terms. French officials used the occasion to engage in commemorative diplomacy, and their most significant gestures in 1988 emphasised the bonds forged between France and Australia during the world wars. In April 1988, French and Australian public servants organised a three-day commemorative program for a group of Australian officials, army officers and four First World War veterans invited to commemorate Anzac Day in France. The program focused exclusively on the Somme battlefields and included the unveiling of a plaque at Bullecourt; the donation of a painting to the same town; visits to the 1st, 2nd and 3rd Division memorials; and an Anzac Day ceremony at Villers-Bretonneux, during which the French minister for Defence decorated the veterans with three Legions of Honor and a Medal of National Merit.[13]

In his account of the ceremonies, Ken Inglis noted that 'Villers-Bretonneux was the right place for a Franco-Australian Bicentennial Anzac Day', because 'exactly seventy years earlier ... men of the 4th and 5th Australian Divisions had captured the town'.[14] But there was more to these ceremonies than celebrating anniversaries of First World War battles. Political issues relating to French nuclear testing in the Pacific and the Hawke government's support of New Caledonian independence had put a strain on Franco-Australian relations, and this influenced the French decision to dedicate a considerable amount of attention and resources to the bicentenary. To hammer home the point, the French

Defence minister André Giraud used a sizable portion of his Anzac Day speech to assert the republic's unity and the importance of France's policy of nuclear deterrence. According to Romain Fathi, these events opened up Villers-Bretonneux as 'a channel through which to address state issues' between France and Australia.[15] After decades of limited interest, the ceremonies and political posturing served to alert Australian officials to the shared site of memory's potential for commemorative diplomacy. Although the events linked to Anzac Day 1988 in France had a minimal impact on the memory of the war at the time, they laid the groundwork for a renewal of Australian commemorative activity in France.

A significant absence in the 1988 itinerary was Belgium. No visit was arranged to the 5th Division's memorial at Polygon Wood, as the monument was apparently 'too far to be involved in this weekend'.[16] The fact that the Belgians had shown no interest in linking their recognition of the bicentenary with Anzac commemoration may have also influenced the final schedule. Their failure to reference the First World War in 1988 is surprising, given that they had drawn on this shared past to engage with Australians previously. For instance, when Henri Fayat had become the first Belgian cabinet minister to officially visit Australia, in 1970, the Belgians had rushed to produce a photograph book, *In Grateful Memory*, to offer their hosts. The book contained a foreword by Belgian prime minister Gaston Eyskens, which stressed that, thanks to the numerous monuments and graves and the recently established Anzac Day ceremony at Ypres, Australia's 'brave countrymen' would 'never be forgotten by a grateful Belgium'.[17] Close to twenty years later, the Anzac Day tradition was still alive and well in Belgian Flanders, but as it lacked an explicit link to the bicentenary celebrations, it received no special attention.

The modern Anzac legend, as politicians from both major parties learned and exploited over the following decades, was not as divisive as Australia Day. Thanks to the works of Bill Gammage, Patsy Adam-Smith and Peter Weir, the contemporary legend had largely been shorn of its imperialist and overtly militarist elements, leaving a powerful narrative of nationhood born out of tragedy and sacrifice. Moreover, with its focus on the landing at Gallipoli, the narrative neatly displaced the symbolic 'birth of the nation' event to foreign shores, far from the increasingly contested history of white settlement in Australia, to which 26 January was inextricably tied. Only two years after the bicentenary, the seventy-fifth anniversary of the Anzac landing at Gallipoli provided Hawke with another, less fraught opportunity to define what it meant to be Australian, and he made the most of it.

In terms of contemporary political involvement in Anzac commemoration, Bob Hawke's 1990 pilgrimage to Gallipoli was a watershed moment. Before then, no prime minister had visited any First World War battlefield for more than fifty years. Perhaps more importantly, no government had ever fully sponsored a pilgrimage to the Dardanelles for ex-servicemen. In 1990, the government spent approximately $10 million on flying the prime minister and an entourage of fifty-eight veterans, eight war widows and eight legatees (children who lost a parent who had served in the Australian Defence Force) to Turkey for three days of services at Gallipoli.[18] For those hoping the pilgrimage would make up for the disappointments of 1988, it was money well spent. Where Hawke's bicentennial rhetoric had been 'rather limited', his utterances at Gallipoli gave the event 'a more distinctively Australian flavour'.[19] His address at Lone Pine asserted that mateship was central to the Anzac tradition and remained central to what it meant to be Australian seventy-five years later:

> At the heart of that [Anzac] tradition lay a commitment. It was a simple but deep commitment to one another, each to his fellow Australian.
>
> And in that commitment ... lies the enduring meaning of ANZAC, then and today and for the future.
>
> It is that commitment ... which defines, and alone defines, what it is to be an Australian. The commitment is all.[20]

The venture, covered by some seventy journalists and broadcast live, received an enormous amount of favourable media exposure. This evidently piqued public interest, as Anzac Day services attracted record crowds that year. Nor was the pilgrimage's influence on Anzac commemoration constrained to 1990; rather, it sparked an interest in mass pilgrimage to Gallipoli. Once again 25 April occupied a central place in the Australian calendar and popular imagination. As one reporter noted, 'Memorial days can't be foisted on to the public, as the lack of national pride in Australia Day demonstrates. Anzac Day now grips the imagination of Australians as our true national day'.[21] In affirming the centrality of Anzac at the heart of Australian identity, the 1990 pilgrimage was not only a popular but a political triumph.

A Tale of Two Returns

In the years following Hawke's Gallipoli pilgrimage, there was an ample number of seventy-fifth anniversaries of other First World War battles to commemorate, had the government been so inclined. The bulk of these, however, passed by with no particular fanfare. The opening of a memorial park commemorating the Australian Imperial Force's battles at Bullecourt on Anzac Day in 1992 was an exception and, once again, demonstrated French nous in attracting Australian attention.[22] The event received little publicity though, as a tussle for the Australian Labor Party leadership saw Paul Keating become Australian prime minister, and he had different commemorative priorities. Whereas Hawke had focused on mateship to disentangle Australia's First World War involvement from its imperial origins, Keating was far more concerned with the Second World War's impact on Australia. Keating hailed from a working-class Irish-Catholic family. He had an active Labor Party background and was a protégé of Jack Lang, the Labor premier of New South Wales who had suspended payments to British lenders during the Depression and was eventually dismissed by the state's British governor for his trouble. Keating had, as one commentator put it, carried pro-Australian, anti-British 'philosophical baggage for a long time'.[23] Moreover, he had a particularly personal connection to Britain's 'betrayal' of Australia at Singapore: his father's brother had been captured by the Japanese during the ill-fated defence of the city and died on the Sandakan death march in 1945. These elements informed Keating's 'radical nationalist' view of Australian history, which saw him assert that it was the Second Australian Imperial Force's struggles against the Japanese in the Pacific theatre that defined the nation.[24] Shortly after the fiftieth anniversary of the fall of Singapore, Keating derided the leader of the opposition, John Hewson, and the member for Bennelong, John Howard, as 'fogies who doffed their lids and tugged the forelock' to the same British establishment that 'decided not to defend the Malayan peninsula, not to worry about Singapore and not to give us our troops back to keep ourselves free from Japanese domination'.[25] Barely two months later, Keating was in Papua New Guinea for his first Anzac Day as prime minster, declaring that it was at Kokoda, not Gallipoli, that 'the depth of the soul of the Australian nation was confirmed'.[26]

Despite Keating's preference for commemorating the Second World War, in 1993 his government was involved in two major initiatives with close links to the Western Front: an official pilgrimage for ex-servicemen to Europe and the interment of the Unknown Soldier at the AWM. The Return to the Western Front Mission benefited from 'support from all shades of the political spectrum' and was cast 'as a national tribute to the sacrifices of Australian service personnel'.[27] The mission's four-day itinerary included visits to all divisional memorials, and the group spent nearly an entire day touring Australian sites of interest in Belgium, with the exception of Hill 60, in Zillebeke. While in Belgium, the veterans participated in wreath-laying ceremonies at Tyne Cot Cemetery and the Menin Gate Memorial, attended a reception hosted by the burgomaster of Ypres, and unveiled two out of eleven plaques – made by Melbourne periodontist Ross Bastiaan and installed on the Western Front with the support of the Department of Veterans' Affairs – at the Menin Gate and Passchendaele.[28] In Australia, the mission received a fair amount of press coverage, and the names of battles that had long since ceased to mean anything to many appeared once again in newspapers. One commentator hopefully suggested that the pilgrimage had, 'perhaps, brought home to new generations of Australians that Gallipoli was not the single event of World War I'.[29] 'Perhaps' was the operative word, as several elements undermined the mission's chances of making a long-lasting impression, especially when compared to Hawke's Gallipoli adventure. The pilgrimage did not take place around Anzac Day, or even Remembrance Day, the only two days related to the First World War that Australians still commemorated. Instead, in a decision reminiscent of interwar triumphalism, the pilgrims' voyage coincided with the seventy-fifth anniversary of the 2nd Division's recapture of Péronne, 'a uniquely Australian victory which was said to have so weakened the German defences that it hastened the end of the war'.[30] Consequently, the pilgrimage's climax, on 3 September, meant little to a public that had forgotten the dates of all but one First World War engagement. Part of the power behind Hawke's trip had resided in the fact that it fell on the most recognisable and ritualised date in the Australian calendar. Conversely, the selection of 3 September emphasised the exceptional nature of the mission rather than suggest it could become an annual event. The 1993 mission was also smaller in scope than the journey to Turkey in nearly every conceivable manner. Although more Australians had fought and died on the Western Front, only fourteen places were made available for returned men, and legatees only received two spots.[31] The contingent's smaller size still could have been offset by the presence of high-ranking officials. Hawke's participation in the ceremonies at Gallipoli had given the occasion added gravitas. Keating, however, did not travel with the 1993 pilgrims. He let the minister for Veterans' Affairs John Faulkner represent him. Given Keating's penchant for theatrics, his absence was a loss for the mission. The previous year, the prime minister had kissed the ground in Papua New Guinea and made provocative statements that placed Kokoda at the heart of the Anzac legend which helped rehabilitate that engagement, and other battles in the Pacific theatre, in collective memory.[32] The pilgrimage to Europe did not throw up such talking points. Faulkner does not appear to have made such grand claims concerning the battles on the Western Front, and if he did, the media seemed more interested in recording the veterans' thoughts and their 'moving' efforts 'to pay a final respect at the graves of mates of their youth'.[33] Deeply touching as the pilgrimage may have been, it lacked memorable speeches or gestures to capture the public's imagination.

The Western Front mission's peregrinations were quickly overshadowed. For nearly three-quarters of a century, Australia's First World War dead had been represented by an Unknown Soldier of the

British Empire buried in Westminster Abbey. Finally, the time came, on Remembrance Day 1993, to replace this 'quaint archaism' with a symbol more fitting of the post-imperial nation Australia had become. Similar proposals had been floated before, but it was only in the early 1990s that officials decided to inter an unidentified soldier in the AWM's Hall of Memory. As opposed to the Western Front mission, which had little potential for public participation, the interment grew into 'an event of national importance' in which Keating and the Department of Veterans' Affairs actively encouraged all Australians to participate. The event generated a substantial amount of public discussion, and on 11 November 1993, 25,000 people lined Anzac Parade to watch the soldier's last journey, while the ABC broadcast the ceremony live. By the time the soldier's tomb was finally sealed, three days later, some 50,000 mourners had entered the Hall of Memory to pay their respects.[34]

There was a Belgian connection to the burial, albeit a barely noticeable one amid the pomp and ceremony. In another example of the increasing significance of northern France in Australian officials' commemorative initiatives, those behind the project had opted to inter in Canberra the remains of an unidentified soldier originally buried at Villers-Bretonneux instead of at Gallipoli. They justified this decision by pointing out that many more Australians had died on the Western Front than in Turkey. The disinterment presented officials with a chance to further consolidate ties with locals at Villers-Bretonneux, but they also took the opportunity to reaffirm links across the Franco-Belgian border. This was achieved by making arrangements to have the soldier's remains lie in state in Ypres' famous cloth hall for one night and by inviting the town's burgomaster (along with the mayor of Villers-Bretonneux) to attend the reburial as an official mourner. This was no more than a deft act of memorial diplomacy undertaken by officials who most likely had their eye on future commemorative ventures. Only about fifty people attended the Last Post service at the Menin Gate Memorial with the disinterred soldier's remains present, and when these were transferred to the cloth hall, the doors of the building were closed, locking out the few Belgians who wished to pay their respects.[35] These minor gestures were lost in the broader context of the entombment in Australia. The burial of the Unknown Soldier commemorated more than Australian sacrifices on the Western Front, or even those in the whole of the First World War. It had the broader aim of honouring 'the memory of all those men and women who laid down their lives for Australia'.[36]

Importing the Last Post

Official interest in commemorating Australian exploits in war did not cease after the entombment of the Unknown Soldier, but events referencing the 1917 engagements in Belgium were few and far between for much of the following decade. In 1994 and 1995, several anniversaries presented Keating with further opportunities to commemorate his preferred global conflict. Accordingly, his government launched Australia Remembers 1945–1995, a nationwide program which commemorated and celebrated the fiftieth anniversary of the end of the Second World War. In 1996, Keating lost the election to John Howard, whose interest in the First World War was markedly greater than his predecessor's. Both Howard's grandfather and father had fought in and survived the conflict, and the appeal that 1914–18 held for the new prime minister went beyond family history. He viewed the first Anzacs' actions at Gallipoli and on the Western Front as having 'carved in stone the virtues and values of the Australian self-image'.[37] By invoking Anzac and its associated values – 'of courage, of valour, of mateship, of decency, of a willingness as a nation to do the right thing, whatever the cost'[38]

– Howard sought to create a coherent, positive and unifying national narrative that countered what he dubbed the 'black armband' interpretations of Australian history that had gained traction after the bicentenary. Later in his prime ministership, Howard mobilised Anzac to legitimate Australia's participation in the war on terror, silencing opposition to the conflict by shrewdly 'shift[ing] his rhetoric away from the pre-war focus on weapons of mass destruction … to the theme of the "liberation of a sorely oppressed people"'.[39] Unsurprisingly then, the official focus of war commemoration swung back to the events of 1914–18 under the Howard government. In addition to Gallipoli, the former battlefields in France were the particular beneficiaries of this change in direction.

Just two years after Howard came to power, the Department of Veterans' Affairs built two memorial parks in France: one at Fromelles, the infamous battlefield where the 5th Division suffered 5533 casualties in twenty-four hours, and the other at Le Hamel, the scene of a clinical victory won by a combined force of Australian and American troops under the command of John Monash. The selection of these locations encapsulated the extremes of the modern Anzac legend, which claimed the war was traumatic and deplorable while simultaneously exalting the triumphs of Australian military manhood. The memorial parks, which would not have existed without the support of French locals and officials who donated the land to the Australian government, opened in July 1998 to coincide with the eightieth anniversary of Le Hamel. Four Australian First World War veterans participated in the ceremonies, and in keeping with the precedent set in 1988, the French government presented them with Legions of Honour for their trouble.[40] Australia's memory footprint in the French landscape was getting deeper.

To the north, all remained relatively quiet on the commemorative front, at least where Australia was concerned. Like the French, Flemish locals were showing a greater interest in promoting their region's First World War history. However, Ypres and its surrounds remained a site of memory for many nations, especially Britain, which had established strong commemorative links with the region during the interwar years. The Belgians did not cater their commemorative efforts explicitly to Australian desires. Locals continued organising small Anzac Day ceremonies at Ypres and Zonnebeke with Australian and New Zealand embassy staffs, but the widely publicised events to commemorate major anniversaries in Belgium from the late 1980s to the early 2000s were far more British than antipodean in character. This was evident in the sites selected for the ceremonies: the Menin Gate Memorial, Tyne Cot Cemetery and St George's Memorial Church were all imperial rather than national memorials. The guests – including members of the royal family, veterans, serving military officers, choirs and bands from Britain – also reflected the British-oriented nature of the ceremonies. Usually limited to the participation of an ambassador or the minister for Veterans' Affairs, the Australian presence at the events was minimal.[41]

Although Australians made little impression on Belgium's memorial landscape at the time, local efforts to commemorate the dead captivated certain Australian officials. Notably, the Last Post ceremony performed at the Menin Gate Memorial for the eightieth anniversary commemorations of third Ypres so impressed Veterans' Affairs minister Bruce Scott that he invited the buglers to tour Australia.[42] This was not the first time the Last Post Committee (later known as the Last Post Association) had received such a request – the buglers had already performed for returned services organisations in Britain and France as early as the 1960s – and they agreed to Scott's proposal.[43] At the end of October 1997, the Last Post Committee's chairperson and three buglers arrived in Australia for a two-week trip, during which they performed in Brisbane, Sydney, Melbourne, Perth, the Gold Coast and Canberra. Exactly what Scott and the Department of Veterans' Affairs aimed to achieve in sponsoring the tour is not clear. It may have briefly raised the profile of Ypres in Australia, but the trip did not shed much light on the Australians' Belgian engagements. In fact, most services at which the buglers performed did not have a clear link to the First World War. Only the Remembrance Day ceremony at the AWM had a direct association with 1914–18. As for the others, the Gold Coast service was organised as 'part of a national reunion of former prisoners of war', one of the two events in Sydney was an observance for 'those who served in the Papua New Guinea campaigns in 1942–45', and the Perth performance marked the reopening of the Western Australian Garden of Remembrance.[44]

The tour suffered from a lack of publicity. The Department of Veterans' Affairs did not promote the buglers' journey as extensively as it did other commemorative initiatives, and there was not much unofficial press interest. With the exception of a government-produced booklet, what little publicity there was cited the usual numbers of killed and missing soldiers in Flanders but contained no explicit references to either Messines or third Ypres.[45] Jenny Macleod has argued that one of the reasons behind the resurgent interest in Anzac Day was the shifting role the press played in explaining the story of the Dardanelles campaign to a younger generation unfamiliar with the legend. In the 1960s, Anzac had received little 'useful or engaging' coverage. Over the following quarter of a century, this 'failure to explain' what had happened at Gallipoli and why it was significant had changed, as newspapers started to fill their columns with 'copious extracts from contemporary diaries and letters and interviews with reminiscing veterans'.[46] By the time the buglers arrived in Australia, such detailed coverage of Anzac exploits was commonplace on 25 April and during other noteworthy events, such as the Return to the Western Front Mission's pilgrimage. The Belgians' journey throughout the Commonwealth was another opportunity to recall the Australian Imperial Force's trials and triumphs through the same means, but no such engaging explanations were forthcoming.

The regularity and professionalism of the contemporary buglers' ritual in Ypres have inspired long-term changes to the AWM's closing ceremony. These were brought about by Brendan Nelson, the AWM's director from 2012 to 2019, who had been a regular at the Last Post Association's nightly renditions during his time as Australian ambassador to Belgium. After taking up his role in Canberra, he reportedly found the AWM's closing ceremony 'wanting' in comparison to the solemn spectacle at Ypres and took it upon himself to institute 'a vastly more elaborate ceremony', including a performance of 'Advance Australia Fair', wreath laying, the telling of a soldier's story, the recital of the 'Ode of Remembrance' and, of course, the Last Post. However, while the source of Nelson's inspiration was clear when the AWM first publicised the ceremony's establishment – 'If they can do that in the city of Ypres, why on earth can't we do this at the Australian War Memorial in the nation's capital?' – there was no recurring mention of the ritual's Belgian origins in the AWM's description.[47]

The Belgian buglers returned to Australia in 2012, 2014 and 2015, and each expedition followed a similar pattern to that of the 1997 voyage, though they were more restricted in scope. They performed at a variety of services that were not specifically related to the Australians' struggles in Belgium, and they received limited press coverage. The AWM was a common location for their performances, but the organisations and individuals who extended invitations to the buglers – including the

Victorian Returned and Services League, a Western Australian senator and three Central Coast high schools – evidently had local objectives in mind when offering to sponsor the trips. As a result, the Belgians only performed in one state capital during each trip – Melbourne in 2012, Perth in 2014 and Sydney in 2015 – and also ended up in lesser known locations, such as Woy Woy, in New South Wales, and the Western Australian town of Yarloop.[48] These local events may have made a deep impression on those who attended them, but they hardly gripped the wider nation.

If neither official nor independent agencies were particularly focused on drawing attention to Messines or third Ypres, it is worth considering why they went to such lengths to bring Belgian buglers to Australia. The playing of the Last Post has long been an integral element of Anzac commemoration, so they did not offer anything markedly different to the ceremonies at which they performed. Undeniably, the buglers, looking 'elegant and a credit to Belgium in their grand uniforms of navy blue with a wealth of golden braid and buttons', gave the services a certain 'panache'.[49] However, their tours did more than superficially embellish familiar ceremonies; they gave the events 'an international feel'.[50] This is important, because ever since a panegyrising dispatch sent by the English war correspondent Ellis Ashmead-Bartlett from Gallipoli helped foster the idea that Australia had finally arrived on the world stage, Australians have sought international recognition for Anzac in order to reaffirm their own commitment to the legend.[51] On the eve of the 1997 trip, Veterans' Affairs minister Bruce Scott claimed the buglers' participation in the Remembrance Day ceremonies of that year would 'assure Australians that the service of those who defended Belgium continue[d] to be remembered and appreciated'.[52] In publicising the Belgians' ongoing appreciation of Anzac sacrifices, the trips legitimised Australia's efforts to commemorate its fallen soldiers, the underlying message being that if Belgians still recognised and regularly commemorated Anzac sacrifice, so too should Australians.

From the Bottom Up

As many historians working in the field of memory studies have noted, in order for state-organised remembrance initiatives to gain traction among the broader population, they must strike a chord with individuals.[53] The controversies surrounding the bicentennial ensured that the 1988 celebrations failed to proffer a widely accepted narrative of Australian nationhood, but like many of those living in other societies experiencing the memory boom, Australians were not deterred from exploring their past. The renewed Anzac legend could offer them a direct connection to it. Accordingly, the Australian government's ramping up of commemorative activity related to Anzac throughout the 1990s was reflected in and reinforced by the broader public's own increasing engagement with the legend. Australians had been turning out in large numbers for key commemorative occasions, and the ranks of marchers at Anzac Day parades swelled as children and grandchildren participated in the stead of their veteran ancestors.[54] At the same time, more and more antipodean tourists were heading to former First and Second World War battlefields, and judging by the ever-widening range of books that referenced Australia's military history, publishers felt the Anzac book market was profitable once again.[55]

The renewed interest in and engagement with Anzac were not due to the profusion of government-orchestrated activities alone. Part of the legend's wider appeal lies in its dynamism and adaptability. While it was never just a celebration of military prowess, the qualities associated with Anzac nowadays – including courage, teamwork and mateship – 'are as much civilian as military'. No longer focusing solely on the world wars and not quite so racially homogenous and male-centric, Anzac also *appears* to be more inclusive. As Joan Beaumont points out in her analysis of the various memorials on Anzac Parade, in front of the Australian War Memorial, the erection of the Hellenic Memorial (1988) was an example of Anzac burnishing its multicultural dimension, while the Australian Service Nurses National Memorial (1999) 'consciously constructed' women (at least nurses) as war heroes.[56] Historian Frank Bongiorno has also noted how tentative steps have been taken to recognise the particularities of Indigenous Australians' service, such as the near-official status accorded to the private plaque 'remembering the Aboriginal people who served in the Australian armed forces' located just outside the AWM's grounds. Anzac's newfound inclusiveness does have limits. As Bongiorno argues, 'If everyone is invited to participate in a national ritual – even if the terms of that inclusion remain unequal – it becomes easier to criticise as ungrateful those who remain aloof, and as disloyal or even dangerous'.[57]

Under Anzac's dynamism runs a sacred undercurrent; as Inglis has convincingly argued, official and unofficial memory work invested in the 'cult of Anzac' from 1915 onwards ensured its elevation to the position of a secular 'civil religion'. Thus, 'in a secular age', many have turned to this civic cult for spiritual nourishment.[58] At a less metaphysical level, the gradually diminishing number of the First Australian Imperial Force's veterans – men who had become sacrosanct bearers of the 'truth' of the First World War experience – may have severed Australia's last living links with the conflict, but their passing also generated an extraordinary amount of publicity for the Anzac legend. From the 1990s onwards, the remaining veterans, by that time frail old men, received concerted media attention on Anzac Day and other significant commemorative ceremonies, including their own state funerals. The ex-servicemen's presence at these events afforded commentators an opportunity to recycle their personal anecdotes, which mostly echoed, and therefore served to affirm, the current popular tropes of the First World War: sacrifice, victimhood and futility.[59] Those who lived the longest even had books published about their life experiences that, unlike the novels of the interwar period, owed more to their tenacity in holding on to life than to the front line.[60]

The concentration on the individual's experience of war has been reflected in the work of family and community historians. As research into the broader Australian public's perceptions of history has shown, overarching, national narratives espoused by official agencies often leave individuals cold, but having personal connections to such narratives can make history more vibrant and compelling.[61] Interest in genealogy and family history has been on the rise in Australia since the 1970s, and straddling the divide between the individual and the collective, the local and the national, the Anzac legend has presented curious researchers with an avenue through which to explore and locate their intimate pasts within that of the nation at large. It has also provided them with 'new reasons for perpetuating the idea that war is central to national identity' in Australia.[62] Given the state's interest in maintaining Anzac as a defining national narrative, official agencies have been only too happy to assist motivated individuals in their quest to discover ancestral or local links to the First World War by providing research support through institutions such as the AWM and the Office of Australian War Graves. Moreover, millions of dollars were spent digitising all First World War service records and other key archives, including Charles Bean's papers, unit diaries and a sample of repatriation files.[63] When John Howard announced in 2007 that the National Archives of

Australia had completed digitising the close to 400,000 service records it held, he called it 'a gift to the nation' that would 'bring extraordinary pleasure and pride to families all around the country'.[64]

Even if the state plays a key role in making sources easily accessible to the public, it does not necessarily follow that independent researchers readily accept the official, nation-affirming Anzac narrative at face value. To understand why this is the case, it is useful to consider Marianne Hirsch's theory of postmemory, as well as the distinction Aleida Assmann makes between her notions of cultural and political memory. Initially devised to explore the impact of trauma on the children of Holocaust survivors, Hirsch's postmemory is concerned with how those with family connections to a violent, traumatic past live in its shadow. This form of memory 'is distinguished from living memory by generational distance and from history by deep personal connection'.[65] Not having experienced a particular event themselves, agents of articulation in postmemory generations draw on a 'legacy of cultural and family affinities' to reinvigorate the representation of past events for the present.[66] In particular, their memory work can tap into what Assmann identifies as cultural memory's archival category, which differentiates cultural from political memory. Although both these types of long-term memory rely on similar modes of transmission – memorials, books and commemorative rituals, among others – political memory is a homogenised conception of the past projected by the state that has a 'bipolar' structure 'defined by a division between what is remembered and what is forgotten'. The archival aspect of cultural memory, on the other hand, refers to information stored in caches, such as libraries, museums and archives, which hovers in a state of 'latency' between being remembered and forgotten.[67] By delving into these caches and bringing erstwhile dormant sources to light, family and local historians not only broaden their understanding of the First World War in Australian history; their research also has the capacity to complicate and even challenge perceptions of the dominant Anzac narrative.[68] This was a key reason why historians such as Bruce Scates pushed for the digitisation of repatriation records during the First World War centenary. According to Scates, engagement with this archive could 'extend the narrative of Anzac into the postwar period, shift the focus from soldier to civilian and demonstrate that war damages a whole society', and this would trouble the political memory of 1914–18, with its emphasis on families deriving 'pleasure and pride' from relatives' war service.[69] Nevertheless, as Bart Ziino argues, it would appear that in the case of Australian First World War remembrance, the relationship between 'family remembering and the public myth of Anzac remains mutually constitutive: Anzac frames and affirms family histories, while at the same time it is proving adaptable to the expanding variety of experiences that emerge in family histories'.[70]

Australians' increased engagement with Anzac has led to a proliferation of books (including a number of republished titles), blogs and local exhibitions. These regularly refer to Messines and third Ypres, but they have ultimately done little to assert the significance or distinctiveness of either engagement. Concentrating on particular individuals or communities, their narrow scope limits their appeal to a broad audience. This can be seen most clearly in the case of published books. Looking for such publications on the National Library of Australia's internet search engine and database, Trove, reveals that after the 1980s there was a rapid rise in the number of published personal narratives and Anzac soldier biographies. Out of hundreds of books, however, only a minority have sold well enough to merit additional reprints or editions, and these exceptional instances were not edited by family members or local historians but by people already established in the publishing industry. A good example of this is Roy Kyle's memoir, *An Anzac's Story*. Kyle's book was neither discernibly distinct from nor better written than other published veterans' accounts. Yet, having been edited by popular Australian author Bryce Courtenay and published by Penguin Books, it had prestige and marketability that other, comparable works lacked and went on to become a bestseller.[71] The vast majority of similar books, on the other hand, have been self-published by unknown compilers, which suggests that established publishers are hardly optimistic about their commercial potential.[72]

Following in the footsteps of Bill Gammage's *The Broken Years* and Patsy Adam-Smith's *The Anzacs*, these works emphasise the war's tragic impact on individuals and the nation. The editors of these histories achieve this by analysing their primary source material through the contemporary notions of futility and trauma, even if that material can be quite oblique when describing the conditions the Anzacs endured. For example, Gilbert Mant's introduction to a collection of edited letters and a manuscript written by an artillery gunner called William Duffell after the war claims,

> The power of the letters lies in their simplicity, a naivety that gradually matures into a kind of shocked realism that reflects the gradual loss of innocence of Gunner Duffell and a more sudden realisation that war was hell, an obscenity. He puts up a protective shield about this towards his family, but the truth is still shattering.[73]

However, it is not necessarily Duffell's letters but the manuscript recounting his experiences that best reveals the 'shattering' truth of 1914–18 to which Mant refers. Written by Duffell when the sacrifices of the formerly 'Great' war were looking increasingly meaningless, in a world engulfed by a second global conflict, it is the manuscript that provides Mant with much of his material detailing 'the full horrors of war'.[74] In personal narratives and biographies that do not have accounts written after the war to draw on, compilers employ words like 'futile', 'horror', 'despair', 'massacre', 'tragedy' and 'misery' on a regular basis.[75] In a handful of instances, editors turn to excerpts of anti-war works, such as those by Erich Maria Remarque and Siegfried Sassoon, if the original source material or their own words do not sufficiently convey the war's pointlessness.[76] As a consequence, these works are often far more pessimistic in their outlook than those discussed in chapter 3: Australian interwar authors were able to find purpose in their war service in spite of the horrors endured. In these more recent publications, most First World War campaigns come across as futile; as such, Messines and third Ypres are just two battles among many costly engagements.

The tendency to fold the 1917 Belgian campaigns into the wider narrative of the war is also apparent in other publications that concentrate on the military events of 1914–18. As discussed in the previous chapter, historians responded positively to Ken Inglis' call to look more closely at war and its legacy for Australia in the 1960s, precipitating what Peter Stanley qualifies as a 'boom' in Australian military history writing.[77] As with many initiatives that have touched on the Anzac legend, official agency has played a role in fostering this boom. The AWM in particular has provided numerous writers and historians with research grants, but it is far from being solely responsible for maintaining the steady stream of publications appearing in Australian bookshops.[78] The field boasts hundreds of titles dissecting the various elements of the First World War written by academics and populist authors. The latter – sometimes dubbed 'storians' – often have a background in journalism, which they put to good use crafting highly readable (and bestselling) tales, although their approach to history has often aggrieved more rigorous, scholarly minded authors.[79] Gallipoli has received an overwhelming amount of attention in these publications, but general overviews of the Australian Imperial Force's battles on the Western Front are not uncommon either.

It is telling that while academic historians and populist storians have dedicated entire books to tackling specific battles from the Australian standpoint, the Belgian engagements, at the time of writing, have not received such in-depth treatment. Antipodean authors have broached Douglas Haig's Flanders campaign in general, and a case could be made that the breadth of fighting in Belgium precludes any approach that focuses solely on the experiences of a single nation's involvement.[80] However, this did not hinder Charles Bean when he wrote the Messines and third Ypres chapters in *The Official History of Australia in the War of 1914–1918*, nor has it posed a problem for New Zealand and Canadian researchers who have analysed the 1917 Flanders campaign from their own nations' perspectives.[81] The same argument could be applied to the Anzacs' other key battles in France, but the Australian actions at Villers-Bretonneux, Le Hamel, Bullecourt and, to a more limited extent, Mont St Quentin were the subjects of one book each by 2016, while Pozières has been dealt with on several occasions.[82] Then there are numerous accounts of Fromelles even though this battle only involved one Australian division and lasted just over a day.[83] That no one wrote a monograph about the third Ypres campaign from a distinctly Australian perspective by the end of the First World War centenary reinforces the impression that it is only marginally important when compared with the Anzacs' experiences in northern France.

Beneath Hill 60

The Belgian battles may not have benefited from any exclusive attention in the vast ocean of Anzac literature, but one element of the fighting did receive special treatment in the influential medium of cinema. In 2010, Jeremy Sims' *Beneath Hill 60* became the first Australian First World War film to grace the silver screen in over twenty years.[84] The film's novelty was not confined to its chronological distance from the films of the 1980s; it was also the first feature-length film to show the Anzacs on the Western Front since the 1930s, and it did not focus on the Australian infantryman's experience. Instead, its protagonists were members of the 1st Australian Tunnelling Company, a handful of whom were based on real-life figures, such as Oliver Woodward. Most of the film's action takes place under Hill 60, in Zillebeke, Belgium, and the Australians' firing of the mine under this eponymous mound is the focus of the film's climax. The infantry's struggles in capturing Messines barely feature, while the Australian Imperial Force's more costly actions at third Ypres fall outside the film's scope.

While the decision to make a film concentrating on tunnellers was relatively original, the portrayal of them has much in common with the post-1980s image of the Anzac infantry. It was not difficult to put those who fought underground on the same pedestal as their mates in the trenches. In European interwar literature, the tunneller was depicted as a master of the material world, which enhanced his military virtues. For soldier-writers, this made him 'a figure of imaginative resolution' distinguished by 'his hardness [and] his invulnerability to the terrors of his imagination'.[85] In his own memoirs, Oliver Woodward did not make such bold assertions concerning the tunnellers' martial prowess. Having experienced the underground war firsthand, he harboured few illusions about the mental strain it caused. Nevertheless, his chronicles contained enough ripping yarns of Australian larrikinism and bravery for *Reveille*, which published excerpts throughout the 1930s.[86] As the popular depiction of the infantryman has evolved, so has that of the miner. In Sebastian Faulks' bestselling novel *Birdsong*, the tunneller is no longer a fierce 'new man' forged out of his terrifying work in the bowels of the earth but an exceedingly vulnerable individual forced to fight in 'a hell within a hell'.[87] Before beginning work on *Beneath Hill 60*, screenplay writer David Roach read *Birdsong*, along with Woodward's memoirs and First World War modernist classics by Siegfried Sassoon, Wilfred Owen and Erich Maria Remarque.[88] Given these sources of inspiration and the Anzac legend's influence in shaping Australian depictions of war, *Beneath Hill 60*'s tunnellers unsurprisingly share traits with both the hardy, resourceful fighter common to interwar literature and his modern, often-powerless counterpart.

The film attempts to balance the tragic and triumphant themes of the Anzac legend in several ways. It includes scenes featuring German miners struggling in the same conditions as the Australians, working desperately to protect the lives of their comrades on the surface. These scenes humanise the Germans, so when the Australians celebrate the death of a young Bavarian sapper who is killed while reading a postcard from his mother, the audience's sympathies are more likely to lie with the mother off-screen who has lost her son, and she represents the millions of mothers, and families in general, of Allied and Central Power soldiers left bereaved by the war. Shortly afterwards, the Australians lose one of their youngest members, the fictional Frank Tiffin, whom Woodward sacrifices when firing the mine under Hill 60. Tiffin's death taints the Australians' accomplishment, costing them what is left of their innocence. The film could have ended at this moment, like Peter Weir's freeze-frame conclusion to *Gallipoli*, but it takes viewers back to

Australia for Woodward's postwar wedding, in order to contemplate the scars 1914–18 left on the nation. The occasion is not a moment of unbridled joy; Woodward and the survivors of his company in attendance wear the strain of the war in hollowed expressions and demeanour; one character is clearly suffering from 'shellshock'. It is far from an optimistic ending, and the text that appears just before the end credits drives this point home when it informs viewers that, despite the Allies' success at Messines, it was only 'a matter of months [before] the Germans had retaken Hill 60'. Ending on such a note, the film makes the tunnellers' achievement a pyrrhic victory, unredeemed by the notion that the nation was born through sacrifice. Yet, the film does not descend into utter futility either, offering consolation through its affirmation of the miners' typical Anzac qualities.

Benefiting from government support, in the form of a grant from Screen Australia, *Beneath Hill 60* was lavishly produced and released just before the ninety-fifth anniversary of the Gallipoli landing.[89] Given the popularity of Anzac, there was surely an expectation that it would be a hit with Australian audiences. However, it did not strike a chord with the public. According to one reviewer, an explanation for the film's average returns may have been that the film did 'its history better than its cinema'.[90] It would appear, then, that Sims and Roach's relatively nuanced approach, combined with a narrative revolving around a unit of specialised troops fighting in a largely forgotten engagement, dulled the film's broader appeal. By the time cinemas stopped screening *Beneath Hill 60*, its performance at the box office had been underwhelming; it only made $3.2 million, falling well short of the $8 million spent putting it together. This was undoubtedly a poor return when measured against the great classic of Australian First World War cinema, *Gallipoli* ($11.74 million). Of course, few Australian films have matched the success of Weir's production, but even when compared to *The Water Diviner* (2014), which starred Russell Crowe and took Australian audiences back to the familiar shores of the Dardanelles, *Beneath Hill 60*'s takings were rather poor.[91] After its release, there were several limited efforts to commemorate the tunnellers, but there were no concerted official attempts to propagate their stories, no visit to Hill 60 by an Australian prime minister and no mention of the site in the itinerary of Belgium Anzac Day commemorations. The most telling example of *Beneath Hill 60*'s negligible impression on the greater commemorative agenda, however, was the fact that no official event was organised to commemorate the 100th anniversary of the Hill 60 mine's detonation.

Returning to Flanders Fields

Several developments starting in the early 2000s commemorated the Australian Imperial Force's role in Messines and third Ypres beyond Australian shores. These initiatives were not all unique to the salient, nor were they on the same scale as those across the Franco-Belgian border. There were, however, two distinctive events that did generate specific, albeit limited, publicity for the AIF's Belgian battles before the centenary commemorations, in 2017: John Howard's visit to Ypres and the discovery of the bodies of five soldiers buried together near the village of Westhoek.

By the time Howard visited Ypres, in 2002, he had already spoken at First and Second World War battlefields in Turkey, France, Thailand and Greece, so he was well accustomed to spruiking the Anzac legend in foreign fields. Unlike the other visits, the Flanders trip did not coincide with Anzac Day, limiting the media's interest in the event. The reports that did appear in the press drew heavily on the tropes of the modern Anzac narrative, focusing on the numbers of Australians killed 'in one of the bloodiest, muddiest and most controversial encounters of World War I'. The media also emphasised Howard's personal connections to the city, in which both his grandfather and father had fought, thereby framing his presence at Ypres not only as a question of statesmanship but as a pilgrimage. Yet, if it was Howard the pilgrim who shed tears under the Menin Gate Memorial, it was Howard the statesman who offered his Belgian hosts a multimedia display for the town's In Flanders Fields Museum.[92] This was a shrewd act of commemorative diplomacy, as Howard was surely aware that a one-off visit to Belgium would be quickly forgotten at home and in Ypres itself. The multimedia display, on the other hand, aimed to shore up the Australian presence in the town over a longer term.

Generating more exposure for the Belgian battles than the visit of a living prime minister was the discovery, during a dig for a gas pipeline, of the 'Westhoek five' (also known as the 'Zonnebeke five') in August 2006 and the attempts made to identify them. Approximately a dozen First World War soldiers, including Australians, are found in Belgium annually, so the discovery of these remains was hardly an exceptional event.[93] Nonetheless, the Westhoek five stood out for several reasons. First, it was uncommon to find several bodies buried together. Second, the well-preserved state of the bodies greatly increased the chances of successfully identifying them, and the chances were further enhanced thanks to an arrangement between Australia and Belgium which saw the latter extract DNA from the remains so that the former might try to match it to living relatives. This was a particularly novel development and one that kept the story in the public eye as the hunt began for relatives of the long-lost men. Finally, the discovery of the remains a year out from the ninetieth anniversary of third Ypres was fortuitous, as it gave investigators a reasonable amount of time to identify the bodies before their interment at a ceremony coinciding with the 2007 commemorations.

The news that five, possibly Australian, soldiers had been discovered filtered through to Australia in September 2006. With little to go on at first, most news outlets were content to reprint the minister for Veterans' Affairs' short press release about the find.[94] In some rare cases, journalists revisited the history of third Ypres in their reports to provide contextual information on the campaign in which the Westhoek five had most likely been killed. These accounts predictably touched on the apparent 'futility' of the battle, the 'absolute misery' experienced by the men who fought in it and the Australian losses. *The Daily Telegraph* was particularly hyperbolic, incorrectly claiming that 'more than half the total number of Australians killed in the Great War' had died in the 'reclaimed swamp' around Passchendaele.[95] Nonetheless, the lack of a personal angle, an element that had become standard fare in many reports appearing on Anzac Day and similar commemorative occasions, explains why so few newspapers dwelled on broad descriptions of third Ypres; an individual Anzac's (or family member's) reminiscences made for more compelling news than generic details about one of the AIF's many battles. It was only as the investigation to identify the men narrowed and the story took on a more personal dimension that it gained traction.

The attempt to match the DNA samples with living Australians provided the Westhoek five story with this personal dimension. The use of DNA to identify 'missing' soldiers from 20th-century wars was not unheard of in 2006, but it was new for Australians. Still, the Australian government's request that the Belgians undertake DNA testing was not immediately made public. This was probably an attempt to avoid prematurely raising expectations that DNA would prove to be a magic bullet in the identification of the men. Even when the field of possibilities narrowed to just seven soldiers, the Australian Army History Unit was 'wary of raising false hopes'.[96] It is also possible the government delayed announcing the use of DNA testing in order to present the public with a fait accompli and thereby avoid any debate about the necessity of going to such lengths to identify the dead and the precedents this might set. Eventually, the ethical and practical implications of the approach were aired after the discovery of a mass grave at Pheasant Wood, Fromelles, in 2008, but the role that DNA played in the identification of the Westhoek five never underwent such scrutiny.

When the government did reveal the use of DNA testing, the procedure's originality, combined with attempts to contact possible relatives, ensured that the Westhoek five did not quickly fade into obscurity. Press reports written after the revelation focused on the exploration of connections between the heroic dead and their living relatives, as well as the broader intersection of personal and national history that DNA identification promised. Family members of three AIF soldiers – Second Lieutenant Leo Corrigan, Private John Hunter and Sergeant George Calder – came forward to offer DNA samples. The stories of Corrigan and Hunter attracted the most media attention, because their deaths still weighed on their families. Deidre Shannon, Corrigan's niece, had often 'heard her uncle spoken of in heroic terms', but the family had 'long given up hope of finding him', while the tale of how Hunter's brother Jim had lovingly wrapped his older brother 'in a blanket tied with signal wire' before burying him in a shallow grave had become family lore.[97] These personal accounts reminded Australians that even though the war had ended close to ninety years beforehand and there were barely any veterans left, it was not part of a distant, ossified past.

The DNA test results did not contain a positive match between Shannon and her uncle. Reportedly 'saddened' by the news, the

Corrigan family was left to confront Leo's loss for a second time. The Hunter and Calder families were more fortunate, and the Department of Defence paid for two members from each family to fly to Belgium so they could attend the reinterment ceremony at Buttes New British Cemetery, at Polygon Wood, on 4 October 2007, the ninetieth anniversary of the battle of Broodseinde. Along with the governor-general Michael Jeffrey, they paid their last respects to relatives they had never met and, in the case of Calder's great-grandnieces, had barely heard of.[98] In Australia, the media concentrated on the process that had culminated in the identification of the men and in this graveside reunion; the fighting during Broodseinde, Polygon Wood (the battle in which Hunter and Calder had been killed) and even third Ypres in general was little more than a footnote in most accounts.[99] It would have been of no surprise if the Westhoek five were never heard of again once the reinterment ceremony was over, but improvements in DNA testing techniques meant that another set of remains was identified in 2007 as belonging to Private George Storey from Western Australia. Again, at the federal government's expense, Storey's great-nephews travelled to Belgium to attend a reinterment ceremony.[100] This time, however, the positive identification made little news outside the Storey family's home state, as far more dramatic developments, in France, overshadowed the event.

The mass grave at Pheasant Wood, Fromelles, in which 250 AIF and British Expeditionary Force soldiers were buried, garnered an enormous amount of attention in public, official and academic spheres. Its discovery was not the result of chance. It was largely thanks to years of dedicated research by Melbourne schoolteacher Lambis Englezos that the grave was uncovered.[101] The elevation of Fromelles in the Anzac narrative had begun in 1998 with the Howard government's opening of a memorial park and unveiling of Peter Corlett's sculpture *Cobbers* in the region. The discovery of the mass grave, the ensuing nationwide attempts to identify the men through DNA testing and their eventual reburial in a new Commonwealth War Graves Commission cemetery firmly anchored the battle within contemporary Australian memory.[102] Conversely, by the time of the war's centenary, the Westhoek five's recovery and the precedent set by the use of DNA to identify them had been all but forgotten.

A Corner of a Foreign Exhibition

A week after the Westhoek five's reinterment, *The Sydney Morning Herald* published an article entitled 'Lest We Forget? What Anzacs at Passchendaele?', by popular historian Jonathan King, promoting the Australian War Memorial's temporary exhibition 'To Flanders Fields'. King briefly recounted the experiences of two men who had fought in 'the bloody battle of Passchendaele' before quoting one of the men's grandsons, who claimed:

> These are the sort of inspiring survival stories we should be teaching our children, instead of focusing on Gallipoli, which always overshadows Passchendaele. Our soldiers won Victoria Crosses there, but the Government never commemorates it despite thousands more casualties than the Gallipoli landing.[103]

This claim was evidently an exaggeration but not entirely without foundation. Gallipoli still dominated the Anzac narrative, and while public and official attention had broadened to include the Western Front, the most significant Australian commemorative projects in Europe revolved around battlefields in France. Nevertheless, starting in 2006, there was a push to strengthen the commemoration and recognition of the AIF's presence in the salient region.

The initial impetus for this expansion was a host of fast-approaching ninetieth anniversaries of major Australian engagements. In the 2006–07 budget, the Australian government allocated $10.5 million to the Department of Veterans' Affairs over four years to honour 'the service and sacrifice of Australians on the Western Front … through a range of projects planned to mark the 90th anniversaries of key battles in France and Belgium'.[104] Three-quarters of the money went towards repairing the Australian Corps Memorial at Le Hamel, which had been plagued by structural and vandalism issues since its unveiling, in 1998. Smaller sums went to the installation of interpretive panels across the Western Front as well as a study into the feasibility of constructing an Australian interpretive centre also on the Western Front. Finally, $300,000 went towards the creation and installation of a project that focused specifically on the Belgian front: an interactive CD-based display for the Commonwealth War Graves Commission's new Tyne Cot Visitor Centre.[105] Publicising the unveiling in its magazine *Vetaffairs*, the Department of Veterans' Affairs declared the display would 'enhance visitors' recognition and understanding of the Australian contribution and sacrifice on the Passchendaele battlefield'.[106] Compared to the construction of memorial parks and the erection of monuments at other sites in Europe, this effort to strengthen Australia's memorial presence in Belgium was not all that impressive.

The Tyne Cot display had far less impact on Australian commemorative patterns than the establishment of a dawn service at the Australian National Memorial at Villers-Bretonneux on Anzac Day the following year. The latter, planned by John Howard's administration but inaugurated under the newly elected government of Kevin Rudd, was the most significant Australian commemorative development on the Western Front between 2006 and 2008. Initially planned as a one-off, such was its success that it became an annual event. This 'huge shift for Australia's commemorative tradition' was beneficial to the government, as it took some pressure off Anzac Day services in Turkey. In recent years, problems related to overcrowding, the perceived rowdiness of young Australians who failed to show proper reverence for the dead and contention over 'ownership' of Gallipoli had complicated Australians' relationship with that 'sacred place'. Villers-Bretonneux, on the other hand, did not pose as many logistical difficulties or attract rowdy backpackers en masse, and its hosts were generally content to placate Australian commemorative desires.[107] Benefiting from substantial publicity, the dawn service was a triumph. Between 3000 and 5000 people attended the 2007 ceremony – quite an achievement, considering that Gallipoli services drew a crowd of 10,000 Australian and New Zealand pilgrims that year.[108] While other sites in France had begun to receive more attention over the preceding years, the dawn service at Villers-Bretonneux firmly asserted the village's position at the centre of official Australian commemoration on the Western Front.

A year later, the Anzac Day commemorative program in Belgium expanded to include a dawn service at the foot of the 5th Division's obelisk in Polygon Wood. Unlike the Villers-Bretonneux service, this ceremony was not an Australian initiative but a Belgian one, and there was a total absence of fanfare in Australia to accompany its inauguration. Lacking notable publicity, the event only managed to draw between 150 and 250 Australians, New Zealanders and locals, while Villers-Bretonneux attracted 3000 attendees. The following year, little had changed, with only approximately 100 early risers making it to Polygon Wood, while Villers-Bretonneux hosted a crowd of 3500 on the same morning.[109] Numbers attending the dawn service and other ceremonies held in Belgium on Anzac Day increased after that, but

Flanders consistently attracted considerably less attention than other First and Second World War sites. A year out from the centenary commemorations, one Australian battlefield tour operator advised those wishing to avoid the hustle and bustle in Turkey or France on Anzac Day to 'head to the Menin Gate in Ieper [Ypres], Belgium, where there is a smaller ... service'.[110]

In the years leading up to the centenary, Australians did not travel to former battlefields just for Anzac Day; they visited them all year round and had been doing so in growing numbers since the Anzac revival. Gallipoli remained the key destination, particularly for young backpackers who saw a trip to Anzac Cove as a rite of passage.[111] While some enthusiastic backpackers also made the trip to Europe, the Western Front did not have the same appeal for young travellers. Northern France and west Belgium were less evocative than Gallipoli's dramatic landscape, and they had not benefited from a century's worth of rhetoric claiming Gallipoli as the birthplace of Australian nationhood. The Western Front was also less backpacker-friendly, and travel around relatively isolated battlefields was not only difficult but expensive. The majority of those Australians who visited sites in France and Belgium were already retired and had the means to travel more comfortably than younger Australians on shoestring budgets; Somme Tourisme even called older Australians 'golden customers', because they spent more money on average than tourists from other countries.[112] Although the reasons for their pilgrimages to the Western Front have not been dissected in as much detail as the backpacker phenomenon, many visited the battlegrounds to explore where their family histories intersected with a national legend.[113]

Young or old, the thousands of Australians who headed to the Western Front each year were less likely to visit the battlefields in Belgium than in France. According to studies into memory tourism in Belgian

Flanders and the French *départements* of Nord, Pas-de-Calais and Somme, 10,500 Australians travelled to the Westhoek, Belgium, in 2014, whereas 25,000 visited First World War sites in France between July 2013 and June 2014. In 2015, Belgian tourism officials noted a marked increase of Australian visitors – 13,500 visited the salient – but this number decreased to 11,300 the following year and fell again to 10,400 in 2017, the centenary year of Messines and third Ypres. By comparison, Somme Tourisme predicted that 40,000 Australians would travel to the French First World War battlefields per year between 2015 and 2018. While Somme Tourisme did not carry out a detailed survey of visitors to the region for the centenary years, visitor numbers to the multimillion-dollar Sir John Monash Centre at Villers-Bretonneux for the eight months it was open in 2018 – close to 50,000 – suggest the projections were accurate, at least as far as that year was concerned.[114]

The concentration of the Australia's commemorative activity in France ensured this stark disparity between the Somme and Ypres with regard to their numbers of Australian visitors. While France had recently seen a proliferation of Australian commemorative and memorial building activity, the major Australian sites in Belgium – Tyne Cot Cemetery, the Menin Gate Memorial, Hill 60 and Polygon Wood – had changed little since the interwar years. This was in spite of agreements being signed by the Department of Veterans' Affairs and the government of Flanders in 2009, and by the Belgian federal government in 2012, professing a 'commitment' to honour the sacrifice of Australians in Belgium and to educate younger generations about the nations' 'shared war history'.[115]

The approaching centenary did little to alter this situation. Although the Australian government increased the Department of Veterans'

Affairs' funding so that it could intensify official commemoration on the Western Front, Belgian sites did not benefit from this as much as those in France. The situation had its roots in past decisions that deprived Australians of a stronger memorial presence in Belgian Flanders, starting with Billy Hughes' refusal to build an Australian national memorial in the salient in 1919. Yet, this alone is not a sufficient explanation, especially given that other neglected sites, such as Bullecourt, Fromelles and Le Hamel, have garnered considerable attention and new monuments since the Anzac revival.

Another crucial difference between the Australian sites in Belgium and those in France is that Ypres and its surrounds are *multinational* sites of memory, while certain French villages give more concentrated focus to Australian exploits. This is particularly evident when analysing the Department of Veterans' Affairs' Australian Remembrance Trail, one of the department's two major centenary projects in Europe (the other being the Sir John Monash Centre at Villers-Bretonneux). Reinforcing other official attempts to shift public attention to the Western Front, the Australian Remembrance Trail aims 'to improve the understanding and appreciation of the achievements and sacrifices of Australians' in Europe. Building on relationships established with local agents in France and Belgium over recent decades, the department injected $10 million into the twelve sites making up the 200-kilometre trail.[116] Of the three Belgian sites, Ypres and Zonnebeke (Polygon Wood and Tyne Cot) were predictable inclusions. Ploegsteert (known as Plugstreet to British troops) was perhaps a little more surprising, given that, with the exception of Australians buried nearby, there is not much of a visible Anzac memorial presence in the area.[117] However, as Joan Beaumont has noted, each site has some 'intrinsic historical importance' related to the AIF's 1917 battles in Flanders, and each has been included in part because there is a First World War museum nearby: in Ypres, the In Flanders Fields Museum; in Zonnebeke, the Memorial Museum Passchendaele 1917; and in Comines-Warneton, the municipality in which Ploegsteert is located, the Plugstreet 14–18 Experience interpretation centre.[118]

The Belgian sites' inclusion in the Australian Remembrance Trail could be a significant step towards recovering the AIF's Flanders struggles from the margins of the Anzac legend. However, these developments need to be put into perspective: not even a tenth of the remembrance trail's funding went to the Belgian sites, which made up a quarter of the initial trail.[119] The money was also used differently in the two countries. In France, a large portion of the remembrance trail funds paid for extensive renovations on, and new displays in, the Jean and Denise Letaille Museum – Bullecourt 1917, the Museum of the Battle of Fromelles and the Franco-Australian Museum in Villers-Bretonneux. While these institutions do not ignore other nations' experiences of war, a considerable amount of exhibition space is dedicated to immersing visitors 'in the private world of the Australian soldiers' who fought in their regions.[120] Finally, the Sir John Monash Centre, at Villers-Bretonneux, managed by the Australian government, was funded separately from the Australian Remembrance Trail but is seen as its 'hub'; it presents a narrow, 'nationalist and soldier-centred vision' of Australia's involvement on the Western Front, for which it has been extensively criticised.[121] Locals running the Belgian museums, on the other hand, have spoken highly of their relationships with the Department of Veterans' Affairs and are keen to attract Australians, but antipodean tourists are not their primary target audience.[122] Consequently, current Anzac displays are not as integral to the Australian Remembrance Trail sites in Belgium. This is particularly evident in the larger museums, at Ypres and Zonnebeke, where Australian content accounts for a fraction of the wider exhibitions.

In the Memorial Museum Passchendaele 1917 and Plugstreet 14–18 Experience, both of which had received approximately $300,000 in remembrance trail funding by 2016, Australian officials and local curators worked together to install Australian exhibits. As with John Howard's gift to the In Flanders Fields Museum and the Tyne Cot installation, a key element of these was an interactive display. In Plugstreet 14–18 Experience, the display is currently the only element drawing specific attention to the AIF's presence in Comines-Warneton in 1917–18. Made up of several touchscreens and containing some 200 photographs and short videos, it offers patient visitors a comprehensive overview of the AIF's time in the vicinity of Ploegsteert Wood and of the Messines engagement in particular. However, in aiming to tell 'the visitor about [the war's] effects in the area of Comines-Warneton, which was devastated by four years of bloody fighting and deprivations', Plugstreet 14–18 Experience's scope extends well beyond Messines.[123] The AIF's presence was not constant in the region throughout the war; therefore, it is hardly surprising that the centre includes numerous other exhibits that focus on the experiences of civilians and soldiers of all nationalities who spent time in the sector. The Australians occupy a significant position, but their story does not dominate, being one among many that Plugstreet 14–18 Experience presents to visitors.

The Australian presence at the Memorial Museum Passchendaele 1917 is also quite visible but nonetheless subsumed within a broader narrative focusing on the military history of the war and third Ypres in particular. Originally, the museum did not have any distinct national displays among its exhibits, but it underwent an expansion in the lead-up to the centenary and added sections with a specific national focus. The nations to benefit from this included Australia, New Zealand, Canada, Great Britain, South Africa, Ireland and Germany. Each section contains explanatory panels providing a brief overview of the particular nation's involvement in the 1917 Flanders campaign, various objects related to that country's experience of war and, in some cases, an interactive display. In the Australian section, an eclectic assortment of equipment, clothing, photographs and community honour boards portrays 'an Australian story' associated with the nation's experience of world war in general but says little about the AIF's experience in the salient (see plates 20 and 21). Those few objects that refer explicitly to third Ypres reflect the modern Anzac narrative, with its emphasis on tragedy, futility and human frailty. These include death plaques of three brothers from the Seabrook family who were killed during the battle of Menin Road and a short video of aged veteran Frank Macdonald describing the chaos of a battle fought over ground that was 'all mud and water'. The interactive display also highlights Australian sacrifices 'in terrible conditions which made the fighting men reach the lowest possible depths of human misery'.[124] Although the section aims to present a distinctive Australian perspective on the First World War and third Ypres, the museum does not give the AIF's history in Belgium any particularly special treatment. The other nation-specific sections are based on the same layout and made up of similar objects. Moreover, given that the description of the general military history of third Ypres appears earlier in the museum's layout, the extra sections can hardly be considered central to the museum's main narrative.

The In Flanders Fields Museum focuses on the wider history of the First World War, and its exhibits emphasise the commonalities of experience and suffering between belligerents. There is little that acknowledges the Australians specifically or presents anything like a unique Australian narrative to visitors. The installation of Howard's interactive gift was an exception to the museum's stance on nationality-based exhibits, but it is telling that when the museum underwent renovations in 2012 it was not reinstalled. Nor did the inclusion of the museum in the Australian Remembrance Trail see the former deviate from its decidedly internationalist objectives. It does not appear to have received remembrance trail funding, but Australian officials have helped develop some content in the newly refurbished exhibitions. Observant visitors to the museum may notice a Brodie helmet bearing the colours of the II ANZAC Corps Mounted Regiment (a combined Australian and New Zealand unit) and an Australian correspondence set, which are displayed alongside other objects in the 'Multicultural War' section of the museum (see plate 22). The museum also presents information about the experiences of individual Australians, such as Fanny Seabrook, mother of the Seabrook brothers. Nonetheless, these are fleeting allusions to the Australians compared to more sustained references in other locations, especially France.

***

The commemoration of the AIF's exploits on the Western Front in general intensified from the 1990s onwards, and while Messines and third Ypres benefited to an extent from this increasing interest, they remained on the fringes of major commemorative projects. Occasionally, they were propelled briefly into the spotlight. The film *Beneath Hill 60*, the discovery of the Westhoek five and the Last Post Association buglers' short tours garnered some attention for the AIF's battles in Belgium. However, they did not inspire any wide-ranging remembrance initiatives with a tangible bearing on Australian memory. Nowhere was this clearer than on the Western Front, where the most significant developments of the period were reserved for French villages. Belgian sites were not entirely ignored in this commemorative turn to Europe;

locals in Zonnebeke, Ypres and Comines-Warneton collaborated with the Department of Veterans' Affairs and its Australian Remembrance Trail project with the expectation that this would attract Australian visitors to Belgian Flanders. Yet, it is clear that none of these *communes* is 'a corner of Australia' in Belgium, like Villers-Bretonneux claims to be in France, but nor do they aim to be; Ypres, Zonnebeke and Comines-Warneton are studded with American, Belgian, British, Canadian, French, German, Indian, Irish and New Zealand memorials. The Ypres salient is a truly multinational site of memory that appeals to visitors from all over the world. This is reflected not only in its monuments but also in the institutions that make up the Australian Remembrance Trail sites in Belgium, where the Australians' are subsumed within larger narratives. Given that Anzac rhetoric elevates the Australian experience of the First World War above all others, it is unsurprising that Australian commemoration on the Western Front has centred on particular French townships instead.

This gap between Australia's evolving memorial presence in France compared to that in Belgium is best captured by one of the In Flanders Fields Museum's final exhibits. As visitors reach the end of the permanent exhibition, they come across a display on commemoration that includes objects related to postwar commemorative activities, such as headstones for soldiers of different nationalities and miniature replicas of memorials. Among the items stands the cast of Charles Web Gilbert's *Digger* statuette, which Australia offered to the town of Ypres in exchange for the Menin Gate lions in 1938 (see plate 23). The *only* model of an Australian digger currently in Belgium, Gilbert's figure is small compared to an average human, and utterly dwarfed by his larger, imposing cousins in France. If the *Digger* could walk, his footprints would make a very shallow impression indeed on the Belgian memorial landscape.

EPILOGUE

The Biggest Stunt in a Century

Zonnebeke and Ypres, 25 September 2017: I arrived at Buttes New British Cemetery early to register for the centenary dawn service and reconnoitre the terrain on which it was to be held. At the Ticketek tent that had been erected on the edge of cemetery, I received a rather generous 'Western Front Centenary 2016–2018' kit, complete with beanie and poncho; thankfully, the infamous salient elements did not intrude on the commemorations. Afterwards, I drove to Ypres, where I met with the ABC's European correspondent to give him a couple of soundbites about the third Ypres campaign. I had sent my details to the Department of Veterans' Affairs in case media outlets might be interested in an historian's perspective for their coverage, but the national broadcaster had been the only one to contact me. (Curiously, the department did contact me on behalf of other media companies the following year, to see if I could say a few words about Villers-Bretonneux.)

Wandering around Ypres' famous ramparts and main square, I heard Australian accents and saw a handful of men dressed in First Australian Imperial Force uniforms. They were the re-enactors who would be overseeing different sections of the 'reflective trail' set up in Polygon Wood especially for the centenary commemorations. They appeared to be older than many of the young men who had passed through the town 100 years before. In fact, judging from the crowd at the Last Post ceremony under the Menin Gate Memorial that night, most Australians at Ypres did not fit the backpacker profile that so marked the Gallipoli pilgrims.

Zonnebeke, 26 September 2017: Dawn services demand an early start. Bleary-eyed, I arrived at a theme park where all commemoration attendees had to park their cars and pass through metal detectors before boarding a bus headed for Polygon Wood. An eager Belgian volunteer announced that the wood was 'just like it was 100 years ago'. I admired his enthusiasm given the hour but doubted that we were in for such an immersive experience. More importantly, did I, or any of my fellow early risers, really wish to experience Polygon Wood as it was in 1917? Thankfully, the wood looked nothing like it had as the men of the 4th and 5th Divisions prepared for battle (see plates 24 and 25). Lush vegetation and trees flanked the wide, dimly lit gravel pathway that led to the butte. At various points along the pathway, there were small stations that made up the reflective trail. Explanatory panels provided contextual information, and the living history re-enactors – 'local amateur history buffs' and Australian enthusiasts – occupied several sections depicting Western Front scenes. These included a machine gun post, a regimental aid post complete with an ahistorical complement of nurses, and a kitchen that was perilously close to the blue lights marking the location of the Australian front line.[1] A few metres on, red lights marked the location of the German front. With the exception of some German soldier re-enactors, once we had gone beyond the Australian lines, re-enactment was replaced with remembrance. Projected onto screens and the remains of a pillbox known as Scott's Post, pale, ethereal faces faded in and out of the woods in the pre-dawn darkness. We were walking among ghosts whose symbolic resting place, on that morning at least, was represented by the final station: a spot-lit field of poppies forming a scarlet pool between the trees.

Once in the cemetery, the VIPs – Australian and Belgian officials – took their seats at the foot of the 5th Division's memorial, while the rest of the crowd was directed towards the back. There were a fair number of empty places in this section. In order to pass the time before the official dawn service started, a film recounting the Australian Imperial Force's experiences on the Western Front was projected onto large screens. This was interspersed with individual stories and musical performances by the Voices of Birralee Choir and a single piece played on didgeridoo by the Indigenous musician David Hudson. Just before the main proceedings kicked off, the names of some of the men killed on the Western Front were read out as their photographs were displayed on the screens. Then came the ceremony proper, complete with catafalque party, speeches by officials, laying of wreaths, the Last Post, a minute of silence and singing of Belgian and Australian anthems. As the official party left, other attendees wandered among the headstones, and the Australian Army Band played First World War songs. So ended the biggest stunt in Polygon Wood for 100 years.

Primarily put together by the well-oiled Department of Veterans' Affairs' commemorative machine, the centenary of the battle of Polygon Wood hit all right notes in the modern Anzac legend: tragedy and trauma infused with pride in the achievements of Australian soldiers above all others. The scale of the organisation – notably, the effort that went into the temporary reflective trail – was impressive. But it was underwhelming within the context of the broader centenary. While it did garner some media interest in Australia, this quickly died down – an outcome that was not all that surprising given the event was sparingly attended. Only 800 or so people passed through Polygon Wood in the early hours of 26 September 2017, making it the smallest of all the Department of Veterans' Affairs' major centenary commemorations in Western Europe. It was utterly dwarfed by the Villers-Bretonneux ceremony on Anzac Day 2018, in particular, which attracted ten times as many attendees.[2]

There was also a distinct lack of star power at Zonnebeke. Although Australian prime minister Malcolm Turnbull stood beside French president Emmanuel Macron at Villers-Bretonneux a few months later, in a demonstration of strong Franco-Australian ties, Australia's sole centenary event in Belgium failed to attract such important figureheads. In lieu of the prime minister, Minister for Veterans' Affairs Dan Tehan and Governor-General Sir Peter Cosgrove were the highest ranking Australian officials present. Princess Astrid, the sister of King Philippe, represented Belgium. The Polygon Wood centenary echoed the battle it commemorated: it was a clinical affair of limited gains.

An Abortive Conclusion to a Bloody Battle

Early in the morning of 12 October 1917, men of Major-General John Monash's 3rd Division began their advance towards Passchendaele. Among them was a subaltern from the 38th Battalion brandishing an Australian flag, which he intended to fly from a ruined building once the Anzacs had captured the Belgian village.[3] The act would be an imitation of a similar stunt that had garnered considerable press attention back in Australia three weeks earlier, when Lieutenant Arthur Hull of the 18th Battalion had planted a flag on top of 'Anzac House', a formidable German pillbox, during the battle of Menin Road (see plate 26).[4] This time round, however, the Australian flag would not fly over a single pillbox seized in the first of the Australians' advances in the salient, but over a village that had become one of the main objectives of the entire third Ypres campaign. So significant was this planned gesture that British headquarters had made arrangements to wire the news of the flag's planting directly to England and Australia. Major-General Sir Charles Harington informed Monash that Field Marshal Sir Douglas Haig was confident that once the flag had been put up, nothing would 'bring it down again'.⁵ It was to be the Australians' crowning achievement of their arduous and costly participation in the 1917 Flanders campaigns, a nation-defining act that would aggressively assert an Australian claim on this Belgian battlefield of 'imperishable memory'.⁶ In the end, there was no such glorious climax to the Australians' participation in third Ypres; the Australian flag did not fly from Passchendaele. The dubious honour of taking the village passed to the Canadians.

As this book has shown, relatively few efforts have been made in the century since the Australians failed to seize Passchendaele to ensure that the battles of Messines and third Ypres did not drift to the margins of the Anzac legend. Caught between the fabled baptisms of fire at Gallipoli and the Somme and the victorious engagements of 1918, the Australian Imperial Force's stunted achievements in Belgium were too costly and too tragic to warrant consistent commemoration for those involved in the campaigns. Ironically, the Belgian battles are not quite tragic enough nowadays. Nor have Australians found the cluttered, multinational commemorative space in Belgian Flanders conducive to the propagation of an Anzac-centric narrative of the First World War (see plate 27). For 100 years, Australians have been quick to affirm their martial sacrifices and achievements on numerous foreign battlefields, but the events of 1917 in the 'Salient of Death' remain largely unclaimed in Australian memory.⁷

NOTES

Foreword
1 *Australian Baptist*, 13 November 1917.

Introduction
1 *Sydney Morning Herald*, 4 August 1914; Gavin Souter, *Lion and Kangaroo: The Initiation of Australia*, new ed. (Melbourne: Text Publishing, 2000), 263; E.M. Andrews, *The Anzac Illusion: Anglo-Australian Relations during World War I* (Cambridge: Cambridge University Press, 1993), 7.
2 Judith Smart, '"Poor Little Belgium" and Australian Popular Support for War, 1914–1915', *War & Society* 12, no. 1 (1994): 27–46; Raymond Evans, *Loyalty and Disloyalty: Social Conflict on the Queensland Homefront, 1914–18* (North Sydney, NSW: Allen & Unwin, 1987), 50–3; John McQuilton, *Rural Australia and the Great War: From Tarrawingee to Tangambalanga* (Carlton South, Vic.: Melbourne University Press, 2001), 21–3.
3 English spellings are used for placenames throughout the text.
4 Ngā Tapuwae New Zealand First World War Trails, New Zealand Ministry for Culture and Heritage, n.d., accessed 23 September 2020, https://ngatapuwae.govt.nz/; *Australian*, 28 and 30 August 2004; Dan Todman, *The Great War: Myth and Memory* (London: Hambledon and London, 2005); Norman Leach, *Passchendaele: Canada's Triumph and Tragedy on the Fields of Flanders; An Illustrated History* (Regina: Coteau Books, 2008); Bill Gammage, *The Broken Years: Australian Soldiers in the Great War*, illus. ed. (Carlton, Vic.: Melbourne University Publishing, 2010); Paul Ham, *Passchendaele: Requiem for Doomed Youth* (North Sydney, NSW: Random House, 2016).
5 Joan Beaumont, *Broken Nation: Australians in the Great War* (Crows Nest, NSW: Allen & Unwin, 2013), 391.
6 For further discussion on the key elements of the memory boom, see Jay Winter, 'The Memory Boom in Contemporary Historical Studies', *Raritan* 21, no. 1 (2001): 52–66; Andreas Huyssen, 'Present Pasts: Media, Politics, Amnesia', *Public Culture* 12, no. 1 (2000): 21–38; Timothy G. Ashplant, Graham Dawson and Michael Roper, 'The Politics of War Memory and Commemoration: Contexts, Structures and Dynamics', in *The Politics of Memory: Commemorating War*, ed. Timothy G. Ashplant, Graham Dawson and Michael Roper (New Brunswick, NJ: Transaction Publishers, 2009), 3–7.
7 Barbara A. Misztal, *Theories of Social Remembering* (Maidenhead, Berks.: Open University Press, 2003), 158.
8 John R. Gillis, 'Memory and Identity: The History of a Relationship', in *Commemorations: The Politics of National Identity*, ed. John R. Gillis (Princeton, NJ: Princeton University Press, 1994), 7; Benedict Anderson, *Imagined Communities: Reflections on the Origin and Spread of Nationalism*, 3rd ed. (London: Verso, 2006).

9   Jay Winter, 'Remembrance of the Great War in British Cultural History since the 1960s', in *Comment (se) sortir de la Grande Guerre? Regards sur quelques pays 'vainqueurs': la Belgique, la France et la Grande-Bretagne*, ed. Stéphanie Claisse and Thierry Lemoine (Paris: L'Harmattan, 2005), 59.
10 Jay Winter and Emmanuel Sivan, 'Setting the Framework', in *War and Remembrance in the Twentieth Century*, ed. Jay Winter and Emmanuel Sivan (Cambridge: Cambridge University Press, 1999), 32–3.
11 Jay Winter, *Sites of Memory, Sites of Mourning: The Great War in European Cultural History* (Cambridge: Cambridge University Press, 1995), 93.
12 Ashplant, Dawson and Roper, 'Politics of War Memory', 7.
13 Eric Hobsbawm, 'Introduction: Inventing Traditions', in *The Invention of Tradition*, ed. Eric Hobsbawm and Terence Ranger (Cambridge: Cambridge University Press, 1983), 1.
14 Marilyn Lake, 'What Have You Done for Your Country?', in *What's Wrong with Anzac? The Militarisation of Australian History*, ed. Marilyn Lake et al. (Sydney: University of New South Wales Press, 2010), 10. See also Honest History Group, 'Centenary Watch', Honest History, 2013, accessed 27 February 2017, http://honesthistory.net.au/wp/category/centenary-watch/; Andrew Bonnell and Martin Crotty, 'Australia's History under Howard', *Annals of the American Academy of Political and Social Science* 617 (2008): 149–65; Frank Bongiorno, 'Anzac and the Politics of Inclusion', in *Nation, Memory and Great War Commemoration: Mobilizing the Past in Europe, Australia and New Zealand*, ed. Shanti Sumartojo and Ben Wellings, 81–97 (Oxford: Peter Lang, 2014); Peter Stanley, 'Monumental Mistake: Is War the Most Important Thing in Australian History?', in *Anzac's Dirty Dozen: 12 Myths of Australian Military History*, ed. Craig Stockings, 260–86 (Sydney: NewSouth Publishing, 2012).
15 Ashplant, Dawson and Roper, 'Politics of War Memory', 9–10; Joan Beaumont, 'Anzac Day to VP Day: Arguments and Interpretations', *Journal of the Australian War Memorial*, no. 40 (2007), accessed 5 November 2020, www.awm.gov.au/journal/j40/beaumont/. See also Andrew Mycock, Shanti Sumartojo and Ben Wellings, '"The Centenary to End All Centenaries": The Great War, Nation and Commemoration', in *Nation, Memory and Great War Commemoration: Mobilizing the Past in Europe, Australia and New Zealand*, ed. Shanti Sumartojo and Ben Wellings (Oxford: Peter Lang, 2014), 22.
16 Ashplant, Dawson and Roper, 'Politics of War Memory', 16–17.
17 Winter and Sivan, 'Setting the Framework', 6.
18 Alistair Thomson, *Anzac Memories: Living with the Legend*, 1st ed. (Melbourne: Oxford University Press, 1994), 9. See also Graham Dawson, *Soldier Heroes: British Adventure, Empire and the Imagining of Masculinities* (London: Routledge, 1994), 24.
19 John Stephens, '"The Ghosts of Menin Gate": Art, Architecture and Commemoration', *Journal of Contemporary History* 44, no. 7 (2009): 7–26.
20 Jenny Macleod, *Reconsidering Gallipoli* (Manchester: Manchester University Press, 2004); Jenny Macleod, ed., *Gallipoli: Making History* (London: Frank Cass, 2004); Raelene Frances and Bruce Scates, eds., *Beyond Gallipoli: New Perspectives on Anzac* (Clayton, Vic.: Monash University Publishing, 2016); Richard Reid, Ian

McGibbon and Sarah Midford, 'Remembering Gallipoli', in *Anzac Battlefield: A Gallipoli Landscape of War and Memory*, ed. Antonio Sagona et al., 192–221 (Port Melbourne, Vic.: Cambridge University Press, 2016); Roger Lee, *The Battle of Fromelles: 1916* (Canberra: Army History Unit, 2010); Christopher Wray, *Pozières: Echoes of a Distant Battle* (Port Melbourne, Vic.: Cambridge University Press, 2016); David Coombes, *A Greater Sum of Sorrow: The Battles of Bullecourt* (Newport, NSW: Big Sky Publishing, 2016).

21 Mark Connelly and Stefan Goebel, *Ypres: Great Battles* (Oxford: Oxford University Press, 2018), 87–8; Beaumont, *Broken Nation*, 389–92.

22 C.E.W. Bean, *The Official History of Australia in the War of 1914–1918*, 12th ed., vol. 3, *The Australian Imperial Force in France in 1916* (Sydney: Angus & Robertson, 1941), 93, 266.

23 Robin Prior and Trevor Wilson, *Passchendaele: The Untold Story*, 2nd ed. (New Haven, Conn.: Yale University Press, 2002); Peter H. Liddle, ed., *Passchendaele in Perspective: The Third Battle of Ypres* (London: Leo Cooper, 1997); John Terraine, *The Road to Passchendaele: The Flanders Offensive of 1917; A Study in Inevitability* (London: Leo Cooper, 1977).

24 Percy Wyndham Lewis cited in Connelly and Goebel, *Ypres*, 49.

25 Prior and Wilson, *Passchendaele*, 23.

26 During this period, the AIF suffered a particularly high-profile casualty. On 2 July 1917, Major-General William Holmes, commander of the 4th Division, was killed by a German shell while escorting New South Wales premier William Holman on a battlefield visit. Although Holmes' death was widely reported in Australia, it did not receive nearly as much attention as that of Major-General William Bridges, at Gallipoli, in 1915. This was due to the Australian government's decision to repatriate Bridge's body and arrange a state funeral for the first commander of the AIF. As Bart Ziino has argued, the appeal of this funeral, which attracted thousands, lay in its sanctioning of 'public expressions of [private] grief'. No such elaborate efforts were made to commemorate Holmes in the war-weary Australia of 1917. Bart Ziino, 'Mourning and Commemoration in Australia: The Case of Sir W.T. Bridges and the Unknown Australian Soldier', *History Australia* 4, no. 2 (2007): 40.5.

27 Quoted in C.E.W. Bean, *The Official History of Australia in the War of 1914–1918*, 11th ed., vol. 4, *The Australian Imperial Force in France in 1917* (Sydney: Angus & Robertson, 1941), 876.

28 The term 'memory footprint' was coined by Joan Beaumont in 'Australia's Global Memory Footprint: Memorial Building on the Western Front, 1916–2015', *Australian Historical Studies* 46, no. 1 (2015): 45–63.

Chapter 1: Bean's Belgium

1 An earlier version of this chapter was published as 'Bean, the Third Battle of Ypres and the Australian Narrative of the First World War', Matthew Haultain-Gall, *Australian Historical Studies*, copyright © 2016 Editorial Board, Australian Historical Studies, reprinted by permission of Taylor & Francis Ltd, http://www.tandfonline.com on behalf of Editorial Board, Australian Historical Studies.

2   Stuart Macintyre, *1901–1942, The Succeeding Age*, vol. 4 of *The Oxford History of Australia*, ed. G.C. Bolton (South Melbourne, Vic.: Oxford University Press, 1990), 189.
3   Joan Beaumont, 'The Politics of a Divided Society', in *Australia's War 1914–1918*, ed. Joan Beaumont (St Leonards, NSW: Allen & Unwin, 1995), 59.
4   Stephen Garton, *The Cost of War: Australians Return* (Melbourne: Oxford University Press, 1996), 39.
5   Samuel Hynes, *A War Imagined: The First World War and English Culture* (London: Pimlico, 1992), ix; Paul Fussell, *The Great War and Modern Memory* (London: Oxford University Press, 1977); Modris Eksteins, *Rites of Spring: The Great War and the Birth of the Modern Age* (Boston: Houghton Mifflin Company, 1989).
6   Jay Winter, *Sites of Memory, Sites of Mourning: The Great War in European Cultural History* (Cambridge: Cambridge University Press, 1995); George Mosse, *Fallen Soldiers: Reshaping the Memory of the World Wars* (New York: Oxford University Press, 1990); Stefan Goebel, *The Great War and Medieval Memory: War, Remembrance and Medievalism in Britain and Germany, 1914–1940* (Cambridge: Cambridge University Press, 2007).
7   Garton, *Cost of War*, 39; Henry Reynolds, 'Are Nations Really Made in War?', in *What's Wrong with Anzac? The Militarisation of Australian History*, ed. Marilyn Lake et al. (Sydney: University of New South Wales Press, 2010), 41–2.
8   K.S. Inglis, *Anzac Remembered: Selected Writings by Ken Inglis* (Melbourne: History Department, University of Melbourne, 1998), 121.
9   Garton, *Cost of War*, 42.
10 For example, see Alistair Thomson, '"Steadfast until Death"? C.E.W. Bean and the Representation of Australian Military Manhood', *Australian Historical Studies* 23, no. 93 (1989): 462–78; E.M. Andrews, 'Bean and Bullecourt: Weaknesses and Strengths of the Official History of Australia in the First World War', *Revue internationale d'histoire militaire* 72 (1990): 25–47; Graham Seal, *Inventing Anzac: The Digger and National Mythology* (St Lucia, Qld: University of Queensland Press, 2004).
11 *From the Australian Front* was a souvenir photo book published for Christmas in 1917. It had no literary content, unlike *The Anzac Book* and *Letters from France*, which was a collection of letters written in mid-1916. For more on these publications, see C.E.W. Bean, ed., *The Anzac Book: Written and Illustrated in Gallipoli by the Men of Anzac*, 3rd ed. (Sydney: UNSW Press, 2010); David Kent, '*The Anzac Book* and the Anzac Legend: C.E.W. Bean as Editor and Image-Maker', *Historical Studies* 21, no. 84 (1985): 376–90; Alistair Thomson, *Anzac Memories: Living with the Legend*, 1st ed. (Melbourne: Oxford University Press, 1994), 64–70; Adrian Caesar, '"Kitch" and Imperialism: The *Anzac Book* Re-visited', *Westerly* 40, no. 4 (1995): 76–85.
12 Michael McKernan, *Here Is Their Spirit: A History of the Australian War Memorial 1917–1990* (St Lucia, Qld: University of Queensland Press in association with Australian War Memorial, Canberra (hereafter *AWM*), 1991), 37.
13 Margaret Hutchison, *Painting War: A History of Australia's First World War Art Scheme* (Cambridge: Cambridge University Press, 2018); Robert Dixon, 'Spotting the Fake: C.E.W. Bean, Frank Hurley and the Making of the 1923 Photographic Record of the War', *History of Photography* 31, no. 2 (2007): 165–79.

14 K.S. Inglis, *Sacred Places: War Memorials in the Australian Landscape*, 3rd ed. (Carlton, Vic.: Melbourne University Press, 2008), 316.
15 Peter Stanley, 'Gallipoli and Pozières: A Legend and a Memorial', *Australian Foreign Affairs Record* 56, no. 4 (1985): 287.
16 C.E.W. Bean, *Letters from France* (London: Cassell, 1917), 113–15. See also McKernan, *Here Is Their Spirit*, 30; Stanley, 'Gallipoli and Pozières', 287.
17 Bill Gammage, 'Introduction', in C.E.W. Bean, *The Official History of Australia in the War of 1914–1918*, 11th ed., vol. 4, *The Australian Imperial Force in France in 1917* (Brisbane: University of Queensland Press, 1983), xxv.
18 Ibid., xxvi.
19 Judith Smart, '"Poor Little Belgium" and Australian Popular Support for War, 1914–1915', *War & Society* 12, no. 1 (1994): 29.
20 Raymond Evans, *Loyalty and Disloyalty: Social Conflict on the Queensland Homefront, 1914–18* (North Sydney, NSW: Allen & Unwin, 1987), 32–3; Kerry McCallum and Peter Putnis, 'Media Management in Wartime', *Media History* 14, no. 1 (2008): 20.
21 John F. Williams, *Anzacs, the Media and the Great War* (Sydney: University of New South Wales Press, 1999), 16.
22 C.E.W. Bean (hereafter *Bean* for archival sources) to 1st Australian Division Headquarters, 27 June 1915, AWM: AWM38, 3DRL 6673/270.
23 Denis Winter, *Making the Legend: The War Writings of C.E.W. Bean* (St Lucia, Qld: University of Queensland Press, 1992), 6–7; Kevin Fewster, ed., *Gallipoli Correspondent: The Frontline Diary of C.E.W. Bean* (Sydney: Allen & Unwin, 1983), 11.
24 C.E.W. Bean, *The Official History of Australia in the War of 1914–1918*, 11th ed., vol. 4, *The Australian Imperial Force in France in 1917* (Sydney: Angus & Robertson, 1941), 833.
25 Michael Piggott, *A Guide to the Personal, Family and Official Papers of C.E.W. Bean* (Canberra: AWM, 1983), 7.
26 Kevin Fewster, ed. *Bean's Gallipoli: The Diaries of Australia's Official War Correspondent*, 3rd ed. (Crows Nest, NSW: Allen & Unwin, 2009), 16.
27 Thomson, *Anzac Memories*, 58–9.
28 Bean, *Official History*, 4:561.
29 Cited in Geoffrey Serle, *John Monash: A Biography*, 2nd paperback ed. (Carlton, Vic.: Melbourne University Press, 2002), 289.
30 Fewster, *Bean's Gallipoli*, 14; Kent, *'Anzac Book'*, 377.
31 *Mercury* (Hobart), 24 July 1916; *Argus* (Melbourne), 26 July 1916; *West Australian* (Perth), 12 August 1916.
32 *Sydney Morning Herald*, 14 June 1917.
33 *Argus*, 11 June 1917.
34 *Sydney Morning Herald*, 12 June 1917.
35 *Argus*, 11 June 1917. For Bean's later accounts of the fighting at Messines, see *West Australian*, 20 August 1917; *Register* (Adelaide), 20 August 1917.
36 E.M. Andrews, 'The Media and the Military: Australian War Correspondents and the Appointment of a Corps Commander, 1918 – A Case Study', *War & Society* 8, no. 2 (1990): 83–103.

37   Bean, Diary, 12, 14, 15 and 18 July 1917, AWM: AWM38, 3DRL 606/82/1.
38   C.E.W. Bean, 'Australia's Records: Preserved as Sacred Things; Pictures, Relics, and Writings', *Anzac Bulletin*, no. 40 (1917): 14.
39   Bean, Diary, 7 and 15 September 1917, AWM: AWM38, 3DRL 606/88/1.
40   *Sydney Morning Herald*, 21 July and 16 August 1917.
41   Mark Connelly and Stefan Goebel, *Ypres: Great Battles* (Oxford: Oxford University Press, 2018), 40–1.
42   *Advertiser* (Adelaide), 3 August 1917; *Argus*, 3 August 1917.
43   Bean, *Official History*, 4:700–8.
44   *Mercury* (Hobart), 7 August 1917.
45   *Age* (Melbourne), 9 November 1917.
46   Winter, *Making the Legend*, 16.
47   Williams, *Anzacs, the Media*, 151; *Commonwealth Gazette*, 27 August 1917, 8 and 23 November 1917, 21 February 1918.
48   Winter, *Making the Legend*, 6.
49   *Argus*, 9 May 1919 (italics added).
50   *Ibid.*, 22 September 1917.
51   For an overview of this battle, see Robin Prior and Trevor Wilson, *Passchendaele: The Untold Story*, 2nd ed. (New Haven, Conn.: Yale University Press, 2002), 111–23.
52   *Argus*, 22 September 1917.
53   Bean, Diary, 21 September 1917, AWM: AWM38, 3DRL 606/88/1.
54   Ibid., 24 September 1917.
55   For example, Ibid., July 1916, AWM: AWM38, 3DRL 606/53/1; and July–August 1916, AWM: AWM38, 3DRL 606/54/1.
56   Bean to Treloar, 7 December 1920, AWM: AWM38, 3DRL 6673/813.
57   *Register*, 11 December 1917; *Sydney Morning Herald*, 27 September 1917.
58   *Argus*, 6 October 1917; *Register*, 8 October 1917.
59   Bean's entry for this battle was not completed until 1932: Diary, 17 March 1932, AWM: AWM38, 3DRL 606/91/1.
60   *Sydney Morning Herald*, 8 October 1917.
61   *Argus*, 8 October 1917; *West Australian*, 8 October 1917.
62   *Sydney Morning Herald*, 8 October 1917; *Argus*, 11 October 1917; *Register*, 13 October 1917.
63   *Register*, 13 October 1917; *Age*, 15 October 1917; *West Australian*, 15 October 1917; *Sydney Morning Herald*, 17 October 1917.
64   Some Australian units did play minor supporting roles during the Canadian advance to Passchendaele. Bean, *Official History*, 4:929–36.
65   Bean, Diary, 13–14 October 1917, AWM: AWM38, 3DRL 606/90/1.
66   Gammage, 'Introduction', xxvii; Andrews, 'Bean and Bullecourt', 27.
67   Bean, Diary, 8 October 1917, AWM: AWM38, 3DRL 606/89/1.
68   Frank Vandiver, 'Field Marshal Sir Douglas Haig and Passchendaele', in *Passchendaele in Perspective: The Third Battle of Ypres*, ed. Peter H. Liddle (London: Leo Cooper, 1997), 33; Jonathan Walker, *The Blood Tub: General Gough and the Battle of Bullecourt, 1917* (Staplehurst, Kent: Spellmont, 1998), 25–6, 107–10.
69   Bean, Diary, 15 November 1917, AWM: AWM38, 3DRL 606/94/1.

70 To further illustrate this point, the subtitle chosen for the article in *The Age* (19 November 1917) was 'A Comparison with Pozieres'. See also *Daily Telegraph* (Sydney), 17 November 1917.
71 C.E.W. Bean, *The Official History of Australia in the War of 1914–1918*, 12th ed., vol. 3, *The Australian Imperial Force in France in 1916* (Sydney: Angus & Robertson, 1941), 862; Bean, *Official History*, 4:946–7.
72 *Advertiser*, 17 October 1917; *Daily Telegraph*, 19 October 1917; *Argus*, 24 October 1917; *Register*, 1 November 1917; *Mercury*, 7 January 1918; *Register*, 24 December 1917.
73 Ashley Ekins, 'The Australians at Passchendaele', in *Passchendaele in Perspective: The Third Battle of Ypres*, ed. Peter H. Liddle (London: Leo Cooper, 1997), 244–5.
74 *Mercury*, 7 January 1918.
75 *West Australian*, 8 January 1918.
76 Michael McKernan, 'Writing about War', in *Australia: Two Centuries of War and Peace*, ed. Michael McKernan and Margaret Browne (Canberra: AWM, 1988), 13; Williams, *Anzacs, the Media*, 265; Kent, '*Anzac Book*', 377; Andrews, 'Bean and Bullecourt', 44; Thomson, *Anzac Memories*, 154.
77 C.E.W. Bean, 'The Writing of the Australian Official History of the Great War: Sources, Methods and Some Conclusions', *Royal Australian Historical Society Journal and Proceedings* 24, no. 2 (1938): 91.
78 Joan Beaumont, 'Anzac Day to VP Day: Arguments and Interpretations', *Journal of the Australian War Memorial*, no. 40 (2007), accessed 5 November 2020, www.awm.gov.au/journal/j40/beaumont/. See also Peter Stanley, *A Stout Pair of Boots: A Guide to Exploring Australia's Battlefields* (Crows Nest, NSW: Allen & Unwin, 2008), 64; Joan Beaumont and Vijaya Joshi, *The Australian Centenary History of Defence*, vol. 6, *Australian Defence: Sources and Statistics* (Melbourne: Oxford University Press, 2001), 2–3; Peter Stanley, 'Reflections on Bean's Last Paragraph', *Sabretache* 24, no. 3 (1983): 4–5; Tony Hastings, 'Writing Military History in Australia', *Melbourne Historical Journal* 13 (1981): 52–4.
79 Gammage, 'Introduction', xxiii; Stanley, *Stout Pair of Boots*, 84–6.
80 Bean, *Official History*, 4:859–60.
81 Gammage, 'Introduction', xxv.
82 Bean, *Official History*, 4:761; Prior and Wilson, *Passchendaele*, 119.
83 Bean, *Official History*, 4:624.
84 Ibid., 4:772.
85 Thomson, '"Steadfast until Death"?', 465–6.
86 Bean, *Official History*, 4:833, 877.
87 Bean called these battles 'Passchendaele I' and 'Passchendaele II' in the *Official History* (4:878, 901). Nowadays, the battle that took place on 9 October is referred to as 'Poelcappelle' and the battle on 12 October as 'first Passchendaele'.
88 Bean, *Official History*, 4:884, 926, 929, 936.
89 Ibid., 4:946–8.
90 Ibid., 3:958.
91 Ibid., 4:948.

Chapter 2: Displaying the Ypres Salient

1 A portion of this chapter is based on 'Same old relics, same old story? Displaying the third battle of Ypres at the Australian War Memorial, past and present', Matthew Haultain-Gall, *History Australia*, copyright © 2017 Australian Historical Association, reprinted by permission of Taylor & Francis Ltd, http://www.tandfonline.com on behalf of Australian Historical Association.
2 K.S. Inglis, *Sacred Places: War Memorials in the Australian Landscape*, 3rd ed. (Carlton, Vic.: Melbourne University Press, 2008), 316; Ann Millar, 'Gallipoli to Melbourne: The Australian War Memorial, 1915–1919', *Journal of the Australian War Memorial*, no. 10 (1987): 34–6.
3 Bean, Further memoir ..., 16 April 1919, AWM: AWM27, 623/1.
4 Michael McKernan, *Here Is Their Spirit: A History of the Australian War Memorial 1917–1990* (St Lucia, Qld: University of Queensland Press in association with AWM, 1991), 86, 152–3.
5 '[Le musée est] un réceptacle et un miroir d'un groupe d'hommes dans le présent qui ... se projette dans le temps'. Romain Fathi, *Représentations muséales du corps combattant de 14–18: l'Australian War Memorial de Canberra au prisme de l'Historial de la Grande Guerre de Péronne* (Paris: L'Harmattan, 2013), 40 (author's translation).
6 Benedict Anderson, *Imagined Communities: Reflections on the Origin and Spread of Nationalism*, 3rd ed. (London: Verso, 2006), 163–4.
7 Susan M. Pearce, *Museums, Objects and Collections: A Cultural Study* (Leicester: Leicester University Press, 1992), 209.
8 Daniel J. Sherman, 'Objects of Memory: History and Narrative in French War Museums', *French Historical Studies* 19, no. 1 (1995): 52–3; Timothy G. Ashplant, Graham Dawson and Michael Roper, 'The Politics of War Memory and Commemoration: Contexts, Structures and Dynamics', in *The Politics of Memory: Commemorating War*, ed. Timothy G. Ashplant, Graham Dawson and Michael Roper (New Brunswick, NJ: Transaction Publishers, 2009), 16–17. See also Andrea Witcomb, *Re-imagining the Museum: Beyond the Mausoleum* (London: Routledge, 2003), 168–9.
9 Matthew Haultain-Gall, 'Same Old Relics, Same Old Story? Displaying the Third Battle of Ypres at the Australian War Memorial, Past and Present', *History Australia* 14, no. 3 (2017): 455.
10 McKernan, *Here Is Their Spirit*, 64–5, 78, 128–9.
11 Jennifer Wellington, *Exhibiting War: The Great War, Museums and Memory in Britain, Canada and Australia* (Cambridge: Cambridge University Press, 2017), 222.
12 Craig Melrose, '"A Praise That Never Ages": The Australian War Memorial and the "National" Interpretation of the First World War, 1922–35', PhD thesis (University of Queensland, 2004), 186.
13 C.E.W. Bean, 'Australia's Records: Preserved as Sacred Things; Pictures, Relics, and Writings', *Anzac Bulletin*, no. 40 (1917): 15.
14 Wellington, *Exhibiting War*, 222–4.
15 AIF Order No. 842, 7 September 1917, AWM: AWM25, 981/3.

Notes

16 AIF Order No. 1238, 17 May 1918, AWM: AWM25, 1013/36.
17 Report on work of Australian War Records Section (hereafter *AWRS*), 30 September 1918, AWM: AWM224, MSS553 part 1.
18 War Trophies and Relics, memo, 6 May 1918, AWM: AWM25, 981/3; McKernan, *Here Is Their Spirit*, 44.
19 Report on work of AWRS, 30 September 1918, AWM: AWM224, MSS553 part 1; AWRS Weekly Report No. 58, 21 April 1919, AWM: AWM16, 4379/1/1 part 8.
20 C.E.W. Bean, *Gallipoli Mission* (Canberra: AWM, 1948).
21 AWRS Weekly Report No. 61, 12 May 1919; and AWRS Weekly Report No. 62, 19 May 1919, AWM: AWM16, 4379/1/1 part 8.
22 Inventory of 3rd Ypres relics, n.d., AWM: AWM333, 2/4/5.
23 Unless noted otherwise, references in this section and the next to the temporary exhibitions and their accompanying guidebooks draw on and quote from Australian War Museum, *Australian War Museum: The Relics and Records of Australia's Effort in the Defence of the Empire, 1914–1918*, booklet (Melbourne: Osboldstone & Co., 1922), 11, 14, 17–18, 24, 25, 27, 31, 67–85; AWM, *Australian War Memorial Museum: The Relics and Records of Australia's Effort in the Defence of the Empire, 1914–1918*, booklet (Sydney: Government Printer, 1927), 20–1, 31, 35, 79–104.
24 This is often spelled as 'Nonne Bosschen'.
25 Plans for Sydney exhibition, n.d. [ca 1925], AWM: AWM93, 6/1/15.
26 'Actual boats': *Sun* (Sydney), 1 April 1923; 'precious war relics': *Sun*, 15 April 1926.
27 *Sun*, 1 April 1923. See also *Argus* (Melbourne), 27 May 1922; *Evening News* (Sydney), 7 April 1925.
28 Bean to Treloar, 14 May 1918, AWM: AWM16, 4372/21/3.
29 Bean to Pearce, 12 June 1922, AWM: AWM38, 3DRL 6673/803.
30 AWRS to Department of Defence, 11 December 1918, AWM: AWM16, 4372/21/3.
31 List of 'War Models', n.d. [ca 1918–19], AWM: AWM16, 4372/21/3.
32 Bean to Pearce, 12 June 1922; and Inquiry into Australian War Memorial Modelling Scheme, 16 February 1923, AWM: AWM38, 3DRL 6673/803.
33 Treloar to Bean, 9 August 1927, AWM: AWM38, 3DRL 6673/802.
34 Press release, 10 December 1924, AWM: AWM93, 20/1/1A.
35 Bain to Treloar, 3 February 1932; and Treloar to Bain, 5 and 22 February 1932, AWM: AWM93, 13/1/37.
36 Caption for *Nonne Boschen* diorama, 27 February 1932, AWM: AWM93, 13/1/37.
37 On the whole, the caption's final sentence was considerably more neutral in Bean's edited version than in the original, which read, 'In the face of this determined onslaught a German who has been lying "doggo" ... decides the time has arrived to "Kamarad"'. Bain to Treloar, 3 February 1932, AWM: AWM93, 13/1/37.
38 *Argus*, 22 September 1917; C.E.W. Bean, *The Official History of Australia in the War of 1914–1918*, 11th ed., vol. 4, *The Australian Imperial Force in France in 1917* (Sydney: Angus & Robertson, 1941), 757n60, 761, 781n148.

39 Anne-Marie Condé, 'A Marriage of Sculpture and Art: Dioramas at the Memorial', *Journal of the Australian War Memorial*, no. 19 (1991): 57–8.
40 Bean, *Official History*, 4:761.
41 Flanders Battlefields caption, n.d. [ca 1922], AWM: AWM315, 566/003/005.
42 Bean, Further memoir …, 16 April 1919, AWM: AWM27, 623/1.
43 Butler to Treloar, 17 September 1922, AWM: AWM93, 13/1/67.
44 Bean, 'Australia's Records', 14; Margaret Hutchison, '"Accurate to the Point of Mania": Eyewitness Testimony and Memory Making in Australia's Official Paintings of the First World War', *Australian Historical Studies* 46, no. 1 (2015): 29, 37–40; Robert Dixon, 'Spotting the Fake: C.E.W. Bean, Frank Hurley and the Making of the 1923 Photographic Record of the War', *History of Photography* 31, no. 2 (2007): 165–79; Martyn Jolly, 'Australian First-World-War Photography Frank Hurley and Charles Bean', *History of Photography* 23, no. 2 (1999): 141–8.
45 Bean cited in Anne-Marie Condé, 'John Treloar, Official War Art and the Australian War Memorial', *Australian Journal of Politics and History* 53, no. 3 (2007): 457.
46 Bernd Hüppauf, 'Modernism and the Photographic Representation of War and Destruction', in *Fields of Vision: Essays in Film Studies, Visual Anthropology, and Photography*, ed. Leslie Devereaux and Roger Hillman (Berkeley: University of California Press, 1995), 102–3; Helen Ennis, *Intersections: Photography, History and the National Library of Australia* (Canberra: National Library of Australia (hereafter *NLA*), 2004), 142.
47 Simon Nasht, *The Last Explorer: Hubert Wilkins, Australia's Unknown Hero* (Sydney: Hodder, 2005), 55.
48 Dixon, 'Spotting the Fake', 177.
49 Bean, Further memoir …, 16 April 1919, AWM: AWM27, 623/1.
50 Margaret Hutchison, '"Gazing on Strange and Terrible Lands": Official War Art and the Australian Experience of the First World War in Belgium, 1916–22', paper presented at Poppies, Propaganda and Passchendaele: Australia, Belgium and the Great War (Sydney: State Library of New South Wales, 21 July 2015); Bean to Pearce, 'Australian War Memorial Pictures (Commissioned)', memo, app. F, 19 April 1919, AWM: AWM27, 623/1.
51 Treloar to Bazley, 2 December 1932, AWM: AWM38, 3DRL 8042/60; J.L. Treloar, *Australian Chivalry: Reproductions in Colour and Duo-Tone of Official War Paintings* (Canberra: AWM, 1933), preface.
52 *First Australian Division Artillery Going into the 3rd Battle of Ypres* and *Bringing Up the Ammunition, Flanders, Autumn 1917* are also known as *Australian Artillery Going into Action Near Ypres* and *In Flanders Mud* respectively. The alternative titles were used in *Australian Chivalry* and the guidebook. Septimus Power, *Bringing Up the Ammunition, Flanders, Autumn 1917*, oil on canvas, 153.0 × 244.5 cm, 1920, AWM: ART03333; Septimus Power, *Bringing Up the Guns*, oil on canvas, 147.3 × 233.7 cm, 1921, AWM: ART03334; Treloar, *Australian Chivalry*, plates 34, 38.
53 Fred Leist, *The Cloth Hall, Ypres*, oil on board, 51.4 × 63.2 cm, 1917, AWM: ART02884; Treloar, *Australian Chivalry*, plates 33, 36.

54 Wheeler's painting was called *'Zero' Hour at Messines* in *Australian Chivalry*. Charles Wheeler, *The Battle of Messines*, oil on canvas, 137 × 229 cm, 1923, AWM: ART03557; Treloar, *Australian Chivalry*, plate 31.
55 David Horner, *The Gunners: A History of the Australian Artillery* (St Leonards, NSW: Allen & Unwin, 1995), 150–4.
56 Maria Tippett, *Art at the Service of War: Canada, Art, and the Great War* (Toronto: University of Toronto Press, 1984), 67–9.
57 Katherine Kovacic, 'Artist at War', *Wartime*, no. 57 (2012): 51; Max J. Middleton, *The Art of Septimus H. Power* (Adelaide: Rigby, 1974), 9–10.
58 Margaret Hutchison, *Painting War: A History of Australia's First World War Art Scheme* (Cambridge: Cambridge University Press, 2018), 112.
59 Tippett, *Art at the Service of War*, 63.
60 Turnour died of his wounds on 28 September 1917. Bean, *Official History*, 4:814n68.
61 *Sunday Times* (Sydney), 27 March 1921.
62 Paul Gough, '"An Epic of Mud": Artistic Interpretations of Third Ypres', in *Passchendaele in Perspective: The Third Battle of Ypres*, ed. Peter H. Liddle (London: Leo Cooper, 1997), 419. For more on Dix's *Flandern* and its allegorical significance, see Laura Brandon, *Art and War* (London: I.B. Tauris, 2007), 54–6; Jay Winter, 'Painting Armageddon: Some Aspects of the Apocalyptic Imagination in Art; From Anticipation to Allegory', in *Facing Armageddon: The First World War Experienced*, ed. Hugh Cecil and Peter H. Liddle (London: Leo Cooper, 1996), 859–63.
63 Septimus Power, *Saving the Guns at Robecq*, oil on canvas, 152.3 × 244.0 cm, 1920, AWM: ART03332;Hutchison, '"Accurate to the Point of Mania"', 44.
64 Winston Churchill cited in Dominiek Dendooven, *Menin Gate and Last Post: Ypres as Holy Ground*, trans. Ian Connerty, 2nd ed. (Koksijde, West Flanders: De Klaproos, 2003), 20.
65 Delphine Lauwers, 'Le saillant d'Ypres entre reconstruction et construction d'un lieu de mémoire: un long processus de négociations mémorielles, de 1914 à nos jours', PhD thesis (European University Institute, 2013), 204–60; Dendooven, *Menin Gate*, 40–4, 59.
66 Bart Ziino, *A Distant Grief: Australians, War Graves and the Great War* (Crawley, WA: University of Western Australia Press, 2007), 105.
67 Hogben to Ware, 13 November 1922, Commonwealth War Graves Commission, Maidenhead (hereafter *CWGC*): WG 219/2/1 pt. 1, box 1010; Bruce cited in Hogben to Ridger, 3 May 1924; Ware to Bruce, 8 May 1924; Cook to Imperial War Graves Commission (hereafter *IWGC*), 14 May 1924; and Principal Assistant Secretary to Ware, 8 December 1924, CWGC: WG 219/2/1 pt. 2, box 1010.
68 *Brisbane Courier*, 26 July 1927; *Register* (Adelaide), 26 July 1927; *Argus*, 26 July 1927; *Weekly Times* (Melbourne), 30 July 1927.
69 Bruce Scates, *Return to Gallipoli: Walking the Battlefields of the Great War* (Cambridge: Cambridge University Press, 2006), 95; John R. Stephens, '"The Ghosts of Menin Gate": Art, Architecture and Commemoration', *Journal of Contemporary History* 44, no. 7 (2009): 8–10.

70 *Western Mail* (Perth), 28 July 1927.
71 *Herald* (Melbourne), 19 January 1928; *Mercury* (Hobart), 1 March 1928; *Sydney Morning Herald*, 1 March 1928.
72 John F. Williams, *The Quarantined Culture: Australian Reactions to Modernism 1913–1939* (Cambridge: Cambridge University Press, 1995), 184.
73 Woolavington to Ryrie, 16 January 1928, National Archives of Australia, Canberra (hereafter *NAA*): A3211, 1962/835 part 1; *West Australian* (Perth), 20 January 1928; *Register*, 20 January 1928; *Brisbane Courier*, 20 January 1928.
74 Bruce to Ryrie, 20 January 1928, NAA: A3211, 1962/835 part 1.
75 Pfister to Trumble, n.d. [ca 1928], NAA: A3211, 1962/835 part 1; Deane to Department of Home and Territories, 12 March 1928, NAA: A1, 1930/2905; Trumble to Prime Minister's Department, n.d. [ca 1928]; 'Presentation to the Commonwealth of Captain W. Longstaff's picture "Ghosts of Menin Gate"', n.d. [ca 1928]; and Treloar to Bean, 17 January and 8 February 1929, AWM: AWM38, 3DRL 6673/307.
76 Jay Winter, *Sites of Memory, Sites of Mourning: The Great War in European Cultural History* (Cambridge: Cambridge University Press, 1995), 58–61.
77 Anne Gray, 'Will Longstaff's *Menin Gate at Midnight*', *Journal of the Australian War Memorial*, no. 12 (1988): 47–8.
78 Draft press release, n.d. [ca 1929], AWM: AWM38, 3DRL 6673/307.
79 Humphrey McQueen, *The Black Swan of Trespass: The Emergence of Modernist Painting in Australia to 1944* (Sydney: Alternative Publishing Cooperative, 1979), 36; McKernan, *Here Is Their Spirit*, 133; Stephens, "'Ghosts of Menin Gate'", 21.
80 Inglis, *Sacred Places*, 262.
81 David W. Lloyd, *Battlefield Tourism: Pilgrimage and the Commemoration of the Great War in Britain, Australia and Canada, 1919–1939* (Oxford: Berg, 1998), 187.
82 *Kalgoorlie Miner*, 9 July 1928; *Western Mail*, 12 July 1928; *West Australian*, 25 July 1928; *Daily News* (Perth), 27 July 1928.
83 *West Australian*, 4 July 1928.
84 *Ibid.*, 31 July 1928.
85 AWM, *'Menin Gate at Midnight': The Story of Captain Will Longstaff's Great Allegorical Painting (Gate of Eternal Memories)*, booklet (Melbourne: AWM, [ca 1929]).
86 Correspondence relating to Monash's presence and press releases, [ca 1929], AWM: AWM93, 6/1/27C; 'Arrangements for unveiling of Captain W.F. Longstaff's painting "Menin Gate at Midnight"', n.d. [ca 1929], AWM: AWM38, 3DRL 6673/307; *Examiner* (Launceston), 26 November 1929; *Argus*, 16 February 1929; *Sunday Mail* (Brisbane), 4 August 1929; *Mercury*, 16 November 1929.
87 *Sydney Morning Herald*, 26 March 1929; *Brisbane Courier*, 8 August 1929; *Advertiser* (Adelaide), 11 July 1929; *Queensland Times* (Ipswich), 27 March 1929.
88 *Advertiser*, 10 July 1929.
89 *Sydney Morning Herald*, 22 March 1929; Inglis, *Sacred Places*, 261–2.
90 *Co-operative News* (Sydney), 1 June 1929.
91 Bazley to Treloar, 18 July 1929, AWM: AWM38, 3DRL 6673/307; untitled note, n.d. [ca 1929], AWM: AWM93, 21/11/23.

92 Treloar to Bean, 11 September 1929, AWM: AWM38, 3DRL 6673/307; *Sydney Morning Herald*, 19 September 1929.
93 *Newcastle Morning Herald and Miners' Advocate*, 21 October 1929; *Examiner*, 27 November 1929.
94 Bean, Treloar and Gullett, correspondence, 1929–30, AWM: AWM38, 3DRL 6673/307.
95 Various sales interview outlines, n.d. [ca 1929–30], AWM: AWM93, 21/11/23 (italics added).

Chapter 3: Belgium Imagined

1 Jay Winter, *War and Remembrance in the Twentieth Century* (Cambridge: Cambridge University Press, 1999), 6.
2 Iwona Irwin-Zarecka, *Frames of Remembrance* (New Brunswick, NJ: Transaction Publishers, 1994), 116.
3 *Argus War Review*, supplement, *Argus* (Melbourne), 6 January 1919.
4 *Brisbane Courier*, 17 December 1918; *Age* (Melbourne), 18 February 1919; *Mercury* (Hobart), 25 June 1919; *Sydney Morning Herald*, 11 November 1919; *West Australian* (Perth), 7 March 1919.
5 John Monash, *The Australian Victories in France in 1918* (London: Hutchinson & Co., 1920), 1–8; F.M. Cutlack, *The Australians: Their Final Campaign, 1918; An Account of the Concluding Operations of the Australian Divisions in France* (London: Sampson Low, Martson, 1918), 17.
6 Monash, *Australian Victories*, 1–8. See also Cutlack, *Australians*, 17.
7 Staniforth Smith, *Australian Campaigns in the Great War: Being a Concise History of the Australian Naval and Military Forces, 1914–1918* (Melbourne: Macmillan & Co., 1919), x, 93–6, 98, 103.
8 Ibid., 117–18.
9 For more on the factors behind the Allies' victory in 1918, see Ashley Ekins, 'The Australians at Passchendaele', in *Passchendaele in Perspective: The Third Battle of Ypres*, ed. Peter H. Liddle (London: Leo Cooper, 1997), 246; Ashley Ekins, ed., *1918: Year of Victory* (Auckland: Exisle Publishing, 2010).
10 Dale Blair, *Dinkum Diggers: An Australian Battalion at War* (Carlton South, Vic.: Melbourne University Press, 2001), 6–7.
11 Barrett, circular, 1922, AWM: AWM184, 9.
12 Ibid; Department of Defence to AIF Trust Fund Trustees, 13 November 1919, AWM184, 9.
13 For example, Bean and Stacy, correspondence, April 1928, AWM: AWM184, 39; Newton to Barrett, 2 June 1924, AWM: AWM184, 48.
14 Wanliss to Bean, 12 April 1928, AWM: AWM184, 50.
15 For example, White to Bean, 20 November 1921, AWM: AWM184, 49; N.G. McNicol, *The Thirty-Seventh: History of the Thirty-Seventh Battalion A.I.F.* (Melbourne: Modern Printing Co., 1936), xxvi.
16 F.W. Taylor and T.A. Cusack, comps., *Nulli Secundus: A History of the Second Battalion, A.I.F., 1914–1919* (Sydney: New Century Press, 1942), 354.

17 E. Gorman, *'With the Twenty-Second': A History of the Twenty-Second Battalion, A.I.F.*, 2nd ed. (Melbourne: History House, 2001), viii.
18 M.B.B. Keatinge, *War Book of the Third Pioneer Battalion* (Melbourne: Specialty Press, 1922), 67. See also McNicol, *Thirty-Seventh*, 139; *The Forty-First: Being a Record of the 41st A.I.F. during the Great War*, facsimile reprint, comp. members of the Intelligence Staff (East Sussex: Naval & Military Press for the Imperial War Museum, 2010), 62.
19 McNicol, *Thirty-Seventh*, 154–7; F.C. Green, *The Fortieth: A Record of the 40th Battalion, A.I.F.* (Hobart: Government Printer, 1922), 93–4.
20 T.D. Bridger, *With the 27th Battery in France: 7th Bde, Australian Field Artillery* (London: St Clements Press, 1919), 63; J.E. Lee, *The Chronicle of the 45th Battalion A.I.F.* (Sydney: Mortons, 1927), 8.
21 Newton Wanliss, *The History of the Fourteenth Battalion, A.I.F.: Being the Story of the Vicissitudes of an Australian Unit during the Great War* (Melbourne: Arrow Printery, 1929), 221.
22 Whether such an opportunity did in fact exist is debatable. Robin Prior and Trevor Wilson, *Passchendaele: The Untold Story*, 2nd ed. (New Haven, Conn.: Yale University Press, 2002), 55–66; Gordon Corrigan, *Mud, Blood and Poppycock: Britain and the First World War* (London: Cassell, 2003), 350–3.
23 Keatinge, *Third Pioneer Battalion*, 59.
24 Arthur Dean and Eric W. Gutteridge, *The Seventh Battalion: Resume of the Activities of the Seventh Battalion in the Great War, 1914–1918* (Melbourne: A. Dean and E.W. Gutteridge, 1933), 93. See also R.H. Chatto, *The Seventh Company (Field Engineers) A.I.F. 1915–1918* (Sydney: Smith's Newspapers, 1936), 97; Gorman, *'With the Twenty-Second'*, 75; W.J. Harvey, *The Red and White Diamond: Authorised History of the Twenty-Fourth Battalion A.I.F.* (Melbourne: Alexander McCubbin, 1920), 185; Green, *Fortieth*, 83.
25 Brian Bond, 'British "Anti-war" Writers and Their Critics', in *Facing Armageddon: The First World War Experienced*, ed. Hugh Cecil and Peter H. Liddle (London: Leo Cooper, 1996), 827. See also Dan Todman, *The Great War: Myth and Memory* (London: Hambledon and London, 2005), 40–1, 81; Corrigan, *Mud, Blood and Poppycock*, 354–5.
26 F.H. Stevens, *The Story of the 5th Pioneer Battalion A.I.F.* (Adelaide: Callotype Co., 1937), 60. See also A.W. Keown, *Forward with the Fifth: The Story of Five Years' War Service, Fifth Inf. Battalion, A.I.F.* (Melbourne: Specialty Press, 1921), 239.
27 'Morass': L.M. Newton, *The Story of the Twelfth: A Record of the 12th Battalion A.I.F. during the Great War of 1914–1918* (Hobart: J. Walch & Sons, 1925), 380; 'quagmire': *History of the 11th Field Company Engineers, Australian Imperial Force* (London: War Narratives Publishing Co., 1919), 18; 'sea of mud': C. Longmore, *'Eggs-a-Cook!' The Story of the Forty-Fourth* (Perth: Colortype Press, 1921), 102.
28 Green, *Fortieth*, 92.
29 Taylor and Cusack, *Nulli Secundus*, 267.
30 Harvey, *Red and White Diamond*, 95.
31 B.V. Stacy, F.J. Kindon and H.V. Chedgey, *The History of the 1st Battalion A.I.F., 1914–1919* (Sydney: History Committee, 1st Battalion, AIF, 1931), 52, 83.

32 McNicol, *Thirty-Seventh*, 263.
33 Peter Dennis et al., *The Oxford Companion to Australian Military History*, 2nd ed. (South Melbourne, Vic.: Oxford University Press, 2008), 425; David Carter, '"Esprit de Nation" and Popular Modernity: *Aussie* Magazine 1920–1931', *History Australia* 5, no. 3 (2008): 74.2–74.5.
34 Graham Seal, *Inventing Anzac: The Digger and National Mythology* (St Lucia, Qld: University of Queensland Press, 2004), 97–104.
35 *Reveille* (New South Wales), July and August 1929.
36 'What the war meant': *Reveille*, June 1929 (italics added); 'plain-speaking': *Duckboard* (Melbourne), September 1929.
37 Humphrey McQueen, 'Emu into Ostrich: Australian Literary Responses to the Great War', *Meanjin Quarterly* 35, no. 1 (1976): 84.
38 Ex-Private X, *War Is War* (London: Victor Gollancz, 1930), 256–8.
39 *Smith's Weekly* (Sydney), 26 April 1930.
40 Graham Seal, 'Unravelling Digger Yarn-Spinning in World War I', *Journal of Australian Studies* 21, no. 53 (1997): 146.
41 *Smith's Weekly*, 5 April 1930.
42 For example, *Duckboard*, September 1934.
43 *Queensland Digger*, 1 April 1929. See also Martin Crotty and Craig Melrose, 'Anzac Day, Brisbane, Australia: Triumphalism, Mourning and Politics in Interwar Commemoration', *Round Table* 96, no. 393 (2007): 683.
44 For example, *Reveille*, July 1930, August 1933, August 1937.
45 *Reveille*, February 1934.
46 Bond, 'British "Anti-war" Writers', 819.
47 *Reveille*, January 1934.
48 Ibid., October 1930 (italics added).
49 Ibid., September and October 1936.
50 *Listening Post* (Western Australia), January 1923.
51 *Aussie*, October 1920.
52 *Smith's Weekly*, 12 April 1930.
53 Ibid., 17 May 1930.
54 Ibid., 28 June 1930.
55 Ibid., 16 August 1930.
56 The heading for this section comes from J. Maxwell, *Hell's Bells and Mademoiselles*, 2nd ed. (Sydney: Angus & Robertson, 1932), 160.
57 Clare Rhoden, *The Purpose of Futility: Writing World War I, Australian Style* (Crawley, WA: UWA Publishing, 2015). See also Carolyn Holbrook, 'The Role of Nationalism in Australian War Literature of the 1930s', *First World War Studies* 5, no. 2 (2014): 215–19; Christina Spittel, 'Remembering the War: Australian Novelists in the Interwar Years', *Australian Literary Studies* 23, no. 2 (2007): 136; Robin Gerster, *Big-Noting: The Heroic Theme in Australian War Writing* (Carlton, Vic.: Melbourne University Press, 1987), 1–16.
58 Holbrook, 'Role of Nationalism', 221; Christina Spittel, 'A Portable Monument? Leonard Mann's *Flesh in Armour* in Australia's Memory of the First World War', *Book History* 14, no. 1 (2011): 199.
59 *Reveille*, April 1936.

60 Rosa Maria Bracco, *Merchants of Hope: British Middlebrow Writers and the First World War, 1919–1939* (Oxford: Berg, 1993), 10–13.
61 Carolyn Holbrook, *Anzac: The Unauthorised Biography* (Sydney: NewSouth Publishing, 2014), 89.
62 Spittel, 'Remembering the War', 130.
63 G.D. Mitchell, *Backs to the Wall: A Larrikin on the Western Front*, new ed. (Sydney: Allen & Unwin, 2007), 147–8, 168, 189–90, 174–5, 314.
64 H.R. Williams, *Comrades of the Great Adventure* (Sydney: Angus & Robertson, 1935), 215–17; H.R. Williams, *The Gallant Company: An Australian Soldier's Story of 1915–1918* (Sydney: Angus & Robertson, 1933), 146.
65 E.J. Rule, *Jacka's Mob* (Sydney: Angus & Robertson, 1933), 257–9, 341.
66 Mitchell, *Backs to the Wall*, 205.
67 J.P. McKinney, *Crucible* (Sydney: Angus & Robertson, 1935), 254–65.
68 T.H. Prince, *Purple Patches: A Tale of the Sappers* (Sydney: Jackson and O'Sullivan, 1935), 259.
69 Gerster, *Big-Noting*, 138.
70 Maxwell, *Hell's Bells*, 13, 138.
71 Mary Tilton, *The Grey Battalion* (Sydney: Angus & Robertson, 1933), 238, 258, 271–2, 275, 287, 309–10.
72 Leonard Mann, *Flesh in Armour*, new ed. (Columbia: University of South Carolina Press, 2008), 82–96, 107–8, 219.
73 W.M. Hughes, *The Splendid Adventure: A Review of Empire Relations within and without the Commonwealth of Britannic Nations* (London: Ernest Benn, 1929), 59, 65–6, 73–5.
74 Todman, *Great War*, 91–2; Andrew Suttie, *Rewriting the First World War: Lloyd George, Politics and Strategy 1914–1918* (Basingstoke, Hants.: Palgrave Macmillan, 2005), 150.
75 *West Australian*, 24 November 1934; David Lloyd George, *War Memoirs of David Lloyd George* (London: Nicholson & Watson, 1934), 4:2211, 2251.
76 Suttie, *Rewriting the First World War*, 150; Lloyd George, *War Memoirs*, 2242.
77 Lloyd George, *War Memoirs*, 2240.
78 F.M. Cutlack, ed. *War Letters of General Monash* (Sydney: Angus & Robertson, 1934), 197–9, 202.
79 *Advertiser* (Adelaide), 4 December 1934; *Courier-Mail* (Brisbane), 5 December 1934; *Daily News* (Perth), 19 December 1934.
80 Maxwell, *Hell's Bells*, 160–8.

Chapter 4: Belgium Experienced

1 Philip Longworth, *The Unending Vigil: A History of the Commonwealth War Graves Commission 1917–1967* (London: Constable & Company, 1967), 36.
2 Minutes, 20 March 1919, NAA: A2909, AGS1/2/1; Extract from Minutes of IWGC Meeting, 15 April 1919, CWGC: WG 219 pt. 2, box 1009; Longworth, *Unending Vigil*, 82–106.
3 For an in-depth analysis of Australia's relationship with the IWGC, see Bart Ziino, *A Distant Grief: Australians, War Graves and the Great War* (Crawley, WA: University of Western Australia Press, 2007), 97–135.

Notes

4   *Reveille* (New South Wales), September 1936.
5   Australian divisional memorials erected in France and Belgium (summary), n.d., AWM: AWM27, 623/2; Minutes, 20 March and 29 April 1919, NAA: A2909, AGS1/2/1.
6   K.S. Inglis, *Sacred Places: War Memorials in the Australian Landscape*, 3rd ed. (Carlton, Vic.: Melbourne University Press, 2008), 247; inscription of 5th Division memorial plaque, Polygon Wood, Zonnebeke (italics added).
7   *Sydney Morning Herald*, 22 July 1938, 9 March 1922.
8   The obelisk design did not suit the men of the 2nd Australian Division, who used their own funds to hire sculptor Charles Web Gilbert to design their memorial.
9   Extracts of Corps Conference, Ham-sur-Heure, 14 March 1919, AWM: AWM27, 623/3.
10 Minutes, 20 March and 29 April 1919, NAA: A2909, AGS1/2/1.
11 Army Order, 12 April 1919, AWM: AWM27, 623/9. See also Minutes, 29 April 1919, NAA: A2909, AGS1/2/1.
12 Minutes, 29 May 1919, NAA: A2909, AGS1/2/1.
13 W.M. Hughes, *The Splendid Adventure: A Review of Empire Relations within and without the Commonwealth of Britannic Nations* (London: Ernest Benn, 1929), 62–5.
14 Bean, Treloar and other Australian officials, correspondence concerning purchase of Pozières windmill site, 1930–34, AWM: AWM38, 3DRL 6673/403.
15 Ingpen to IWGC London, 4 October 1919; and Hogben to Ware, 3 February 1920, CWGC: WG 857/3/1, box 1060.
16 Director of Works to Land and Legal Adviser, 24 February 1920, CWGC: WG 857/3/1, box 1060.
17 Consulting Engineer to AIF HQ London, 25 March 1920, NAA: A2909, AGS6/1/5 part 1; Land and Legal Adviser to Ingpen, 31 May 1920, CWGC: WG 857/3/1, box 1060.
18 Neither NAA nor CWGC records specify when or by whom the gum trees were planted. *West Australian* (Perth), 27 February 1925.
19 Correspondence concerning return of crosses to Australia, 1924–30, CWGC: WG 1406/3, box 1087.
20 Summary of Australian Memorials in France and Belgium, n.d., NAA: CP103/22, 23A; Seccombe to CO Australian Graves Services, 30 August – 4 September 1920, NAA: A2909, AGS6/1/5 part 2; Memo concerning 1st Tunnelling Company Memorial, Hill 60, 6 January 1922, NAA: A6006, 1922/1/6.
21 *Brisbane Courier*, 15 November 1923; *Advertiser* (Adelaide), 11 November 1927; *Reveille*, June 1933; *Courier-Mail* (Brisbane), 26 September 1933.
22 Romain Fathi, *Our Corner of the Somme: Australia at Villers-Bretonneux* (Cambridge: Cambridge University Press, 2019), 30–98; Linda Wade, "'By Diggers Defended, by Victorians Mended": Searching for Villers Bretonneux', PhD thesis (University of Wollongong, 2008), 100–263.
23 *Argus* (Melbourne), 4 November 1922.
24 *Reveille*, April and July 1935; *Sydney Morning Herald*, 10 August 1929.
25 Joan Beaumont, *Broken Nation: Australians in the Great War* (Crows Nest, NSW: Allen & Unwin, 2013), xix–xx; Wade, "'By Diggers Defended'", 285–6; Fathi, *Our Corner of the Somme*, 112–34.

26 Ian Hay, *The Ship of Remembrance* (London: Hodder and Stoughton, 1926), 12.
27 David W. Lloyd, *Battlefield Tourism: Pilgrimage and the Commemoration of the Great War in Britain, Australia and Canada, 1919–1939* (Oxford: Berg, 1998), 7–8; John R. Stephens, 'Sacred Landscapes: Albany and Anzac Pilgrimage', *Landscape Research* 39, no. 1 (2014): 31–2; Daniel J. Sherman, *The Construction of Memory in Interwar France* (Chicago, Ill.: University of Chicago Press, 1999), 16–17; George Mosse, *Fallen Soldiers: Reshaping the Memory of the World Wars* (New York: Oxford University Press, 1990), 152–3; *Argus*, 4 November 1922; *Brisbane Courier*, 15 November 1923; *Advertiser*, 19 November 1924; *West Australian*, 18 March 1937.
28 Mosse, *Fallen Soldiers*, 92; Mark McKenna and Stuart Ward, '"It Was Really Moving, Mate": The Gallipoli Pilgrimage and Sentimental Nationalism in Australia', *Australian Historical Studies* 38, no. 129 (2007): 141–51; Jay Winter, *Sites of Memory, Sites of Mourning: The Great War in European Cultural History* (Cambridge: Cambridge University Press, 1995), 52–3; Bruce Scates, *Return to Gallipoli: Walking the Battlefields of the Great War* (Cambridge: Cambridge University Press, 2006); Ziino, *Distant Grief*, 163–86.
29 *Argus*, 11 October 1923; *Sydney Morning Herald*, 13 February 1928; *Reveille*, July 1928; *Queensland Digger*, January 1930; *Reveille*, September 1930.
30 Wade, '"By Diggers Defended"', 253–4; Fathi, *Our Corner of the Somme*, 85–6.
31 Lloyd, *Battlefield Tourism*, 177–8.
32 *Mercury* (Hobart), 8 and 10 October 1919, 24 December 1929; *Advertiser*, 10 February 1921; *Argus*, 2 October 1937; Lloyd, *Battlefield Tourism*, 113.
33 William Pulteney and Beatrix Brice, *The Immortal Salient: An Historical Record and Complete Guide for Pilgrims to Ypres* (London: J. Murray for the Ypres League, 1925), 79–80; Scates, *Return to Gallipoli*, 67–74, 138–9.
34 For more on the history of this ceremony at Ypres, see chapter 5.
35 Richard White, 'The Soldier as Tourist: The Australian Experience of the Great War', *War & Society* 5, no. 1 (1987): 68; Jay Winter, 'Communities in Mourning', in *Authority, Identity and the Social History of the Great War*, ed. Frans Coetzee and Marilyn Shevin Coetzee (Providence: Berghahn Books, 1995), 349–50; Ziino, *Distant Grief*, 174–5.
36 Martin Crotty and Craig Melrose, 'Anzac Day, Brisbane, Australia: Triumphalism, Mourning and Politics in Interwar Commemoration', *Round Table* 96, no. 393 (2007): 681.
37 *West Australian*, 23 October 1928; *Reveille*, October 1936.
38 Ziino, *Distant Grief*, 174–5.
39 Victoria Cross citation, 1917, copy, NAA: B2455, Jeffries Clarence Smith, first published in *London Gazette*, 18 December 1917.
40 *West Australian*, 2 August 1933.
41 *Argus*, 8 August 1933.
42 *West Australian*, 2 August 1933.
43 *Advertiser*, 19 November 1924; *Register News-Pictorial* (Adelaide), 12 December 1929; *Argus*, 12 November 1938.
44 *Mercury*, 5 September 1929; *Ballarat Courier*, 22 September 1928. See also *Mercury*, 2 October 1920; *West Australian*, 17 November 1926; *News* (Perth), 11 November 1929.

45 For example, *Mercury*, 25 March 1930.
46 *Advertiser*, 8 December 1919.
47 *Herald* (Melbourne), 10 May and 16 September 1929; Scates, *Return to Gallipoli*, 88–98; Lloyd, *Battlefield Tourism*, 196–8.
48 *Herald* (Melbourne), 16 September 1929.
49 *West Australian*, 21 May 1932.
50 J.C. Waters, *Crosses of Sacrifice: The Story of the Empire's Million War Dead and Australia's 60,000* (Sydney: Angus & Robertson, 1932), 6, 73–5; *West Australian*, 21 May 1932; *News* (Perth), 2 July 1932; *Duckboard* (Melbourne), August 1932.
51 *Argus*, 29 November 1920; Ziino, *Distant Grief*, 21.
52 *Where the Australians Rest: A Description of Many of the Cemeteries Overseas in Which Australians – Including Those Whose Names Can Never Be Known – Are Buried*, booklet (Melbourne: Government Printer, 1920), 5, 12–27.
53 Bean to Trumble, 7 January and 18 February 1920, AWM: AWM38, 3DRL 6673/371.
54 *Advertiser*, 20 December 1924; *Brisbane Courier*, 7 April 1930; *Sydney Morning Herald*, 5 December 1930.
55 Ziino, *Distant Grief*, 174.
56 *Brisbane Courier*, 1 January 1924.
57 *West Australian*, 27 February 1925. See also Australia House to Stanley Bruce, 16 October 1924, NAA: A458, T337/7.
58 *Argus*, 25 April 1925; *Sydney Morning Herald*, 25 April 1925.
59 *Sydney Morning Herald*, 5 December 1930; *Age* (Melbourne), 8 December 1930.
60 *Argus*, 21 June 1935; *Courier-Mail*, 21 June 1935; *Advertiser*, 22 June 1935.
61 *Argus*, 27 August 1935.
62 Ziino, *Distant Grief*, 12–35.
63 *Mercury*, 4 October 1923; *Argus*, 31 December 1923; *West Australian*, 21 June 1927; *Courier-Mail*, 21 June 1935; *Advertiser*, 22 June 1935.
64 *Argus*, 21 June 1935.
65 Ibid., 25 December 1920; *Sydney Morning Herald*, 22 July 1938.
66 *Argus*, 26 August 1921 (italics added).
67 *Sydney Morning Herald*, 31 December 1923.
68 Longworth, *Unending Vigil*, 73–127; Jonathan F. Vance, *Death So Noble: Memory, Meaning and the First World War* (Vancouver, BC: UBC Press, 1997), 64–5.
69 Note attached to Prime Minister's Anzac Day message for 25th April 1924, 3 April 1924, NAA: A458, R337/7 (italics added).
70 Soldiers' Graves Press Release and Prime Minister's Anzac Day message for 25th April 1924, 3 April 1924, NAA: A458, R337/7.
71 *West Australian*, 16 November 1937.
72 *Telegraph* (Brisbane), 14 November 1927.
73 *Mercury*, 4 October 1923, 5 September 1929; *Advertiser*, 11 November 1927.
74 *Reveille*, February 1935.
75 *Sydney Morning Herald*, 2 February 1922.
76 *Mercury*, 4 October 1923.
77 *Listening Post* (Western Australia), September 1938.
78 *Reveille*, April 1935.

79 *Advertiser*, 27 October 1926. For other examples, see *Mercury*, 4 October 1923; *Sydney Morning Herald*, 25 June 1927; *Listening Post*, October 1930.
80 *Geelong Advertiser*, 21 March 1928.
81 *Sydney Morning Herald*, 2 February 1922.
82 *West Australian*, 16 November 1937; *Reveille*, February 1931; Mosse, *Fallen Soldiers*, 90.
83 *Sydney Morning Herald*, 25 June 1927.
84 *Reveille*, April 1935.
85 Ibid., February 1938.
86 *Sydney Morning Herald*, 10 August 1929; *Highlander: Monthly Magazine of the 30th Battalion, N.S.W. Scottish Regiment*, August 1938.
87 *Listening Post*, November 1934. See also *Advertiser*, 11 November 1927; *Sydney Morning Herald*, 10 August 1929; *Mercury*, 5 September 1929; *Reveille*, June 1933, January 1934, July 1935.
88 *Reveille*, November 1934.
89 For example, see *West Australian*, 23 October 1928, 20 September 1933; *Reveille*, February 1935, April 1935.
90 *Mercury*, 5 September 1929.
91 The *Brooding Soldier* was designed by Frederick Clemesha. Ibid; *West Australian*, 23 October 1928; *Reveille*, January 1934.
92 *Listening Post*, November 1934; *Reveille*, April 1935, January 1934.
93 *West Australian*, 2 August 1929; *Brisbane Courier*, 2 August 1929; *Mercury*, 2 August 1929.
94 Tom Lawson, '"The Free-Masonry of Sorrow"? English National Identities and the Memorialization of the Great War in Britain, 1919–1931', *History & Memory* 20, no. 1 (2008): 100; Lloyd, *Battlefield Tourism*, 108–9.
95 *Argus*, 26 July 1927; *West Australian*, 21 June 1927; *Advertiser*, June 1927; *Queensland Digger*, November 1927.
96 Prime Minister's Department to Official Secretary in Great Britain, 9 March 1937, NAA: A664, 462/401/253; Scates, *Return to Gallipoli*, 141; Lloyd, *Battlefield Tourism*, 207.
97 Military Board Instructions, 30 November 1936, NAA: A664, 462/401/253; Lloyd, *Battlefield Tourism*, 208–9.
98 *Herald*, 10 April 1937; Bruce to Australian Government, cablegram, 22 April 1937; and Prime Minister Lyons (London), cablegram, 18 May 1937, NAA: A705, 226/1/417.
99 *Le Sud* (Ypres), 30 May 1937.
100 Lloyd, *Battlefield Tourism*, 107–9, 198–208; Vance, *Death So Noble*, 57.
101 *Herald* (Melbourne), 10 April 1937; *Courier-Mail*, 6 May 1937; *Mercury*, 13 May 1937; *Age*, 8 July 1937.
102 *Mercury*, 13 May 1937; *Advertiser*, 13 May 1937; *Courier-Mail*, 13 May 1937.
103 *Age*, 26 May 1937; *Le Sud*, 30 May 1937; *Examiner* (Launceston), 2 July 1937; *Queensland Digger*, September 1937; *Sydney Morning Herald*, 22 May 1937; *Mercury*, 24 May 1937; *Argus*, 29 June 1937. For more on the Vimy Ridge pilgrimage, see Vance, *Death So Noble*, 57.
104 *Queensland Digger*, September and October 1937. See also *Mercury*, 2 July 1937.
105 *Age*, 29 June and 8 July 1937.

Chapter 5: Dead Trees and Withering Memories

1. 5th Division Memorial – Polygon Wood, 2 November 1944, CWGC: WG 857/3/1, box 1060.
2. Marc Augé, *Oblivion* (Minneapolis: University of Minnesota Press, 2004), 17.
3. Jan Assmann and John Czaplicka, 'Collective Memory and Cultural Identity', *New German Critique*, no. 65 (1995): 128–31.
4. *Courier-Mail* (Brisbane), 31 October 1939.
5. *Mercury* (Hobart), 12 December 1939.
6. *Courier-Mail*, 4 November 1939.
7. *West Australian* (Perth), 14 October 1939; *Chronicle* (Adelaide), 30 November 1939; *Argus* (Melbourne), 28 September 1939; *News* (Adelaide), 16 October 1939.
8. *Argus*, 5 June 1941.
9. *Sydney Morning Herald*, 25 April 1945.
10. Joan Beaumont, 'The Anzac Legend', in *Australia's War 1914–1918*, ed. Joan Beaumont (St Leonards, NSW: Allen & Unwin, 1995), 174; K.S. Inglis, *Sacred Places: War Memorials in the Australian Landscape*, 3rd ed. (Carlton, Vic.: Melbourne University Press, 2008), 331–3, 349; Joan Beaumont, Lachlan Grant and Aaron Pegram, 'Remembering and Rethinking Captivity', in *Beyond Surrender: Australian Prisoners of War in the Twentieth Century*, ed. Joan Beaumont, Lachlan Grant and Aaron Pegram (Carlton, Vic.: Melbourne University Press, 2015), 1–2; Stephen Garton, *The Cost of War: Australians Return* (Melbourne: Oxford University Press, 1996), 7.
11. Beaumont, Grant and Pegram, 'Remembering and Rethinking Captivity', 2.
12. Graham Seal, *Inventing Anzac: The Digger and National Mythology* (St Lucia, Qld: University of Queensland Press, 2004), 147–9.
13. Inglis, *Sacred Places*, 343, 356–7.
14. *Evening News* (Sydney), 25 April 1922.
15. *Age* (Melbourne), 25 April 1947.
16. Inglis, *Sacred Places*, 331.
17. E.M. Andrews, *The Anzac Illusion: Anglo-Australian Relations during World War I* (Cambridge: Cambridge University Press, 1993), 162.
18. Beaumont, 'Anzac Legend', 174.
19. *Reveille* (New South Wales), September 1945.
20. *Argus*, 10 November 1945.
21. Seal, *Inventing Anzac*, 105–16.
22. This conceptualisation of social memory is clearly based on Jan Assmann's communicative memory. Aleida Assmann, 'Memory, Individual and Collective', in *The Oxford Handbook of Contextual Political Analysis*, ed. Robert E. Goodin and Charles Tilly (Oxford: Oxford University Press, 2006), 213–15; Assmann and Czaplicka, 'Collective Memory and Cultural Identity', 126–8; Jay Winter and Emmanuel Sivan, 'Setting the Framework', in *War and Remembrance in the Twentieth Century*, ed. Jay Winter and Emmanuel Sivan (Cambridge: Cambridge University Press, 1999), 16.
23. Assmann, 'Memory, Individual and Collective', 216; Kerwin Lee Klein, 'On the Emergence of Memory in Historical Discourse', *Representations* 69 (2000): 130.

24　Assmann, 'Memory, Individual and Collective', 215–17; Assmann and Czaplicka, 'Collective Memory and Cultural Identity', 130–1.
25　Paula Hamilton, 'Memory Studies and Cultural History', in *Cultural History in Australia*, ed. Richard White and Hsu-Ming Teo (Sydney: University of New South Wales Press, 2003), 88.
26　Dan Todman, *The Great War: Myth and Memory* (London: Hambledon and London, 2005), 219.
27　Graeme Davison, 'The Habit of Commemoration and the Revival of Anzac Day', *Australian Cultural History*, no. 23 (2003): 81.
28　*Argus*, 16 September 1944; *Advertiser* (Adelaide), 5 May 1945; *Mail* (Adelaide), 21 July 1945.
29　H.V. Johnson to Cabinet, 13 January 1947, NAA: A2700, 1208A; *West Australian*, 27 February 1925.
30　Menzies to McBride, 2 September 1952, NAA: A663, O190/1/45.
31　Allen to Prime Minister's Department, 28 August 1952, NAA: A663, O190/1/45.
32　Defence Committee, minute at meeting, 2 October 1952, NAA: A663, O190/1/45.
33　Press release, 5 February 1953, NAA: A705, 226/1/525 part 1; Geoff Browne, 'Herring, Sir Edmund Francis (Ned) (1892–1982)', *Australian Dictionary of Biography*, National Centre of Biography, Australian National University, n.d., accessed 30 March 2016, http://adb.anu.edu.au/biography/herring-sir-edmund-francis-ned-12626.
34　Treasury Minute Paper, 13 January 1953, NAA: A571, 1952/2868.
35　Poole to High Commissioner, London, 14 February 1928; Blamey to Murdoch, 10 May 1928; Abbott to Archbishop of Sydney, 1 February 1929; Secretary to Archbishop of Melbourne, n.d.; and Archbishop of Sydney to Bruce, 21 June 1929, NAA: A664, 487/401/24; Murdock to General Secretary, RSSILA, 7 June 1928; and RSSILA to Murdock, 19 June 1928, NLA: MS 6609, series 1, box 35, item 3884.
36　'The Friends of St. George's Memorial Church, Ypres', pamphlet, 1955, NLA: MS 6609, series 1, box 35, item 3884.
37　*Age*, 27 June 1953; *Reveille*, June 1953.
38　*Age*, 27 June 1953.
39　Minutes, 24–25 February 1953, NLA: MS 6609, series 3, box 389; *Ypersche Nieuws* (Ypres), 4 July 1953.
40　*West Australian*, 8 September 1951; *Advertiser*, 24 November 1954.
41　*Sydney Morning Herald*, 26 January 1952.
42　Jenny Macleod, 'The Fall and Rise of Anzac Day: 1965 and 1990 Compared', *War & Society* 20, no. 1 (2002): 150–3, 157–8; Alistair Thomson, *Anzac Memories: Living with the Legend*, 1st ed. (Melbourne: Oxford University Press, 1994), 189.
43　Ric Throssell, *For Valour: Ric Throssell's Play* (Sydney: Currency Press, 1976).
44　Alan Seymour, *The One Day of the Year* (London: Angus & Robertson, 1962).
45　Alrene Sykes and Keith Richards, 'Another Look at the Old War-Horse: Alan Seymour's "The One Day of the Year"', *Australasian Drama Studies* 2, no. 2 (1984): 66; Carina Donaldson and Marilyn Lake, 'Whatever Happened to

the Anti-war Movement?', in *What's Wrong with Anzac? The Militarisation of Australian History*, ed. Marilyn Lake et al. (Sydney: University of New South Wales Press, 2010), 86.

46 Geoffrey Serle, 'The Digger Tradition and Australian Nationalism', *Meanjin Quarterly* 24, no. 2 (1965): 158.

47 Jeffrey Grey, 'In Every War but One? Myth, History and Vietnam', in *Zombie Myths of Australian Military History*, ed. Craig Stockings (Sydney: University of New South Wales Press, 2010), 201.

48 Ann Mari Jordens, 'Conscription and Dissent: The Genesis of Anti-war Protest', in *Vietnam Remembered*, ed. Gregory Pemberton (Sydney: Weldon Publishing, 1990), 81; Ashley Ekins, '"Not One Scintilla of Evidence"? The Media, the Military and the Government in the Vietnam Water Torture Case', *Australian Journal of Politics and History* 42, no. 3 (1996): 354, 357.

49 Ann Curthoys, 'History and Reminiscence: Writing about the Anti-Vietnam-War Movement', *Australian Feminist Studies* 7, no. 16 (1992): 127–8; Grey, 'In Every War but One?', 201.

50 Peter Cochrane, 'At War at Home: Australian Attitudes during the Vietnam Wars', in *Vietnam Remembered*, ed. Gregory Pemberton (Sydney: Weldon Publishing, 1990), 176, 180–1; Robin Gerster, *Big-Noting: The Heroic Theme in Australian War Writing* (Carlton, Vic.: Melbourne University Press, 1987), 246; Carina Donaldson, '"The Book Is Inspired by the Australian Soldier": The Wounds of War and the Literary Rehabilitation of the Australian Soldier in Vietnam War Writing', *Journal of Australian Studies* 36, no. 4 (2012): 474–6.

51 Joan Beaumont, 'Australian Citizenship and the Two World Wars', *Australian Journal of Politics and History* 53, no. 2 (2007): 173.

52 David Goldsworthy, 'Australian External Policy and the End of Britain's Empire', *Australian Journal of Politics and History* 51, no. 1 (2005): 18; Neville Meaney, 'Britishness and Australia: Some Reflections', *Journal of Imperial and Commonwealth History* 31, no. 2 (2003): 125.

53 James Curran and Stuart Ward, *The Unknown Nation: Australia after Empire* (Carlton, Vic.: Melbourne University Press, 2010), 15–16; Goldsworthy, 'Australian External Policy', 19.

54 Stuart Ward, *Australia and the British Embrace: The Demise of the Imperial Ideal* (Carlton South, Vic.: Melbourne University Press, 2001), 10–11, 260–1.

55 Curran and Ward, *Unknown Nation*, 198–9.

56 K.S. Inglis, 'The Anzac Tradition', *Meanjin Quarterly* 24, no. 1 (1965): 34.

57 Russel Ward, *The Australian Legend*, 2nd ed. (South Melbourne, Vic.: Oxford University Press, 2003), 228–35; Michael McKernan, 'Writing about War', in *Australia: Two Centuries of War and Peace*, ed. Michael McKernan and Margaret Browne (Canberra: AWM, 1988), 16.

58 Bart Ziino, 'The First World War in Australian History', *Australian Historical Studies* 47, no. 1 (2016): 119–20.

59 K.S. Inglis, *Anzac Remembered: Selected Writings by Ken Inglis* (Melbourne: History Department, University of Melbourne, 1998), 31; Bruce Scates, *Return to Gallipoli: Walking the Battlefields of the Great War* (Cambridge: Cambridge University Press, 2006), 125–9.

60 Memo to External Affairs Minister, 16 October 1967, NAA: A1838, 25/1/3/25 part 1.
61 *Reveille*, September 1967.
62 Circular No. 2, April 1970, NAA: A1838, 1516/6/313 part 1.
63 Scates, *Return to Gallipoli*, 152; *Reveille*, February 1971.
64 Hasluck to Cahill, 15 May and 9 August 1967; and External Affairs, memo, 16 January 1968, NAA: A1838, 25/1/3/25 part 1; Scates, *Return to Gallipoli*, 148–9.
65 *Reveille*, February 1971.
66 Anderson to Gorton, September 1970; Greet to Birch, 23 June 1971; and Birch to Greet, 6 July 1971, NAA: A1838, 1516/6/313 part 1.
67 Matthew Graves, 'Memorial Diplomacy in Franco-Australian Relations', in *Nation, Memory and Great War Commemoration: Mobilizing the Past in Europe, Australia and New Zealand*, ed. Shanti Sumartojo and Ben Wellings (Oxford: Peter Lang, 2014), 170–2.
68 Cahill to Dehem, 29 January 1968, Stadsarchief Ieper, Ypres (hereafter *SI*): TOE/48 252; Piper to Secretary, External Affairs, 20 February 1968, NAA: A1838, 25/1/3/25 part 1; Draft Itinerary, April 1970, NAA: A1838, 1516/6/313 part 1.
69 Piper to Secretary, External Affairs, 20 February 1968, NAA: A1838, 25/1/3/25 part 1; Draft Itinerary, April 1970, NAA: A1838, 1516/6/313 part 1.
70 Prime Minister, Brief message, 6 May 1968; and Walker to Secretary, External Affairs, 15 May 1968, NAA: A1838, 25/1/3/25 part 1; Circular No. 3, September 1970; and Order of Ceremony for Unveiling of Mont St Quentin Memorial, 2 September 1971, NAA: A1838, 1516/6/313 part 1.
71 Cahill to Hasluck, 4 June 1968; and Walker to Secretary, External Affairs, 15 May 1968, NAA: A1838, 25/1/3/25 part 1.
72 Greet to Secretary, Foreign Affairs, 20 September 1971, NAA: A1838, 1516/6/313 part 1.
73 Walker to Secretary, External Affairs, 12 December 1967, NAA: A1838, 25/1/3/25 part 1.
74 Dehem to Harry, 4 March 1967; Harry to Dehem, 23 March 1967; and Knight to Annoot, 11 April 1967, SI: TOE/64 404.
75 Norrish to Dehem, 15 March 1968, SI: TOE/64 410.
76 Linda Wade, '"By Diggers Defended, by Victorians Mended": Searching for Villers Bretonneux', PhD thesis (University of Wollongong, 2008), 184, 190–2.
77 Cook to Bruce, 16 August 1926; Rosenthal to mayor of Mont St Quentin (translation), 26 August 1926; mayor of Mont St Quentin to Cook (extract of translation), 26 August 1926; and Phillips to Official Secretary, Australia House, 5 August 1927, NAA: A461, D370/1/15.
78 Romain Fathi, *Our Corner of the Somme: Australia at Villers-Bretonneux* (Cambridge: Cambridge University Press, 2019), 101–7.
79 Rupert Brooke, 'The Soldier', in *1914 and Other Poems*, London: Sidgwick & Jackson, 1915, 15.
80 David W. Lloyd, *Battlefield Tourism: Pilgrimage and the Commemoration of the Great War in Britain, Australia and Canada, 1919–1939* (Oxford: Berg, 1998), 108.
81 *Brisbane Courier*, 21 May 1920.

82 Lloyd, *Battlefield Tourism*, 36; Mark Connelly and Stefan Goebel, *Ypres: Great Battles* (Oxford: Oxford University Press, 2018), 125–8.
83 *Ypres Times*, 1 October 1921.
84 Ibid., 1 January 1922, 1 July 1923, 1 April 1924, 1 April 1925; Mark Connelly, 'The Ypres League and the Commemoration of the Ypres Salient, 1914–1940', *War in History* 16, no. 1 (2009): 59–60.
85 *Argus*, 16 June 1922; *Ypres Times*, 1 July 1922, 1 October 1922, 1 October 1923.
86 *Het Yperse* (Ypres), 21 March 1925, 9 October 1926.
87 Dominiek Dendooven, *Menin Gate and Last Post: Ypres as Holy Ground*, trans. Ian Connerty, 2nd ed. (Koksijde, West Flanders: De Klaproos, 2003), 113–16.
88 *Reveille*, February 1928, June 1930; *Geraldton Guardian*, 10 April 1930; *Examiner* (Launceston), 1 January 1935; *Sun* (Sydney), 15 June 1935; *Herald* (Auckland), 29 May 1935; *West Australian*, 18 March 1937; *Age*, 11 November 1939.
89 Connelly and Goebel, *Ypres*, 156–7.
90 *Advertiser*, 3 October 1963; *Sydney Morning Herald*, 22 January 1964; Annoot to Till, 16 October 1963, SI: TOE/55 336.
91 McKinnon to Dehem, 23 January 1964; Davidson to Dehem, 24 January 1964; Johnson to Service de Tourisme Ypres, 22 January 1964; and Cooke to Dehem, 22 January 1964, SI: TOE/55 336.
92 Knight to Dehem, 27 October 1966; Harry to Dehem, 27 February 1967; and Dehem to Harry, 4 March 1967, SI: TOE/64 404.
93 *Ypersche Nieuws*, 21 April 1967.
94 Norrish to Dehem, 15 March 1968; Davis to Dehem, 19 March 1969; and Norrish to Dehem, 2 April 1970, SI: TOE/64 410; *Ypersche Nieuws*, 23 April 1971; *Wekelijks Nieuws* (Poperinghe), 20 April 1979, 21 April 1989.
95 Franky Bostyn et al., *Passchendaele 1917: The Story of the Fallen and Tyne Cot Cemetery* (Roeselare, West Flanders: Roularta Books, 2007), 315.
96 Eric Hobsbawm, 'Introduction: Inventing Traditions', in *The Invention of Tradition*, ed. Eric Hobsbawm and Terence Ranger (Cambridge: Cambridge University Press, 1983), 4–5.
97 Unless noted otherwise, this section refers to and quotes from Bill Gammage, *The Broken Years: Australian Soldiers in the Great War*, 1st ed. (Ringwood, Vic.: Penguin Books, 1975), 52–113, 84, 147–204, 276–9; Patsy Adam-Smith, *The Anzacs* (Melbourne: Thomas Nelson, 1978), vii, ix, 1, 58–149, 190–207, 216–20, 244–51, 280–92.
98 C.E.W. Bean, *The Official History of Australia in the War of 1914–1918*, 11th ed., vol. 4, *The Australian Imperial Force in France in 1917* (Sydney: Angus & Robertson, 1941), 620.
99 Carolyn Holbrook, *Anzac: The Unauthorised Biography* (Sydney: NewSouth Publishing, 2014), 128–9; Anne-Marie Condé, 'Imagining a Collection: Creating Australia's Records of War', *reCollections* 2, no. 1 (2007), http://recollections.nma.gov.au/issues/vol_2_no_1/papers/imagining_a_collection.
100 C.E.W. Bean, *The Official History of Australia in the War of 1914–1918*, 1st ed., vol. 6, *The Australian Imperial Force in France during the Allied Offensive, 1918* (Sydney: Angus & Robertson, 1942), 1094–5.
101 Macleod, 'Fall and Rise', 163.

102 Bart Ziino, '"A Lasting Gift to His Descendants": Family Memory and the Great War in Australia', *History & Memory* 22, no. 2 (2010): 130.
103 Christina Twomey, 'Trauma and the Reinvigoration of Anzac: An Argument', *History Australia* 10, no. 3 (2013): 87, 107.
104 Todman, *Great War*, 81.
105 Joan Beaumont and Vijaya Joshi, *The Australian Centenary History of Defence*, vol. 6, *Australian Defence Sources and Statistics* (Melbourne: Oxford University Press, 2001), 273.
106 Curran and Ward, *Unknown Nation*, 224; Stuart Ward, 'The "New Nationalism" in Australia, Canada and New Zealand: Civic Culture in the Wake of the British World', in *Britishness Abroad: Transnational Movements and Imperial Cultures*, ed. Kate Darian-Smith, Patricia Grimshaw and Stuart Macintyre (Carlton, Vic.: Melbourne University Publishing, 2007), 259.
107 J.G. Fuller, *Troop Morale and Popular Culture in the British and Dominion Armies, 1914–1918* (Oxford: Clarendon Press, 1990), 167.
108 Joy Damousi, 'War and Commemoration: "The Responsibility of Empire"', in *Australia's Empire*, ed. Deryck M. Schreuder and Stuart Ward (Oxford: Oxford University Press, 2008), 308–9.
109 *Gallipoli*, directed by Peter Weir (Australia: Roadshow Film, 1981); Holbrook, *Anzac*, 138.
110 Peter Weir, 'Gallipoli: "I Felt Somehow I Was Really Touching History"', *Literature/Film Quarterly* 9, no. 4 (1981): 213–17.
111 John Cribbin, comp., *The Making of Anzacs* (Sydney: Collins/Fontana, 1985), 49.
112 *Anzacs*, episode 5, 'Now, There Was a Day …', directed by John Dixon, George Miller and Pino Amenta, produced by Geoff Burrowes, Burrowes-Dixon Company, screenplay by John Dixon and John Clarke (Pyrmont, NSW: Roadshow Entertainment, 2014), DVD.
113 Ibid., episode 2, 'The Big Push'.
114 Graeme Turner, 'ANZACS: Putting the Story Back in History', in *War: Australia's Creative Response*, ed. Anna Rutherford and James Weiland (Sydney: Allen & Unwin, 1997), 232.
115 *Anzacs*, episode 3, 'The Devil's Arithmetic'.
116 Ibid.; and episode 4, 'Fields of Fire'.

Chapter 6: Lost in a Surfeit of Memory

1 It is unlikely the lions were still in place when the AIF arrived in Belgium for third Ypres. Treloar to Murphy, 27 January 1937; and Murphy to Treloar, 12 February 1937, AWM: AWM315, 748/022/001 01; Elizabeth Burness, 'The Menin Gate Lions', *Sabretache* 29, no. 2 (1988): 12–13. For more on the gifting of the Menin Gate lions to Australia, see Matthew Haultain-Gall, 'Lions and Kangaroos: Mobilising the Anzac Legend in the Ypres Salient', *Journal of Belgian History*, forthcoming.
2 Treloar to Murphy, 18 June 1936 and 4 October 1935, AWM: AWM315, 748/022/001 01. See also Bruce and Bourgmestre of Ypres, correspondence, 1936, NAA: A1, 1936/1567.

3   Department of Veterans' Affairs to McKernan and Flemming, memo, 10 October 1985, AWM: AWM315, 748/022/001 part 2.
4   Brown to Treloar, 14 July 1947; Treloar to Brown, 16 July 1947; Joseph to McGrath, 5 April 1962; and Allan to Lancaster, 20 January 1970, AWM: AWM315, 748/022/001 01; Robert Kellet to Alfred Caenepeel, 8 October 1976, In Flanders Fields Museum Research Centre, Ypres (hereafter *IFFM*): MAP 1004.
5   Department of Veterans' Affairs to McKernan and Flemming, memo, 10 October 1985; and McAuslan and Stanley to McKernan, 11 October 1985, AWM: AWM315, 748/022/001 part 2.
6   Bruce to Bourgmestre of Ypres, 31 January 1936, NAA: A1, 1936/1567.
7   Flemming to Burness, 16 October 1985, AWM: AWM315, 748/022/001 part 2.
8   Treloar to Bowles, 13 September 1947, AWM: AWM315, 748/022/001 01.
9   Joan Beaumont, 'Remembering the Heroes of Australia's Wars: From Heroic to Post-heroic Memory', in *Heroism and the Changing Character of War*, ed. Sibylle Scheipers (Houndmills, Hants.: Palgrave Macmillan, 2014), 334.
10 Marilyn Lake, 'How Do School Children Learn about the Spirit of Anzac?', in *What's Wrong with Anzac? The Militarisation of Australian History*, ed. Marilyn Lake et al. (Sydney: University of New South Wales Press, 2010), 139–47; Bill Gammage, 'The Anzac Cemetery', *Australian Historical Studies* 38, no. 129 (2007): 124–40.
11 Mark McKenna, 'Anzac Day: How Did It Become Australia's National Day?', in *What's Wrong with Anzac? The Militarisation of Australian History*, ed. Marilyn Lake et al. (Sydney: University of New South Wales Press, 2010), 114–16.
12 Tony Bennett, 'Introduction', xviii; John Hutchinson, 'State Festivals, Foundation Myths and Cultural Politics in Immigrant Nations', 17; and Peter Cochrane and David Goodman, 'The Great Australian Journey: Cultural Logic and Nationalism in the Postmodern Era', 189, in *Celebrating the Nation: A Critical Study of Australia's Bicentenary*, ed. Tony Bennett et al. (Sydney: Allen & Unwin, 1992).
13 *Vetaffairs* (Australia), June 1988; K.S. Inglis, *Anzac Remembered: Selected Writings by Ken Inglis* (Melbourne: History Department, University of Melbourne, 1998), 90–2.
14 Inglis, *Anzac Remembered*, 92.
15 Romain Fathi, *Our Corner of the Somme: Australia at Villers-Bretonneux* (Cambridge: Cambridge University Press, 2019), 113.
16 Inglis, *Anzac Remembered*, 91.
17 Annoot to Coombs, 5 December 1969, SI: TOE/64 410; In Grateful Memory …, commemorative volume of photographs, January 1970, AWM: AWM225, 2.
18 *Vetaffairs*, January–February 1990; *Canberra Times*, 21 April 1990; Jenny Macleod, 'The Fall and Rise of Anzac Day: 1965 and 1990 Compared', *War & Society* 20, no. 1 (2002): 154.
19 James Curran, *The Power of Speech: Australian Prime Ministers Defining the National Image* (Melbourne: Melbourne University Press, 2004), 180.
20 Bob Hawke, 'Speech at Lone Pine Ceremony, 25 April, 1990', Department of the Prime Minister and Cabinet, n.d., accessed 12 October 2020, https://pmtranscripts.pmc.gov.au/sites/default/files/original/00008010.pdf.
21 *Sydney Morning Herald*, 25 April 1990.

22 Ibid., 27 April 1992.
23 *Canberra Times*, 29 February 1992.
24 For more on Keating's relationship with Anzac, see James Curran, 'The "Thin Dividing Line": Prime Ministers and the Problem of Australian Nationalism, 1972–1996', *Australian Journal of Politics and History* 48, no. 4 (2002): 482–4; Carolyn Holbrook, 'Commemorators in Chief', in *Anzac Day Then and Now*, ed. Tom Frame (Sydney: UNSW Press, 2016), 223–4.
25 Commonwealth of Australia, *Parliamentary Debates*, House of Representatives, no. 182, 27 February 1992, 374 (Paul Keating).
26 *Canberra Times*, 27 April 1992.
27 *Vetaffairs*, December 1992; *Sydney Morning Herald*, 4 September 1993.
28 *Australians on the Western Front: August 29 – September 3 1993; Order of Service*, program (Canberra: Department of Veterans' Affairs, 1993).
29 *Sydney Morning Herald*, 4 September 1993.
30 *Vetaffairs*, April–May 1993.
31 Ibid., March 1993.
32 Jo Hawkins, '"What Better Excuse for a Real Adventure": History, Memory and Tourism on the Kokoda Trail', *Public History Review* 20 (2013): 5.
33 *Canberra Times*, 30 August and 2 September 1993; *Sydney Morning Herald*, 4 September 1993.
34 K.S. Inglis, 'The Unknown Australian Soldier', *Journal of Australian Studies* 23, no. 60 (1999): 15–16; *Vetaffairs*, September 1993; *Sydney Morning Herald*, 19 October and 12 November 1993; Bart Ziino, 'Mourning and Commemoration in Australia: The Case of Sir W.T. Bridges and the Unknown Australian Soldier', *History Australia* 4, no. 2 (2007): 40.13.
35 Johan Durnez, 'The Johan and Hilde Newsletter', e-newsletter (privately distributed, 7 November 2013).
36 *Reveille* (New South Wales), January/February 1994.
37 Curran, *Power of Speech*, 242.
38 John Howard, 'Address at Anzac Day Parade Canberra', 25 April 2003, Department of the Prime Minister and Cabinet, n.d., accessed 31 October 2020, pmtranscripts.pmc.gov.au/release/transcript-20549.
39 Mark McKenna, 'Howard's Warriors', in *Why the War Was Wrong*, ed. Raimond Gaita (Melbourne: Text Publishing, 2003), 173.
40 Bruce Scott (Minister for Veterans' Affairs), 'Australian Sacrifice Recalled: $1.34m for Western Front Memorial Parks', media release 157/97 (Department of Veterans' Affairs, 28 October 1997); *Vetaffairs*, June and November 1998; Bruce Scott, 'Address by the Minister for Veterans' Affairs the Honourable Bruce Scott MP at the Dedication of the Fromelles Memorial Park' (Fromelles, 5 July 1998).
41 Ephemera from 1987 and 1992 commemorative events at Ypres, IFFM: MAP 1074 (1); Ephemera from 11 November 1998 and 25,000th Last Post (31 October 2011) commemorative events, IFFM: MAP 1074 (2); Franky Bostyn et al., *Passchendaele 1917: The Story of the Fallen and Tyne Cot Cemetery* (Roeselare, West Flanders: Roularta Books, 2007), 309–13.
42 *Vetaffairs*, August 1997.

Notes

43 Ian Connerty, *The Last Post: 30,000 Daily Tributes to the Fallen* (Tielt, West Flanders: Lannoo Publishers, 2014), 138–42.
44 Bruce Scott (Minister for Veterans' Affairs), 'Buglers from Belgium Arrive in Australia', media release 162/97 (Department of Veterans' Affairs, 31 October 1997); *Sydney Morning Herald*, 6 November 1997; *Office of Australian War Graves Journal 1997–98* (Phillip, ACT: Office of Australian War Graves, 1998), 41.
45 Richard Reid, *'He Is Not Missing. He Is Here!' Australians and the Menin Gate: Visit to Australia by Buglers from the Menin Gate, Ieper, Belgium*, booklet (Canberra: Department of Veterans' Affairs, 1997); *Sydney Morning Herald*, 6 November 1997; *Herald Sun* (Melbourne), 10 November 1997; *Canberra Times*, 11 November 1997; *Australian*, 11 November 1997; *West Australian* (Perth), 19 November 1997.
46 Macleod, 'Fall and Rise of Anzac Day', 156–7.
47 *Sydney Morning Herald*, 17 April 2013; AWM, 'Last Post Ceremony', AWM, n.d., accessed 14 September 2020, www.awm.gov.au/commemoration/last-post-ceremony.
48 Last Post Association, 'A Delegation of the Last Post Association (Ieper-Belgium) Travels to Australia for Armistice', www.lastpost.be/en/news/54/a-delegation-of-the-last-post-association-ieper-belgium-travels-to-australia-fo, Last Post Association, n.d., accessed 14 September 2016; Last Post Association, 'A Delegation of the Last Post Association (Ieper-Belgium) Travels to Australia (Perth & Canberra)', www.lastpost.be/en/news/58/a-delegation-of-the-last-post-association-ieper-belgium-travels-to-australia-pe, Last Post Association, n.d., accessed 14 September 2016; Last Post Association, 'A Delegation of the Last Post Association (Ieper-Belgium) Travels to Woy Woy (NSW) Australia for Armistice', www.lastpost.be/en/news/95/a-delegation-of-the-last-post-association-ieper-belgium-travels-to-woy-woy-nsw, Last Post Association, n.d., accessed 14 September 2016; Commonwealth of Australia, *Parliamentary Debates*, Senate, no. 4, 24 March 2014, 1894–7 (Christopher Back); and 24 November 2015, 8858–61 (Deborah O'Neill).
49 *Canberra Times*, 12 November 1997, 14 November 2012.
50 New South Wales, *Parliamentary Debates*, Legislative Assembly, 12 November 2015, 5883–4 (David Mehan).
51 John F. Williams, *The Quarantined Culture: Australian Reactions to Modernism 1913–1939* (Cambridge: Cambridge University Press, 1995), 86–7, 93; Fathi, *Our Corner of the Somme*, 5–8. For more on Ellis Ashmead-Bartlett and his association with the Anzac legend, see Fred Brenchley and Elizabeth Brenchley, *Myth Maker: Ellis Ashmead-Bartlett, the Englishman Who Sparked Australia's Gallipoli Legend* (Milton, Qld: John Wiley & Sons, 2005).
52 Scott, 'Buglers from Belgium'.
53 For example, see Jay Winter, 'The Memory Boom in Contemporary Historical Studies', *Raritan* 21, no. 1 (2001): 53; Alistair Thomson, *Anzac Memories: Living with the Legend*, 2nd ed. (Clayton, Vic.: Monash University Publishing, 2013), 318.
54 K.S. Inglis, *Sacred Places: War Memorials in the Australian Landscape*, 3rd ed. (Carlton, Vic.: Melbourne University Press, 2008), 412–13.
55 Jo Hawkins, *Consuming Anzac: The History of Australia's Most Powerful Brand* (Crawley, WA: UWA Publishing, 2018), 49–50.

56 Beaumont, 'Remembering the Heroes', 334, 340–1.
57 Frank Bongiorno, 'Anzac and the Politics of Inclusion', in *Nation, Memory and Great War Commemoration: Mobilizing the Past in Europe, Australia and New Zealand*, ed. Shanti Sumartojo and Ben Wellings (Oxford: Peter Lang, 2014), 86–90, 97.
58 Inglis, *Sacred Places*, 433–45; Bruce Scates, *Return to Gallipoli: Walking the Battlefields of the Great War* (Cambridge: Cambridge University Press, 2006), 196.
59 See, for example, *Advertiser* (Adelaide), 23 June 2001; John Howard, 'Transcript of the Prime Minister the Hon John Howard MP Address at the State Funeral Service of Alec William Campbell', 24 May 2002, Department of the Prime Minister and Cabinet, n.d., accessed 9 December 2017, http://pmtranscripts.pmc.gov.au/release/transcript-12946; *Daily Telegraph* (Sydney), 17 May 2002; *Courier-Mail* (Brisbane), 21 March 2003; *Australian Financial Review*, 22 April 2005; Paula Hamilton, 'Memory Studies and Cultural History', in *Cultural History in Australia*, ed. Richard White and Hsu-Ming Teo (Sydney: University of New South Wales Press, 2003), 86–8.
60 Jonathan King, *Gallipoli: Our Last Man Standing; The Extraordinary Life of Alec Campbell* (Milton, Qld: John Wiley & Sons, 2003); Lynette Ramsay Silver, *Marcel Caux: A Life Unravelled* (Milton, Qld: John Wiley & Sons, 2005); Tony Stephens, *The Last Anzacs: Lest We Forget*, rev. ed. (North Fremantle, WA: Fremantle Press, 2009).
61 Paul Ashton and Paula Hamilton, *History at the Crossroads: Australians and the Past* (Ultimo, NSW: Halstead Press, 2007), 20; Anna Clark, 'Private Lives, Public History: Navigating Historical Consciousness in Australia', *History Compass* 14, no. 1 (2016): 2–3.
62 Peter Dennis et al., *The Oxford Companion to Australian Military History*, 2nd ed. (South Melbourne, Vic.: Oxford University Press, 2008), 42. See also Joy Damousi, 'Why Do We Get So Emotional about Anzac?', in *What's Wrong with Anzac? The Militarisation of Australian History*, ed. Marilyn Lake et al. (Sydney: University of New South Wales Press, 2010), 103.
63 National Archives of Australia and Archives New Zealand, 'About', Discovering Anzacs, National Archives of Australia, 2007, accessed 15 December 2016, https://discoveringanzacs.naa.gov.au/about/. See also Department of Veterans' Affairs, 'The Office of Australian War Graves', Department of Veterans' Affairs, n.d., accessed 15 December 2016,www.dva.gov.au/commemorations-memorials-and-war-graves/office-australian-war-graves; AWM, 'Researching Family History', AWM, n.d., accessed 23 September 2020, www.awm.gov.au/collection/understanding-the-memorials-collection/researching-family-history.
64 John Howard, 'Transcript of the Prime Minister the Hon John Howard MP Address at the Launch of a Gift to the Nation', 12 April 2007, NAA, 2007, archived by NLA, 2 June 2011, accessed 16 September 2020, https://webarchive.nla.gov.au/awa/20110602085221/http://www.naa.gov.au/Images/Howard-transcript_tcm2-8345.pdf.
65 Marianne Hirsch, *Family Frames: Photography, Narrative and Postmemory* (Cambridge, Mass.: Harvard University Press, 1997), 22.

66 Andrea Liss, *Trespassing through Shadows: Memory, Photography and the Holocaust* (Minneapolis: University of Minnesota Press, 1998), 86.
67 Aleida Assmann, 'Memory, Individual and Collective', in *The Oxford Handbook of Contextual Political Analysis*, ed. Robert E. Goodin and Charles Tilly (Oxford: Oxford University Press, 2006), 220–1.
68 Carolyn Holbrook and Bart Ziino, 'Family History and the Great War in Australia', in *Remembering the First World War*, ed. Bart Ziino (Abingdon, Oxon.: Routledge, 2015), 39–40.
69 Bruce Scates, 'How War Came Home: Reflections on the Digitisation of Australia's Repatriation Files', *History Australia* 16, no. 1 (2019): 198–9.
70 Bart Ziino, '"A Lasting Gift to His Descendants": Family Memory and the Great War in Australia', *History & Memory* 22, no. 2 (2010): 140.
71 Kyle's book was one of the top-selling adult non-fiction books between April 2003 and March 2005. Roy Kyle, *An Anzac's Story* (Camberwell, Vic.: Penguin Books, 2003); 'Bestsellers 1 April 2003 to 31 March 2004', *Australian Bookseller & Publisher* 83, no. 2 (2004): 62–3; 'Bestsellers 4 Weeks to 26 March 2005', *Australian Bookseller & Publisher* 84, no. 10 (2005): 30. See also E.P.F. Lynch, *Somme Mud: The War Experiences of an Infantryman in France 1916–1919* (North Sydney, NSW: Random House, 2008); Stephen Dando-Collins, *Crack Hardy: From Gallipoli to Flanders to the Somme, the True Story of Three Australian Brothers at War* (North Sydney, NSW: Vintage Books, 2011).
72 Carolyn Holbrook, *Anzac: The Unauthorised Biography* (Sydney: NewSouth Publishing, 2014), 151.
73 Gilbert Mant, ed. *Soldier Boy: The Letters of Gunner W.J. Duffell, 1915–18* (Kenthurst, NSW: Kangaroo Press, 1992), 9.
74 For example, see the difference between the language of Duffell's letters and that of his manuscript concerning third Ypres in ibid., 9, 97–111.
75 'Futile': W.H. Downing, *To the Last Ridge* (Sydney: Duffy & Snellgrove, 1998), xv; 'horror': Patrick Wilson, ed. *So Far from Home: The Remarkable Diaries of Eric Evans, an Australian Soldier during World War I* (East Roseville, NSW: Kangaroo Press, 2002), 1; 'despair': Kyle, *Anzac's Story*, 16; 'massacre': Jillian Oppenheimer, *Horses and Guns: Poss Nivison's War with the Australian Field Artillery Brigades, on the Western Front, 1915–1919* (Walcha, NSW: Ohio Productions, 2005), x; 'tragedy': Maurice Campbell and Graeme Hoskens, eds., *Four Australians at War: Letters to Argyle, 1914–19* (Kenthurst, NSW: Kangaroo Press, 1996), 8; 'tragedy' and 'misery': Noel Carthew, *Voices from the Trenches: Letters to Home* (Frenchs Forest, NSW: New Holland, 2002), 165, 175, 183, 184, 212.
76 Carthew, *Voices from the Trenches*, 234; K.M. Lyall, ed. *Letters from an Anzac Gunner* (East Kew, Vic.: Lyall's Yarns, 1990), 174.
77 Peter Stanley, 'War without End', in *Australian History Now*, ed. Anna Clark and Paul Ashton (Sydney: NewSouth Publishing, 2013), 91.
78 Michael McKernan, 'Making History', *Journal of the Australian War Memorial*, no. 19 (1991): 40–1; Stanley, 'War without End', 91–6.
79 Martin Crotty and Craig Stockings, 'The Minefield of Australian Military History', *Australian Journal of Politics and History* 60, no. 4 (2014): 588–9; Stanley, 'War without End', 101–2; Jeffrey Grey, 'Cuckoo in the Nest? Australian

Military Historiography: The State of the Field', *History Compass* 6, no. 2 (2008): 458–60.
80 Robin Prior and Trevor Wilson, *Passchendaele: The Untold Story*, 2nd ed. (New Haven, Conn.: Yale University Press, 2002); Paul Ham, *Passchendaele: Requiem for Doomed Youth* (North Sydney, NSW: Random House, 2016).
81 Daniel G. Dancocks, *Legacy of Valour: The Canadians at Passchendaele 1917* (Edmonton: Hurtig Publishers, 1986); Glyn Harper, *Massacre at Passchendaele: The New Zealand Story* (Auckland: HarperCollins Publishers, 2000).
82 Peter FitzSimons, *Victory at Villers-Bretonneux: Why a French Town Will Never Forget the Anzacs* (North Sydney, NSW: Penguin Random House Australia, 2016); John Laffin, *The Battle of Hamel: The Australians' Finest Victory* (East Roseville, NSW: Kangaroo Press, 1999); David Coombes, *A Greater Sum of Sorrow: The Battles of Bullecourt* (Newport, NSW: Big Sky Publishing, 2016); Peter Stanley, *Men of Mont St Quentin: Between Victory and Death* (Carlton North, Vic.: Scribe, 2009); Meleah Hampton, *Attack on the Somme: 1st Anzac Corps and the Battle of Pozières Ridge, 1916* (Solihull: Helion & Company, 2016); Peter FitzSimons, *Fromelles & Pozières: In the Trenches of Hell* (North Sydney, NSW: William Heinemann, 2015); Christopher Wray, *Pozières: Echoes of a Distant Battle* (Port Melbourne, Vic.: Cambridge University Press, 2016); Scott Bennett, *Pozières: The Anzac Story* (Brunswick, Vic.: Scribe, 2012); Peter Charlton, *Pozieres 1916: Australians on the Somme* (North Ryde, NSW: Methuen Haynes, 1986).
83 For example, FitzSimons, *Fromelles & Pozières*; Carole Wilkinson, *Fromelles: Australia's Bloodiest Day at War* (Fitzroy, Vic.: Black Dog Books, 2012); Roger Lee, *The Battle of Fromelles: 1916* (Canberra: Army History Unit, 2010); Patrick Lindsay, *Fromelles: The Story of Australia's Darkest Day; The Search for Our Fallen Heroes of World War One* (Prahan, Vic.: Hardie Grant, 2007); Robin S. Corfield, *Don't Forget Me, Cobber: The Battle of Fromelles, 19/20 July 1916; An Inquiry* (Rosanna, Vic.: Corfield and Company, 2000).
84 *Beneath Hill 60*, directed by Jeremy Sims, produced by Bill Leimbach, Silence Productions, screenplay by David Roach (Australia: Paramount Pictures, 2010).
85 Eric Leed, *No Man's Land: Combat and Identity in World War I* (Cambridge: Cambridge University Press, 1979), 140–8.
86 *Reveille*, August 1932 – June 1936.
87 Leed, *No Man's Land*, 148; Sebastian Faulks, *Birdsong* (London: Vintage, 2004), x, 121–4.
88 David Roach, 'Based on a True Story: Writing *Beneath Hill 60*', *Teaching History* 44, no. 3 (2010): 18.
89 Screen Australia, *Annual Report 08/09*, Screen Australia, 2009, accessed 11 October 2016, www.screenaustralia.gov.au/getmedia/5c43905b-da1d-43ea-a237-8b51c9b6c1c4/SA-Annual-Report-2008-2009.pdf?ext=.pdf), 93.
90 Daniel Reynaud, 'Digging Up New Anzac Legends', *History Australia* 7, no. 2 (2010): 40.2.
91 Screen Australia, 'Top 100 Australian Feature Films of All Time', Screen Australia, n.d., accessed 31 October 2016, www.screenaustralia.gov.au/fact-finders/cinema/australian-films/top-films-at-the-box-office; *Sydney Morning Herald*, 15 April 2010.

92 *Age* (Melbourne), 11 July 2002; *Australian*, 10 July 2002; *Sydney Morning Herald*, 12 July 2002; *Daily Telegraph*, 12 July 2002.
93 Jean-Noel Ducasse, 'Didier Pontzeele & Senator Glenn Sterle – Belgian War Graves', SBS French, 9 October 2013, accessed 28 October 2016, www.sbs.com.au/yourlanguage/french/en/content/didier-pontzeele-senator-glenn-sterle-belgian-war-graves.
94 Bruce Billson (Minister Assisting the Minister for Defence), 'Discovery of Remains on the Western Front', media release VA097 (Department of Defence, 18 September 2009).
95 *Canberra Times*, 20 September 2006; *Mercury* (Hobart), 20 September 2006; *Daily Telegraph*, 11 November 2006.
96 Bruce Billson (Minister Assisting the Minister for Defence), 'Army Progress in Bid to Identify WW1 Remains', media release MINASSIST 014/2007 (Department of Defence, 9 March 2007); *Age*, 21 April 2007.
97 *Canberra Times*, 25 August and 8 September 2007; *Sydney Morning Herald*, 5 October 2007.
98 *Age*, 5 September 2007; Bruce Billson (Minister Assisting the Minister for Defence), 'Missing World War One Diggers Identified through DNA', media release MINASSIST 048/2007 (Department of Defence, 5 September 2007); *Canberra Times*, 5 September 2007; *Age*, 5 October 2007.
99 For example, *Herald Sun*, 4 October 2007; *Sydney Morning Herald*, 5 October 2007; *Courier-Mail*, 5 October 2007.
100 Bruce Billson (Minister Assisting the Minister for Defence), 'New Development in Identification of Australian WW1 Soldiers', media release 053/2007 (Department of Defence, 17 October 2007); *West Australian*, 30 September and 1 October 2008.
101 For more on Englezos' role, see Lindsay, *Fromelles*.
102 Joan Beaumont, *Broken Nation: Australians in the Great War* (Crows Nest, NSW: Allen & Unwin, 2013), 196–200.
103 *Sydney Morning Herald*, 12 October 2007.
104 *Vetaffairs*, June 2006.
105 *Office of Australian War Graves Journal 2005–2006* (Phillip, ACT: Office of Australian War Graves, 2006), 79–80; Repatriation Commission, National Treatment Monitoring Committee and Department of Veterans' Affairs, *Annual Report, 2006–2007* (Canberra: Department of Veterans' Affairs, 2007), 125; Repatriation Commission, Military Rehabilitation and Compensation Commission, National Treatment Monitoring Committee and Department of Veterans' Affairs, *Annual Reports, 2007–2008* (Canberra: Department of Veterans' Affairs, 2008), 125.
106 *Vetaffairs*, September 2007.
107 *Sydney Morning Herald*, 8 September 2007; Bart Ziino, 'Who Owns Gallipoli? Australia's Gallipoli Anxieties 1915–2005', *Journal of Australian Studies* 30, no. 88 (2006): 4–12; Gammage, 'Anzac Cemetery', 138–40; John McQuilton, 'Gallipoli as Contested Commemorative Space', in *Gallipoli: Making History*, ed. Jenny Macleod (London: Frank Cass, 2004), 151–4; Fathi, *Our Corner of the Somme*, 145–6.

108 *Australian*, 8 September 2007; *Sydney Morning Herald*, 25 October 2007; *West Australian*, 21 February 2008; *Vetaffairs*, June 2008.
109 Repatriation Commission, Military Rehabilitation and Compensation Commission, National Treatment Monitoring Committee and Department of Veterans' Affairs, *Annual Reports, 2008–2009* (Canberra: Department of Veterans' Affairs, 2009), 155; Freddy Declerck (former chairman of the Memorial Museum Passchendaele 1917), email to author, 10 March 2017; Repatriation Commission, Military Rehabilitation and Compensation Commission and Department of Veterans' Affairs, *Annual Reports, 2009–2010* (Canberra: Department of Veterans' Affairs, 2010), 202; Johan Durnez, 'Anzac Day in Belgium Pt 1', Family and Friends of the First AIF Inc., 28 April 2010, accessed 9 November 2016, http://fffaif.org.au/?p=8485.
110 *Sydney Morning Herald*, 20 April 2013.
111 Scates, *Return to Gallipoli*, 199–201.
112 Somme Tourisme, 'Workshops-Australie', Somme Tourisme, n.d., accessed 22 November 2016, www.somme-tourisme.org/Vos-outils/Commercialisation/Les-groupes/Workshops-Australie (webpage deleted); Observatoire de Tourisme Westtoer, *Tourisme de mémoire – Great War: départements Nord, Pas-de-Calais, Somme* (Westtoer: Observatoire de Tourisme Westtoer, 2015), 44, 54; Kenniscentrum Westtoer, *Wereldoorlog I bezoekers in de Westhoek: resultaten bezoekersonderzoek 2013-2014-2015*, Kenniscentrum Westtoer, 2016, accessed 21 November 2016, http://corporate.westtoer.be/sites/westtoer_2015/files/westtoer_corporate/kenniscentrum/ra-woi-bezoekers_westhoek_bezoekersonderzoek_2013-2014-2015.pdf, 123–4; Jennifer Stephenson (first secretary, Department of Veterans' Affairs, France and Belgium), interview with the author, 9 June 2016.
113 Observatoire de Tourisme Westtoer, *Tourisme de mémoire*, 75; Kenniscentrum Westtoer, *Wereldoorlog I bezoekers*, 124; Scates, *Return to Gallipoli*, 100–21.
114 Observatoire de Tourisme Westtoer, *Tourisme de mémoire*, 12; Kenniscentrum Westtoer, *Wereldoorlog I bezoekers*, 18; Kenniscentrum Westtoer, *Wereldoorlog I herdenkinstoerisme in de Westhoek: volumes en evoluties 2013–2018*, Kenniscentrum Westtoer, 2019, accessed 9 December 2019, https://corporate.westtoer.be/sites/westtoer_2015/files/westtoer_corporate/kenniscentrum/ra-woi-herdenkingstoerisme_wh_volumes_evoluties_2013-2018.pdf, 23; Somme Tourisme, 'Workshops-Australie'; Somme Tourisme, 'Les sites de visite: tableau de bord 2017 2018 2019', Somme Tourisme, 2020, accessed 12 October 2020, www.somme-tourisme.org/app/download/12080969012/Tableau+de+bord+2018+2019+2020.pdf?t=1600174176.
115 Alan Griffin (Minister for Veterans' Affairs), 'Historic Agreement between Flanders and Australia Recognises Shared War History', media release VA027 (Department of Veterans' Affairs, 22 April 2009); Warren Snowdon (Minister for Veterans' Affairs), 'Shared History Helps Forge Stronger Ties with Belgium', media release VA099 (Department of Veterans' Affairs, 23 November 2012).
116 The Australian Remembrance Trail sites in France are Fromelles, Bullecourt, Thiepval, Pozières (1st Australian Division memorial and the windmill), Villers-Bretonneux, Le Hamel, Mont St Quentin and Bellenglise. Department of Veterans' Affairs, 'Australians on the Western Front 1914–1918', Department

of Veterans' Affairs, 19 July 2008, archived by NLA, 19 July 2008, accessed 12 October 2020, https://webarchive.nla.gov.au/awa/20080718164527/http://www.ww1westernfront.gov.au/.

117 Australians fought in the vicinity of Ploegsteert Wood during the battle of Messines, and the nearby CWGC Toronto Avenue Cemetery is the only all-Australian cemetery in Belgium.

118 Joan Beaumont, 'Australia's Global Memory Footprint: Memorial Building on the Western Front, 1916–2015', *Australian Historical Studies* 46, no. 1 (2015): 62.

119 Department of Veterans' Affairs, 'Australians on the Western Front'.

120 Joffrey Levalleux, 'Discoveries: At Bullecourt 1917, Immerse Yourself in the Private World of the Australian Soldiers', Arras Pays d'Artois Tourisme, n.d., accessed 9 October 2020, www.arraspaysdartois.com/en/remembrance/visit-bullecourt-1917-museum/; *Vetaffairs*, Spring and Summer 2014.

121 Sir John Monash Centre, n.d., accessed 24 September 2020, https://sjmc.gov.au/; Bruce Scates, 'Remembering and Forgetting the First World War at the Sir John Monash Centre', in *The Great War: Aftermath and Commemoration*, ed. Carolyn Holbrook and Keir Reeves (Sydney: University of New South Wales Press, 2019), 197. For a French perspective on the Sir John Monash Centre, see Romain Fathi, 'Le prosélytisme mémoriel australien dans la Somme et le nouveau Centre Sir John Monash', *Revue d'histoire* 3, no. 143 (2019): 129–47.

122 Toerisme Vlaanderen and Westtoer, *Toeristisch marketingplan 100 jaar Groote Oorlog*, (Brussels: Toerisme Vlaanderen and Westtoer, 2012), 7; Peter Slosse (business director of In Flanders Fields Museum and head of tourism for Ypres), interview with the author, 30 September 2015; Steven Vandenbussche (curator of Memorial Museum Passchendaele 1917 and tourism officer for Zonnebeke), interview with the author, 30 September 2015; Anny Beauprez (founding member of Plugstreet 14–18 Experience and former president of tourism for Comines-Warneton) and François Maekelberg (founding member of Plugstreet 14–18 Experience and president of local returned services associations in Comines-Warneton), interview with the author, 2 October 2015; Caroline Winter, 'The Multiple Roles of Battlefield War Museums: A Study at Fromelles and Passchendaele', *Journal of Heritage Tourism* 13, no. 3 (2018): 215.

123 Plugstreet 14–18 Experience, 'Presentation', Plugstreet 14–18 Experience, n.d., accessed 2 December 2016, www.plugstreet1418.be/en/presentation.

124 'Australians at Passchendaele', interactive display, Memorial Museum Passchendaele 1917, Zonnebeke, 30 October 2015.

Epilogue

1 Wereldoorlog I in de Westhoek, 'Centenary of the Battle of Polygon Wood: Reflective Program – Zonnebeke – 26/09/2017', Wereldoorlog I in de Westhoek, September 2017, accessed 27 December 2019, www.wo1.be/en/youwerethere/11649/centenary-of-the-battle-of-polygon-wood-reflective-program.

2 Repatriation Commission, Military Rehabilitation and Compensation Commission and Department of Veterans' Affairs, *Annual Reports, 2017–2018* (Canberra: Department of Veterans' Affairs, 2018), 71.

3   N.G. McNicol, *The Thirty-Seventh: History of the Thirty-Seventh Battalion A.I.F.* (Melbourne: Modern Printing Co., 1936), 148; Geoffrey Serle, *John Monash: A Biography*, 2nd paperback ed. (Carlton, Vic.: Melbourne University Press, 2002), 294.
4   *Evening News* (Sydney), 22 September 1917; *Age* (Melbourne), 24 September 1917; *Brisbane Courier*, 24 September 1917; C.E.W. Bean, *The Official History of Australia in the War of 1914–1918*, 11th ed., vol. 4, *The Australian Imperial Force in France in 1917* (Sydney: Angus & Robertson, 1941), 112n770.
5   Harington to Monash, 11 October 1917, AWM: 3DRL 2316, RCDIG0000622.
6   *Advertiser* (Adelaide), 3 August 1917.
7   James Pollard, 'War Cobbers', unpublished manuscript, [ca 1934], AWM: MSS1356.

BIBLIOGRAPHY

This bibliography is divided into two sections: the first contains archival sources grouped under the relevant repository, and the second lists all other sources consulted for this book, with the exception of author correspondence and interviews, newspapers and periodicals, which are cited only in the Notes.

Archival Sources

Australian War Memorial, Canberra (AWM)
3DRL/2316, Monash, Sir John KCMG KCB (General, b. 1865 – d. 1931), 1914–19.
AWM16, Australian War Records Section registry files and register of file titles, 1914–18 War.
        4372/21/3, Proposal re scheme of models required for Australian War Museum, 1918–19.
        4379/1/1 part 8, Weekly reports Australian War Records Sub-section France – reports number 52 to 67 covering weeks ending 16 March 1919 to 22 June 1919 and related correspondence, 1919.
AWM25, Written records, 1914–18 War.
        981/3, Australian War Records Section. Correspondence, memos, and instructions regarding collection of war specimens and trophies, 1918.
        1013/36, Notes in connection with war record work in Egypt and Palestine, 1917–18.
AWM27, Records arranged according to AWM Library subject classification, ca 1 January 1927 – ca 31 December 1970.
        623/1, Further memoir by C E W Bean, concerning the official records and history of the AIF and the establishment of a memorial, 16 April 1919.
        623/2, Divisional memorials – General, 1930.
        623/3, Australian Corps and miscellaneous memorials, 1919.
        623/9, Army Order – Memorials on battlefields, 1919.
AWM38, Official History, 1914–18 War: Records of C E W Bean, Official Historian.
        3DRL 606/53/1, Diary, July 1916.
        3DRL 606/54/1, Diary, July–August 1916.
        3DRL 606/82/1, Diary, July 1917.
        3DRL 606/84/1, Diary, August 1917.
        3DRL 606/88/1, Diary, September 1917.
        3DRL 606/89/1, Diary, September–October 1917.
        3DRL 606/90/1, Diary, October 1917.

3DRL 606/91/1, Diary, October 1917.
3DRL 606/94/1, Diary, November–December 1917.
3DRL 6673/270, Correspondence, 1914–16.
3DRL 6673/307, Correspondence, 1928–31.
3DRL 6673/371, Correspondence, 1919–20.
3DRL 6673/403, Papers, 1930–35.
3DRL 6673/802, Correspondence, 1920–56.
3DRL 6673/803, Papers, 1922–26.
3DRL 6673/813, Correspondence, 1920–21.
3DRL 8042/60, Letters, 1932.

AWM93, AWM registry files – First series, 1 January 1902 – 31 December 1993.
6/1/15, Layout of Collections in Exhibition Building, Sydney, 1925–26.
6/1/27C, Exhibition in Melbourne of 'Menin Gate at Midnight', 1929.
13/1/37, Battlefield models – General file, 1925–40.
13/1/67, Model illustrating the chain of evacuation of the wounded, 1922–23.
20/1/1A, Publicity – AWM, Newspapers, 1922–36.
21/11/23, Various drafts and other papers relating to distribution of Menin Gate pictures, 1930.

AWM184, AIF publications and Anzac Book Trust Fund files ('unit histories correspondence'), 1915–47.
9, Applications by unit historians for advances from Anzac Book Trust Fund, 1919–41.
39, 1st Battalion, 1919–31.
48, 12th Battalion, 1920–31.
49, 13th Battalion, 1921–24.
50, 14th Battalion, 1919–32.

AWM224, Unit manuscript histories, 1 August 1914 – 31 December 1946.
MSS553 part 1, Australian War Records Section: Report on the work, May 1917 – September 1918.

AWM225, Records presented to the AWM by heads of state and other official visitors, 1917–2000.
2, In Grateful Memory: from the Prime Minister of Belgium His Excellency Gaston Eyskens to the Prime Minister of Australia His Excellency John Gorton on the occasion of the first official visit of a Belgian Cabinet Minister to Australia His Excellency Henri Fayat, January 1970 (commemorative volume of photographs relating to the Ypres salient offensives, June–October 1917).

AWM315, AWM registry files – Second series, 1917–90.
566/003/005, Models: Plan model of Flanders Battlefield, 1922–34.
748/022/001 01, Exhibits: Relics – Official – Other Allies – Menin Gate Lions presented to AWM by the Belgian Government, 1935–71.
748/022/001 part 2, Lions presented to AWM by Belgium Government (Menin Gate Lion), 1985–87.

AWM333, Records of the documentation, control and exhibition of the AWM relics collection, ca 1917 – ca 1951.

2/4/5, Descriptions and notes for captions, Relics – 3rd Battle of Ypres – Winter 1917/18, 1920–50.
MSS1356, James Pollard, unpublished manuscript entitled 'War Cobbers' entered in the RSSILA Centenary War Novel Competition, ca 1934.

Commonwealth War Graves Commission, Maidenhead (CWGC)

WG 219 pt. 2, box 1009, Memorials to the Missing, 1920–23.
WG 219/2/1 pt. 1, box 1010, Memorials to the Missing – Tyne Cot & Menin Gate, 1920–23.
WG 219/2/1 pt. 2, box 1010, Memorials to the Missing - Tyne Cot & Menin Gate, 1923–29.
WG 857/3 pt. 1, box 1124, Battle Exploit Memorials – Australia, 1919–34.
WG 857/3/1, box 1060, Battle Exploit Memorials Australians 5th Div. Polygon Wood, 1919–56.
WG 1406/3, box 1087, Memorial Crosses and Unit Memorials – Australians, 1924–30.

In Flanders Fields Museum Research Centre, Ypres (IFFM)

MAP 1004, Australische Troepen (1), n.d.
MAP 1074, Menenpoort plechtigheden (Ieper) (1), n.d.
MAP 1074, Menenpoort plechtigheden (Ieper) (2), n.d.

National Archives of Australia, Canberra (NAA)

A1, Department of Home Affairs [II] (Central Office), Correspondence files, annual single number series, 1890–1969.
    1930/2905, 'Ghosts of Menin Gate' – Presentation of picture to the Commonwealth, 1928–30.
    1936/1567, AWM Sculptured Lion from Ypres, 1936–37.
A458, Department of External Affairs, Correspondence files, multiple number series, second system, 1899–1939.
    R337/7, Graves. Visit of Mr Bruce, 1924.
    T337/7, Defence. Graves in France and Belgium. Visit of Mrs Allan, 1924.
A461, Prime Minister's Department, Correspondence files, multiple number series (third system), 1901–50.
    D370/1/15, War memorials abroad – Divisional memorials in France, 1919–47.
A571, Department of the Treasury, Correspondence files, annual single number series, 1901–78.
    1952/2868, Coronation of Her Majesty Queen Elizabeth the Second, June 1953, 1952–55.
A663, Department of Defence, Correspondence files, multiple number series with 'O' prefix, 1939–90.
    O190/1/45, Australian Coronation Contingent, 1953.
A664, Department of Defence, Correspondence files, multiple number series, 1912–42.
    462/401/253, Australian Coronation Contingent, 1936–38.
    487/401/24, Ypres Memorial Church Fund – Correspondence, 1924–29.

A705, Department of Air, Correspondence files, multiple number (Melbourne) series, 1912–88.
    226/1/417, Coronation Contingent, 1936–41.
    226/1/525 part 1, Coronation Contingent 1953 – Policy, 1952–53.
A1838, Department of External Affairs, Correspondence files, multiple number series, 1914–93.
    25/1/3/25 part 1, France – Battle of the Somme Pilgrimage, 1967–76.
    1516/6/313 part 1, Visit overseas – Pilgrimage to Mt St Quentin 1971, 1970–71.
A2700, Curtin, Forde and Chifley Ministries – folders of Cabinet minutes and agenda, 1941–49.
    1208A, Australian Divisional Memorials in France and Belgium, 1947.
A2909, Australian High Commission, United Kingdom – War Memorial Section, Australian Graves Services, 1916–.
    AGS1/2/1, Australian Battle Memorials and Soldiers' Graves Committee – Minutes, 1919.
    AGS6/1/5 part 1, Memorials – Western Theatre General, 1918–20.
    AGS6/1/5 part 2, Memorials – Western Theatre, 1920–25.
A3211, Australian High Commission, United Kingdom, Correspondence files, annual single number series, 1960–.
    1962/835 part 1, Picture 'Ghosts of Menin Gate' by Captain Longstaff, 1928–51.
A6006, Cabinet Office, Folders of copies of Cabinet Papers, 1901–.
    1922/1/6, 1st Tunnelling Company Memorial, Hill 60, 1922.
B2455, First Australian Imperial Force Personnel Dossiers, 1914–20.
    JEFFRIES Clarence Smith, 1914–20.
CP103/22, Prime Minister's Department, Miscellaneous correspondence, 1901–32.
    23A, Papers regarding Australian war memorials in France and Belgium, and war cemeteries, 1923.

National Library of Australia, Canberra (NLA)

MS 6609, Records of the Returned and Services League of Australia, 1916–97.
    Series 1, box 35, item 3884, Ypres Memorial Church Fund, 1928.
    Series 3, box 389, Minutes of the Federal Executive, 1950–58.

Stadsarchief Ieper, Ypres (SI)

TOE/48 252, Stadsbestuur Ieper, Toerisme, Organisatie van activiteiten ihkv de herdenking van de Eerste Wereldoorlog, Stukken betreffende bezoeken in het kader van de herdenking van de Eerste Wereldoorlog, 1965–69.
TOE/55 336, Stadsbestuur Ieper, Toerisme, Organisatie van activiteiten ihkv de herdenking van de Eerste Wereldoorlog, Correspondentie betreffende de herdenking van 50 jaar Eerste Wereldoorlog, gerangschikt per land, 1964.
TOE/64 404, Stadsbestuur Ieper, Toerisme, Organisatie van activiteiten ihkv de herdenking van de Eerste Wereldoorlog, Dossier inzake de organisatie van Anzac Day, 1967–69.

TOE/64 410, Stadsbestuur Ieper, Toerisme, Organisatie van activiteiten ihkv de herdenking van de Eerste Wereldoorlog, Dossier inzake de organisatie van Anzac Day, 1970.

Other Sources

Adam-Smith, Patsy. *The Anzacs*. Melbourne: Thomas Nelson, 1978.

Anderson, Benedict. *Imagined Communities: Reflections on the Origin and Spread of Nationalism*. 3rd ed. London: Verso, 2006.

Andrews, E.M. *The Anzac Illusion: Anglo-Australian Relations during World War I*. Cambridge: Cambridge University Press, 1993.

———. 'Bean and Bullecourt: Weaknesses and Strengths of the Official History of Australia in the First World War.' *Revue internationale d'histoire militaire* 72 (1990): 25–47.

———. 'The Media and the Military: Australian War Correspondents and the Appointment of a Corps Commander, 1918 – A Case Study.' *War & Society* 8, no. 2 (1990): 83–103.

Anzacs (mini-series). Directed by John Dixon, George Miller and Pino Amenta. Produced by Geoff Burrowes, Burrowes-Dixon Company. Screenplay by John Dixon, John Clarke and James Mitchell. Pyrmont, NSW: Roadshow Entertainment, 2014. DVD. First aired 27 October 1985 on Nine Network.

Ashplant, Timothy G., Graham Dawson and Michael Roper. 'The Politics of War Memory and Commemoration: Contexts, Structures and Dynamics.' In *The Politics of Memory: Commemorating War*, edited by Timothy G. Ashplant, Graham Dawson and Michael Roper, 3–85. New Brunswick, NJ: Transaction Publishers, 2009.

Ashton, Paul, and Paula Hamilton. *History at the Crossroads: Australians and the Past*. Ultimo, NSW: Halstead Press, 2007.

Assmann, Aleida. 'Memory, Individual and Collective.' In *The Oxford Handbook of Contextual Political Analysis*, edited by Robert E. Goodin and Charles Tilly, 210–26. Oxford: Oxford University Press, 2006.

Assmann, Jan, and John Czaplicka. 'Collective Memory and Cultural Identity.' *New German Critique*, no. 65 (1995): 125–33.

Augé, Marc. *Oblivion*. Minneapolis: University of Minnesota Press, 2004.

Australian War Memorial (AWM). *Australian War Memorial Museum: The Relics and Records of Australia's Effort in the Defence of the Empire, 1914–1918*. Booklet. Sydney: Government Printer, 1927.

———. 'Last Post Ceremony.' AWM, n.d. Accessed 14 September 2020. www.awm.gov.au/commemoration/last-post-ceremony.

———. *'Menin Gate at Midnight': The Story of Captain Will Longstaff's Great Allegorical Painting (Gate of Eternal Memories)*. Booklet. Melbourne: AWM, ca 1929.

———. 'Researching Family History.' AWM, n.d. Accessed 23 September 2020. www.awm.gov.au/collection/understanding-the-memorials-collection/researching-family-history.

Australian War Museum. *Australian War Museum: The Relics and Records of Australia's Effort in the Defence of the Empire, 1914–1918*. Booklet. Melbourne: Osboldstone & Co., 1922.

Australians on the Western Front: August 29 – September 3 1993; Order of Service. Program. Canberra: Department of Veterans' Affairs, 1993.

AWM. *See* Australian War Memorial.

Bean, C.E.W. (Charles Edwin Woodrow), ed. *The Anzac Book: Written and Illustrated in Gallipoli by the Men of Anzac*. 3rd ed. Sydney: UNSW Press, 2010.

———. 'Australia's Records: Preserved as Sacred Things; Pictures, Relics, and Writings.' *Anzac Bulletin*, no. 40 (1917): 14–15.

———. *Gallipoli Mission*. Canberra: AWM, 1948.

———. *Letters from France*. London: Cassell, 1917.

———. *The Official History of Australia in the War of 1914–1918*. 12th ed. Vol. 3, *The Australian Imperial Force in France in 1916*. Sydney: Angus & Robertson, 1941.

———. *The Official History of Australia in the War of 1914–1918*. 11th ed. Vol. 4, *The Australian Imperial Force in France in 1917*. Sydney: Angus & Robertson, 1941.

———. *The Official History of Australia in the War of 1914–1918*. 1st ed. Vol. 6, *The Australian Imperial Force in France during the Allied Offensive, 1918*. Sydney: Angus & Robertson, 1942.

———. 'The Writing of the Australian Official History of the Great War: Sources, Methods and Some Conclusions.' *Royal Australian Historical Society Journal and Proceedings* 24, no. 2 (1938): 85–112.

Beaumont, Joan. 'Anzac Day to VP Day: Arguments and Interpretations.' *Journal of the Australian War Memorial*, no. 40 (2007). Accessed 5 November 2020. www.awm.gov.au/journal/j40/beaumont/.

———. 'The Anzac Legend.' In *Australia's War 1914–1918*, edited by Joan Beaumont, 149–80. St Leonards, NSW: Allen & Unwin, 1995.

———. 'Australian Citizenship and the Two World Wars.' *Australian Journal of Politics and History* 53, no. 2 (2007): 171–82.

———. 'Australia's Global Memory Footprint: Memorial Building on the Western Front, 1916–2015.' *Australian Historical Studies* 46, no. 1 (2015): 45–63.

———. *Australia's War 1914–1918*. St Leonards, NSW: Allen & Unwin, 1995.

———. *Broken Nation: Australians in the Great War*. Crows Nest, NSW: Allen & Unwin, 2013.

———. 'The Politics of a Divided Society.' In *Australia's War 1914–1918*, edited by Joan Beaumont, 35–63. St Leonards, NSW: Allen & Unwin, 1995.

———. 'Remembering the Heroes of Australia's Wars: From Heroic to Post-heroic Memory.' In *Heroism and the Changing Character of War*, edited by Sibylle Scheipers, 334–48. Houndmills, Hants.: Palgrave Macmillan, 2014.

Beaumont, Joan, Lachlan Grant and Aaron Pegram. 'Remembering and Rethinking Captivity.' In *Beyond Surrender: Australian Prisoners of War in the Twentieth Century*, edited by Joan Beaumont, Lachlan Grant and Aaron Pegram, 1–17. Carlton, Vic.: Melbourne University Press, 2015.

Beaumont, Joan, and Vijaya Joshi. *The Australian Centenary History of Defence*. Vol. 6, *Australian Defence: Sources and Statistics*. Melbourne: Oxford University Press, 2001.

Beneath Hill 60 (film). Directed by Jeremy Sims. Produced by Bill Leimbach, Silence Productions. Screenplay by David Roach. Australia: Paramount Pictures, 2010.

Bennett, Scott. *Pozières: The Anzac Story*. Brunswick, Vic.: Scribe, 2012.

Bibliography

Bennett, Tony. 'Introduction: National Times.' In *Celebrating the Nation: A Critical Study of Australia's Bicentenary*, edited by Tony Bennett, Pat Buckridge, David Carter and Colin Mercer, xiii–xviii. Sydney: Allen & Unwin, 1992.

Billson, Bruce (Minister Assisting the Minister for Defence). 'Army Progress in Bid to Identify WW1 Remains.' Media release MINASSIST 014/2007. Department of Defence, 9 March 2007.

———. 'Discovery of Remains on the Western Front.' Media release VA097. Department of Defence, 18 September 2009.

———. 'Missing World War One Diggers Identified through DNA.' Media release MINASSIST 048/2007. Department of Defence, 5 September 2007.

———. 'New Development in Identification of Australian WW1 Soldiers.' Media release 053/2007. Department of Defence, 17 October 2007.

Blair, Dale. *Dinkum Diggers: An Australian Battalion at War*. Carlton South, Vic.: Melbourne University Press, 2001.

Bond, Brian. 'British "Anti-war" Writers and Their Critics.' In *Facing Armageddon: The First World War Experienced*, edited by Hugh Cecil and Peter H. Liddle, 817–30. London: Leo Cooper, 1996.

———. 'Passchendaele: Verdicts, Past and Present.' In *Passchendaele in Perspective: The Third Battle of Ypres*, edited by Peter H. Liddle, 479–88. London: Leo Cooper, 1997.

Bongiorno, Frank. 'Anzac and the Politics of Inclusion.' In *Nation, Memory and Great War Commemoration: Mobilizing the Past in Europe, Australia and New Zealand*, edited by Shanti Sumartojo and Ben Wellings, 81–97. Oxford: Peter Lang, 2014.

Bonnell, Andrew, and Martin Crotty. 'Australia's History under Howard.' *Annals of the American Academy of Political and Social Science* 617 (2008): 149–65.

Bostyn, Franky, Kristof Blieck, Freddy Declerck, Frans Descamps and Jan Van der Fraenen. *Passchendaele 1917: The Story of the Fallen and Tyne Cot Cemetery*. Roeselare, West Flanders: Roularta Books, 2007.

Bracco, Rosa Maria. *Merchants of Hope: British Middlebrow Writers and the First World War, 1919–1939*. Oxford: Berg, 1993.

Brandon, Laura. *Art and War*. London: I.B. Tauris, 2007.

Brenchley, Fred, and Elizabeth Brenchley. *Myth Maker: Ellis Ashmead-Bartlett, the Englishman Who Sparked Australia's Gallipoli Legend*. Milton, Qld: John Wiley & Sons, 2005.

Bridger, T.D. *With the 27th Battery in France: 7th Bde, Australian Field Artillery*. London: St Clements Press, 1919.

Brooke, Rupert. *1914 and Other Poems*. London: Sidgwick & Jackson, 1915.

Browne, Geoff. 'Herring, Sir Edmund Francis (Ned) (1892–1982).' *Australian Dictionary of Biography*. National Centre of Biography, Australian National University, n.d. Accessed 30 March 2016. http://adb.anu.edu.au/biography/herring-sir-edmund-francis-ned-12626. First published in hardcopy by Melbourne University Press in 2007.

Burness, Elizabeth. 'The Menin Gate Lions.' *Sabretache* 29, no. 2 (1988): 10–19.

Caesar, Adrian. '"Kitch" and Imperialism: The *Anzac Book* Re-visited.' *Westerly* 40, no. 4 (1995): 76–85.

Campbell, Maurice, and Graeme Hoskens, eds. *Four Australians at War: Letters to Argyle, 1914–19*. Kenthurst, NSW: Kangaroo Press, 1996.

Carter, David. '"Esprit de Nation" and Popular Modernity: *Aussie* Magazine 1920–1931.' *History Australia* 5, no. 3 (2008): 74.1–74.22.

Carthew, Noel. *Voices from the Trenches: Letters to Home*. Frenchs Forest, NSW: New Holland, 2002.

Charlton, Peter. *Pozieres 1916: Australians on the Somme*. North Ryde, NSW: Methuen Haynes, 1986.

Chatto, R.H. *The Seventh Company (Field Engineers) A.I.F. 1915–1918*. Sydney: Smith's Newspapers, 1936.

Clark, Anna. 'Private Lives, Public History: Navigating Historical Consciousness in Australia.' *History Compass* 14, no. 1 (2016): 1–8.

Cochrane, Peter. 'At War at Home: Australian Attitudes during the Vietnam Wars.' In *Vietnam Remembered*, edited by Gregory Pemberton, 164–85. Sydney: Weldon Publishing, 1990.

Cochrane, Peter, and David Goodman. 'The Great Australian Journey: Cultural Logic and Nationalism in the Postmodern Era.' In *Celebrating the Nation: A Critical Study of Australia's Bicentenary*, edited by Tony Bennett, Pat Buckridge, David Carter and Colin Mercer, 175–90. Sydney: Allen & Unwin, 1992.

Commonwealth of Australia. *Parliamentary Debates*. House of Representatives, no. 182, 27 February 1992.

———. *Parliamentary Debates*. Senate, no. 4, 24 March 2014.

———. *Parliamentary Debates*. Senate, no. 14, 24 November 2015.

Condé, Anne-Marie. 'Imagining a Collection: Creating Australia's Records of War.' *reCollections* 2, no. 1 (2007). Accessed 5 November 2020. http://recollections.nma.gov.au/issues/vol_2_no_1/papers/imagining_a_collection.

———. 'John Treloar, Official War Art and the Australian War Memorial.' *Australian Journal of Politics and History* 53, no. 3 (2007): 451–64.

———. 'A Marriage of Sculpture and Art: Dioramas at the Memorial.' *Journal of the Australian War Memorial*, no. 19 (1991): 56–9.

Connelly, Mark. 'The Ypres League and the Commemoration of the Ypres Salient, 1914–1940.' *War in History* 16, no. 1 (2009): 51–76.

Connelly, Mark, and Stefan Goebel. *Ypres: Great Battles*. Oxford: Oxford University Press, 2018.

Connerty, Ian. *The Last Post: 30,000 Daily Tributes to the Fallen*. Tielt, West Flanders: Lannoo Publishers, 2014.

Coombes, David. *A Greater Sum of Sorrow: The Battles of Bullecourt*. Newport, NSW: Big Sky Publishing, 2016.

Corfield, Robin S. *Don't Forget Me, Cobber: The Battle of Fromelles, 19/20 July 1916; An Inquiry*. Rosanna, Vic.: Corfield and Company, 2000.

Corrigan, Gordon. *Mud, Blood and Poppycock: Britain and the First World War*. London: Cassell, 2003.

Cribbin, John, comp. *The Making of Anzacs*. Sydney: Collins/Fontana, 1985.

Crotty, Martin, and Craig Melrose. 'Anzac Day, Brisbane, Australia: Triumphalism, Mourning and Politics in Interwar Commemoration.' *Round Table* 96, no. 393 (2007): 679–92.

Crotty, Martin, and Craig Stockings. 'The Minefield of Australian Military History.' *Australian Journal of Politics and History* 60, no. 4 (2014): 580–91.

Curran, James. *The Power of Speech: Australian Prime Ministers Defining the National Image*. Melbourne: Melbourne University Press, 2004.

———. 'The "Thin Dividing Line": Prime Ministers and the Problem of Australian Nationalism, 1972–1996.' *Australian Journal of Politics and History* 48, no. 4 (2002): 469–86.

Curran, James, and Stuart Ward. *The Unknown Nation: Australia after Empire*. Carlton, Vic.: Melbourne University Press, 2010.

Curthoys, Ann. 'History and Reminiscence: Writing about the Anti-Vietnam-War Movement.' *Australian Feminist Studies* 7, no. 16 (1992): 116–36.

Cutlack, F.M. *The Australians: Their Final Campaign, 1918; An Account of the Concluding Operations of the Australian Divisions in France*. London: Sampson Low, Martson, 1918.

———, ed. *War Letters of General Monash*. Sydney: Angus & Robertson, 1934.

Damousi, Joy. 'War and Commemoration: "The Responsibility of Empire".' In *Australia's Empire*, edited by Deryck M. Schreuder and Stuart Ward, 288–311. Oxford: Oxford University Press, 2008.

———. 'Why Do We Get So Emotional about Anzac?' In *What's Wrong with Anzac? The Militarisation of Australian History*, edited by Marilyn Lake, Henry Reynolds, Mark McKenna and Joy Damousi, 94–109. Sydney: University of New South Wales Press, 2010.

Dancocks, Daniel G. *Legacy of Valour: The Canadians at Passchendaele 1917*. Edmonton: Hurtig Publishers, 1986.

Dando-Collins, Stephen. *Crack Hardy: From Gallipoli to Flanders to the Somme, the True Story of Three Australian Brothers at War*. North Sydney, NSW: Vintage Books, 2011.

Davison, Graeme. 'The Habit of Commemoration and the Revival of Anzac Day.' *Australian Cultural History*, no. 23 (2003): 73–82.

Dawson, Graham. *Soldier Heroes: British Adventure, Empire and the Imagining of Masculinities*. London: Routledge, 1994.

Dean, Arthur, and Eric W. Gutteridge. *The Seventh Battalion: Resume of the Activities of the Seventh Battalion in the Great War, 1914–1918*. Melbourne: A. Dean and E.W. Gutteridge, 1933.

Dendooven, Dominiek. *Menin Gate and Last Post: Ypres as Holy Ground*. 2nd ed. Translated by Ian Connerty. Koksijde, West Flanders: De Klaproos, 2003.

Dennis, Peter, Jeffrey Grey, Ewan Morris, Robin Prior and Jean Bou. *The Oxford Companion to Australian Military History*. 2nd ed. South Melbourne, Vic.: Oxford University Press, 2008.

Department of Veterans' Affairs. 'Australians on the Western Front 1914–1918.' Department of Veterans' Affairs, 19 July 2008. Archived by National Library of Australia, 19 July 2008. Accessed 12 October 2020. https://webarchive.nla.gov.au/awa/20080718164527/http://www.ww1westernfront.gov.au/.

———. 'The Office of Australian War Graves.' Department of Veterans' Affairs, n.d. Accessed 15 December 2016. www.dva.gov.au/commemorations-memorials-and-war-graves/office-australian-war-graves.

Dixon, Robert. 'Spotting the Fake: C.E.W. Bean, Frank Hurley and the Making of the 1923 Photographic Record of the War.' *History of Photography* 31, no. 2 (2007): 165–79.

Donaldson, Carina. '"The Book Is Inspired by the Australian Soldier": The Wounds of War and the Literary Rehabilitation of the Australian Soldier in Vietnam War Writing.' *Journal of Australian Studies* 36, no. 4 (2012): 473–86.
Donaldson, Carina, and Marilyn Lake. "Whatever Happened to the Anti-war Movement?' In *What's Wrong with Anzac? The Militarisation of Australian History*, edited by Marilyn Lake, Henry Reynolds, Mark McKenna and Joy Damousi, 71–93. Sydney: University of New South Wales Press, 2010.
Downing, W.H. *To the Last Ridge*. Sydney: Duffy & Snellgrove, 1998.
Ducasse, Jean-Noel. 'Didier Pontzeele & Senator Glenn Sterle – Belgian War Graves.' SBS French, 9 October 2013. Accessed 28 October 2016. www.sbs.com.au/yourlanguage/french/en/content/didier-pontzeele-senator-glenn-sterle-belgian-war-graves.
Durnez, Johan. 'Anzac Day in Belgium Pt 1.' Family and Friends of the First AIF Inc., 28 April 2010. Accessed 9 November 2016. http://fffaif.org.au/?p=8485.
———. 'The Johan and Hilde Newsletter.' E-newsletter. Privately distributed, 7 November 2013.
Ekins, Ashley, ed. *1918: Year of Victory*. Auckland: Exisle Publishing, 2010.
———. 'The Australians at Passchendaele.' In *Passchendaele in Perspective: The Third Battle of Ypres*, edited by Peter H. Liddle, 227–54. London: Leo Cooper, 1997.
———. '"Not One Scintilla of Evidence"? The Media, the Military and the Government in the Vietnam Water Torture Case.' *Australian Journal of Politics and History* 42, no. 3 (1996): 345–64.
Eksteins, Modris. *Rites of Spring: The Great War and the Birth of the Modern Age*. Boston: Houghton Mifflin Company, 1989.
Ennis, Helen. *Intersections: Photography, History and the National Library of Australia*. Canberra: National Library of Australia, 2004.
Evans, Raymond. *Loyalty and Disloyalty: Social Conflict on the Queensland Homefront, 1914–18*. North Sydney, NSW: Allen & Unwin, 1987.
Fathi, Romain. 'Le prosélytisme mémoriel australien dans la Somme et le nouveau Centre Sir John Monash.' *Revue d'histoire* 3, no. 143 (2019): 129–47.
———. *Our Corner of the Somme: Australia at Villers-Bretonneux*. Cambridge: Cambridge University Press, 2019.
———. *Représentations muséales du corps combattant de 14–18: l'Australian War Memorial de Canberra au prisme de l'Historial de la Grande Guerre de Péronne*. Paris: L'Harmattan, 2013.
Faulks, Sebastian. *Birdsong*. London: Vintage, 2004.
Fewster, Kevin, ed. *Bean's Gallipoli: The Diaries of Australia's Official War Correspondent*. 3rd ed. Crows Nest, NSW: Allen & Unwin, 2009.
———, ed. *Gallipoli Correspondent: The Frontline Diary of C.E.W. Bean*. Sydney: Allen & Unwin, 1983.
Fitzsimons, Peter. *Fromelles & Pozières: In the Trenches of Hell*. North Sydney, NSW: William Heinemann, 2015.
———. *Victory at Villers-Bretonneux: Why a French Town Will Never Forget the Anzacs*. North Sydney, NSW: Penguin Random House Australia, 2016.
The Forty-First: Being a Record of the 41st A.I.F. during the Great War. Facsimile reprint. Compiled by members of the Intelligence Staff. East Sussex: Naval &

Military Press for Imperial War Museum, 2010. First published by Australian Commonwealth Military Forces, ca 1920.

Frances, Raelene, and Bruce Scates, eds. *Beyond Gallipoli: New Perspectives on Anzac.* Clayton, Vic.: Monash University Publishing, 2016.

Fuller, J.G. *Troop Morale and Popular Culture in the British and Dominion Armies, 1914–1918.* Oxford: Clarendon Press, 1990.

Fussell, Paul. *The Great War and Modern Memory.* London: Oxford University Press, 1977.

Gallipoli (film). Directed by Peter Weir. Australia: Roadshow Film, 1981.

Gammage, Bill. 'The Anzac Cemetery.' *Australian Historical Studies* 38, no. 129 (2007): 124–40.

———. *The Broken Years: Australian Soldiers in the Great War.* 1st ed. Ringwood, Vic.: Penguin Books, 1975. Illustrated ed. Carlton, Vic: Melbourne University Publishing, 2010.

———. 'Introduction.' In C.E.W. Bean, *The Official History of Australia in the War of 1914–1918.* Vol. 4, *The Australian Imperial Force in France in 1917*, xxi–xxx. Brisbane: University of Queensland Press, 1983.

Garton, Stephen. *The Cost of War: Australians Return.* Melbourne: Oxford University Press, 1996.

Gerster, Robin. *Big-Noting: The Heroic Theme in Australian War Writing.* Carlton, Vic.: Melbourne University Press, 1987.

Gillis, John R. 'Memory and Identity: The History of a Relationship.' In *Commemorations: The Politics of National Identity*, edited by John R. Gillis, 3–26. Princeton, NJ: Princeton University Press, 1994.

Goebel, Stefan. *The Great War and Medieval Memory: War, Remembrance and Medievalism in Britain and Germany, 1914–1940.* Cambridge: Cambridge University Press, 2007.

Goldsworthy, David. 'Australian External Policy and the End of Britain's Empire.' *Australian Journal of Politics and History* 51, no. 1 (2005): 17–29.

Gorman, E. *'With the Twenty-Second': A History of the Twenty-Second Battalion, A.I.F.* 2nd ed. Melbourne: History House, 2001. First published in 1919.

Gough, Paul. '"An Epic of Mud": Artistic Interpretations of Third Ypres.' In *Passchendaele in Perspective: The Third Battle of Ypres*, edited by Peter H. Liddle, 409–21. London: Leo Cooper, 1997.

Graves, Matthew. 'Memorial Diplomacy in Franco-Australian Relations.' In *Nation, Memory and Great War Commemoration: Mobilizing the Past in Europe, Australia and New Zealand*, edited by Shanti Sumartojo and Ben Wellings, 169–87. Oxford: Peter Lang, 2014.

Gray, Anne. 'Will Longstaff's *Menin Gate at Midnight*.' *Journal of the Australian War Memorial*, no. 12 (1988): 47–50.

Green, F.C. *The Fortieth: A Record of the 40th Battalion, A.I.F.* Hobart: Government Printer, 1922.

Grey, Jeffrey. 'Cuckoo in the Nest? Australian Military Historiography: The State of the Field.' *History Compass* 6, no. 2 (2008): 455–68.

———. 'In Every War but One? Myth, History and Vietnam.' In *Zombie Myths of Australian Military History*, edited by Craig Stockings, 190–212. Sydney: University of New South Wales Press, 2010.

Griffin, Alan (Minister for Veterans' Affairs). 'Historic Agreement between Flanders and Australia Recognises Shared War History.' Media release VA027. Department of Veterans' Affairs, 22 April 2009.

Ham, Paul. *Passchendaele: Requiem for Doomed Youth*. North Sydney, NSW: Penguin Random House Australia, 2016.

Hamilton, Paula. 'Memory Studies and Cultural History.' In *Cultural History in Australia*, edited by Richard White and Hsu-Ming Teo, 81–97. Sydney: University of New South Wales Press, 2003.

Hampton, Meleah. *Attack on the Somme: 1st Anzac Corps and the Battle of Pozières Ridge, 1916*. Solihull: Helion & Company, 2016.

Harper, Glyn. *Massacre at Passchendaele: The New Zealand Story*. Auckland: HarperCollins Publishers, 2000.

Harvey, W.J. *The Red and White Diamond: Authorised History of the Twenty-Fourth Battalion A.I.F.* Melbourne: Alexander McCubbin, 1920.

Hastings, Tony. 'Writing Military History in Australia.' *Melbourne Historical Journal* 13 (1981): 51–5.

Haultain-Gall, Matthew. 'Lions and Kangaroos: Mobilising the Anzac Legend in the Ypres Salient.' *Journal of Belgian History*, forthcoming 2021.

———. 'Same Old Relics, Same Old Story? Displaying the Third Battle of Ypres at the Australian War Memorial, Past and Present.' *History Australia* 14, no. 3 (2017): 444–60.

Hawke, Bob. 'Speech at Lone Pine Ceremony, 25 April, 1990.' Department of the Prime Minister and Cabinet, n.d. Accessed 12 October 2020. https://pmtranscripts.pmc.gov.au/sites/default/files/original/00008010.pdf.

Hawkins, Jo. *Consuming Anzac: The History of Australia's Most Powerful Brand*. Crawley, WA: UWA Publishing, 2018.

———. '"What Better Excuse for a Real Adventure": History, Memory and Tourism on the Kokoda Trail.' *Public History Review* 20 (2013): 1–23.

Hay, Ian. *The Ship of Remembrance*. London: Hodder and Stoughton, 1926.

Hirsch, Marianne. *Family Frames: Photography, Narrative and Postmemory*. Cambridge, Mass.: Harvard University Press, 1997.

History of the 11th Field Company Engineers, Australian Imperial Force. London: War Narratives Publishing Co., 1919.

Hobsbawm, Eric. 'Introduction: Inventing Traditions.' In *The Invention of Tradition*, edited by Eric Hobsbawm and Terence Ranger, 1–14. Cambridge: Cambridge University Press, 1983.

Holbrook, Carolyn. *Anzac: The Unauthorised Biography*. Sydney: NewSouth Publishing, 2014.

———. 'Commemorators in Chief.' In *Anzac Day Then and Now*, edited by Tom Frame, 214–31. Sydney: UNSW Press, 2016.

———. 'The Role of Nationalism in Australian War Literature of the 1930s.' *First World War Studies* 5, no. 2 (2014): 213–31.

Holbrook, Carolyn, and Bart Ziino. 'Family History and the Great War in Australia.' In *Remembering the First World War*, edited by Bart Ziino, 39–55. Abingdon, Oxon.: Routledge, 2015.

Honest History Group. 'Centenary Watch.' Honest History, 2013. Accessed 27 February 2017. http://honesthistory.net.au/wp/category/centenary-watch/.

Horner, David. *The Gunners: A History of the Australian Artillery*. St Leonards, NSW: Allen & Unwin, 1995.
Howard, John. 'Address at Anzac Day Parade Canberra.' 25 April 2003. Department of the Prime Minister and Cabinet, n.d. Accessed 31 October 2020. https://pmtranscripts.pmc.gov.au/release/transcript-20549.
———. 'Transcript of the Prime Minister the Hon John Howard MP Address at the Launch of a Gift to the Nation.' 12 April 2007. National Archives of Australia, 2007. Archived by National Library of Australia, 2 June 2011. Accessed 16 September 2020. https://webarchive.nla.gov.au/awa/20110602085221/http://www.naa.gov.au/Images/Howard-transcript_tcm2-8345.pdf.
———. 'Transcript of the Prime Minister the Hon John Howard MP Address at the State Funeral Service of Alec William Campbell.' 24 May 2002. Department of the Prime Minister and Cabinet, n.d. Accessed 9 December 2017. http://pmtranscripts.pmc.gov.au/release/transcript-12946.
Hughes, W.M. *The Splendid Adventure: A Review of Empire Relations within and without the Commonwealth of Britannic Nations*. London: Ernest Benn, 1929.
Hüppauf, Bernd. 'Modernism and the Photographic Representation of War and Destruction.' In *Fields of Vision: Essays in Film Studies, Visual Anthropology, and Photography*, edited by Leslie Devereaux and Roger Hillman, 94–124. Berkeley: University of California Press, 1995.
Hutchinson, John. 'State Festivals, Foundation Myths and Cultural Politics in Immigrant Nations.' In *Celebrating the Nation: A Critical Study of Australia's Bicentenary*, edited by Tony Bennett, Pat Buckridge, David Carter and Colin Mercer, 3–25. Sydney: Allen & Unwin, 1992.
Hutchison, Margaret. '"Accurate to the Point of Mania": Eyewitness Testimony and Memory Making in Australia's Official Paintings of the First World War.' *Australian Historical Studies* 46, no. 1 (2015): 27–44.
———. '"Gazing on Strange and Terrible Lands": Official War Art and the Australian Experience of the First World War in Belgium, 1916–22.' Paper presented at Poppies, Propaganda and Passchendaele: Australia, Belgium and the Great War. Sydney: State Library of New South Wales, 21 July 2015.
———. *Painting War: A History of Australia's First World War Art Scheme*. Cambridge: Cambridge University Press, 2018.
Huyssen, Andreas. 'Present Pasts: Media, Politics, Amnesia.' *Public Culture* 12, no. 1 (2000): 21–38.
Hynes, Samuel. *A War Imagined: The First World War and English Culture*. London: Pimlico, 1992.
Inglis, K.S. *Anzac Remembered: Selected Writings by Ken Inglis*. Melbourne: History Department, University of Melbourne, 1998.
———. 'The Anzac Tradition.' *Meanjin Quarterly* 24, no. 1 (1965): 25–44.
———. *Sacred Places: War Memorials in the Australian Landscape*. 3rd ed. Carlton, Vic.: Melbourne University Press, 2008.
———. 'The Unknown Australian Soldier.' *Journal of Australian Studies* 23, no. 60 (1999): 8–17.
Irwin-Zarecka, Iwona. *Frames of Remembrance*. New Brunswick, NJ: Transaction Publishers, 1994.

Jolly, Martyn. 'Australian First-World-War Photography Frank Hurley and Charles Bean.' *History of Photography* 23, no. 2 (1999): 141–8.
Jordens, Ann Mari. 'Conscription and Dissent: The Genesis of Anti-war Protest.' In *Vietnam Remembered*, edited by Gregory Pemberton, 60–81. Sydney: Weldon Publishing, 1990.
Keatinge, M.B.B. *War Book of the Third Pioneer Battalion*. Melbourne: Specialty Press, 1922.
Kenniscentrum Westtoer. *Wereldoorlog I bezoekers in de Westhoek: resultaten bezoekersonderzoek 2013-2014-2015*. Kenniscentrum Westtoer, 2016. Accessed 21 November 2016. http://corporate.westtoer.be/sites/westtoer_2015/files/westtoer_corporate/kenniscentrum/ra-woi-bezoekers_westhoek_bezoekersonderzoek_2013-2014-2015.pdf.
———. *Wereldoorlog I herdenkinstoerisme in de Westhoek: volumes en evoluties 2013–2018*. Kenniscentrum Westtoer, 2019. Accessed 9 December 2019. https://corporate.westtoer.be/sites/westtoer_2015/files/westtoer_corporate/kenniscentrum/ra-woi-herdenkingstoerisme_wh_volumes_evoluties_2013-2018.pdf.
Kent, David. '*The Anzac Book* and the Anzac Legend: C.E.W. Bean as Editor and Image-Maker.' *Historical Studies* 21, no. 84 (1985): 376–90.
Keown, A.W. *Forward with the Fifth: The Story of Five Years' War Service, Fifth Inf. Battalion, A.I.F.* Melbourne: Specialty Press, 1921.
King, Jonathan. *Gallipoli: Our Last Man Standing; The Extraordinary Life of Alec Campbell*. Milton, Qld: John Wiley & Sons, 2003.
Klein, Kerwin Lee. 'On the Emergence of Memory in Historical Discourse.' *Representations* 69 (2000): 127–50.
Kovacic, Katherine. 'Artist at War.' *Wartime*, no. 57 (2012): 50–3.
Kyle, Roy. *An Anzac's Story*. Camberwell, Vic.: Penguin Books, 2003.
Laffin, John. *The Battle of Hamel: The Australians' Finest Victory*. East Roseville, NSW: Kangaroo Press, 1999.
Lake, Marilyn. 'How Do School Children Learn about the Spirit of Anzac?' In *What's Wrong with Anzac? The Militarisation of Australian History*, edited by Marilyn Lake, Henry Reynolds, Mark McKenna and Joy Damousi, 135–56. Sydney: University of New South Wales Press, 2010.
———. 'What Have You Done for Your Country?' In *What's Wrong with Anzac? The Militarisation of Australian History*, edited by Marilyn Lake, Henry Reynolds, Mark McKenna and Joy Damousi, 1–25. Sydney: University of New South Wales Press, 2010.
Lake, Marilyn, Henry Reynolds, Mark McKenna and Joy Damousi, eds. *What's Wrong with Anzac? The Militarisation of Australian History*. Sydney: University of New South Wales Press, 2010.
Last Post Association. 'A Delegation of the Last Post Association (Ieper-Belgium) Travels to Australia for Armistice.' Last Post Association, n.d. Accessed 14 September 2016. www.lastpost.be/en/news/54/a-delegation-of-the-last-post-association-ieper-belgium-travels-to-australia-fo.
———. 'A Delegation of the Last Post Association (Ieper-Belgium) Travels to Australia (Perth & Canberra).' Last Post Association, n.d. Accessed 14 September 2016. www.lastpost.be/en/news/58/a-delegation-of-the-last-post-association-ieper-belgium-travels-to-australia-pe.

———. 'A Delegation of the Last Post Association (Ieper-Belgium) Travels to Woy Woy (NSW) Australia for Armistice.' Last Post Association, n.d. Accessed 14 September 2016. www.lastpost.be/en/news/95/a-delegation-of-the-last-post-association-ieper-belgium-travels-to-woy-woy-nsw.

Lauwers, Delphine. 'Le saillant d'Ypres entre reconstruction et construction d'un lieu de mémoire: un long processus de négociations mémorielles, de 1914 à nos jours.' PhD thesis. European University Institute, 2013.

Lawson, Tom. '"The Free-Masonry of Sorrow"? English National Identities and the Memorialization of the Great War in Britain, 1919–1931.' *History & Memory* 20, no. 1 (2008): 89–120.

Leach, Norman. *Passchendaele: Canada's Triumph and Tragedy on the Fields of Flanders; An Illustrated History*. Regina: Coteau Books, 2008.

Lee, J.E. *The Chronicle of the 45th Battalion A.I.F.* Sydney: Mortons, 1927.

Lee, Roger. *The Battle of Fromelles: 1916*. Canberra: Army History Unit, 2010.

Leed, Eric. *No Man's Land: Combat and Identity in World War I*. Cambridge: Cambridge University Press, 1979.

Levalleux, Joffrey. 'Discoveries: At Bullecourt 1917; Immerse Yourself in the Private World of the Australian Soldiers.' Arras Pays d'Artois Tourisme, n.d. Accessed 9 October 2020. www.arraspaysdartois.com/en/remembrance/visit-bullecourt-1917-museum/.

Liddle, Peter H., ed. *Passchendaele in Perspective: The Third Battle of Ypres*. London: Leo Cooper, 1997.

Lindsay, Patrick. *Fromelles: The Story of Australia's Darkest Day; The Search for Our Fallen Heroes of World War One*. Prahan, Vic.: Hardie Grant, 2007.

Liss, Andrea. *Trespassing through Shadows: Memory, Photography and the Holocaust*. Minneapolis: University of Minnesota Press, 1998.

Lloyd, David W. *Battlefield Tourism: Pilgrimage and the Commemoration of the Great War in Britain, Australia and Canada, 1919–1939*. Oxford: Berg, 1998.

Lloyd George, David. *War Memoirs of David Lloyd George*. Vol. 4. London: Nicholson & Watson, 1934.

Longmore, C. *'Eggs-a-Cook!' The Story of the Forty-Fourth*. Perth: Colortype Press, 1921.

Longworth, Philip. *The Unending Vigil: A History of the Commonwealth War Graves Commission 1917–1967*. London: Constable & Company, 1967.

Lyall, K.M., ed. *Letters from an Anzac Gunner*. East Kew, Vic.: Lyall's Yarns, 1990.

Lynch, E.P.F. *Somme Mud: The War Experiences of an Infantryman in France 1916–1919*. North Sydney, NSW: Random House, 2008.

Macintyre, Stuart. *1901–1942, The Succeeding Age*. Vol. 4 of *The Oxford History of Australia*, edited by G.C. Bolton. South Melbourne, Vic: Oxford University Press, 1990.

Macleod, Jenny. 'The Fall and Rise of Anzac Day: 1965 and 1990 Compared.' *War & Society* 20, no. 1 (2002): 149–68.

———, ed. *Gallipoli: Making History*. London: Frank Cass, 2004.

———. *Reconsidering Gallipoli*. Manchester: Manchester University Press, 2004.

Mann, Leonard. *Flesh in Armour*. Columbia: University of South Carolina Press, 2008. First published in 1932 by Phaedrus.

Mant, Gilbert, ed. *Soldier Boy: The Letters of Gunner W.J. Duffell, 1915–18*. Kenthurst, NSW: Kangaroo Press, 1992.

Maxwell, J. *Hell's Bells and Mademoiselles*. 2nd ed. Sydney: Angus & Robertson, 1932.
McCallum, Kerry, and Peter Putnis. 'Media Management in Wartime.' *Media History* 14, no. 1 (2008): 17–34.
McKenna, Mark. 'Anzac Day: How Did It Become Australia's National Day?' In *What's Wrong with Anzac? The Militarisation of Australian History*, edited by Marilyn Lake, Henry Reynolds, Mark McKenna and Joy Damousi, 110–34. Sydney: University of New South Wales Press, 2010.
———. 'Howard's Warriors.' In *Why the War Was Wrong*, edited by Raimond Gaita, 167–200. Melbourne: Text Publishing, 2003.
McKenna, Mark, and Stuart Ward. '"It Was Really Moving, Mate": The Gallipoli Pilgrimage and Sentimental Nationalism in Australia.' *Australian Historical Studies* 38, no. 129 (2007): 141–51.
McKernan, Michael. *Here Is Their Spirit: A History of the Australian War Memorial 1917–1990*. St Lucia, Qld: University of Queensland Press in association with AWM, 1991.
———. 'Making History.' *Journal of the Australian War Memorial*, no. 19 (1991): 40–1.
———. 'Writing about War.' In *Australia: Two Centuries of War and Peace*, edited by Michael McKernan and Margaret Browne, 11–21. Canberra: AWM, 1988.
McKinney, J.P. *Crucible*. Sydney: Angus & Robertson, 1935.
McNicol, N.G. *The Thirty-Seventh: History of the Thirty-Seventh Battalion A.I.F.* Melbourne: Modern Printing Co., 1936.
McQueen, Humphrey. *The Black Swan of Trespass: The Emergence of Modernist Painting in Australia to 1944*. Sydney: Alternative Publishing Cooperative, 1979.
———. 'Emu into Ostrich: Australian Literary Responses to the Great War.' *Meanjin Quarterly* 35, no. 1 (1976): 78–87.
McQuilton, John. 'Gallipoli as Contested Commemorative Space.' In *Gallipoli: Making History*, edited by Jenny Macleod, 150–8. London: Frank Cass, 2004.
———. *Rural Australia and the Great War: From Tarrawingee to Tangambalanga*. Carlton South, Vic.: Melbourne University Press, 2001.
Meaney, Neville. 'Britishness and Australia: Some Reflections.' *Journal of Imperial and Commonwealth History* 31, no. 2 (2003): 121–35.
Melrose, Craig. '"A Praise That Never Ages": The Australian War Memorial and the "National" Interpretation of the First World War, 1922–35.' PhD thesis. University of Queensland, 2004.
Middleton, Max J. *The Art of Septimus H. Power*. Adelaide: Rigby, 1974.
Millar, Ann. 'Gallipoli to Melbourne: The Australian War Memorial, 1915–1919.' *Journal of the Australian War Memorial*, no. 10 (1987): 33–42.
Misztal, Barbara A. *Theories of Social Remembering*. Maidenhead, Berks.: Open University Press, 2003.
Mitchell, G.D. *Backs to the Wall: A Larrikin on the Western Front*. New ed. Sydney: Allen & Unwin, 2007. First published in 1937 by Angus & Robertson.
Monash, John. *The Australian Victories in France in 1918*. London: Hutchinson & Co., 1920.
Mosse, George. *Fallen Soldiers: Reshaping the Memory of the World Wars*. New York: Oxford University Press, 1990.
Mycock, Andrew, Shanti Sumartojo and Ben Wellings. '"The Centenary to End All Centenaries": The Great War, Nation and Commemoration.' In *Nation, Memory and*

Bibliography

Great War Commemoration: Mobilizing the Past in Europe, Australia and New Zealand, edited by Shanti Sumartojo and Ben Wellings, 1–24. Oxford: Peter Lang, 2014.

Nasht, Simon. *The Last Explorer: Hubert Wilkins, Australia's Unknown Hero*. Sydney: Hodder, 2005.

National Archives of Australia and Archives New Zealand. 'About.' Discovering Anzacs. National Archives of Australia, 2007. Accessed 15 December 2016. https://discoveringanzacs.naa.gov.au/about/.

New South Wales. *Parliamentary Debates*. Legislative Assembly, 12 November 2015.

Newton, L.M. *The Story of the Twelfth: A Record of the 12th Battalion A.I.F. during the Great War of 1914–1918*. Hobart: J. Walch & Sons, 1925.

Ngā Tapuwae New Zealand First World War Trails. New Zealand Ministry for Culture and Heritage, n.d. Accessed 23 September 2020. https://ngatapuwae.govt.nz/.

Observatoire de Tourisme Westtoer. *Tourisme de mémoire – Great War: départements Nord, Pas-de-Calais, Somme*. Westtoer: Observatoire de Tourisme Westtoer, 2015.

Office of Australian War Graves Journal 1997–98. Phillip, ACT: Office of Australian War Graves, 1998.

Office of Australian War Graves Journal 2005–2006. Phillip, ACT: Office of Australian War Graves, 2006.

Oppenheimer, Jillian. *Horses and Guns: Poss Nivison's War with the Australian Field Artillery Brigades, on the Western Front, 1915–1919*. Walcha, NSW: Ohio Productions, 2005.

Pearce, Susan M. *Museums, Objects and Collections: A Cultural Study*. Leicester: Leicester University Press, 1992.

Piggott, Michael. *A Guide to the Personal, Family and Official Papers of C.E.W. Bean*. Canberra: AWM, 1983.

Plugstreet 14–18 Experience. 'Presentation.' Plugstreet 14–18 Experience, n.d. Accessed 2 December 2016. www.plugstreet1418.be/en/presentation.

Prince, T.H. *Purple Patches: A Tale of the Sappers*. Sydney: Jackson and O'Sullivan, 1935.

Prior, Robin, and Trevor Wilson. *Passchendaele: The Untold Story*. 2nd ed. New Haven, Conn.: Yale University Press, 2002.

Pulteney, William, and Beatrix Brice. *The Immortal Salient: An Historical Record and Complete Guide for Pilgrims to Ypres*. London: J. Murray for the Ypres League, 1925.

Reid, Richard. *'He Is Not Missing. He Is Here!' Australians and the Menin Gate: Visit to Australia by Buglers from the Menin Gate, Ieper, Belgium*. Booklet. Canberra: Department of Veterans' Affairs, 1997.

Reid, Richard, Ian McGibbon and Sarah Midford. 'Remembering Gallipoli.' In *Anzac Battlefield: A Gallipoli Landscape of War and Memory*, edited by Antonio Sagona, Mithat Atabay, C.J. Mackie, Ian McGibbon and Richard Reid, 192–221. Port Melbourne, Vic.: Cambridge University Press, 2016.

Repatriation Commission, Military Rehabilitation and Compensation Commission and Department of Veterans' Affairs. *Annual Reports, 2009–2010*. Canberra: Department of Veterans' Affairs, 2010.

———. *Annual Reports, 2017–2018*. Canberra: Department of Veterans' Affairs, 2018.

Repatriation Commission, Military Rehabilitation and Compensation Commission, National Treatment Monitoring Committee and Department of Veterans' Affairs. *Annual Reports, 2007–2008*. Canberra: Department of Veterans' Affairs, 2008.

———. *Annual Reports, 2008–2009*. Canberra: Department of Veterans' Affairs, 2009.

Repatriation Commission, National Treatment Monitoring Committee and Department of Veterans' Affairs. *Annual Report, 2006–2007.* Canberra: Department of Veterans' Affairs, 2007.

Reynaud, Daniel. 'Digging Up New Anzac Legends.' *History Australia* 7, no. 2 (2010): 40.1–40.2.

Reynolds, Henry. 'Are Nations Really Made in War?' In *What's Wrong with Anzac? The Militarisation of Australian History*, edited by Marilyn Lake, Henry Reynolds, Mark McKenna and Joy Damousi, 24–44. Sydney: University of New South Wales Press, 2010.

Rhoden, Clare. *The Purpose of Futility: Writing World War I, Australian Style.* Crawley, WA: UWA Publishing, 2015.

Roach, David. 'Based on a True Story: Writing *Beneath Hill 60*.' *Teaching History* 44, no. 3 (2010): 15–19.

Rule, E.J. *Jacka's Mob.* Sydney: Angus & Robertson, 1933.

Scates, Bruce. 'How War Came Home: Reflections on the Digitisation of Australia's Repatriation Files.' *History Australia* 16, no. 1 (2019): 190–209.

———. 'Remembering and Forgetting the First World War at the Sir John Monash Centre.' In *The Great War: Aftermath and Commemoration*, edited by Carolyn Holbrook and Keir Reeves, 193–207. Sydney: University of New South Wales Press, 2019.

———. *Return to Gallipoli: Walking the Battlefields of the Great War.* Cambridge: Cambridge University Press, 2006.

Scott, Bruce (Minister for Veterans' Affairs). 'Address by the Minister for Veterans' Affairs the Honourable Bruce Scott MP at the Dedication of the Fromelles Memorial Park.' Fromelles, 5 July 1998.

———. 'Australian Sacrifice Recalled: $1.34m for Western Front Memorial Parks.' Media release 157/97. Department of Veterans' Affairs, 28 October 1997.

———. 'Buglers from Belgium Arrive in Australia.' Media release 162/97. Department of Veterans' Affairs, 31 October 1997.

Screen Australia. *Annual Report 08/09.* Screen Australia, 2009. Accessed 11 October 2016. www.screenaustralia.gov.au/getmedia/5c43905b-da1d-43ea-a237-8b51c9b6c1c4/SA-Annual-Report-2008-2009.pdf?ext=.pdf.

———. 'Top 100 Australian Feature Films of All Time.' Screen Australia, n.d. Accessed 31 October 2016. www.screenaustralia.gov.au/fact-finders/cinema/australian-films/top-films-at-the-box-office.

Seal, Graham. *Inventing Anzac: The Digger and National Mythology.* St Lucia, Qld: University of Queensland Press, 2004.

———. 'Unravelling Digger Yarn-Spinning in World War I.' *Journal of Australian Studies* 21, no. 53 (1997): 146–56.

Serle, Geoffrey. 'The Digger Tradition and Australian Nationalism.' *Meanjin Quarterly* 24, no. 2 (1965): 148–59.

———. *John Monash: A Biography.* 2nd paperback ed. Carlton, Vic.: Melbourne University Press, 2002.

Seymour, Alan. *The One Day of the Year.* London: Angus & Robertson, 1962.

Sherman, Daniel J. *The Construction of Memory in Interwar France.* Chicago, Ill.: University of Chicago Press, 1999.

———. 'Objects of Memory: History and Narrative in French War Museums.' *French Historical Studies* 19, no. 1 (1995): 49–74.
Silver, Lynette Ramsay. *Marcel Caux: A Life Unravelled*. Milton, Qld: John Wiley & Sons, 2005.
Sir John Monash Centre. n.d. Accessed 24 September 2020. https://sjmc.gov.au/.
Smart, Judith. '"Poor Little Belgium" and Australian Popular Support for War, 1914–1915.' *War & Society* 12, no. 1 (1994): 27–46.
Smith, Staniforth. *Australian Campaigns in the Great War: Being a Concise History of the Australian Naval and Military Forces, 1914–1918*. Melbourne: Macmillan & Co., 1919.
Snowdon, Warren (Minister for Veterans' Affairs). 'Shared History Helps Forge Stronger Ties with Belgium.' Media release VA099. Department of Veterans' Affairs, 23 November 2012.
Somme Tourisme. 'Les sites de visite: tableau de bord 2017 2018 2019.' Somme Tourisme, 2020. Accessed 12 October 2020. www.somme-tourisme.org/app/download/12080969012/Tableau+de+bord+2018+2019+2020.pdf?t=1600174176.
———. 'Workshops-Australie.' Somme Tourisme, n.d. Accessed 22 November 2016. www.somme-tourisme.org/Vos-outils/Commercialisation/Les-groupes/Workshops-Australie (webpage deleted).
Souter, Gavin. *Lion and Kangaroo: The Initiation of Australia*. New ed. Melbourne: Text Publishing, 2000.
Spittel, Christina. 'A Portable Monument? Leonard Mann's *Flesh in Armour* in Australia's Memory of the First World War.' *Book History* 14, no. 1 (2011): 187–220.
———. 'Remembering the War: Australian Novelists in the Interwar Years.' *Australian Literary Studies* 23, no. 2 (2007): 121–39.
Stacy, B.V., F.J. Kindon and H.V. Chedgey. *The History of the 1st Battalion A.I.F., 1914–1919*. Sydney: History Committee, 1st Battalion, AIF, 1931.
Stanley, Peter. 'Gallipoli and Pozières: A Legend and a Memorial.' *Australian Foreign Affairs Record* 56, no. 4 (1985): 280–9.
———. *Men of Mont St Quentin: Between Victory and Death*. Carlton North, Vic.: Scribe, 2009.
———. 'Monumental Mistake: Is War the Most Important Thing in Australian History?' In *Anzac's Dirty Dozen: 12 Myths of Australian Military History*, edited by Craig Stockings, 260–86. Sydney: NewSouth Publishing, 2012.
———. 'Reflections on Bean's Last Paragraph.' *Sabretache* 24, no. 3 (1983): 4–11.
———. *A Stout Pair of Boots: A Guide to Exploring Australia's Battlefields*. Crows Nest, NSW: Allen & Unwin, 2008.
———. 'War without End.' In *Australian History Now*, edited by Anna Clark and Paul Ashton, 90–106. Sydney: NewSouth Publishing, 2013.
Stephens, John R. '"The Ghosts of Menin Gate": Art, Architecture and Commemoration.' *Journal of Contemporary History* 44, no. 7 (2009): 7–26.
———. 'Sacred Landscapes: Albany and Anzac Pilgrimage.' *Landscape Research* 39, no. 1 (2014): 21–39.
Stephens, Tony. *The Last Anzacs: Lest We Forget*. Rev. ed. North Fremantle, WA: Fremantle Press, 2009.
Stevens, F.H. *The Story of the 5th Pioneer Battalion A.I.F.* Adelaide: Callotype Co., 1937.

Suttie, Andrew. *Rewriting the First World War: Lloyd George, Politics and Strategy 1914–1918.* Basingstoke, Hants.: Palgrave Macmillan, 2005.
Sykes, Alrene, and Keith Richards. 'Another Look at the Old War-Horse: Alan Seymour's "The One Day of the Year".' *Australasian Drama Studies* 2, no. 2 (1984): 65–89.
Taylor, F.W., and T.A. Cusack, comps. *Nulli Secundus: A History of the Second Battalion, A.I.F., 1914–1919.* Sydney: New Century Press, 1942.
Terraine, John. *The Road to Passchendaele: The Flanders Offensive of 1917; A Study in Inevitability.* London: Leo Cooper, 1977.
Thomson, Alistair. *Anzac Memories: Living with the Legend.* 1st ed. Melbourne: Oxford University Press, 1994. 2nd ed. Clayton, Vic.: Monash University Publishing, 2013.
———. '"Steadfast until Death"? C.E.W. Bean and the Representation of Australian Military Manhood.' *Australian Historical Studies* 23, no. 93 (1989): 462–78.
Throssell, Ric. *For Valour: Ric Throssell's Play.* Sydney: Currency Press, 1976.
Tilton, Mary. *The Grey Battalion.* Sydney: Angus & Robertson, 1933.
Tippett, Maria. *Art at the Service of War: Canada, Art, and the Great War.* Toronto: University of Toronto Press, 1984.
Todman, Dan. *The Great War: Myth and Memory.* London: Hambledon and London, 2005.
Toerisme Vlaanderen and Westtoer. *Toeristisch marketingplan 100 jaar Groote Oorlog.* Brussels: Toerisme Vlaanderen and Westtoer, 2012.
Treloar, J.L. *Australian Chivalry: Reproductions in Colour and Duo-Tone of Official War Paintings.* Canberra: AWM, 1933.
Turner, Graeme. 'ANZACS: Putting the Story Back in History.' In *War: Australia's Creative Response*, edited by Anna Rutherford and James Weiland, 229–38. Sydney: Allen & Unwin, 1997.
Twomey, Christina. 'Trauma and the Reinvigoration of Anzac: An Argument.' *History Australia* 10, no. 3 (2013): 85–108.
Vance, Jonathan F. *Death So Noble: Memory, Meaning and the First World War.* Vancouver, BC: UBC Press, 1997.
Vandiver, Frank. 'Field Marshal Sir Douglas Haig and Passchendaele.' In *Passchendaele in Perspective: The Third Battle of Ypres*, edited by Peter H. Liddle, 30–44. London: Leo Cooper, 1997.
Wade, Linda. '"By Diggers Defended, by Victorians Mended": Searching for Villers Bretonneux.' PhD thesis. University of Wollongong, 2008.
Walker, Jonathan. *The Blood Tub: General Gough and the Battle of Bullecourt, 1917.* Staplehurst, Kent: Spellmont, 1998.
Wanliss, Newton. *The History of the Fourteenth Battalion, A.I.F.: Being the Story of the Vicissitudes of an Australian Unit during the Great War.* Melbourne: Arrow Printery, 1929.
Ward, Russel. *The Australian Legend.* 2nd ed. South Melbourne, Vic.: Oxford University Press, 2003. First published in 1958.
Ward, Stuart. *Australia and the British Embrace: The Demise of the Imperial Ideal.* Carlton South, Vic.: Melbourne University Press, 2001.
———. 'The "New Nationalism" in Australia, Canada and New Zealand: Civic Culture in the Wake of the British World.' In *Britishness Abroad: Transnational Movements and Imperial Cultures*, edited by Kate Darian-Smith, Patricia Grimshaw and Stuart Macintyre, 231–63. Carlton, Vic.: Melbourne University Publishing, 2007.

Waters, J.C. *Crosses of Sacrifice: The Story of the Empire's Million War Dead and Australia's 60,000*. Sydney: Angus & Robertson, 1932.

Weir, Peter. 'Gallipoli: "I Felt Somehow I Was Really Touching History".' *Literature/Film Quarterly* 9, no. 4 (1981): 213–17.

Wellington, Jennifer. *Exhibiting War: The Great War, Museums and Memory in Britain, Canada and Australia*. Cambridge: Cambridge University Press, 2017.

Wereldoorlog I in de Westhoek (The Great War in Flanders Fields). 'Centenary of the Battle of Polygon Wood: Reflective Program – Zonnebeke – 26/09/2017.' Wereldoorlog I in de Westhoek, September 2017. Accessed 27 December 2019. www.wo1.be/en/youwerethere/11649/centenary-of-the-battle-of-polygon-wood-reflective-program.

Where the Australians Rest: A Description of Many of the Cemeteries Overseas in Which Australians – Including Those Whose Names Can Never Be Known – Are Buried. Booklet. Melbourne: Government Printer, 1920.

White, Richard. 'The Soldier as Tourist: The Australian Experience of the Great War.' *War & Society* 5, no. 1 (1987): 63–76.

Wilkinson, Carole. *Fromelles: Australia's Bloodiest Day at War*. Fitzroy, Vic.: Black Dog Books, 2012.

Williams, H.R. *Comrades of the Great Adventure*. Sydney: Angus & Robertson, 1935.

———. *The Gallant Company: An Australian Soldier's Story of 1915–1918*. Sydney: Angus & Robertson, 1933.

Williams, John F. *Anzacs, the Media and the Great War*. Sydney: University of New South Wales Press, 1999.

———. *The Quarantined Culture: Australian Reactions to Modernism 1913–1939*. Cambridge: Cambridge University Press, 1995.

Wilson, Patrick, ed. *So Far from Home: The Remarkable Diaries of Eric Evans, an Australian Soldier during World War I*. East Roseville, NSW: Kangaroo Press, 2002.

Winter, Caroline. 'The Multiple Roles of Battlefield War Museums: A Study at Fromelles and Passchendaele.' *Journal of Heritage Tourism* 13, no. 3 (2018): 211–23.

Winter, Denis. *Making the Legend: The War Writings of C.E.W. Bean*. St Lucia, Qld: University of Queensland Press, 1992.

Winter, Jay. 'Communities in Mourning.' In *Authority, Identity and the Social History of the Great War*, edited by Frans Coetzee and Marilyn Shevin Coetzee, 326–55. Providence: Berghahn Books, 1995.

———. 'The Memory Boom in Contemporary Historical Studies.' *Raritan* 21, no. 1 (2001): 52–66.

———. 'Painting Armageddon: Some Aspects of the Apocalyptic Imagination in Art; From Anticipation to Allegory.' In *Facing Armageddon: The First World War Experienced*, edited by Hugh Cecil and Peter H. Liddle, 854–78. London: Leo Cooper, 1996.

———. 'Remembrance of the Great War in British Cultural History since the 1960s.' In *Comment (se) sortir de la Grande Guerre? Regards sur quelques pays 'vainqueurs': la Belgique, la France et la Grande-Bretagne*, edited by Stéphanie Claisse and Thierry Lemoine, 59–75. Paris: L'Harmattan, 2005.

———. *Sites of Memory, Sites of Mourning: The Great War in European Cultural History*. Cambridge: Cambridge University Press, 1995.

———. *War and Remembrance in the Twentieth Century*. Cambridge: Cambridge University Press, 1999.
Winter, Jay, and Emmanuel Sivan. 'Setting the Framework.' In *War and Remembrance in the Twentieth Century*, edited by Jay Winter and Emmanuel Sivan, 6–39. Cambridge: Cambridge University Press, 1999.
Witcomb, Andrea. *Re-imagining the Museum: Beyond the Mausoleum*. London: Routledge, 2003.
Wray, Christopher. *Pozières: Echoes of a Distant Battle*. Port Melbourne, Vic.: Cambridge University Press, 2016.
X, Ex-Private (A.M. Burrage). *War Is War*. London: Victor Gollancz, 1930.
Ziino, Bart. *A Distant Grief: Australians, War Graves and the Great War*. Crawley, WA: University of Western Australia Press, 2007.
———. 'The First World War in Australian History.' *Australian Historical Studies* 47, no. 1 (2016): 118–34.
———. '"A Lasting Gift to His Descendants": Family Memory and the Great War in Australia.' *History & Memory* 22, no. 2 (2010): 125–46.
———. 'Mourning and Commemoration in Australia: The Case of Sir W.T. Bridges and the Unknown Australian Soldier.' *History Australia* 4, no. 2 (2007): 40.1–40.17.
———. 'Who Owns Gallipoli? Australia's Gallipoli Anxieties 1915–2005.' *Journal of Australian Studies* 30, no. 88 (2006): 1–12.

INDEX

I ANZAC Corps 29
II ANZAC Corps 28
  Mounted Regiment 241
8 August 1918 99, 103, 159, 164

Adam-Smith, Patsy 187, 188–9, 190–1, 192, 193, 194, 197, 204, 221
  Anzacs (book) 187, 188–192, 193, 221
adoptive kinship 136, 137–8, 139, 142–6, 147, 155
Advertiser (newspaper) 119
Albert I of Belgium, King 72, 73, 181
Allan, Stella 142–3
Amiens 56, 144–5, 160, 163, 175, 177, 178
Anderson, Benedict 50
Angus & Robertson 110
anti-war movement 173
Anzac Book Trust Fund 90–1
Anzac Day 41, 84, 85, 136, 145–6, 163, 164–5, 172, 179, 185, 205, 206, 207, 208, 213–14, 216, 217, 229
  in Belgium 16, 179–180, 181, 185–6, 197, 203, 212, 227, 234–5
  decline 171–2
  at Gallipoli 234, 235
  at Villers-Bretonneux 180–1, 202–3, 233–4, 245
Anzac House 246
Anzac legend 4, 9, 15, 17, 21, 22, 30, 42–3, 48, 51, 62, 82, 85, 89, 97–8, 119, 123, 137, 152, 215, 225, 232, 240, 245, 247
  characteristics of 21, 31–2, 59, 68–9, 95, 104, 105, 108, 110, 136, 187–8, 193, 194, 204–5, 210–11, 216–17
  declining interest 16, 158, 165, 171–4, 186–7, 197
  and family history 17, 189, 216, 218–19, 220, 221–2, 232, 235

and national identity 100–1, 200–1, 204–5, 206, 217, 218
reinterpretation 165, 166, 186–192, 193–4, 197, 206
resurgence 6, 17, 159, 187, 200, 216
rhetoric 85, 136, 144–5, 160, 161–3, 164, 174, 235, 242
Anzac Parade, Canberra 209, 217
Anzacs (miniseries) 194–7
ANZUS Treaty 168
Argus (newspaper) 164
Armentières 10
artillery 22, 23, 181, 196
  Australian 30–2, 64, 66–7
  see also Ypres, third battle of
Ashmead-Bartlett, Ellis 215
Ashplant, Timothy 7
Assmann, Aleida 165, 219
Astrid of Belgium, Princess 246
Augé, Marc 157
Aussie (magazine) 98, 101, 106–7
Australia Day 201–2, 204, 205
Australia House *see* Australian High Commission
Australia Remembers 1945–1995 210
Australian Army Band 245
Australian Army History Unit 230
Australian Battle Memorials and Soldiers' Graves Committee 127, 128
Australian Bicentennial Authority 201
Australian Broadcasting Corporation 209, 243
Australian Corps 28, 87, 88–9, 118, 123, 131, 164, 195
Australian Corps Memorial Park, Le Hamel 233
Australian embassy
  Brussels 16, 179, 185, 212
  Paris 176, 177, 178
Australian flag 246, 247

307

Australian government   25, 33, 172, 193
  and the AIF memorials   125, 126, 129, 131, 166–7, 180
  and Anzac resurgence   200–1, 210–11, 216, 231–2
  and the AWM   48, 51
  funds provided for commemoration   233, 236–7, 238
  and the Menin Gate Memorial   71, 72
  relations with Belgians   203, 228, 229, 236
  relations with the French   180, 202–3, 211
  and St George's Memorial Church   168
  support for pilgrimages   134, 152–3, 167, 174–8, 204, 207, 231
  Villers-Bretonneux dawn service   233–4
Australian Graves Detachment   53, 130
Australian High Commission, London   129
Australian Historical Mission   53
Australian Imperial Force (AIF)   1–2, 10–11, 17, 21, 22, 38, 39, 41–2, 48, 49, 53, 59, 86, 87, 89, 130, 146, 159–160, 161, 173, 214, 239, 245
  and the third battle of Ypres   2, 3, 7, 11–15, 23, 29–30, 34–5, 37, 39, 40, 46, 143, 161, 237–8, 247
Australian Imperial Force (units)
  1st Australian Tunnelling Company   12, 28, 93, 129, 130, 149–150, 224
  Battalions
    4th Machine Gun Battalion   168–9
    5th Infantry Battalion   39
    8th Infantry Battalion   194, 195, 196
    18th Infantry Battalion   246
    38th Infantry Battalion   246
    40th Infantry Battalion   104
    48th Infantry Battalion   29
    59th Infantry Battalion   68

  Brigades
    4th Brigade   87
    9th Brigade   175
  Divisions
    1st Division   3, 11, 13, 14, 33, 142
    2nd Division   11, 13, 14, 33, 46, 142, 175–6, 207
    3rd Division   12, 14, 15, 27, 28, 46, 87, 94, 121–2, 142, 175, 246
    4th Division   11, 12, 13–14, 94, 142, 202, 244
    5th Division   11, 13–14, 35, 89, 129, 142, 202, 211, 244
  see also unit histories
Australian Labor Party   19–20, 205–6
Australian national identity   100, 174, 200, 201, 205, 218
Australian National Memorial, Villers-Bretonneux   21, 71, 125, 126–7, 129, 131, 132, 233–4
  unveiling   134–5, 144, 147, 155, 159
Australian official war art scheme   22, 48, 61, 62, 64–5, 69–70
Australian Remembrance Trail   8, 237–240, 241–2
Australian War Memorial (AWM)   15, 21, 48–50, 51, 52, 54, 81–2, 98–9, 130, 165, 187 213, 232
  conception   22, 48
  family history   218
  Hall of Memory   209
  Last Post ceremony   214
  Menin Gate at Midnight tour   15–16, 49, 50, 70, 73, 74–6, 78–81, 82–3, 150
  Menin Gate lions   198–200
  research support   222
  temporary interwar exhibitions (Melbourne and Sydney)   7, 15, 49–50, 51, 144, 160
    arrangement   51–2, 54–5, 59–60, 62, **plate 4**
    models (dioramas)   56–61
    objects   55–6
    paintings   56, 61–2, 65–70
    photographs   56, 61–4

INDEX

Australian War Records Section 22, 29, 48, 51, 52–4, 74

backpackers 234, 235, 243
Barrett, Charles 91
Bastiaan, Ross 207
Battle Exploit Memorials Committee 127–8
battlefield tourism *see* pilgrimage
Bazley, Arthur 80, 91
Bean, Charles 8, 15, 21–2, 23, 29, 34, 165
  Anzac Book 22
  and the Anzac legend 22, 23, 30–2, 43, 44–5, 187
  appointment as official correspondent 24–5
  and the AWM 22, 29, 48, 49, 51, 52, 53, 81–2
    Menin Gate at Midnight tour 76, 80
    modelling scheme 56, 57–8
  battlefield tour (1950) 170–1
  censorship 24–5, 26, 33, 42
  composite images 61–2, 63
  correspondence 7, 23, 24–6, 40
    on Broodseinde 35–6, 39–40
    on first Passchendaele 37, 40
    on Fromelles 27
    on Menin Road 32–3
    on Messines 27–8
    on Poelcappelle 36–7, 40
    on Polygon Wood 34–5, 39
    on Pozières 27, 32, 33, 35, 37, 39
    on third Ypres 29–31, 32, 39, 44
  criticism of Monash 28
  diaries 23, 26, 29, 38, 218
    on Broodseinde 38
    on Menin Road 33, 34
    on Messines 28–9
    on Poelcappelle and first Passchendaele 37–9
    on Pozières 29, 33, 34, 39
    on third Ypres 34
  Official History 7, 21, 23, 26, 40–3, 44–5, 48, 92, 102, 144, 187–8, 194, 196, 223
    on Bullecourt 42, 43
    on Messines 42
    on Pozières 42, 46
    on third Ypres 42, 43–6, 47, 54, 59, 160
    on Second World War 161
  unit histories 91–2
  view of Pozières 22–3, 34, 39, 171
  view of third Ypres 23, 34, 40, 47
  on *Where the Australians Rest* 142
Beaumont, Joan 3, 9–10, 132, 191–2, 217, 237
Belgium
  Belgian Relief 1
  German invasion 1, 24
  government 236
  'Poor little' Belgium 1
  relations with Australia 72, 177, 203, 228, 229, 246
  see also Ypres
Beneath Hill 60 (film) 224–7, 241
Bennett, Brigadier-General, H. Gordon 107–8
Bicentenary of Australia 5, 16, 201–3, 204, 211, 216
Birdwood, Lieutenant-General Sir William Birdwood 29, 30
blockhouses *see* Ypres, third battle of
Blomfield, Sir Reginald 70, 71, 181
Bond, Brian 95, 102
Bongiorno, Frank 217
British Broadcasting Corporation 72
British Empire 2, 30, 72–3, 126, 145, 156, 158, 163, 173, 181, 183, 193
British Empire Service League 169
British Expeditionary Force 30, 33, 42, 78, 181, 183
  62nd Division (2nd West Riding) 91
  British Fifth Army 13, 32
  British Second Army 13, 32, 37
British Legion pilgrimage 151, 154
Broodseinde 14, 15, 35–6, 38, 39–40, 45, 54, 57, 88, 93, 95, 97, 103, 108, 121, 140, 150, 196, 231

309

proposed national memorial at   127–9,
    237, **plate 16**
Brooke, Rupert   181
Bruce, Stanley   71–2, 74, 142–3, 144–6,
    198, 199
Bruce government   71
Bullecourt   29, 200, 202, 237
    battles of   2, 11, 32, 38–9, 42, 43,
        55, 91–2, 102, 122, 223
    Jean and Denise Letaille
        Museum   238
    Memorial Park   205
Bullecourt (diorama)   59
Burrage, A.M.   100
Burrowes, Geoff   194, 197
Butler, Colonel Graham   61
Buttes New British Cemetery *see* Polygon
    Wood

Cahill, Fred   176, 177
Calder, George   230, 231
Canada   3, 33, 35, 48, 104, 153, 154,
    164, 168, 223, 239, 247
    Brooding Soldier memorial (Saint-
        Julien)   150–1
Canberra Times (newspaper)   175
Caporetto   40
Caterpillar mine   28
Channel Nine   194
Chifley, Ben   163
Churchill, Winston   71
civil religion   217
Cochrane, Peter   201
collective memory *see* memory
Comines-Warneton   238, 239, 241–2
commemorative diplomacy   177–8,
    202–3, 209–10, 228
Commonwealth War Graves
    Commission   232, 233; *see also*
    Imperial War Graves Commission
Condé, Anne-Marie   59
Connelly, Mark   9–10
conscription   19–20, 23, 25, 40, 46, 161,
    172
Corbie   180
Corlett, Peter   232

Corrigan, Leo   230–1
Cosgrove, Peter   246
Courier-Mail (newspaper)   159
Courtenay, Bryce   221
Cross of Sacrifice   125
Crotty, Martin   136
Crowe, Russell   227
Crowle, W.   138
Curran, James   173
Cutlack, Frederic   148–9
    The Australians (book)   86–7
    War Letters of General Monash
        (book)   119, 121–2

Daily Telegraph (newspaper)   229
Dawson, Graham   7
Dean, Arthur   95
decolonisation   173
Dehem, Albert   185
Department of Defence   90, 231
Department of Veterans' Affairs   199,
    201, 207, 209, 211, 212–13, 233,
    236–7, 238, 243, 245; *see also* Australian
    Remembrance Trail
Dernancourt (diorama)   60
digitisation of war records   218–19, 220
Dix, Otto
    Flandern (painting)   69, **plate 11**
Dixon, Robert   63–4
Doyle, Arthur Conan   182
Duffell, William   221
Dyett, Gilbert   151–2
Dyson, Will   64–5

Edward VIII, King   182
Eksteins, Modris   20
Elizabeth II, Queen   167
Englezos, Lambis   231
European Economic Community   173–4
Eyskens, Gaston   203

family history   16, 210, 218–220, 235
Fathi, Romain   132, 203
Faulkner, John   208
Faulks, Sebastian
    Birdsong (book)   225

Index

Fayat, Henri 203
films 8, 159, 187, 192–4, 224, 226–7
First World War centenary 16–17, 220, 223, 227, 235, 236, 237, 243, 245
FitzSimons, Peter 9
Flemming, Jim 199
Flers 46, 62
Foch, Ferdinand 180
French, Field Marshall Sir John 78, 182
French government 202–3, 211
Fromelles 159, 200, 231–2, 237
    Australian Memorial Park 211, 231–2
    battle of 2, 11, 17, 27, 54, 97, 111, 211, 223
    Museum of the Battle of Fromelles 238
    Pheasant Wood mass grave 230, 231–2
Fussell, Paul 20

Gallant Legion series 110
Gallipoli 1, 17, 41, 53, 87, 101, 116, 120, 159, 209, 223, 234
    Anzac Day 132, 204–5, 234, 235
    and the Anzac legend 9, 20, 22, 30, 42, 55, 85, 96–7, 163–4, 173, 187, 192, 195, 197, 200, 204–5, 206, 210, 215, 232, 247
    pilgrimage destination 3, 133, 135, 145, 146, 174–5, 176, 204–5, 207–8, 235
    press reports 25, 27, 33, 213–4, 215
Gallipoli (film) 193–4, 225, 226
Gammage, Bill 23, 42, 193, 194, 197, 204
    The Broken Years (book) 187–8, 189–192, 194, 221, **plate 3**
Garton, Stephen 21
gas 12, 33, 150
Gee, Emma (pseudonym) 103, 104–5
genealogy *see* family history
George, Sydney 106–7, 108
    'Ypres' (poem) 106–7, **plate 14**

George V, King 30, 73, 182
George VI, King 134, 155
Gilbert, Charles Web 180
    Digger (statuette) 242, **plate 23**
Giraud, André 202–3
Glencorse Wood 140
Godley, Lieutenant-General Sir Alexander 28–9
Goebel, Stefan 9–10, 20
Goodman, David 201
Gorton, John 178
Gough, General Sir Hubert 13, 32, 38
Government of Flanders 236
Graves, Robert
    Goodbye to All That (book) 99
Gray, Anne 75
Great Depression 134, 143, 206
Green, Frank 96, 103–4, 116
grief and mourning 6, 72–3, 75–77, 84, 117, 125, 134, 135, 136–7, 138–9, 142, 143, 149, 155
Gueudecourt (diorama) 59
gum trees 130, 157, 167
Gutteridge, Eric 95

Haig, Field Marshal Sir Douglas 11, 13, 14, 26–7, 32, 36, 37, 120, 195–6, 223, 246–7
Ham, Paul
    Passchendaele (book) **plate 3**
Hampson, Alfred 141
    Where the Australians Rest (booklet) 141–2, **plates 18 and 19**
Harington, Major-General Sir Charles 38, 246–7
Harry, Ralph 185
Hasluck, Paul 176
Hawke, Bob 204–5, 206 208
Hawke government 201, 202, 204
Hay, Ian
    Ship of Remembrance (book) 133
Hazebrouck 56, 160
Hell Fire Corner 140
Herald (newspaper) 139–40
Herring, Sir Edmund 167, 170
Hewson, John 206

high diction   21, 97, 140, 162–3
Hill 60 (Zillebeke)   9, 28, 93, 141, 148, 207, 224, 225, 226, 227, 236
   1st Australian Tunnelling Company memorial   125, 129, 130–1, 136, 149–150, 156, 179
Hindenburg Line   56, 112
Hirsch, Marianne   219
histories   7, 8, 16, 216
   academic histories   9, 41, 187, 191–2, 222–3
   family histories   220–2
   general histories   86–9, 122–3
   popular histories   9, 187, 188, 222–3
   unit histories   7, 8, 16, 41, 85, 89–90, 91, 92–3, 97–8, 99, 100, 119, 123, 160
      1st Infantry Battalion   97
      2nd Infantry Battalion   92, 96
      3rd Pioneer Battalion   93, 94
      5th Pioneer Battalion   95
      7th Infantry Battalion   95
      14th Infantry Battalion   91–2, 94
      22nd Infantry Battalion   92
      24th Infantry Battalion   97
      37th Infantry Battalion   97
      40th Infantry Battalion   96, 103, 116
   on Messines   90, 93–4
   on Pozières   97
   on third Ypres   90, 93, 94–6, 97
   see also Bean, Charles
Hobbs, Major-General Sir Joseph Talbot   128
Hobsbawm, Eric
   The Invention of Tradition (book)   6, 186
Howard, John   206, 210–11, 218–19, 227, 228, 240
Howard government   231–2, 233
Hudson, David   245
Hughes, William   19, 25, 99, 126, 127, 128, 129, 132, 142, 144, 160–1, 237
   The Splendid Adventure (book)   119–20, 122, 128
Hull, Arthur   246

Hunter, John   230, 231
Hurley, Frank   61, 62, 63–4
   official photographs   3, **plates 1 and 2**
   The Morning of Passchendaele (photograph)   63, **plate 6**
Hutchison, Margaret   70
Hynes, Samuel   20

Imperial War Graves Commission (IWGC)   70–2, 124, 125–6, 128, 129–130, 138, 141, 182
   cemeteries   2, 125–6, 137, 140–1, 142–4, 145, 148, 156, 166, 181
In Flanders Fields Museum   228, 238, 239, 240–1, 242, **plate 22**
In Grateful Memory (book)   203
Indigenous Australians   201, 217
Inglis, Ken   76, 126–7, 174, 175, 202, 217, 222
Irwin, Les   176
Irwin-Zarecka, Iwona   85

Jacka, Albert   112–13
Jeffrey, Michael   231
Jeffries, Barbara   137
Jeffries, Clarence   137
Joshi, Vijaya   191–2

Keating, Paul   206, 208, 209, 210
Keating government   206–7 210
Kiggell, Lieutenant-General Sir Launcelot   190, 196
King, Jonathan   232
Kokoda   161, 206, 208
Kyle, Roy
   An Anzac's Story (book)   221

Lang, Jack   206
Last Post Association   212, 214
Last Post Committee   184
   buglers' tours of Australia   212–3, 214–6, 241
   see also Last Post Association
Le Hamel   200, 211, 223, 237; *see also* Australian Corps Memorial

Index

Leist, Fred   65, 66, 68
   Australian Infantry Attack in Polygon Wood (painting)   66, 68–9, 80   **plate 9**
Lind, Edmund   154–5
literature   7, 8, 16, 216
   'anti-war' books   99, 107, 109, 110, 222, 225
   novels and memoirs   85, 109–118, 119–22, 123, 160–1, 165, 220–2
Lloyd George, David   195–6
   War Memoirs of David Lloyd George (book)   119, 120–1, 122, 160–1
Lone Pine   32, 204
Longstaff, Will   74, 75
   Menin Gate at Midnight (painting)   9, 49, 70, 73–7, 79–80, 81, 82, **plate 12**; *see also* Australian War Memorial
Ludendorff, General Erich   159, 164
Lyons, Enid   143
Lyons, Joseph   142, 143–4

Macdonald, Frank   240
Macfarlane, Andrew   157
McGee, Sergeant Lewis   103
McKenna, Mark   201
McKinney, Jack
   Crucible (book)   109–10, 113–14
Macleod, Jenny   213
McQueen, Humphrey   99
Macron, Emmanuel   246
Macswan, Norman   175
Mann, Leonard   114, 117
   Flesh in Armour (book)   109–10, 114–15, 116, 117–18
Mant, Gilbert   221–2
Massey, John   148
Maxwell, Joseph   114
   Hell's Bells and Mademoiselles (book)   114–16, 123
media   7–8, 24–6, 36, 41, 86, 122, 136, 170, 213–14, 243
   Menin Gate Memorial coverage   70, 72, 76–80
   pilgrimage coverage   139, 153–4, 175, 205, 207, 227–8
   Westhoek five coverage   229, 230, 231
   see also Bean, Charles
Melrose, Craig   51, 136
memorial diplomacy *see* commemorative diplomacy
Memorial Museum Passchendaele 1917   238, 239–240, **plates 20 and 21**
memorials   3, 5, 6, 7, 49, 84, 85, 124–5, 126, 133, 135, 137, 139 150–1, 162, 212, 217, 219, 233, 236, 237, 242
   AIF divisional memorials   126–8, 129, 131–2, 166–7, 207, **plate 15**
   1st Australian Division (Pozières)   202
   2nd Australian Division (Mont St Quentin)   157, 175, 176, 180, 202
   3rd Australian Division (Sailly-le-Sec)   202
   see also Polygon Wood
   Australian Service Nurses National Memorial   217
   Hellenic Memorial   217
   plaques   129, 139, 144, 168–170, 202, 207, 217, 233
   smaller unit memorials   130
memory   4–8, 84, 133–4, 157, 216
   collective memory   4, 5–8, 133–4, 177
   collective remembrance   8, 84–5, 137
   cultural memory   158, 165–6, 219–20
   memory boom   4, 216
   and museums   50–1
   political memory   165, 219, 220
   postmemory   219
   social memory   165
Menin Gate lions   198–200, 242
Menin Gate Memorial   2, 9, 70–2, 73, 76, 78, 81, 82, 126, 135–6, 140, 150, 156, 168, 179, 181, 207, 212, 228, 235, 236, **plate 13**
   Last Post ceremony   136, 137, 150, 154, 177, 183–4, 210, 212, 214, 243
   unveiling   72–3, 75, 185

Menin Road 75, 104, 140, 198
   battle of 13, 32–3, 34, 43, 54, 57, 58–9, 88, 93, 94–5, 108, 150, 196, 240, 246, **plate 26**
Menzies, Robert 167
Mercury (newspaper) 119
Messines 10, 29, 53, 140, 141, 177
   battle of 1–2, 3, 9, 11–13, 23, 26–7, 28, 60, 65, 66, 85, 130, 195, 200, 224, 226, 239, 247
     at the AWM 52, 55, 57, 60, 61, 62–3, 64
     Bean's accounts 26–7, 28–9, 36, 42
     published accounts 86, 87, 89, 90, 93–4, 102, 111–12, 113, 122–3, 150, 190–1, 222, 223
missing soldiers
   commemoration of 2, 71–2, 124–5, 126, 130, 137, 139, 141, 143
   DNA identification 228, 229–231, 232
   see also Menin Gate Memorial
Mitchell, George 102, 111
   Backs to the Wall (book) 111–12, 113
modernism 20, 21, 62, 65, 67, 69, 95, 102, 104, 109, 189, 225
Monash, General Sir John 27, 28, 78, 89, 100, 195, 211, 246
   The Australian Victories in France (book) 41, 86–7, 92, 110
   War Letters of General Monash (book) 119, 121–2
Mont St Quentin 157, 163, 175, 177, 178, 180, 223
Mont St Quentin (diorama) 60
Mouquet Farm 11, 171
Mosse, George 20
multiculturalism 201, 217, 241

Nash, Paul
   The Menin Road (painting) 69, **plate 10**
National Archives of Australia 218–19
National Library of Australia 220
nationalism 20–1, 50, 133–4, 188
   'new nationalism' 158, 173–4, 192–3

Nelson, Brendan 214
New Zealand 3, 27, 130, 169, 179–180, 185–6, 212, 223, 234, 239, 241, 242
Ngā Tapuwae New Zealand First World War Trails 3, **plate 3**
Nonne Boschen (diorama) 55, 57–60, 68, **plate 5**
Nord (French *département*) 236

Office of Australian War Graves 218
Officer, Keith 180
Owen, Wilfred 225

Pas-de-Calais (French *département*) 236
Passchendaele 11, 13, 15, 97, 108, 117, 140, 149, 160, 207, 229
   first battle of 15, 36–7, 38, 40, 45, 54, 86, 96, 103–4, 117, 121–2, 137, 246–7
   see also Ypres, third battle of
Passchendaele (film) 3
Penguin Books 221
Percival, C.H. 106
Péronne 129, 175, 178, 180, 207
photography 3, 22 , 48, 49, 56, 59, 61–4, 239, 240, 245
pilgrimage 2, 7–8, 9, 76, 98, 124, 125, 133–8, 142–3, 147, 155–6, 159, 170–1, 182, 205, 216, 228, 235–6
   1965 Gallipoli pilgrimage 174–5, 176
   1990 Gallipoli pilgrimage 204–5, 207–8
   2nd Division Western Front pilgrimage 175–8, 179
   9th Brigade Western Front pilgrimage 175–8, 179
   Australian War Graves Pilgrimage 134, 138–9, 140, 151
   coronation (Elizabeth II) tour 167–8, 170
   coronation (George VI) pilgrimage 134, 152–5, 167
   Return to the Western Front Mission 207–8, 209, 214
   see also veterans

Index

Ploegsteert 237, 238, 239
Plugstreet Experience 14–18
 interpretation centre 238, 239
Plumer, General Sir Herbert 12, 13–15, 32, 38, 72–3, 190
Poelcappelle 14, 15, 36–7, 38, 40, 45, 54, 86
Pollard, Jas 103, 104, 105–6, 108
Polygon Wood 33, 236, 237, **plate 24**
 5th Australian Division Memorial 9, 35, 125, 127–9, 131–2, 136, 149, 156, 157, 167, 179, 203, 244
 Anzac Day 186, 234–5
 battle of 13–14, 34–5, 39, 54, 59, 68–9, 87–8, 91, 93, 94–5, 104, 112–13, 231
 Buttes New British Cemetery 129–130, 148, 231, **plate 17**
 centenary 243–6, **plate 25**
Power, Septimus 65, 66, 67–8, 69
 First Australian Division Artillery Going into the 3rd Battle of Ypres (painting) 66, 67, 80, 105, **plate 8**
Pozières 129, 147, 180, 181
 battle of 2, 11, 17, 96–7, 111, 116, 195, 196, 223
 Bean's view 22–3, 27, 29, 32, 33, 34, 35, 37, 39, 42–3, 46, 171
 objects from 29, 55–6
Prince, Thomas 114
 Purple Patches (book) 114–15
prisoners of war 44, 62, 64, 99, 161–2, 173, 213
propaganda 24, 68

radio 24, 72, 78
Ranger, Terence
 The Invention of Tradition (book) 6, 186
re-enactors 243, 244
Remarque, Erich Maria 222, 225
 All Quiet on the Western Front (book) 65, 99
Remembrance Day 207, 209, 213, 215

Returned and Services League (RSL) 162, 167, 168–70, 171, 174, 175, 186, 215
Returned Sailors' and Soldiers' Imperial League of Australia (RSSILA) 19–20, 49, 74–5, 98, 148, 151, 152, 164–5, 168
returned services publications 8, 7, 16, 85, 98–108, 109, 111, 119, 121, 122, 123, 148, 149, 154
 Duckboard (magazine) 98, 99, 101
 Listening Post (magazine) 98, 105, 149–150
 Queensland Digger (magazine) 98, 101, 111
 Reveille (magazine) 98, 99, 101–2, 111, 164, 224–5
Rhoden, Clare 109
Roach, David 225, 226
Robb, Leonard 151
Roper, Michael 7
Rudd government 233
Rule, Edgar
 Jacka's Mob (book) 112–13
Russian Revolution 40

Sailly-le-Sec 180
St George Memorial Church, Ypres 168–170, 179, 182–3, 212
Sassoon, Siegfried 222, 225
Scates, Bruce 220
Scott, Bruce 212–3, 215
Scott's Post 244
Screen Australia 226
Scullin, James 142, 143
Seabrook family 240, 241
Seal, Graham 162
Seccombe, Clarence 147, 148
Second World War 16, 156, 158, 159–162, 163–4, 166, 173, 180, 184, 206, 210
 Pacific theatre 161, 170, 206, 208
 Singapore 164, 173, 206
Serle, Geoffrey 172
Seymour, Alan 172
 The One Day of the Year (play) 172
Shannon, Deidre 230

315

Sims, Jeremy   224, 226
Sir John Monash Centre   236, 237, 238
Sivan, Emmanuel   8
Slater, Henry   148, 149
Smith, Staniforth
   Australian Campaigns in the Great War (book)   86, 87–9
Smith's Weekly (newspaper)   98, 100–1, 106, 107–8
social history   174, 187
Somme   3, 11, 39, 46, 53, 59, 62, 124, 128–9, 145, 147, 175, 176, 178, 181, 182, 202, 247
   first battle of the Somme   10–11, 30, 161
   French *département*   236
Somme Tourisme   235, 236
spiritualism   70, 75, 76–7
Stillman, Geoff   147
Stone of Remembrance   125–6
Storey, George   231
strikes   19
Sydney Morning Herald (newspaper)   48, 127, 232

Tehan, Dan   246
Telegraph (newspaper)   146
television   8, 24, 159, 172, 187, 192–3, 205
Thomson, Alistair   8
Throssell, Hugo   172
Throssell, Ric
   For Valour (play)   172
Tilton, Mary   114, 116
   The Grey Battalion (book)   114–15, 116–17
Tobruk   161, 168
Todman, Dan   165–6
   The Great War (book)   **plate 3**
traditionalism   20–1, 51, 52, 59, 62, 63, 65, 67, 69–70, 82, 104, 110, 136, 140, 162–3, 172, 173
trauma   4, 189–190, 219, 221, 245
Treloar, John   51, 52, 54, 57, 61, 67, 70, 74–5, 80, 81, 83 165, 198, 199
   Australian Chivalry (art folio)   65–6, 67, 68, 69 **plate 7**

Turnbull, Malcolm   246
Turnour, Lieutenant J.E.   68
Twomey, Christina   189–190
Tyne Cot Cemetery, Zonnebeke   2, 137, 139, 140–1, 143, 149, 151–2, 186, 207, 212, 233, 236, 237, 239

Unit History Scheme   90–2
United States of America   153, 163, 168, 172–3
   battle of Le Hamel   211
Unknown Australian Soldier   207, 209–10
Unknown Soldier, Westminster Abbey   208–9

Vandenbraambussche, Pierre   183–4
Vetaffairs (magazine)   233
veterans   6, 8, 74, 81, 84, 90, 162, 164, 184, 185–6, 188–9, 213, 240
   battlefield pilgrimages   133, 135, 146–56, 170–1, 174–8, 179, 202, 204–5, 207–8, 211, 212
   passing away   158, 164–6, 172, 197, 216, 217–8
   see also returned services publications
Vietnam War   158, 166, 172–3, 186
Villers-Bretonneux   17, 53, 132, 144, 147, 154–5, 159, 160, 163, 177, 178, 180–1, 200, 202–3, 209, 223, 234, 236, 242, 243
   Anzac Day   85, 132, 180–1, 233–4
   centenary   245, 246
   Franco-Australian Museum of Villers-Bretonneux   238
   see also Australian National Memorial
Voices of Birralee Choir   245

Wade, Linda   132
Wanliss, Harold   113
Wanliss, Newton   91, 94
war on terror   211
Ward, Russel
   Australian Legend (book)   174
Ward, Stuart   173
Ware, Fabian   71–2

Index

Water Diviner (film)   227
Waters, John   139–140
  Crosses of Sacrifice (book)   140–1
Weir, Peter   193–4, 197, 204
West Australian (newspaper)   77, 84, 124, 137
Western Front   3, 10–11, 13, 30, 32, 41, 51–2, 55, 62, 70, 86, 110, 126, 191, 207, 210, 223, 235, 242
  declining interest   156, 158, 166, 167, 170, 176, 194, 197
  rediscovery of   158, 200, 232–4, 241
Westhoek five   227, 228–231, 232, 241
Wheeler, Charles   65, 66
White Australia   158, 173
Wilkins, Hubert   62, 63
Williams, Harold   112
Williams, John   24, 31, 73–4
Winter, Jay   6, 8, 20
Woodward, Oliver Holmes   224–6
Woolavington, Lord   73, 74
Wyndham Lewis, Percy   67
Wytschaete   141

Ypres   124–5, 126, 135, 147, 150, 155–6, 164, 175, 177, 214, 235, 236, 237–8, 241–2, 243
  Anzac Day   16, 179–180, 181, 185–6, 197, 203, 212, 227
  British site of memory   30, 70, 71, 72, 78–9, 126, 140–1, 156, 181–5, 212
  Cloth Hall   68, 138, 209, 210
  criticism of locals   148, 183, 184
  first battle of   30, 183
  local authorities   183, 198, 199, 209–10, 238, 242
  multinational site of memory   211–2, 237, 242, 247, **plate 27**
  official Australian visits   142, 143–4, 153–4, 155, 207, 227–8
  second battle of   30, 33
  third battle of   2, 11–15, 86, 87–8, 102, 113, 115, 116–18, 122–3, 195, 200, 222, 223, 229, 232, 239, 246–7

artillery   12, 14, 23, 38, 43, 45, 47, 57, 59, 93, 95, 104, 108, 116, 120
  in British memory   11, 160–1
  criticism of British leadership   37–8, 43, 45–6, 95, 118, 119–122, 196
  objectives   11, 13
  pillboxes   43–5, 57–8, 59, 63, 68–9, 93, 118, 143, 196, 246
  state of terrain   11, 13, 14, 37, 45, 59, 60, 63, 69, 95–6, 105–6, 114, 118, 120, 140, 149, 190, 240
Ypres League   182–3
Ypres Times (newsletter)   182

Ziino, Bart   137, 220
Zonnebeke   33, 140, 212, 237, 238, 241–2, 243, 244, 246